The Teachings of a Perfect Master

Books by Henry Bayman
The Station of No Station (2001)
The Secret of Islam (2003)
The Black Pearl (2005)

Online books
The Meaning of the Four Books

Science, Knowledge, and Sufism

Websites
hbayman.angelfire.com
hbayman.blogspot.com

The Teachings of a Perfect Master

An Islamic Saint for the Third Millennium

~

By
HENRY BAYMAN

ANQA PUBLISHING ♦ OXFORD

Published by Anqa Publishing
PO Box 1178
Oxford OX2 8YS, UK
www.ibn-arabi.com

© Henry Bayman, 2012
First published 2012
Reprinted 2015

Henry Bayman has asserted his moral right
under the Copyright, Designs and Patents Act, 1988,
to be identified as the author of this work.

All rights reserved. No part of this publication
may be reproduced, stored in a retrieval system,
or transmitted, in any form or by any means,
without the prior permission in writing of the publisher.

British Library Cataloguing in Publication Data.
A catalogue record for this book is available from the British Library.

ISBN: 978 1 905937 44 8

Cover design:
Henry Bayman and Michael Tiernan

Printed and bound in the USA by
Edwards Brothers, Inc.

Contents

Preface   xi

Prologue   1
The Impossible Human 2; Central Asia 3; Central Anatolia 4; The Perfect Human Being 5; My encounter with the Master 8; His life 10; Remarks by those who knew him 11; His views of others 13; Miraculous feats 14; His teachings 17; The Holy Grail and the Fisher King 18; St. Francis, the 'Peace Prayer,' and democracy 22; Light on astrology 25; The emancipation of humankind 28; The Wisdom Base 29; An Islamic wisdom manual 30; Methodology 31; Important notes 33

The Wisdom Base

Introduction   39
Ascension 39; Hidden Knowledge 40

I GENERAL   47

The foundation   49
Why did God create the universe? 49; Divine unity 53; The sun of love 54; Religion and brotherhood 56; The best of times, the worst of times 57; Material and spiritual 58; The light of reason 59; Thanksgiving 60; The school of wisdom 61

Compassion and Mercy   63
Compassion without Mercy 65; Mercy without Compassion 65

Universality   67
The universal religion 67; The Prophet 67; The Book 68; The Ka'ba 69

The door of hope   71

The audition   73
The Peace Prayer 73; O humankind 75

Four poles, four elements   79
The four poles 79; The four elements 80; The tomb of the body 82

Ethics — 85

The First Pillar of Islam 85; Good and evil 85; Ethics and knowledge 86; Attitude to others 87; What is necessary 88; Emulate the Names of God 88; Work ethics 90; The white stones 91; Towards one's spouse 92; Towards children 93; Towards parents 93; Forbidden versus Allowed 95

The mind and the heart — 97

Kinds of minds 97; The captain and the engineer 99

Faith — 101

Courtesy — 103

Admirable conduct 103; Animal rights 106

Political secularism (laicism) — 109

No reformation in Islam 113; Democracy 113; Terrorism 113

Knowledge/science, art — 115

Religious/spiritual sciences 116; Practice makes perfect 118; Distribute, don't fail to teach 119; Teaching methods 119; Useless knowledge 119; Intuitive knowledge in animals 120; Science Fiction 121; Music, art 121

Closing the Two Doors — 123

Taking the Permanent Ablution 125

The Base Self — 129

Levels of selfhood 131; The pet snake 132; The beggar of God 132; The three fears of the self 132; Never mind Paradise 135; The two guards 135; The three organs 136; Madmen of the belly 137; The wrath of God versus the wrath of the self 138; Food for the spirit 138; The fly that defeated the eagle 140; The seven orifices 141; The spirit 141; The vain peacock 142; The eight gates 142; Satan 143

The Divine Law — 147

Overflow 150; Mercy versus justice 151; Some important Verses 151

Charity — 153

The three hoarders 153; The road to Paradise 154; The Alms-tax 155; Alms-tax as charity 156; Live longer by charity 157; A Robin Hood example 159

Destiny — 161

Total Will, Partial Will 163; Precaution versus predestination 163

Death, afterlife, the Apocalypse — 167
Earthly retribution 167; Death and resurrection 168; The Mahdi 169; Doomsday 170; The Third Adam 172; The pen is mightier than the sword 173; The way out 173

Miscellaneous topics — 175
Politics 175; A lesson in politics 176; Being chief 176; Timing 176; Economics 177; To a man whose business was failing 178; Interest 178; Christianity 180; Prayers (supplication) 181; Women 182; Leavening of humanity 183; Superstition 183; Try it yourself 184

II THE INWARD PATH: SUFISM — 185

Sufism — 187
Introduction to Sufism 187; Having two wings 188; The blind men and the elephant 188; The chicks and ducklings 188; Wisdom 189; Balance 189; Read my mind 189; The garbage collectors 190; Enlightened by beans 190; The secret of the fragrance 191; The best thing 192; Stages in Sufism 193; A drop in the sea 193; I'm not the sun, I'm *in* the sun 195; The fish in the sea 195; Miscellaneous 196

The beginning — 197
The three prerequisites 197; The three enemies, the three friends 197; Practice makes perfect 199; You're the traveler 200; God in search of man 200; God-ish: the language of the Quran 201; Sainthood 202

The essence of man — 205
The master 207; False masters 208; Those without a master 209; The requirements for a master 209; Prayerless masters 210; The guidance of the master 211; The flying frog 212; The responsibilities of the disciple 212; One performs the Ascension through the master 214; The graft 214; The jeweler's apprentice 215; Gossip and men of religion 215

The Paths (Orders) — 217
Spiritual schools 217; Unity in diversity 217; Discussions 220; My yoke is light 220; God 221; Love 222; Work 224; The shepherd who was enlightened by a thorn 226; Patience 228

Worship — 231
Ablution 231; Prayer 232; Prayer and Invocation 242; Invocation 244

The secret and the sublime 249

Die before you die 249; Unveiling 249; Miraculous deeds and asceticism 250; Spacefolding 251; The child of the spirit 253; How to see the world 254; Hidden Knowledge 255; The flight of the gryphon 256; Subtleties (*lata'if*) 257; The human body maps the universe 257; The Guarded Tablet 258; Uniting the heart and the mind 260

III DESCENT OF THE LIGHT (WHO'S WHO IN ISLAM) 263

The prophets 265

Introduction 265; Adam 268; Hud 270; Abraham 271; Lot 274; Moses 275; Solomon 285; Ezra 289; Jonah 289; Luqman 290; Jesus 292

The Prophet 295

His life 295; Childhood 296; Arbitrator for the Black Stone 296; Announcing his prophethood 297; The challenge 298; Be truthful 299; The poor 299; The blind man 300; How to recognize a prophet 300; Declaration of faith is enough 301; How to see an angel 301; Don't fall for the same trick twice 302; The thanksgiving servant 303; Health matters 303; The importance of work 304; Egalitarianism 304; Give good names to children 304; I've come to improve, not to kill 305; The highest knowledge 305; Compassion 306; Don't embarrass people 306; The first Prayer-call 307; Miracles 307; The unforgettable wife 308; Self-reliance 309; The morality of the Quran 309; Love me with all your heart 309; The meaning of the Ascension 310; The Prophet in his cosmic aspect 312; The Prophet's household 316

The caliphs 317

Abu Bakr 317; Omar 317; Ali 322; Early history of Islam 328

The scholars 331

The four schools of Islamic law 331; Abu Hanifa 331; Ghazali 340; Bukhari 341

The saints 345

The Saintlight 345; Khidr 348; Aq Shamsuddin 355; Ibn 'Arabi 355; Bayazid of Bistam 363; Bahlul the Wise 364; Muhammad Birgivi of Bursa 367; Sirri Saqati 369; Junayd of Baghdad 370; Shaykh Shibli 370; Ashraf Rumi 372; Hajji Bayram Wali 373; Niyazi Misri 374; Hajji Bektash Wali 375; Mansur al-Hallaj 377; Ahmed Ibn Hanbal 378;

Hassan of Basra 379; Rabia Adawiya 380; Hatim al-Ta'i 380; Muhammad Abdullah al-Tunisi 382; Ibrahim Adham 385; Ismail Hakki of Bursa 388; Kuddusi Baba 389; Mahmud Hudayi 389; Mawlana Jalaluddin Rumi 391; Shams of Tabriz 394; Nasruddin Hodja 397; Nur-ul Arabi 403; Shaykh Sha'ban Wali 404; Hafiz of Shiraz 404; Yunus Emre 405; Yusuf Bahri 408

The Chain 411
General 411; Abdul Qadir Gilani 411; Bahauddin Naqshband 421; Khalid Baghdadi 423; Ibrahim Hakki of Erzurum 424; Ali Sebti 424; Mahmud Samini 425; Othman Badruddin 427; Musa Kâzim Efendi 430; Hajji Ahmet Kaya Efendi (Keko) 431; Hajji Ahmet Kayhan 442

Epilogue 455
Once upon a dream 456

Appendix: Some important formulas 461

Index 463

Preface

This book is about the life, teachings and thought of a Sufi saint, the Grand Master Ahmet Kayhan, who bore the Saintlight for most of the latter part of the twentieth century. I was privileged to enjoy his presence for twenty years.

No one taught Sufism like Master Kayhan did. Nobody taught Islam like him, either. He took these two and fused them together, out of which fusion flowed a vital, rejuvenating spiritual water that was the balm of injuries and a grace to all hearts it touched. It is no exaggeration to say that this is what true Islam and true Sufism are all about.

Two things about this book distinguish it from its predecessors in this field: content and format.

The content is culled from the daily conversations of the Master. I have read many books on Islam and Sufism, but nowhere have I seen many of the expositions in this book, and never with such force. Even brief passages are enough to demonstrate the Master's originality as well as authenticity.

The way in which the Master delivered these teachings was an integral part of the teaching and cannot be reproduced here. Very gently, he would lay out his explanations in a soft voice, speaking slowly as though he had all the time in the world. This cannot be emulated on the printed page. Instead, I have topically organized the entire range of his teachings spanning two decades. If science is organized knowledge, what is presented here is the science of Sufism, the pinnacle of spiritual sciences. A certain statement he made on one occasion may be completed by something he uttered years before or later. The present format allows the Master's thought to be perceived at a glance. I have called this the 'Wisdom Base.' The sequencing of subjects arose naturally out of my records of his discourses – they seemed to suggest the present order in particular.

Both in terms of form and content, then, this book stands out among its peers. The Master was peerless, incomparable, and of necessity this quality is carried over to the book of which he was, in a very real sense, the 'author.'

The Master was a virtuoso of Sufi teaching stories. Examples of these are recorded throughout the book. Questions and remarks by those present, and the Master's responses, are included where called for. An

Appendix includes the original Arabic formulas – presented in italicized translations in the text – from the Koran and tradition used by the Master, both in transliteration and translation into English.

What comments I have as editor/translator are confined to textual devices such as brackets and footnotes, thus clearly separating them from the Master's own words.

I have shunned special terms wherever possible. These are common in Sufic texts, but the interruptions, while scholarly, detract from proper appreciation of the text. Instead, I have substituted translations that can be easily understood. This has obviated the need for a glossary.

All my earlier books have been scholarly in nature. A serious attempt was made in them to back up the text with academic resources. Here, the Master's words speak for themselves. He had the knack of explaining the most difficult concepts in the simplest terms, so there is nothing daunting here and the main text can be read easily by all but the illiterate.

Non-Muslims will gain a perspective on true Islam and true Sufism as never before. Muslims may discover a deeper dimension to their faith. In the end, I believe that the lives of all who read it will be enriched.

The greatest Sufi masters of old recorded their teachings in books, but many of these are hundreds of years old and do not really address problems of the modern world. It is a great blessing to have found a Sufi master who proclaimed the highest wisdom in a readily comprehensible, contemporary idiom. Nor is this proselytizing, for these discourses are not aimed at conversion – they are 'in-group' discussions. We are invited to a front seat in all the Master's most important discourses, and allowed to judge his teachings for ourselves. This is probably the closest, and only, glimpse we are ever going to get of the highest reaches of contemporary Islam/Sufism. It is a book of labor and love, to be cherished by all who seriously understand its message.

To present a public account of such an illustrious master would have been my duty to humankind in any case. But ever since the horrible events of 9/11, this task has taken on an added urgency. In the wrong hands, the teachings of a religion can be perverted, distorted and rendered out of all recognition. In the teachings of Master Kayhan, and to my knowledge nowhere else, lies the antidote to a dangerous strain of Islam that promises nothing but more strife and pain for the future of humankind. This should not even be termed 'Islam' but rather, to call a spade a spade, the abuse of Islam for political ends.

PREFACE

'Islam,' observed the historian Herbert J. Muller, 'had no real political doctrine.' Lest this be deemed an isolated view, let us hear it categorically from Professor Claude Cahen, doyen of historians of Islam: 'there was no Islamic political doctrine.'[1] This is the reason why, as Professor Muller again remarks: 'The spiritual unity of Islam failed to inspire political unity.'[2] (This includes even Arab unity, which is the first thing one would ordinarily expect.) It also explains why Muslims borrowed the political and bureaucratic structures of the Roman and Persian empires wholesale at their first opportunity. Islam is a religion, not a political ideology. I know there are those who believe that there can be such a thing as 'political Islam,' but they are mistaken.

Islam is a world religion and will remain so. It transcends, as it must, any merely local and historical political forms. Like Christianity and Buddhism, it has adherents in many countries irrespective of borders. When the Prophet instructed his followers to proclaim the religion in other lands, he did not tell them to take over the governments of those lands. Such a thought never even crossed the Prophet's mind. As for the caliphate, it was a transitional device for the first thirty years (as foretold in a Saying of the Prophet), after which it slowly dissipated its power and outlived its usefulness in a few centuries, if not much earlier.

To put it simply: *Roma* (empire) and *Amor* (love) don't mix. State/politics and religion, which is based on love and compassion, don't mix. It is for this reason that Islam is a civic religion. There was never a church in Islam, so positing a 'mosque and state' parallel to the Christian 'church and state' would be a gross misrepresentation. The Prophet was the sole authority in the emergent Medinan community. He was forced to wage wars of self-defense. His political successors were four caliphs. These were necessary if Islam was to survive. To generalize from this limited period to all time is, as I have noted elsewhere, to radically misinterpret the office of prophethood – and also of the caliphate. It is like clinging on to the eggshell once the chick has come out. After the Prophet, political authority and spiritual authority were separated, and spiritual authority was left to whoever

---

1. Quoted in L. Carl Brown, *Religion and State: The Muslim Approach to Politics*, New York: Columbia University Press, 2000, p. 57.

2. Herbert J. Muller, *The Loom of History*, New York: New American Library (Mentor Books), c.1958, pp. 333, 334. The fact that Muller's remarks were made about half a century ago highlights another fact: Islam did not have, and was not perceived as having, a political doctrine for almost all of its first fourteen centuries. The many attempts by Muslims in the last fifty years to invent such a doctrine out of thin air may be sincere, but are also misguided.

were the most righteous, the most spiritual, the most humane. It was never formally organized and enshrined in a church.

The content differs from earlier books in at least two important respects. The first is that an English-language account of the Sufis of Central Anatolia has not been forthcoming in recent decades. (The only exception may be Reshad Feild's earlier writings such as *The Last Barrier*, now out of print.) Yet their version of Sufism, descending directly from the earlier Sufis of Central Asia, is of the utmost importance.

Second, and even more important, the Master's discourse *redefines Islam for the twenty-first century*. In a conversational tone (because taken from his actual conversations), he expounds the purest, highest form of Islam/Sufism, in a way that transcends all Orders and Schools. He always attached greater importance to Islam (the whole) than to Sufism (its part), and spoke of 'Mohammedanhood' as the desired goal, which is a synthesis of the first two: it is what existed before they were 'electrolyzed' into a couple of apparently distinct components. In his conception, Islam is not just the external (exoteric) teaching of behavior, of 'going through the motions,' of rote and mindless repetition. Fused with Sufism, it is shot through and through with spirituality, with love and tenderness and everything that makes a religion worthwhile.

Let me end by expressing my thanks to Stephen Hirtenstein, Michael Tiernan and, last but not least, John White, for having made this book possible.

Henry Bayman

Prologue

> If I could ask don Juan one final question, I would ask,
> How did he move me so? How did he touch my spirit so that
> every beat of my heart is filled with the feeling of this path?
> Every beat of my heart.
>
> Carlos Castaneda[1]

King Arthur! Who can deny the appeal of the legendary king, who has captured the imagination of generations? What would you think if, wandering through the woods one fine day, you came upon Camelot – not its ruins, but thanks to some sort of time tunnel, *Camelot itself* – where King Arthur lived with his Knights of the Round Table? In the 1960s musical of the same name, Camelot was depicted whimsically as a place where the summers cannot be too hot, the winters too cold, or the days rainy.

And for me, Camelot was Ankara. It was exactly as described above: a long Indian summer followed by a few brief months of winter, not very severe; mild summers, especially in later years; light snowfall from the same weather fronts that were claiming lives elsewhere. It was as if an invisible shield had been placed over the city, protecting it from harsh extremes.

But that was not the reason why Ankara was Camelot. This state of affairs was the consequence and not the cause. For in Ankara there lived a king; an unknown, unsung, yet once and future king. A king not of the physical, but of the spiritual realm.

Do you think it's possible to live a legend in real life, in three-dimensional, physical existence? Throughout the fifteen years between 1983 and 1998, I lived various parts of at least three legends. I was there, if only partially, on Olympus, in Camelot and on the trail of the Holy Grail. And I was there, not just for myself, but for us all.

But no retelling of a myth can ever substitute for living, actually experiencing, the myth itself. Had I not lived it and seen it with my own eyes, I, too, would have refused to believe it. The colors of the rainbow do not exist in this gray world we inhabit, these boggy badlands, this spiritual desert, this emotional flatland. As its denizens, we cannot conceive of colors other than black and white and shades of

---

1. http://www.nagualism.com/an-encounter-with-carlos-castaneda.html, interview with *The Sun*, September 1997. (Accessed 16 March 2012.)

gray. Yet they exist nonetheless. Beyond three dimensions there is a fourth, and beyond four dimensions there is a fifth, and so on.

You may feel at times that what is being related is fiction, make-believe. Yet it is not. It all took place in a bustling city on earth, in real time and space, as the second millennium AD drew to a close.

What other true-life stories were experienced in the past, yet went unrecorded because there was no one to recount them for our convenience? In the end, we are left with our inevitable partial knowledge and human ignorance. This does not mean that we are allowed to compensate by assuming all kinds of absurdities. But it does mean that we should be prepared for the unexpected. Someday, somewhere, it may stare you in the face, and you might not be able to recognize it. As Heraclitus said a long time ago: 'He who does not expect the unexpected cannot detect it.' It was because Schliemann expected it that he discovered Troy.

Do not take anything for granted. But equally, do not sneer if, one day, you too happen to stumble upon ... *the Truth*.

The Impossible Human

This is the story of the Impossible Man. When I say 'Impossible,' I don't mean it in the sense of 'impossible to get along with' or anything of that sort. No. If that were the case, the solution would be trivial, and there would be no need for an account.

The Impossible Man is the person who, by any and all known laws of science, ought not to exist.

Theoretically, his existence should be impossible. And yet he *exists*...[2]

Had I not chanced to encounter him, I too would have refused to believe in his existence. Therefore, I have no right to expect you to do so. All I can do is set down the facts, and leave the decision to you.

The Impossible Man, which can also mean the Impossible Woman (the state is not gender-specific), is one who has been *blessed beyond belief*. For him (or her), nature's laws get bent, the impossible becomes possible, a solution materializes where there should by rights be none, cavities appear in a solid block.

---

2. Or rather, existed. These lines were written at the end of July 1998, shortly before the Master passed away.

It should not be surmised that the Impossible Man (or Woman) does these things himself (or herself). No: they are done *for him*, and he cannot help marveling as they happen. Nor can he help feeling very small and extremely unworthy of the grace that has been sent to his doorstep. All he can do is weep and give thanks – weep at the vastness of the gift when compared to his insignificance, give thanks because he has, without deserving it, received something which not even the greatest efforts can secure. It is God's gift to him, freely given, without the expectation of anything in return. It is a present, wholly free and wholly undeserved.

Does he suffer? Yes, he does. Does he die? Yes, he does – the Impossible Man is only, and entirely, human. Yet the vicissitudes of life fail to faze him, because he knows that, if his time is not yet up, saving grace will suddenly arrive from the most unexpected quarters. He tries, unsuccessfully, to be worthy of all the aid he is given. But this is a vain hope. For no amount of struggle, no matter how valiant, can ever earn infinite bounty, which is what arrives.

As for you, I can wish upon you nothing more sublime, nothing more to your good, and nothing more wonderful, than that you should become an Impossible Human yourself. May God's grace be upon you, and may you go with God – or God go with you.

Central Asia

It is like the rolling plains of the Midwest USA. You travel for miles and miles, and there is not the slightest sign of a hill. It is as if someone had taken a gigantic iron and ironed out the wrinkles in the geography. Nor will you meet many people in this part of the world; it is one of the more sparsely populated regions of the planet.

Suddenly, from the center of this vast, flat expanse, rises a structure that is as imposing as it is startling. Startling, because so unexpected. Why should it be there, in the middle of flatland? Nowadays, there is a village that has sprung up around it. To view it in proper perspective, you have to approach it from the north, from a distance of hundreds of miles. South of it, the Tien Shan (the 'God Mountains') blend slowly into the Himalayas.

We are in southern Kazakhstan. The village is called Turkestan (earlier known as Yasa). And the imposing structure, shooting so starkly skyward, is the mausoleum where the tomb of Ahmet Yasawi, the Sufi saint, rests. For pilgrims from all over Asia, it is the second Mecca.

Who was Ahmet Yasawi? What manner of man was he? What caused people to remember him, to commit his poems to their hearts and souls, and to revere him for hundreds of years?

The truth is that unless you find *a living example* of such a person, you will never really know how they were able to inspire such veneration.

This is the story of how I was fortunate enough to find one. It is the story of the Sufis, but it is also much more. It is the story of the meaning of the universe, of the worth of man, and of how the two are interlinked. It is the greatest story ever told, and retold countless times, as it will be till the end of time.

Central Anatolia

It is a medium-sized mosque in a village near Ankara, not too small, not too large, dressed in white. As you approach it, at one point it appears as if its dome were proceeding downwards from its single minaret. Every day, when the time for one of the Five Daily Prayers arrives, a beautiful Prayer-call issues from the loudspeakers, even if there is no one there. These 'calls without a Caller (*muezzin*)' have been made possible by the students of the Master, who have equipped the mosque with a computer system that switches on the sound on schedule.[3] As in the Ottoman mosques of old, the intonation (*maqam*) for each Prayer-time is different. A digital recording and playback system has endowed each summons with a musical quality of great depth and beauty.

Enter the adjoining small mausoleum (*turba*), and you will find a large wooden casket, two-and-a-half yards beneath which lies the body of my Master, Ahmet Kayhan. Here, as in tombs of saints around the world, you may chance upon displays of adoration and respect that border on worship, yet you will not be able to understand the reason for this. What cause on earth could drive human beings to such extremes of adulation – superstition, illusion, piety? Visit as many saint-tombs as you like, but the living will be unable to justify their behavior to you, nor are they necessarily willing to do so. As for the saints themselves, it is highly doubtful that you will be able to see them rise from their graves and greet you.

---

3. This practice has been discontinued in recent times.

This book explains, among other things, *why* saints are held in such high esteem. In order to understand this, you have to look not at the casket itself, but behind and beyond it. You have to look, not at the silence of the grave, but backward to the time when that saint strolled the earth. For the roots of veneration were sown when the saint was alive, and walked with God; in his loving kindness to those who visited him, in his selfless service to all creatures coming to his door. As the child is father to the man, so the man is father to his post-mortem reputation. Meticulously inspecting the tomb, carefully measuring its dimensions, will teach you nothing in this regard.

The Perfect Human Being

'If the gurus and yogis of India knew what masters are in Turkey,' a Sufi sage once said, 'they would come over here and throw themselves at their feet.'

The Sufi saints are those who have taken Jesus' call: 'Be perfect, even as your Father in heaven is perfect' (*Matthew* 5:48) to heart. A central concept of the Sufis is the 'Perfect Human Being' (*al-insan al-kamil*), representing the full flowering of all human and cosmic potentialities. Let us try to understand who a Perfect Human Being is by recourse to the famous poem by mystical poet Francis Thompson, which has been called the greatest ode written in the English language.[4] The following extract contains the gist of it:

> I fled Him, down the nights and down the days;
> I fled Him, down the arches of the years;
> I fled Him, down the labyrinthine ways
> Of my own mind; and in the mist of tears
> I hid from Him … [But God spoke to me and said:]
>
> 'All things betray thee, who betrayest Me …
> Naught shelters thee, who wilt not shelter Me …

---

4. *The Hound of Heaven* (1890). The 'hound' in the title has frequently been taken as referring – to put this delicately – to the Higher Powers, but I reckon Francis Thompson to be scarcely capable of such discourtesy. Rather, it is *himself* he is referring to, for he has fled God as a hound flees its master out of fear of punishment. In Thompson's case, it is the love of worldly things that distracts him, so he refuses to befriend his Lord and Master, who is in reality his only true friend. By analogy, the 'hound' also refers to anyone else in the same situation.

> Lo, naught contents thee, who content'st not Me ...
> Lo, all things fly thee, for thou flyest Me!
> Strange, piteous, futile thing!
> Wherefore should any set thee love apart?
> Seeing none but I make much of naught ...
> And human love needs human meriting:
> How hast thou merited –
> Of all man's clotted clay the dingiest clot?
> Alack, thou knowest not
> How little worthy of any love thou art!
> Whom wilt thou find to love ignoble thee,
> Save Me, save only Me?...
> Ah, fondest, blindest, weakest,
> I am He whom thou seekest!
> Thou dravest love from thee, who dravest Me.'

Truly a great poem. Now, from this I would like to single out the following lines (changing the language slightly):

> All things betray thee, who betrayest Me
> Naught shelters thee, who will not shelter Me
> Nothing contents thee, who do not content Me
> Lo, all things fly thee, for thou flyest Me!

Now the Perfect Human Being is a person who possesses the exact opposite of these attributes so ably pinpointed by Francis Thompson. And for that reason, nothing betrays such a person who never betrays God. For one has become a Friend of God, a saint, who is always loyal to God. Because one's heart has become the abode, the shelter of God, everything shelters one. Because one has pleased God, and because one is content with little, everything contents one. And because one flies *to* God instead of flying *from* God, everything rushes to the Perfect Human Being, who is a wonder to contemplate and marvelous to behold.

Of the friends of God, it is said repeatedly in the Quran: 'No fear is upon them, neither shall they sorrow' (2:62, 2:262, 2:274, 3:170, etc.). In a Sacred Saying of the Prophet, God says: 'The heavens and the earth contain Me not, yet the Heart of My faithful servant does.' And in the Quran it is proclaimed: 'Contented Soul, return to your Lord, Pleased (with Him) and Pleasing (to Him)' (89:27–8). Furthermore, it states: 'Fly/flee to God' (51:50). In other words, the circumstances advocated by these Sacred Verses and Saying are precisely the reverse of those identified by Francis Thompson as distancing humans from God. And this can only lead to proximity to God, to entering the Company of the Elect who always praise and give thanks to God.

The light of God shines on such a person's face. S/he has become transmuted, transformed from an ordinary human being into a person who has won Divine approval. Just as St. Francis of Assisi had a special relationship with birds and animals, even lesser creatures will befriend such a person. Here is a true-life story from one of the Sufi saints, related by Abu Ali Farmadi, one of the great Sufi saints of the Naqshbandi Order:

> During a trip, we had approached a mountain. Suddenly, a very large snake confronted us. We were all scared and fled. Shaykh Abu Sa'id was there, too. He dismounted from his horse and approached the snake. I was with the Shaykh. The snake rubbed its head on the ground before him, making movements as if to show respect. The Shaykh addressed the snake: 'You went to a lot of trouble.' Then the snake departed and returned to the mountain. Whereupon we asked the Shaykh what this had been all about. He replied: 'When I was at this mountain [in seclusion], we were in the same place with this snake for several years. When it sensed that we were passing by, it came and renewed its friendship. The beauty of the covenant comes from faith. Towards one of good temper, everything is good-tempered. Abraham was well-tempered, so the fire was well-behaved towards him, too: it didn't burn him.'[5]

So how does one go about becoming such a person? Well, there's a whole battery of methods, but one of them is to invoke God's name constantly. The Arabic word *zikr* (or *dhikr*) means both invocation and remembrance, so that we should constantly remember God, and invoking His name is remembering. Verses from the Quran indicate the importance of this: 'Believers, invoke God often' (33:41). 'Hearts find tranquility by invoking God, and only by invoking God do hearts find rest' (13:21). 'Whoever turns away from My invocation will have a constricted life' (20:124). 'Invoke God with much invocation' (33:41). 'Invoke Me so that I will remember you, and give thanks to Me' (2:152).

---

5. Translated from www.biriz.biz/evliyalar/ea0551.htm, a Turkish-language site, accessed 11/16/2010. For the reference to Abraham, see the Quran: 'God saved him from the fire' (29:24). 'O fire, be coolness and peace to Abraham' (21:69).

Similarly, the Prophet has remarked: 'One who loves something much invokes it often. And the love of God becomes evident through invocation/remembrance. Hearts become rusty just as iron rusts. Their polish is to recite the Quran and to invoke God frequently.' One can invoke God even in one's own language, using such words as 'Dieu' (French) or 'Gott' (German), for example. (The Master told an artist who asked for an invocation formula, 'Say "God" in your own language, say "God" in English. Say "God" and stroke the paintbrush [on the canvas].')

My encounter with the Master

Ever since my youth, I have been in quest of Truth. My interests have led me from paranormal events to yoga, from science to philosophy to mysticism, from East Asian religions to monotheism. It was in 1975 that I first encountered a Sufi master whom I shall call Saladin. I still remember the most important detail of that meeting:

'Do you want to *talk* about Sufism, or to *be* a Sufi?' Saladin asked.

'Being seems of greater value than talking,' I replied.

That was the prelude to a training period of three years, after which, in the spring of 1978, Saladin took me to visit Ahmet Kayhan. He was tall, lean, of arresting appearance, and had had jet-black hair in his youth, which never turned entirely white even in advanced old age. Accomplished Sufi masters have nonverbal ways of communicating their stations to those who visit them, and in a few minutes I became aware that I was in the presence of an extraordinary human being. Little did I realize at the time that this encounter would lead to a life-long immersion in the Master's teachings.

In my earlier books, I have described Grandpa Ahmet as 'the flawless human being.' He was flawless not physically, but spiritually. Honesty, courage, love, humility, intelligence, and all the other most adorable human qualities were combined in him to an unprecedented degree. Such people, who stand above what we come to expect from the average level of humanity, force us to redefine what it means to be human. But the Master ('Efendi') was the ultimate example, second to none, of a superior human being.

After being in his presence under the closest circumstances for fifteen years, all I can say is this: if he was human, we are all subhuman. If we are human, he was superhuman. Since the majority determines the generic, it follows that the latter must have been the case. The fact is that he was a saint, a Friend of God, who combined all the most wonderful human qualities within himself. And he took pains to stress that this was the fruit of superior moral conduct, of following God's Law to the letter.

Every sentence he uttered was the summary of many books, and I was able to judge them as true because I happened to have read some of those books. What was all the more amazing was that his knowledge was not based on book-knowledge. He learned to read and write during his military duty, and of course he read books after that. But when he pronounced on subjects about which he had not, and could not have, read anything at all, it was quite uncanny how accurate he could be. Call it what you will – intuitive knowledge, inner discernment, or whatever you like.

Let me give just one example. A brother who was into New Age philosophy and whose nickname was 'the Buddhist' experimented with psychedelic drugs years ago. Whereupon the Master told him: 'You picked up the phone, you got the message. Now hang up the phone and come here.'

As soon as I heard about this, I was immediately reminded of Alan Watts' dictum: 'When you get the message, you hang up the phone.'[6] It is the last word on artificially induced altered states of consciousness. According to Watts, psychedelic substances (entheogens) are tools that provide a glimpse into genuine mystical insight, to be discarded and replaced by more methodical meditation techniques once that glimpse is obtained. Watts was speaking from direct experience, as well as incorporating other people's experiences and the results of scientific research. The Master, on the other hand, never had any experience with psychedelics – he lived in a culture where these were totally unknown and nonexistent, not just physically but even conceptually. Yet his remark to our friend was dead on target, identical with expert opinion.

No book can foretell events that have not yet come to pass, and yet the Master had that knowledge, too. When we look at a wall, ordinary people cannot see beyond it. Yet the Master saw beyond that wall, and beyond the walls beyond it, and his very first pronouncement would be the end result, the conclusion, of an initially indefinite matter that would take months or years to resolve itself in real time.

---

6. This statement occurs in the Prologue, written nine years later, to Watts' book, *The Joyous Cosmology* (1962). We have it on the authority of Huston Smith that Ram Dass is the originator of this phrase.

What I am trying to do, however, is a contradiction in terms. I am trying to describe the indescribable, the truth of which one could pass judgment on only by encountering the Master oneself. But since he is no longer among us this is an impossibility, and so I must refrain from saying more. Instead, in this book I will try to achieve the next best thing, by allowing him to describe the Perfect Human in his own words.

His life

Master Kayhan was born around early 1898 in a village called Aktarla (Mako) in the province of Malatya, Turkey, and died in August 1998 in Ankara. He married his wife, Mother Hajar, in 1937. They had four children and many grandchildren.

The biographical details surrounding his saga are unexciting. They are quite ordinary – like any average human being, he lived, married, had children, worked, had health problems, and so on. No amount of detail in this regard is going to help us unravel his mystery. The mundane details of a sage's life really do not explain anything. This means we must look elsewhere if we are to understand how a human being becomes a saint.

This can be directly attributed to his encounter with his own Master, Hajji Ahmet Kaya, also called 'Keko' – Kurdish for 'father' – by those who knew him. Keko was in the grand tradition of the greatest Sufi saints, of the Naqshbandi Order, who traced their roots to Central Asia and from there, all the way to the Prophet.

To human beings, Keko was like a magnet. He attracted many, just as a magnet attracts iron filings. And among these, there was one of such purity and effort that he was capable of becoming a magnet exactly like Keko. Another simile might be inductive resonance. Over a short distance, an alternating current flowing in a coil can induce a similar current in another coil (the basis for wireless power transfer). Among the thousands of human beings who came to visit him, Keko 'electrified' one to such an extent that he became a source of electricity himself. That person was Ahmet Kayhan.

Remarks by those who knew him

As many of the persons involved are still alive, I shall refrain from naming names.

There was an Alawi Grandfather[7] in the city of Sivas. He was 117 years old and blind in both eyes. The Master was walking on a road in winter. The Grandfather told his sons: 'A light is going there in the riverbed. Bring him to me.' They went and looked; it was a stranger. They brought him in. The Grandfather pressed the Master to his bosom and exclaimed: 'You're my light, you're the one I've been seeking for years!'

It is related of an Italian professor of Turcology that, after seeing the Master, she met a couple of Turkish women who were looking for a teacher. She told them: 'What are you looking for? There is such a person in Ankara that I've seen Moses, Jesus and Muhammad combined in him.'

A friend who is now also dead: 'He lived in modesty, he died in modesty.'

A doctor:

It was from him that we learned how to love – to love human beings, to love animals. But we couldn't learn enough. That is what torments us. He told me: 'We gave you a house, a car, a spouse. What did you bring us?' I hung my head. He said: 'These are human. Become attributed with the attributes of God.'

A friend describes an event that occurred during a visit to the Master:

A person came. He entered with his shoes[8] and crossed his legs. Then he said, 'I'm the grandson[9] of Abdul Qadir Gilani [the Grand Saint]. There's supposed to be someone here who claims he's his inheritor. Show him to me!'

Grandpa doesn't say anything, he just rolls a cigarette.

---

7. The Alawis are a heterodox Islamic sect in the Middle East. Their spiritual elders are called 'Father' or 'Grandfather.'

8. An act of ill manners in a clean household where everyone performs the prostration and hence wears slippers or socks.

9. That is, his descendant. This kind of phrase is often used in the Middle East. Some translators of the Quran, unaware of this fact, have mistranslated Verses and then imputed error to the Quran itself. For example, Mary is called the 'sister' of Aaron (19:28), a temporal impossibility. But this simply means 'belonging to the same family.'

The man held the flame of a lighter under his hand, his palm, and said, 'See? This is the way that's done.' Grandpa says: 'What's he saying? Interpret for me.'

Grandpa: 'My child, come and sit down over here. First of all, [giving him the cigarette he had rolled] light a cigarette. Why do you scold us? You've invoked Abdul Qadir Gilani's name, how can we say anything against you?'

The man took two drags from the cigarette. Suddenly he said: 'Friends, have I done anything discourteous?' He kneeled before the Master, 'Sir, have I done anything rude? I'm the grandson of Abdul Qadir Gilani, but you're his inheritor.'

Grandpa told us: 'This man is in dire straits, he's out of money, let's all pitch in. He's invoked the great saint Gilani's name, let's give whatever we can.'

Of this (or a comparable) encounter, Efendi said: 'He spewed and declaimed, this place was all crowded. I said, "You've tired yourself. Have a cup of tea." He said: "Okay. But you didn't oppose anything I said, you just showed your assent," he said. I said "Yes." When he left I told the rest: "This man is freaked out, don't mind him."'

The friend continues:

I and [another friend] took Grandpa to a doctor. When we got there, Grandpa decided against it, he said 'No' and was on his way out. The doctor was very angry. 'Just a moment,' he said. 'They call me "Crazy So-and-so," I throw a patient on the floor and still I examine him.'

Grandpa said: 'My child, they call me "Grandpa Ahmet," I remove one's fire just as water extinguishes this cigarette in my hand with a *hiss*.'

The man stopped for a moment, he came out of that state, there was no trace of anger left in him. 'Grandpa,' he said, 'I'd be ashamed to examine you.'

He told me, 'My last will to you: Build a Heart, don't break it. Don't tear down the Ka'ba [the sacred sanctuary of the Heart]. Serve the Heart you've broken until you mend it. If you demolish the Ka'ba, how can you prostrate towards it?'

His views of others

The Master's view of human beings transcended ordinary religious lines and divisions. He called Yitzhak Rabin, the Israeli prime minister who was later assassinated by an extremist, 'a Muslim' because of his efforts to establish peace in the Middle East. He even called Mikhail Gorbachev, the head of the former Soviet Union, 'the saint of the age' because he worked for world peace. It was what a person was and did that counted, rather than categorizations and labels that pigeonhole.

Of the Japanese, he said: 'Now only the Japanese remain in the world who hold on to religion. No matter what they worship. They're the only ones who possess a religion.'

Regarding Americans, his comments were as follows:

> Science was lacking in the Ottomans, they have it. America has become an enormous empire in 250 years. It vanquished Europe, then only Russia remained to confront it. Now it's fallen, too. How did America do this? By hard work.
>
> How did America come about? How did they achieve all this in 250 years? Never mind earlier times, Istanbul is a six hundred-year old city during the [Ottoman] Empire. In spite of this, Istanbul is like a village beside their cities. So is Izmir [Smyrna]. What is the secret of this?
>
> Hard work, sir. God says, 'I love those who work, I'm with the righteous.' They worked hard physically and spiritually. That's the crux of the matter.
>
> Americans are outside by the time of the Dawn Prayer, they're going to work. Hardworking nations are like that. They assume the leadership of all nations. [A friend] went to Izmir five or ten years ago, he saw Americans there, going to work at the time of the Dawn Prayer-call. When the Prayer-call started, they all stopped, bowed their heads and listened. They continued on their ways after the Prayer-call was over. Go home, look at your national ID cards. It says 'Muslim' there. Be ashamed of that. Just sit lazily at home and say, 'We're Muslims'! If America were to become Muslim, it would be paradise on earth.
>
> What a beautiful name they've taken! A, M, K [vocalization of letters in 'America']. They're all [initials of] the Divine Names of God.[10]

---

10. Also: Allah, Muhammad, Koran (Quran).

Miraculous feats

Out of countless examples, I shall relate only a few. This is the subject that attracts the most attention, but it is also the most superficial. It is incorrect to ground the truth of a religion or the veracity of a saint on miraculous events. It is better not to dwell upon them at all. What is much more important is morality, courtesy and meticulously carrying out God's commandments.

First, consider the following observations of Ptolemy Tompkins regarding 'the Adult-Unlike-Other-Adults' – a person radically different from other people.

> This person could be either a man or a woman, but let's say for the moment that he is a man. Things fall into place for this man in a way that they don't for others. Doors open and shut for him as if they had known just when he was coming. Trains and buses pull up when he needs them to. Even the weather changes to suit his needs – though, due to his extraordinary and inexplicable contentedness, those needs tend to be modest in the extreme. Unlike most people, who struggle and chafe against a world that is all too often at odds with their desires, this individual seems to have struck up a secret agreement with life when no one was looking, as a result of which events just seem to go his way. Wanting next to nothing, he receives everything.[11]

Now compare this with the following account. If you visit a certain doctor who presently lives in Istanbul, and he is inclined to tell you, you will learn that on one occasion, the Master went with him to a hospital to visit an acquaintance in the Emergency Ward. This was perhaps the best-guarded section of the hospital, and the doctor was glad to be there to help the Master, since he was highly placed in his own hospital's hierarchy. He expected that he could overcome any obstacles they might encounter. What happened next is a case for the books.

The Master took his hand, and they began to walk. To his mounting amazement, doors swung open before them at just the right time, normally forbidding hospital personnel smiled and made way, the Master – who had never been in that hospital before – proceeded as if he knew exactly where he was going (which, of course, he did), and the

---

11. Ptolemy Tompkins, 'The Wisdom Eaters,' *Lapis* No. 8, in www.seriousseekers.com/News%20and%20Articles/article_tompkins_p_wisdomeaters.htm, accessed 11/16/2010.

doctor realized, with a shock, that it was the Master who was leading *him* through his own hospital rather than *he* leading the Master. The Master went straight to the patient as if all those obstacles had never existed, and they began to talk as though nothing extraordinary had happened.[12]

A few more accounts of the same sort follow.

A family member:

Ten or fifteen days before he died ... he was lying down in the front part of the house. We, the rest of the family, were in the back. Something important occurred. When he got up, he asked: 'What happened?' I said 'Nothing happened,' whereupon he told me the event exactly as it took place, as if he had been there. He said, 'I have an eye behind me, I saw it with that eye.'

He gave his last pension (90 million Liras) to Mother Hajar. She hid this, but lost it. We looked everywhere and couldn't find it. Mother Hajar pressed him – she said, 'Find this for me.' 'Go,' he said, 'behind the door to her room, she has an old dress. Look in its pocket.'

But I had already looked there, and Mother Hajar had dismissed the money we found. 'That's my daily allowance,' she'd said, 'put it back.' We went back to where he told us and counted it. There were 90 million Liras. But my father had never entered my mother's room in his life, and its only key always stayed in her pocket.'

A prominent politician:

The first time we went to visit Grandpa was in 1976, together with [a famous journalist and another friend]. He seated me beside him, they were sitting facing us. I had some questions in my mind about Sufism, but couldn't bring myself to ask them. I especially wanted to ask about the Unity of Being [Ibn 'Arabi's famous concept].

A little later, Grandpa took a paper out of his pocket, gave it to me and said simply, 'Read.' I looked at it, it was about the Unity of Being. When I finished reading, he asked: 'Okay?' 'Okay,' I said. 'What's that?' [the journalist] asked. 'It's not for you,' said Grandpa, and put the paper back in his pocket.

---

12. I haven't used quotation marks since I don't have his detailed account written down.

On another occasion: 'One day, my friends exasperated me, and I rushed out to visit him. As soon as I was through the door, he said: "Come on in. Why do they vex you like this?"'

An acquaintance: 'One day, Grandpa was performing his Prayer in the back, and we were sitting here talking. A fourteen-year-old girl said: "I saw Grandpa and this place in a dream, and came straight over without asking anyone anything."'

In a dream, a family member saw Noah's Ark. Its captain was Grandpa. It was two stories from the outside, but many floors from within. One floor was the North and South Poles, another floor was America.

A couple who knew the Master for many years:

The wife: 'We were driving on an intercity highway in the wee hours of the morning. My husband was driving the car. I was in the back seat and in constant vigil so he wouldn't fall asleep and cause an accident. Suddenly, I saw the Master's face leaning over the front windshield and waving at us with his hand. I noticed that my husband had begun to nod his head. It was a signal for him to wake up.'

The husband: 'I was driving when I seem to have drowsed off imperceptibly. Suddenly, in my dream, I saw the Master lean over the front windshield from the top of the car and wave his hand. I immediately woke up.'

In other words, one saw in reality exactly what the other saw in a dream.

The next time they visited the Master, before they could say anything, he remarked: 'You tire me. Am I supposed to watch out for you all the time?'

On another occasion, after he folded space while riding in a friend's car – the car appeared to have moved an impossible distance in a split-second – he told him: 'Don't be preoccupied with such things. These are for children.'

Paranormal abilities are merely the object of contempt for such people, who regard them as childish. As Tompkins observes, 'the message that the Adult-Unlike-Other-Adults holds out is one of uncompromising singularity and seriousness.'[13]

---

13. Tompkins, ibid.

His teachings

'Man is not God, and God is not man. But man is close to God, and God is close to man.' Like Alexander cutting the Gordion Knot, the Master put an end with these words to centuries of sterile theological debate, which had got caught between the manifestation of the Divine in a human being and the outright denial that such a self-contradictory statement leads to. On the one hand, this formula avoids the pitfalls, the logical contradictions, of equating a man or men with God. On the other hand, it democratically brings God within the easy reach of all human beings.

It is said in the Psalms: 'Fear of the Lord is the beginning of wisdom' (Psalms 111:10, Proverbs 9:10). But why? Why is fear the door to wisdom?

The way the Master explained it, fear of God leads to obeying His orders. And obeying his orders makes the love of God blossom in one's Heart. This the Master stated explicitly. What was implicit in his teachings was the following: when God becomes Beloved to one, one fears offending the Beloved by violating His commandments. This causes one to be more careful, and hence one's love of God increases. As a result, love and fear constitute two perpendicular fields, similar to the electromagnetic field, that cause one's wisdom to spiral ever upwards.

When the Master spoke of 'Sufism,' he meant Islam, and when he said 'Islam' he meant Sufism. To him, the two were identical. What was important was that the Divine Law should be considered as the foundation, the basis, of spiritual development. The precepts, morals and actions of the Divine Law constituted the infrastructure upon which the skyscraper of Unification, of Sufic mysticism, would rise, and could not otherwise be built. Even assuming for a moment that it could be achieved by other means, such an achievement would merely be a temporary State (*hal*) and not a permanent Station (*maqam*). Thus, 'Islam' and 'Sufism' were two sides of the same coin. But what should we call the coin itself? What everybody ordinarily understands by these two words is so variegated and so misleading that another term seems called for, in the same way that we call the synthesis of oxygen and hydrogen 'water.' If I were to follow the Eastern tradition, perhaps I would call it 'Tao' or 'Nirvana.' If I follow the Western tradition, I should call it 'wisdom.' In the end, names are unimportant – 'a rose by any other name would smell as sweet.' What counts is the fragrance, the experience: inhale first, worry about labels afterwards. But this *is* what has traditionally been taught by Islam and Sufism.

The Master took pure Sufism, like democracy, with a pinch of salt. His preferred term was 'Muhammadanhood,' that is, living a Muhammadan life.

I should perhaps clarify what is meant by 'Muhammadanhood.' A Muhammadan is a follower of Muhammad. In the past, some people have objected to this term. Seeing a parallel between 'Muhammadan' and 'Christian,' they have concluded that it implies an equation of Muhammad with God, in the same way that Jesus Christ is regarded as God or the son of God in Christianity. But this is not the case. 'Muhammadan' simply means a follower in the path of Muhammad, nothing else. Similarly, 'Muhammadanhood' denotes the state of being such a follower. It is not correct to call this 'Muhammadanism,' because one follows not only the thought and faith of Muhammad but also his deeds, and because the '-ism' suffix has been usurped by ideologies.

Why is this term necessary at all? Because the term 'Muslim' has of late come to lack this emphasis on the importance of the Prophet. But without the Prophet, of course, right understanding of the Quran – and right action based on it – would be impossible. We have to remember that the best guide to a religion is the one who founded it in the first place.

The Holy Grail and the Fisher King

On July 9, 1994, the Master suffered an accident at a resort hotel in Yalova, Turkey. Stepping out of a bathtub, he fell on the slippery floor. His right thigh (the top of the femur, to be precise) was broken as a result.

He was operated on three days later, but the break never healed satisfactorily, which was perhaps to be expected considering that he was ninety-six at that time. Until his departure in 1998, the wound would make its effect felt. Not that this had any adverse effect on his flock – they showered him all the more with their attention, although this became an unbearable burden at his great age and perhaps hastened that event by which we all have to go someday.

In this section, I shall digress from the normally factual account I have been giving and delve into the symbolism of myth. Yet this is not out of place, for it will be apparent to anyone who is knowledgeable that what I experienced with the Master for his last four years – that is, after his leg was broken – is an instance in real life of the myth of the Fisher King. Of course, there is nothing extraordinary in knowing a lame person. If we consider the myth in detail, however, we shall discover that there is more here than meets the eye.

I am aware that there are many versions of the Holy Grail/Fisher King story, and that various separate legends became conflated over the course of time. Rather than mull over their minutiae, I shall present a short, sorted-out version that appears to make the greatest sense to me. First the story, then the interpretation.

The Grail is supposed to be the chalice in which the blood of the Holy Prophet Jesus was collected. It could also be the cup of the Last Supper, and thus associated with the Eucharist. 'Grail' derives from the Old French 'graal' or 'greal,' and 'san greal' (St. Grail) came to be read as 'sang real' (royal blood) in the later Middle Ages. It has also been associated with the Philosopher's Stone (*lapis elixir*, Stone of the Elixir of Life).

The cup, originally in the possession of Joseph of Arimathea, is transported to Britain, entrusted to the Grail King or Fisher King, and guarded in the splendid Grail Castle atop the Mount of Salvation. The king, however, suffers an injury in his thigh, after which he begins to waste away.

In the Bible, Jacob struggles with the dark angel during which his thigh is dislocated (Genesis 32:24–32). Job is tested with illness and calamity, while Joseph of Arimathea is wounded by a black angel. 'This assault by the dark aspect of [creation] against a chosen human being who is called upon to grapple with the dark [power] and at the same time to serve as a vessel for the realization of the totality of God is therefore an ever-recurring motif in the history of Judeo-Christian religious consciousness.'[14]

Meanwhile, King Arthur has heard of the Grail, and sends his knights off in search of it. But the Grail can be accessed only by the purest, and in one version of the tale it is Percival (Parsifal) who visits the Fisher King and sees the Grail. The king's illness and the sighting call for a response which, however, Percival is unable to make, and as a result he suffers a setback due to which his quest is postponed by many years.

In the meantime the Fisher King dies, and his land becomes a Waste Land. Only the hero who discovers the Grail will be able to rejuvenate the land, making it prosperous and happy again. After a long, arduous struggle, Percival is finally able to achieve this goal.

---

14. Emma Jung and Marie-Louise von Franz, *The Grail Legend*, Andrea Dykes (tr.), Princeton, NJ: Princeton University Press (Bollingen Series), 1998 [1960], p. 211.

What was the response demanded by the event? One is suggested by the legends: Percival should have inquired about the Grail and how it could be obtained. There is no simple answer because many can be given, but the one I prefer is *lack of courtesy*. It is necessary to observe courtesy (*adab*) at all times, under all conditions and especially in the presence of such an august king. Percival should have shown the Fisher King a little more compassion, should have inquired about his health and perhaps tried to heal him.

As for the vision of the Grail, let us try to understand it via the so-called 'legend of the Fisher King.' The story's symbolism as it has come down to our age is a little garbled, and I have tried to straighten it out partially in what follows.

Once there was a boy who wanted to be king, and in a trial of ordeals he spent a night alone in a forest. Lucky boy that he was, the holy vision of the Grail, the symbol of Grace, appeared to him. A voice told the child: 'You will be the Grail's Guardian. It will heal men's hearts.' But the boy, blinded by the prospect of a life full of power, beauty and glory, could only think of the omnipotence the Grail would confer on him. In this state of mind he touched the Grail, which seared his hand and disappeared.

From that day the boy is wounded, both materially and spiritually. He grows to be a young man, a king, but he is sullen and listless; life has no meaning, no purpose. His knights return empty-handed from every search for the Grail. One day, as he lies dying, he is offered a drink by another person. His wound is healed. He looks at the cup, and recognizes it as the Holy Grail. He asks: 'How were you able to find the Grail, which neither I as king, nor my knights have ever been able to?' The person replies: 'I did not know you were a king. I only saw your suffering.' It is he who has become Guardian of the Grail.

Thus the Grail will not be found by those who search for it out of selfish desire. It is again compassion, the urge to help others in need, that will cap our spiritual quest. Such power is entrusted only to those who are willing and able to give, not those who will block or misappropriate it.

We can now attempt to decipher the Grail legend. The actual physical existence of such a cup, now or in the past, is of no concern to us here. We are concerned only with its symbolism. (Others have already noted the similarity between the Grail chalice and the cup of Jamshid in Persian–Arabian legend.)[15]

---

15. See 'Sufism: The case of the Cryptic Wineglass' in my online book *Science,*

Let us start with the Fisher King. As psychologist Carl G. Jung has observed, he is a 'fisher of men,' a spiritual guide who leads lost souls to salvation. But what does the Grail mean? What does it signify? For centuries people have toiled to find an answer. I shall offer a Sufic analysis below.

From time immemorial, people have believed that blood embodies the life-principle and is the seat of the soul.[16] In Old Arabic, blood also meant the self. The chalice into which the precious blood – that is, the selfhood – of Jesus is poured is thus the 'Christ-bearer,' the *christophoros* (from which the English name Christopher is derived). But who is Christ, exactly? He is the Messiah, the Mahdi, the spiritual leader of his time. And in Sufic terminology, the same function is implemented by the Saintlight (since the Age of Prophets is now long past).

What is the Saintlight? It began as the Light of Prophethood on the forehead of Adam. It was carried on from prophet to prophet as a light on their foreheads, reaching its greatest intensity with Muhammad. Muhammad combined the attributes of prophethood and sainthood within himself. Though no new religion and hence new prophet will appear, the Light of Prophethood now continues down through the saints as the Light of Sainthood, or Saintlight.

The blood of Jesus, then, is an equivalent symbol for the Saintlight, and the vessel – the *human* vessel – that bears it is the Heartmind of the Sufi saint, the Fisher King. Thus, the Grail and the Fisher King, who is the Guardian of the Grail, are two sides of the same coin. And the next guardian, whoever he may be, *must discover the Saintlight within his own Heartmind* and personally become the Grail's Sufic version.

Now the amazing thing is that all this fit the Master to a 'T.' He was not a mythical figure, a figment of anyone's imagination. Instead, he was already a Sufi saint, already a spiritual king, already a fisher or savior of men – saving them from being drowned in the vicissitudes of this world. But the parallels became overwhelming once his leg was broken. Perhaps Jung would have said that an archetype was unfolding, was being acted out, in real life.

Myths are not supposed to actualize themselves in real life. Yet this one did.

But why? Why did such a marvelous person suffer such an injury? The Master himself gave various explanations at different times, such

---

Knowledge, and Sufism, also published in *The Secret of Islam*, Berkeley, CA: North Atlantic Books, 2003.

16. *The Grail Legend*, p. 92.

as that he had gone hunting in his youth without any genuine need. Perhaps all of these indeed played a part. But to my mind, they do not explain why a mere legend that arose, as far as we know, in the twelfth century, should be enacted across a span of eight hundred years in the real world, at the end of the twentieth century, at a very different level of technology and civilization.

St. Francis, the 'Peace Prayer,' and democracy

Perhaps the significance of the Grail, in the present context, is to serve as a pointer to the affinities between the Master and St. Francis of Assisi, a contemporary of the Grail legend.

Echoing widespread opinion, Ernest Renan wrote of St. Francis that he was 'the only perfect Christian since Christ ... Francis really *was* a second Christ, or, rather, he was a faithful mirror of Christ.'[17] In the same way, the Master was a faithful reflection of God and His Prophet. We might say of them both that they were Grail-realized persons, and any similarity between Francis and the Master cannot fail to highlight a corresponding affinity between Jesus and Muhammad.

During the years I was visiting Saladin, I was also translating wisdom texts into Turkish, such as Desiderata, Plato's allegory of the Cave and selections from the Upanishads. I would show these translations to Saladin and ask him to comment on them. I always received exceptional insights from the Sufic standpoint.

Among these texts, there was a lovely poem generally attributed to St. Francis of Assisi.[18] It is widely known:

> Lord, make me an instrument of Thy peace.
> Where there is hatred, let me sow love
> Where there is injury, pardon
> Where there is doubt, faith
> Where there is despair, hope
> Where there is darkness, light;
> And where there is sadness, joy.
> O Divine Master, grant that I may not so much seek

---

17. Quoted in Roy M. Gasnick (comp., ed.), *The Francis Book*, New York: Macmillan, 1980, p. 135.

18. Attributed, but it cannot be traced, to St. Francis. A Google search reveals that this 'Peace Prayer' first surfaced in a 1912 French magazine. The author is anonymous, to the best of my knowledge.

To be consoled as to console;
To be understood, as to understand;
To be loved, as to love.
For it is in giving that we receive,
It is in pardoning that we are pardoned,
And it is in dying
That we are born to eternal life.

I translated it, and Saladin liked it so much that he showed it to the Master, who was likewise impressed. However, he also thought it could be improved on when viewed from a Sufic perspective, so Saladin worked on the poem until they arrived at an enhanced Sufic version of the text. This the Master would distribute to all visitors, saying that it was composed entirely of verses from the Quran and the sayings of the Prophet. Of a special prayer of the Prophet, he remarked 'This is democracy' more than once, and of St. Francis' poem, he said the same thing many times.

The Master thought that this poem captured an essential aspect of religion, whether it be Christianity, Islam, or any other. He regarded it as the essence of democracy. In this he was fully in agreement with one of Francis' most astute biographers, G. K. Chesterton, who called Francis 'the world's one quite sincere democrat' and a 'very genuine democrat.' One might say that the Master's uncanny discernment pierced through to the very heart of Francis' thought as expressed in this poem.

The Master always used sources from within the Islamic tradition. This poem and Edouard Schuré's text on Hermeticism were the only exceptions to this rule, so his use of them is evidence of the high regard in which he held both.

As a footnote to this anecdote, Ziauddin Sardar has written about St. Francis:

There is considerable common ground behind the teachings of St Francis and those of the Sufis. Indeed, some people argue that during his stay in Cairo St Francis became a Sufi. This is one explanation why the caliph gave him complete freedom to travel in Muslim lands and come and go as he wished. Some people even go so far as to say that the nine months when he is supposed to have disappeared he actually spent in a Sufi *tariqa* [Order].[19]

---

19. http://web.archive.org/web/20030822132230/http://www.others.com/assisi.htm, accessed 11/16/2010.

Thus, in using Francis' poem, the Master was perhaps actually reclaiming lent property. Whatever the truth of the matter, there is no doubt that Francis' version of Christianity and Sufism share a common ground.

Chesterton brings up the notion of *courtesy* in relation to St. Francis – unaware as he may have been of Sufism, in which courtesy is held to be of paramount importance. Francis, he says, treated everyone like a king, even the lowliest:

> He honored all men; that is, he not only loved but also respected them all. What gave him his extraordinary personal power was this: that from the pope to the beggar, from the sultan of Syria in his pavilion to the ragged robber crawling out of the wood, there was never a man who looked into those brown burning eyes without being certain that Francis Bernardone was really interested in *him*; in his own individual life from the cradle to the grave; that he himself was being valued and taken seriously ...
>
> Now for this particular moral and religious idea there is no external expression except courtesy. Exhortation does not express it, for it is not mere abstract enthusiasm; beneficence does not express it, for it is not mere pity. It can be conveyed only by a certain grand manner that may be called good manners. We may say if we like that Saint Francis, in the bare and barren simplicity of his life, had clung to one rag of luxury: the manners of a court. But whereas in a court there is one king and a hundred courtiers, in this story there was one courtier, moving among a hundred kings, for he treated the whole mob of men as a mob of kings.[20]

Here, Chesterton has captured the essence of courtesy. This dovetails with the Master's following statement: 'Everybody calls me "Master," but every person who enters through this door is my master.' The one nuance Chesterton's penetrating observation fails to note is that a person is able to become a spiritual king only by treating other people as kings and queens. In the movie and play *My Fair Lady* (based on Bernard Shaw's *Pygmalion*), Colonel Pickering treats even a flower-girl like a duchess, whereas Professor Higgins (on his own admission) treats even a duchess like a flower-girl. It is in Pickering's approach – and not Higgins' – that nobility of soul shines forth. It is through honoring others that one becomes oneself ennobled. And

---

20. Quoted from Chesterton, *St. Francis of Assisi* (1923) in *The Francis Book*, pp. 40–1.

here we glimpse one of the democratic promises of Islam: nobility is not a matter of blue blood, even a beggar can become a king.

The entire text of the Sufi-enhanced version of St. Francis' poem is reproduced in the following pages in 'The audition,' interspersed with comments by the Master.

This should not lead one to suppose that he viewed democracy as an unalloyed blessing. His main complaint, however, was perhaps about excesses committed in the name of democracy, even in opposition to its true spirit. (Plato, too, had much earlier pointed out how freedom too often degenerates into license.) In particular, he held that the splintering of political parties turned 'wife against husband and father against son.' He said: 'Democracy tries to unite, whereas the multi-party system tries to fragment, to tear apart. One builds up, the other tears down.' This may represent a failing of the democratic process that has yet to be resolved by political science. 'Democracy works well in America [the USA] and Britain,' he observed, 'because they have strong constitutions and firm laws. They arrest criminals.'

More dangerous, however, were the two points he always returned to: illicit gain (e.g., 'Thou shalt not steal') and illicit sex (e.g., 'Thou shalt not covet thy neighbor's wife'),[21] which democracy failed to provide adequate safeguards against. This failure was due to a blind spot in democracy which prevented the necessity of these primary prohibitions of God from being perceived. It was this failure that would ultimately lead to ruin.

Light on astrology

The Master's discourse 'fired my neurons,' as it were. It had an immensely stimulating and liberating effect on my mental processes, allowing me to discover connections between things I knew that I had never imagined before. I have written about these in earlier books.

Take, for example, the case of astrology, not discussed previously.

'That the sky does something to man is obvious enough,' wrote Kepler, who practised both astronomy and astrology, 'but what it does specifically remains hidden.'[22] Kepler's words ring no less true today

---

21. Of course, in addition to these two Commandments, there are many other forms that illicit gain and sex take.

22. Quoted in Arthur Koestler, *The Sleepwalkers*, Harmondsworth: Penguin, 1968 [1959], p. 245.

than when they were written five centuries ago. Astrology is a subject over which skeptics and believers remain sharply divided.

For decades, I too followed the subject with interest. I noted with sorrow the fate of the French scientist Michel Gauquelin, who was driven to suicide by his detractors for claiming that more athletes are born under Mars than any other planet. I suspended judgment until, one day, a third possibility came up that cast the debate in an entirely different light. This was due to a remark belonging to Giordano Bruno, a contemporary of Kepler.

Bruno spoke of 'the celestial images on which all things below depend.'[23] This immediately brought to my mind what Master Ahmet Kayhan had said during our summer excursion to Ayvalik in 1996. The Master's explanations acted as a catalyst in making the necessary associations between the sources I shall be presenting.

We had been reading the section on 'Spacewarps, Timewarps' in his last magnum opus, *Study in the School of Wisdom*. This section deals with the Sufic concept of 'the folding of space and time.' When we came to the part where the teleportation example given in the Quran (27:40) is discussed, he interrupted us to give a lengthy explanation as to how this was indeed possible, but only for the very few who have gone through decades of training. In *The Bezels of Wisdom*, Ibn 'Arabi himself mentions that such instantaneous relocation is effected, not at the ordinary physical level, but at the level of the 'Essential Realities' (*al-a'yan al-thabita*).

Probably the easiest way to think of this is to look at what ufologist Jacques Vallée says: 'If you think of [reality] as the software for the universe, all it would take is for someone to change a comma in the program and the chair you are sitting in wouldn't be a chair at all.'[24] Or else, the chair would not be here, but elsewhere. And indeed, it was the throne of the Queen of Sheba that was teleported in the Quranic example. Obviously 'reality' here means a higher order of reality than what we're accustomed to, and if you replace that term by 'Essential Realities,' you will see more or less what I'm getting at.

What caught my attention in Bruno's statement, however, was that he was not referring simply to 'the stars' (or planets), as any latter-day astrologer might be prone to do. Rather, he was speaking of 'celestial

---

23. Quoted from Frances Yates, *Giordano Bruno and the Hermetic Tradition*, London: Routledge & Kegan Paul, 1978, pp. 232–2, in Michael Baigent and Richard Leigh, *The Elixir and the Stone*, London: Penguin, 1997, p. 182.

24. 1995 interview posted on www.conspire.com/val3html, accessed 10/17/1998.

images' in the same way (and perhaps even in the same sense) that Ibn 'Arabi spoke of 'Essential Realities.' Bruno more probably meant the signs of the Zodiac, but his statement can be interpreted in another manner as well.

Once we make this connection, the meaning and import of astrology stands revealed. Astronomers have long taken astrologers to task because the gravitational and electromagnetic influences of distant astronomical objects are too faint to make a significant difference in the destiny or propensity of individuals on earth. But if we take the heavenly entities to refer, not to the stars and planets in physical space, but to Essential Realities in 'ontological space' or 'reality space,' and think of the elevation as taking place not in the third dimension (physical 'up') but in the fifth dimension (noetic 'up,' counting time as a fourth), we immediately see that understood in this sense, the claims of astrology hold true, and not just for human births alone, but for all phenomena unfolding on the 'movie screen' before our eyes. For their reality, including spatiotemporal location, is determined on higher levels of reality than that which we inhabit, on the film moving in front of the movie projector and not on the screen itself.

Ever since scientists fell out with churchmen (perhaps even before), Western civilization has abandoned faith in anything other than the physical. The fifth dimension has been collapsed onto the third, 'angels' and 'elves' have become 'aliens,' and Essential Realities have been replaced with stars, planets and sun signs. (Whether ordinary astrology works is a moot point, but the interpretation presented here is the truth it points to.) It is simply our error if, seeing a shadow, we fail to infer the entity it belongs to merely because we cannot see the entity, and impute substance to the shadow itself. There are higher orders of reality, ontological levels that are 'more real,' and it does not serve our benefit to ignore their existence just because statistically, the majority of human beings are not 'tuned' to the 'wavelengths' at which they can be perceived. Quite without such supernormal perception, our mental faculties themselves should suffice to infer their existence, but unfortunately these faculties, too, have shriveled to the point where they are incapable of contemplating any exit from the physical.

The emancipation of humankind

The Master's wisdom also allowed me to catch a glimpse of how Islam could possibly be the last religion. He once mentioned that the Prophet had great difficulty in explaining even the simplest things to the ignorant people around him, but now such explanations had become much easier due to a general improvement in the receptivity of humankind. The seeds that earlier fell on stone, as it were, now fell on tilled soil.

This led me to conjecture that humanity had been developing not simply since the Prophet's time, but since the dawn of man. It then became possible to view the prophets as coming at appropriate times to appropriate societies, aiding – perhaps even catalyzing – the emancipation of the human race.

Finally, a universal religion came that differed in two important respects from its predecessors. First, the great spiritual leavening of humanity had come to a point where every individual could now be entrusted with his or her own spiritual destiny. There was no longer any need for a chaperone, a church, and this was one of the prime distinctions between Islam and other religions with a claim to universality. From this point on, a sacerdotal organization was not required, and one could, by using the revealed instructions, work out one's own salvation oneself. In this, God was removing all intermediaries between Himself and a human being. Though religious instructors still existed, they stood beside the individual, not between him and God, and they were not organized into a class set apart.

The second difference was that this latest version of revelation – Islam is at pains to emphasize this continuity of revelation, which invited all societies to the Sacred – no longer required an update. Humanity, and the revelation that came to it, had reached a point where further developments could take place within this last version, for it bore answers that met the entire spectrum of possibilities inherent within the human condition. A helpful analogy may be of humanity as 'hardware' and religion as 'software.' For a given set of hardware, the software develops until it reaches its most perfect, best-suited form. Any further change would require a change of the hardware itself – not a viable option in the case of humanity.

The Wisdom Base

Database.
Information Base.
Knowledge Base.
And now, finally: Wisdom Base.

In 1987, I returned from a trip to England armed with a pocket tape recorder. It was my intention to tape, and then decipher, the Master's conversations. For years, I had waited for this opportunity to tape his voice. Over the preceding years, though I had taken scanty notes, I had by and by come to the realization that here was this veritable Amazon flowing out to sea with no chance of retrieval. Something had to be done to capture every drop of wisdom issuing from his mouth. His words had wings – they had the power to elevate you, whether you realized it or not. The Master encouraged the taking of notes, saying that memory is prone to forgetfulness and that his words should be recorded: 'The mind forgets, but writing does not forget.'

I had to discontinue taping the Master before a year had passed, for the following reasons: (1) The Master sometimes spoke very softly, so that some words dropped out of the voice range of the recorder, and (2) transcribing the proceedings of a day every evening was taking up too much of my time. Doing this was necessary because I had only a limited number of minicassettes I could cycle through.

So I decided to carry a pocket notepad, and take down every word of the Master I could. I exhausted more than two dozen writing pads in this way before the Master's departure.

I was very careful in taking these notes. If I could not catch every single word but was forced to record the general meaning, this was indicated. If I missed only one word and had to substitute an equivalent, this was also recorded. So it is quite clear which words belonged to the Master and which did not. Generally, I did not record the names of persons asking questions but only the Master's responses, because it was the latter which were important.

One difference between these notes and the audio transcriptions is that I was not able to take down every word. Fortunately, however, there was a certain redundancy in the Master's speech. Some sentences he would repeat twice, some words more times. Together with the pauses in his speech, which was itself unhurried, this allowed me sufficient time to take down the salient points of his discourse.

These 'field notes,' together with the earlier transcribed material, constitute a meticulous recording of the Master's teachings over more than a decade. This is unique, for while many people took notes, no one else was able to record the Master's conversations so copiously or faithfully. There is ample material in these recordings to form an idea of what the Master thought and taught.

This is of the first importance, because although the Master published four books in Turkish (I helped him in preparing these), distributed many pamphlets and more than a hundred sheets, nowhere is there a full statement of his own views. The books were anthologies, selections from sources he considered valuable or simply useful. The only full-length piece belonging to him in these books – which he personally dictated to me one night – is the Introduction to *The Meaning of the Four Books*.

An Islamic wisdom manual

Now, *for the first time*, we have at hand the actual teachings of perhaps the greatest Muslim/Sufi saint of the age, flowing straight from his mouth. Not only that, but the material has been organized so that you can start on the first page and continue through to the end in one smooth flow. This argues against a chronological arrangement, which would not be as useful or accessible. And in fact, the chronological records are just a disconnected jumble of snippets.

I have also included a few reports from reliable people who were able to quote verbatim from the Master. These ring true and do not distort his teachings in any way. Indeed, some of them are corroborated by my own records.

The reader thus enjoys an advantage that no one who visited the Master, not even myself, ever was able to glimpse before – the big picture, the complete range of his oral teachings, painstakingly pieced together like a jigsaw puzzle. As the puzzle gradually took shape, the grand design of the Master's teachings began to emerge. Against this, of course, has to be set the advantage of having seen him in person. Which is preferable? I think the latter, without a doubt. But failing that, the record we have on hand is invaluable in that it sets down the highest wisdom teaching as it was elaborated in the contemporary world, moment by moment. To all those interested in 'Islam,' here is the true Islam, and to all those interested in Sufism, here is the true Sufism, as set forth by one of their greatest exponents in modern times.

Methodology

In performing this arduous task, I am aware of the tremendous burden resting on my shoulders. It is of the essence that I reflect his teachings as accurately as possible, ideally with zero distortion. Hence, utmost care was exercised in processing the Master's legacy.

How many times have we wished that we could tell which speaker was Plato, and which Socrates, in the *Dialogues*? Well, we have that kind of an opportunity, here and now. In what follows, I shall not tamper with the Master's words in any way. My own comments will be confined to footnotes, to (*italics in parentheses*) and to [brackets] where the text flow may be interrupted. These clearly mark out which is the Master's voice and which the compiler/editor's. The latter I have tried to keep to a minimum. In general, bracketed expressions are part of the main text, while italicized remarks are comments about the text. Questions and comments by various people have also been typeset in *italics*. Any longish statements by others will be presented in indented paragraphs.

The Master once indicated his trust in me as follows: '[He] says what I say. He doesn't say anything more than what I say.' I shall try to live up to that trust. He also instructed me to take only his religious/spiritual statements and to discard the rest, and I have also tried to abide by this. This is only logical, for the small talk of everyday life – or the private affairs of other people, for example – has no place in these pages. What follows does not exhaust the Master's utterances, it is what I am able to bring together at present within a coherent book.

Since this is not a 'critical edition,' the exact words of the Master and those not used by him but nevertheless faithful to his general meaning have been 'homogenized.' This is done in order to obtain a flowing text unencumbered by extensive textual devices. Overall, I would estimate that ninety-nine percent of the text serving as basis for the translation consists of the Master's very own words. As for the remainder, it is only 'connective tissue,' providing continuity without introducing external or different meanings. Chapter and section headings belong to me, but I have at times used phrases from the Master for these.

During the period when I was taking these notes, the Master naturally returned to some points numerous times. Hence a story might be retold in a number of different ways. This was a very important aspect of the Master's use of stories, and there was a reason for it. He would tailor the stories to fit the needs of a particular visitor. Thus he might conclude a classic story with a radically different ending. This was his way of providing 'medicine' for a specific individual at a specific time. Sometimes he also answered unvoiced questions in this way.

On the other hand, I would sometimes take down the same story with varying degrees of detail. If it had often been heard – or recorded – I might be content with a brief summary of the highlights.

Hence, the following procedure was implemented:

1. The notes were converted into electronic format using word-processing software.
2. All stories and all the variants of each story were collated using a tree structure.
3. The fullest or most representative version of a story was selected as template.
4. This was then translated into English.
5. Elements missing from that version were searched for in other variants, and relevant material was brought in and introduced – by tweezers or with a pipette, as it were.
6. Thus, a composite was obtained representing the fullest and richest version of that story.

The same method has been utilized in other cases as well. In translations, I have valued clarity and ease of understanding over accuracy, but neither has the latter been sacrificed entirely. In any case, the letter of the original may be changed, but not the meaning.

The discussions and stories have been topically arranged. The result is a collage of expressions and sentences uttered by the Master. Stories that fall in the same category have been placed together, as far as possible. The 'Mosaic cycle' of stories, for example, brings together stories that deal with Moses *from within the Islamic/Sufi tradition*. And some of his teaching stories were very similar to the parables of Jesus. These and others, I am sure, will be of great interest not just to Muslims or Sufis alone. In this practice I am actually following a lead of the Master, who sometimes concatenated several stories involving the same person.

I have included the Introduction to *Body and Spirit*, which also served as Introduction to *The Meaning of the Four Books*. This piece was dictated to me by the Master himself word for word, and is the only such extensive piece available. Its inclusion here serves not only as a yardstick regarding how the Master himself would have gone about writing a book, but also completes the present book by serving to bring all of the Master's most important statements under one cover.

Stories presented in earlier books are included here: (1) for the sake of completeness; (2) because those were recalled from memory and are therefore different variants; and (3) because those books included other stories from Sufi lore and what came directly from the Master was not explicitly indicated.

What we have here is a cookbook. All the recipes are here, all the ingredients are indicated, all the exquisite flavors are described, straight from the highest authority. There's only one catch – you have to cook it yourself. And therein lies the rub, for it's easy on paper but not in real life.

Important notes

1. What the Master has imparted to us is 'received tradition.' *Received tradition* – tradition as it has come down to our day, as we received it from the Master, as he received it from his own Master and so on. It may not suit our opinions, or may even clash with what we know. This fact should not prevent us from benefiting from what is essential in his message. Take what you need, what is beneficial to you – leave the rest if you want to. Don't throw out the baby with the bathwater. Certainly this editor cannot be blamed for remaining faithful to the main thrust of the teachings. I want to make it clear that I have not 'sanitized' them – this is actually what the Master taught. This material was intended strictly for internal consumption. In general, there is no proselytization to anyone outside the fold, so this is no propaganda tract.

2. A note on factuality: It is very important to distinguish between what is related as historical fact and what constitutes a Sufi teaching story. For example, characters who cannot have been together in real life because they lived in different ages may be cast together in such a story. I would caution the reader that in such cases, what is important is the lesson to be drawn rather than who actually met whom or did what in physical life. Details may vary, attributions may change, but as a rule the core message of a Sufi story remains invariant. I say this in order to avoid fruitless quibbling over details. After all, these are only stories. A Nobel Prize-winning physicist (I withhold his name) was once presented with a copy of Dostoevsky's *Crime and Punishment*.

When he finished it, his only comment was: 'The sun rises twice on the same day.' For God's sake let's not get stuck in this mode, shall we?

3. Another important point to note concerns translations of Quranic verses (called simply 'Verses') and the Traditions ('Sayings') of the Prophet. Arabic, in which the Prophet articulated both, is an extremely complex, rich and textured language. It is commonly accepted among scholars that the Quran cannot be translated properly, because of the multiple meanings of various Arabic words. By the same token, this also applies to the Traditions. Hence, like translations from the Chinese-language *Tao Te Ching*, every attempt to tease out the meaning of verses or sayings in another language is at best an interpretation or commentary. This is applicable especially in the case of verses whose meanings have been classified as 'indefinite' (*mutashabih*). This is why Arthur J. Arberry, for example, called his rendition of the Quran *The Koran Interpreted*. It is also why reading the Quran from the original is emphasized over reading a translation of it in Muslim countries, despite the fact that the reader may not understand Arabic at all – it is less hazardous to recite a text not understood than to make a translation that may sometimes be erroneous, but is always condemned to be incomplete. Hence, when we say 'the meaning of a Verse' or 'the meaning of a Tradition/Saying' in what follows, we mean such an *interpretation or commentary*, which may not be immediately apparent from a literal-minded, bare-bones 'translation' of the Arabic original. For the same reason, we never use the expression 'translation of a Verse/Saying.' The meanings given here, coming from the highest level of wisdom, also serve as guidelines regarding which (kinds of) interpretations ought to be favored over others.

4. Although I have tried to isolate subjects as far as possible, the Master's wisdom is an *integral teaching*, seamlessly interwoven and integrated. It is precisely this rich interrelatedness that holds the greatest interest for us and makes the teaching holistic. I have tried to avoid repetitions, but may not have succeeded entirely in this endeavor as a result. In places I have left pointers intentionally, to serve as links to other subjects and to allow a glimpse into the Master's multidimensional ('hyperlinked,' to use an Internet concept) discourse which, in order to obtain this wisdom base, I have had to segregate.

5. It is well known that there are seven stages of the self in Sufism. Whenever 'the self' is used without a qualifier, this almost invariably defaults to the Base Self, which is the self in its natural, unpurified state. I have sometimes used words like 'ego,' 'egotistical' and 'selfishness' in order to clarify this.

6. Throughout the Master's grand narrative, certain stories are so well-placed that I hadn't the heart to pry them away from their surroundings. They're like inlaid jewels. I myself have sometimes taken the liberty of using an exceptionally apt story in the appropriate place, but such occasions are few.

7. 'Formal Prayer' or 'Ritual Prayer' is too cumbersome a term for the five-times daily prayer of *salat/namaz* when frequently referred to. I have attempted a workaround by capitalizing the letter P in order to distinguish (Formal) Prayer from ordinary supplication. Similarly, the convention of capitalizing first letters is adopted in order to distinguish Quranic Verses and Prophetic Sayings from ordinary verses and sayings. The first letters of special terms such as Unclean/Illicit/Forbidden (*haram*), Invocation (*zikr*) and so on have also been capitalized.

8. 'We,' the first person plural form used by God in the Quran and indicative of His majesty, has been replaced in translating the Master's discourse with the first person singular, 'I,' in order to ease comprehension in English.

9. Emphases and exclamatory remarks of the Master have been italicized. In addition, formulas (such as the profession of faith or mantras used in Invocation), prayers and Verses which he articulated in Arabic, have also been italicized when translating into English. The most important of these are collected in an appendix for easy reference, together with their Arabic transliterations.

The
Wisdom Base

Introduction

Ascension

As everyone knows, each and every one of the prophets has ascended to God. We are not going to explain these Ascents here in detail, but rather will summarize them briefly. There has been no prophet without ritual Prayer, nor without Ascension (*mi'raj*). Many of them have ascended twice.

Adam had his first Ascension when his spirit was created by God. His second Ascent occurred at the mountain of Arafat together with our mother Eve.

Idris (Enoch), in accordance with the Quranic verse – 'We raised him to a high place' – ascended and did not come back. Noah, at the time of the Flood associated with his name, ascended while on the ship he made by God's command.

Abraham ascended to heaven twice: First, when he was thrown into the fire, and second, at the moment when he was about to sacrifice his beloved son Ishmael. These two are very important points.

Jonah, at the time when he was swallowed by the whale, was inspired by God Almighty with the verse: 'There is no god but You. Glory be to You, I have been of the wrongdoers' [21:87]. By repeating this verse, he made his Ascension in the belly of the whale.

King Solomon, the son of David, told his father he would accept prophethood on two conditions. He said to him: 'If God Almighty grants the prophethood on both physical and spiritual grounds, I will accept it.' God was pleased with these words of Solomon, and his request was granted. This became his Ascension, because he wanted it that way.

As for Moses, he also performed two Ascensions. In his first ascent, right after his birth his mother placed him in a basket of bulrushes and set him adrift on the Nile. His second ascent occurred on Mount Sinai [Horeb].

Jesus also had two Ascensions. In the first one, the Virgin Mary was asked: 'How did you get pregnant?' Jesus answered from his mother's womb: 'My mother's words are the truth, heed my mother.' His second ascent happened during the Crucifixion (his ascension was spiritual).[1]

---

1. According to Islamic belief, Jesus was not crucified, but was lifted bodily out of

The Ascension of the Prophet Muhammad was superior to those of the other prophets. Crossing the Seven Heavens, he performed his Ascension starting from the seventh, conversed with God, and returned with the greatest good news to his community and all mankind.

Hidden Knowledge

Hidden Knowledge [*'ilm al-ladun*: literally, 'knowledge from Our side'[2] – esoteric or inner knowledge of things conferred by God], with the permission and order of God Almighty, fills the whole earth and the heavens. I, humble person that I am, cannot explain this here. However, we may be content to give a few ciphers.

Do all prophets possess Hidden Knowledge, or don't they?

According to legend, after gathering his entire army, Alexander the Great, with a sign from the Esoteric, started looking for the Elixir of Life in order to achieve immortality. After a considerable amount of exploration, two soldiers set out from the camp one day to continue the search, with the understanding that they would return and report if they happened to find the Elixir.

Around noon they arrived at a river. In order to have lunch, they took out some dried fishes and proceeded to eat. When they threw the remaining skeleton of a fish into the river, an amazing thing happened. The skeleton regained life, took on flesh and appeared to them in the form of a living fish.

The one known as Khidr[3] peeled a fish, ate its meat and, holding the skeleton from its tail, immersed it in the water. The fish immediately reconstituted, regained life and started squirming in his hand. To his friend, Elias [Elijah], he said: 'We have found the Elixir.' They drank from the water, and also watered their horses. Their human attributes disappeared, and sublime, divine attributes came over them.

---

physical space. Someone else was crucified instead, most likely Judas for his betrayal. The Master is saying that in addition, Jesus ascended to God in spirit on this occasion. For further details, see below, The prophets/Jesus.

2. This is a very difficult term to translate and has been rendered here as 'esoteric', but should not be confused with the general use of the term 'esoteric' (*batini*). *Ladun* points to a higher and more specialized form of *batin*.

3. The pronunciation is very close to 'Hizzer.' *Khidr* means 'the Green One,' and he is said to travel throughout the world, helping those in distress. For further information see below, p. 348.

This is the story. Now for the truth:

This water was a flowing water, a river. Whoever drank from this water should have become like Khidr and Elias. However, *since their goal was the Elixir*, only these two ascended, only they could ascend by this water.

The story goes on:

The two friends returned to the army of Alexander the Great, but they did not tell Alexander about their discovery. Instead, they requested permission to leave the army and go back. Alexander did not grant their request, since he did not want his army to break ranks. In spite of their leader's ban, however, Khidr and Elias left the army and started off. Alexander sent his army after them, and ordered their capture. However, during a close pursuit, both of them were suddenly lost from sight.

Did the earth swallow them up, or were they raised to the sky?

All the attempts of Alexander's men to find them met with failure. So they went back, and reported to Alexander the Great.

Alexander then said:

'I overexerted myself and my army in order to achieve immortality, yet the Elixir fell to their lot. Mine was only a rebellion against the will of God.'

This brings us to Moses and Khidr [see the Quran, 18:60–5].

Moses, with the permission of God Almighty, attained a very high level in his knowledge of the Outward and Inward sciences. In spite of this, God declared:

'Moses, you must learn Hidden Knowledge.'

Moses asked:

'My Lord, is Hidden Knowledge beyond the Outward and Inward sciences you have given me?'

God answered:

'O Moses, Hidden Knowledge is superior to all the other sciences. The time has now come for you to discover this. Go to the place where the two seas meet [to a designated pier on the banks of the Red Sea]. There, you will see a man of such-and-such a description. Tell him: "I have come to learn esoteric knowledge from you."'

The man described by God was none other than Khidr.

So Moses went and found Khidr, who answered to the description. After greeting him, he told him about the above order. Khidr said:

'I was waiting for you here on God's orders.'

They became companions, and soon boarded a ship. Although he was a great prophet, Moses was now taking orders from Khidr. While the ship was sailing on the high seas, Khidr at one point said:

'Let's go downstairs together.'

They went to the lowest deck of the ship. Khidr said to Moses:

'Take this hammer and make a hole through the ship's hull with this nail.'

Moses objected:

'There are many people and animals on this ship.'

Khidr repeated: 'Just be patient, make a hole.'

So Moses obeyed. Water started flowing into the ship. A short while later, they were invaded by pirates. But by this time, the water had already flooded the first deck. Upon seeing this, the pirates fled, among shouts: 'The ship is sinking,' and so saved themselves. On the other hand, the people on board had panicked. The captain of the ship was shouting orders: 'What are you waiting for? Abandon ship!' Just as they were about to do so, Moses and Khidr plugged the hole with a wooden peg. Water stopped flowing in, the water in the ship was bailed out and they all continued their voyage.

When Moses and Khidr got off the ship, they landed in another town. While they were disembarking, youngsters were playing ball just as they do today in a field adjacent to the port.

Khidr came face to face with a young man about eighteen years old. Khidr looked at him with a stern face, whereupon the young man attacked him. The friends of the young man tried to separate them from each other. Khidr struck the jugular vein on the young man's neck, and he died immediately. Moses and Khidr escaped through the crowd in the ensuing commotion.

During evening hours they called on a town. No matter which door they knocked on, nobody would open.

By then it was midnight. Moses, being human, was hungry and cold. Khidr, since he had drunk of the Elixir with the permission of God, was affected neither by hunger nor by cold.

Presently they came across a ruined wall, on the verge of falling down. Khidr said: 'Let's repair this wall.'

Moses: 'What are you talking about? I'm cold and hungry. We've been driven from every door in this town. And now you want to repair this ruined wall!'

Khidr said: 'Don't argue with me, just help me do our work.'

Moses had no choice; he began to work. They repaired and restored the wall. But inwardly, Moses was getting very angry with Khidr. He made this apparent by saying:

'What are you trying to accomplish?'

Khidr sighed, and answered him as follows:

'Moses, you have been too impatient. You could not stand three events. Now, I am going to explain them to you.

'We drilled a hole in the hull of the ship. You saw with your own eyes what happened next: pirates invaded the ship. They were going to rob the ship and kill us all. The ship owner's money was honestly earned. I felt pity and saved them.

'The young man I killed was the son of a prominent man. He was rebellious towards his parents. He also belittled the people of that town. If one day he were to rule there, he would have oppressed the people. We killed one man, and saved a hundred thousand from harm.

'Consider now this wall. The man who built this house was a righteous man. He built this house with money earned honestly. He put the remaining money in a jug, and buried it near the wall we repaired. (Khidr pointed with his hand:) Right here, beneath this foundation.

'The father and mother passed away, the uncle took custody of the children, and the house was ruined. The kids are still young. After they leave their uncle they will build a house on this lot, and this money will then be their share.'

Khidr continued:

'I think you now understand the reasons for the things we did. But you were too impatient; our companionship is at an end. We must now depart.'

Khidr gave his hand to Moses, and they shook hands. Moses began to weep and wail:

'If you leave me here now, where am I going to go? I don't know my way back. Please don't leave me.'

Khidr said:

'Don't worry. If you are wise, we will be together all the time. Give your hand to me and shut your eyes tight. Open them when I say so.'

Moses gave him his hand. Khidr said 'close your eyes' and 'open them,' in immediate succession. Moses looked around; he was in front of his house.

This, with the permission, grant and favor of God, is referred to as 'the folding of space' (*tayy al-makan*).

With the permission of God and the approval of His Messenger, a number of saints from the School of Muhammad have become friends with Khidr. Moreover, they still continue to do so.

I would like to give you an example.

During the Second World War, I used to live in a village known as Mako [its new name is Aktarla]. On the 20th of June, I wished to visit my Master, Hajji[4] Ahmet Efendi. The distance between us was about five hours. Half the way I needed to walk was uphill; the remaining half was downhill.

By the time I reached the hilltop, I was tired. I wanted to catch my breath, and sank to my knees. Looking downward, I saw two persons, a man and a woman, cutting grass for animals and petting each other from time to time. I could not take my eyes off them. Suddenly, I heard my Master's voice:

'Strangers at play. What is that to you?'

I got up right away, and continued on my way without a backwards glance. However, when I left home my wish had been: 'Today, on the hill, let me see Khidr on my way.'

When I passed the peak and started descending, I came across a familiar couple, a husband and wife. We said hello, chatted for a while and departed.

I said to myself: 'These can't be Khidr. Khidr travels alone and lives alone.' And I did not meet anyone else until I reached the blissful residence of my Master.

I went directly to the guest room. He was sitting alone. I greeted him and kissed his blessed hand. After exchanging a few words, he said:

'Hamid Efendi from your town has been waiting here for two days. (I knew this man.) He was very insistent, saying: "I will not go anywhere if you don't show me Khidr." He just would not leave. I told him to get out half an hour before you came in, and shut the door on him. And now you've come. I felt pity for the poor man. He was coming in, going out and asking for Khidr, all the while that he was sitting right next to Khidr.'

If you were in my place, what would you make of this conversation?

But I, poor Ahmet Kayhan that I am, understood nothing. It did not even occur to me that I should at least have kissed his hand again.

---

4. *Hajji*: A title of respect used for persons who have performed the Pilgrimage (*hajj*) to Mecca.

You, my brothers and sisters, don't be heedless and careless like I was. Try to love and understand the people you see and admire.

I hope these words of mine will not sound strange to you: He who is a saint, he who is a Friend of God (*wali*), is with Khidr every instant.

Hajji Ahmet Kayhan

I

General

The foundation

This earth, the sun, are not as you think they are. They constantly revolve around a nebula, only we can't see it.[1]

The Prophet of God

Why did God create the universe?[2]

Greetings and peace upon all the living and all who are dead.

What is this, this universe, how does it revolve without cease? Everything has been going on in its proper place for billions of years. If one side were to bend just a little bit, *whoosh*, it's all over. When was this planet established? How long has it been since the first human on earth? What good is man, what did God create him for?

Why did God create the human being? In order to let Himself be found. So that the human may say, 'God exists.'
God is not in need of anything. Yet He does have one need. What is that? Nobody knows God. God created man in order to be known.[3]
When a host invites a guest, he prepares all kinds of feasts. God, too, is the same. He decked out the globe and handed it to the service of man. He created everything else and created the human only then. The creation of man – at least fifteen thousand years. The earth, billions of years. What's the name of the first organism? Then the forests. The animals. That is, *He decorated the world*. Why? For man. Our earth found its taste with man, it will lose its taste with man. It was honored with the human, it is dishonored by the human. Man goes. The world remains where it is.

---

1. 'Nebula' is the correct translation for *bulut* (cloud) in an astronomical context. The solar system orbits the Milky Way galaxy once every 240 million years, a fact not discovered by physical science until the second half of the twentieth century. This epigraph belongs to the Master, I have not inserted it from elsewhere.

2. The Master begins by answering the central question of philosophy: Why is there something rather than nothing?

3. A reference to the Holy Tradition: 'I was a hidden treasure, and loved to be known …'

The universe has an owner. His name is God. Let's eat, drink, have children, suffer their worries and get out of here. Is *this* all we came here for? We came to search for the owner of the universe. You haven't found the master of the house yet. We need to find the owner of the cosmos. And for this, calmness is necessary, patience is necessary, work is necessary.

When we go somewhere for a visit, we wait for the owner of the house. Half an hour. We see him for ten, fifteen minutes, and leave. We wait for sixty, seventy years, yet we don't look for the owner of this house, this body. This house, this body has an Owner! Let's fortify this with Verse and Saying so it's firm: 'I was with you. Who were you with?'

Don't forget. Don't forget what is said. This came at the most important point. It came at the point of telling you about yourself, of making you know yourself.

God says: 'Whatever is in the world and in space, I created for you.' Can we live without the sun? Can we live without air? Can we live without earth? Can we survive without water? One has to meditate like this.

Don't give thanks to the belly. Give thanks to *God*. In a Holy Tradition, the Prophet of God says: 'If you knew yourselves, you would prostrate to yourselves.' Man is *that* valuable. Man is higher than the angels, if he knows his worth. Otherwise, he's lower than an animal. He gave humans a morality higher than the angels.

A Saying states, 'If man knew the divine, exalted secrets given him by God, he would prostrate to himself.' The meaning of a Saying: 'Every human is influential on a Divine Name.' There is a Name upon each human being, only we can't see it.

'I am pleased with My servants, as long as they're pleased with Me.' What does that mean? One must work.

God has placed all He has given at the disposal of human beings. 'Whatever is on earth and in heaven, I created for you.' For your survival.

Does God love man more, or does man love God more? God loves man so much that He gave man everything, then He couldn't stand it, couldn't resist it and gave *even Himself*. There, we just said the highest. If our lifespan were a thousand years, it would still not be enough if we were to thank God for a thousand years for bearing a human spirit, for possessing a human frame. An hour of meditation is better than a year of worship. If you were to live a thousand years, if this exchange of love between God and man were to last a thousand years, it still wouldn't be finished.

This body is a world. That's the main issue. It has treasures within. Deserts, forests, they're all this body. Nor are we going to set out and deal with desert and forest on the outside. We're going to transcend them all here, in this body.

Behind this mind God has given us, there is an infinite dam. A dam that is beneficial to everything, to animals, to plants. Don't be a candle, be a thousand-watt lightbulb. You distribute light with [fiber-optic] cable. Give to the spiritual cable as well, distribute light with that too. This is very important, the light of the Heart, the cable of the Heart.

The eighteen thousand worlds are mentioned in the Book (i.e., the Quran).[4] Yunus Emre says:

> *Within a mountain, I beheld*
> *The eighteen thousand worlds.*

He saw his own body. 'Mountain' means the body. Another lover of God, Hajji Bayram Wali, said:

> *Upon two columns* [pointing to his legs] *I beheld*
> *The eighteen thousand worlds.*

Now there's a fine point here. Leave aside the eighteen thousand worlds, did God create this world with all its creatures, its paraphernalia, for us, or did He create us for them? He says, 'I created everything for you, and you I created for Myself.' The thing is to be able to come to the latter, God willing. 'I created the eighteen thousand worlds for you, and you I created for Myself.' To whoever understands. I've set it down before you. Eat if you want, don't eat if you don't.

Don't bring darkness to mind, say 'There is light, I am light.' Don't think of pessimism and despair. Love life, be in love with life.

God says to man, 'I am in you.' Whoever says 'God' – he doesn't know a thing – whoever says 'God is One,' God is his visitor. Both the believer and the unbeliever. If the faithless person says 'God,' God is his visitor, too. God is everywhere, He is with you wherever you go.

---

4. 'The Lord of the worlds' (1:1). Eighteen thousand is not an exact number, but denotes a great multiplicity of worlds or realms.

But what about you? Are *you* with God wherever you go? 'Whoever says "God" will not go wanting.' So says a Tradition. If you say it *even once*, you won't go lacking. But if you say it a thousand times, that has its own reward.

God is enough for you. God loves you, so love God. Try to love God.

Kuddusi Baba is of the Qadiri Order. He lived in Niğde [pron. *knee-day*] two hundred years ago. One day he prays to God:

> *Whereas a Name of yours is 'Forgiver,'*
> *'Coverer' of shames* – the whole universe! –
> *To whom shall I go when I have You?*

That is, 'To whom shall I tell my troubles? You know them already.'

Now Kuddusi brings together the soil of the earth, the animals, the plants and then returns to himself. Then the body, inside and outside. He returns to his own reality. The bodily situation: A tiny lentil in the eye, if there aren't mountains and fields in its way, will see a thousand miles. A tiny lentil! There, with sound heart and sound mind, a mountain walks on two feet. Yes, this human body is a mountain. The human voice is great. A human being is one or two meters tall, his voice can be heard several miles away. His eye is tiny, but if there's no obstruction, it can see two or three hundred miles. The ear hears in the same way. The human being is puny, yet great.

What business is this? Man is of greatest worth, the most powerful; again, man is the weakest. What mystery is this? Man is in charge of everything, man again is the weakest. Man is a stranger away from his homeland. Man is like nothing else. If he has material means but no spirituality, he's ruined anyway. That's why man is away from his homeland.

As Kuddusi is taking account like that, he says: 'My God, thank you.' That is, praise. 'Thanks for the sun, thanks for the stars, thanks for a flower,' whatever is beneficial to human beings. Thanks and praise, thanks and praise, other prayers, all night long he continues. He dived inside, delved into meditation. That is, 'Thank you for granting me all these. These are for me. Who am *I* for?' Namely, he delved into Sufism.

He looked up when the Dawn Prayer-call was being issued. He said: 'My God, if I were to live a *thousand* years, and were to thank you at every breath, it still wouldn't be enough.'

We too should give thanks in this way. For our food, our drink, our fuel and so on. To live with this faith. At the end, '*My God,*' together with meditation, 'Did You create all these for my survival? Yes. Yes, You created all these divine paraphernalia for me, You've bestowed them on me. Thank You, praise be to You. For whom did You create me, Your weak servant?' Yes! He has bestowed with compassion, with kindness. Who are you, what are you all about? The whole universe revolves for your sake. What are you? As Kuddusi says, if we were to live a thousand years and not raise our heads from prostration during that time, we still couldn't give proper thanks for this body. Just the body, the body alone. Let's be intelligent, God willing.

If we were to study and search for twenty, thirty, fifty years, this is what we're going to find. This is the essence.

Divine unity

Unity[5] has many categories, the most important is that Unity is a name of God ['the One': *al-Ahad*]. Second, it is knowledge. But in the end, nothing is beyond unity. The sun is the largest, it is within unity no less than a flower, whether real or artificial. So is the scholar, so is the barfly. But the drunkard has lost his way, he's not outside unity. We're not going to deny him either. Rather, we're going to try and save him. This is general unity. Special unity is what is in Islam.

Let's explain this with the grace of God, as well as we know how, and whoever wants can listen.

'I created the universe for you, and you I created for Myself.'

This last is divine unity. This is a general unity, they call it divine unity.

The details we have gone into are also divine unity, but this is the real unity. We're going to do the other, too. *There is no god but God, Muhammad is the Messenger of God* – we're going to do that [say the Word of Unity]. But it's important to enter *divine* unity. Meditate on this, God willing, meditate on it all. *In accordance with that*, we're going to give thanks to God.

The Five Pillars of Islam are: pronouncing the Word of Witnessing, Prayer, Fasting, Pilgrimage, Alms-tax. And this is the science of unification. A person who does not delve into this unity does not know the true worth of humanity. He does not know the value of this lump

---

5. *Tawhid* can mean both unification and unity.

of flesh [the heart], he doesn't know the value of the snake, the lion, the honeybee. The worth of man, of a piece of wood, of a tiny animal, is understood *after* one delves into this unity. Yes, that's what we need. It's all for us, to help man stand. Could we survive without the sun? Could we survive without the air, without clouds and rain? If it weren't for these divine blessings you see and hear across this globe could you live? No, you couldn't. This totality is serving you, this totality.

Let me give another example. Do water and oil mix? They don't. The oil rises to the top. You too, when you pass into this divine unity, this meditation, will prove your humanity everywhere and always rise to the top, God willing. Because there isn't anything greater, there's only God. And God's Prophet. This is how you approach divine unity. The other unifications are for bringing us to this one: Prayer is for this purpose, so is worship, the Glorious Quran is for this – that is, they're all for entering this divine unity. To know that it is from the Real, to accept the Real, to prostrate to the Real. There is no other way.

With meditation. This universe in general, the realm of space, the globe of the Earth, 'I created for you.' For you, so that you may stand. 'And you,' He says, 'only for Myself.' What does this call for? Sacrificing ourselves. We can't resolve this if we live and give thanks for a thousand years. It is necessary to say 'God is Greatest' with the Attribute of Compassion, the Attribute of Mercy, and to prostrate. We can only do it in prostration. A praise.

We're at great fault. To prostrate to God, but to prostrate *consciously*. And to give creatures their rights, as well. 'My God, did You create all these for me?' 'Yes.' 'I can't really give thanks for them, but I can fulfill my servanthood and prostrate to You.' To thank the sun, to thank the air, the water, the earth, the ant, the plant. If we don't do this, we will have failed to acknowledge their rights, and we'll go in error.

He says, 'I'm pleased with My servant, so long as he's pleased with Me.' This part is very difficult. One has to search, to learn. To fulfill God's orders. Until: 'My God, You created the entire universe.'

The sun of love

Love, love one another. Love one another for God. There is no other salvation.

Be thoughtful of others. Be thoughtful of everyone and everything. If you see a sick person on the bus, give him your seat. Prayer alone won't do, these are all Prayer. Don't disturb anyone. Always be the one who is disturbed.

Work, give something to humanity.

Let's not bear this burden for naught. To work correctly. Let's benefit all humankind in general, let's be beneficial to the owner of the Torah, to the owner of the Gospel.[6] Let us be useful to animals, from an ant to a whale – larger than an elephant – that is, to all living things from small to large. From a blade of grass to an oak tree, a pine tree. From the president down to a menial worker in tatters with failing eyesight. I'm saying this to all of you. Let's be useful.

Be a sun, be a sun. Be a sun in knowledge, in worship, in piety, in faith. Be givers, be givers. Let everyone benefit. Whoever says 'Hello' to us should be like the sun. With us there is no veil! To be a sun, to be superior materially and spiritually. Be useful to your country, your nation, and to humanity. To animals and plants, down to an ant.

Wake them up. Awaken even a stone. Let us build up even a weed and a brook. Let us make people love them. Without plants and animals, what would man do?

I told you to serve human beings. You find that there are no human beings left to serve, everyone's doing it. Serve animals. You find that's not left either, raise a flower. Cultivate a garden or something. Always work, serve, don't stay idle. Together with knowledge. Always to work.

'God,' they say, 'didn't create an atom in vain.' God says, 'I didn't create anything ugly. I created everything in its proper place. Good/bad, beautiful/ugly, are so only according to human beings,' He says.

If we are good, everything will be good. If we're good, the universe is good. If we see the universe as bad, this or that, know that we're bad. When man is corrupted, the entire world becomes corrupt.

Everyone will be accountable for himself. No one will be responsible for another. Human beings are the best of the best of the best. If only we knew their worth.

To be enlightened. To love, to cause others to love, to know, to find. To be materially and spiritually enlightened.

Whoever says 'Hello' to me should throw away the thorns. S/he should remain as a pure rose, should be a rose without thorns, so that

---

6. That is, Jews and Christians. The Master never used the terms 'Old Testament' and 'New Testament.' When he speaks of the Torah, the Psalms and the Gospel, he means the holy books revealed to Moses, David and Jesus, respectively. These are the originals of the Torah, the Psalms and the Gospels as we know them today.

when someone reaches out, they won't get pricked. You have to put on the brakes. Selfish desires need to be curbed.

God loved human beings very much. 'Search, find' – for this, in order to make Himself loved, He sent prophets and holy books. What a pity if man remains with his self. It's no use if he owns the whole world. May God protect us all, may He bestow on us all.

'Because I love human beings, I serve man by the hand of man.' So the one who serves the most is God.

Animals, plants all serve us. Who do we serve, I wonder? If we serve God, creation will be pleased with us, God will be pleased with us, and so we will pass on.

A child has need of a mother and father until fifteen years of age, until education is finished. If s/he finds work, the burden of the mother and father will ease a little bit. All of us here are at the service of the ego. We haven't escaped from it yet.

Religion and brotherhood

Religion is humanity. Religion is what creates man out of nothing. It is what separates water from earth.

Love one another. Where does love come from? Again, it comes from religion. 'Hatred does not cease by hatred, hatred ceases by love'[7] – this is the meaning of Verse and Saying. 'The heart of all religion is love'[8] – this, too, is the meaning of Verse and Saying.

Love one another, and God will love you.

We're human. We're all brethren. All human beings aren't relatives, they're brothers and sisters. From one father and one mother. We're not going to say 'Go over there' to non-Muslims. We're going to love them, too. They're brethren even if they don't accept us.

Our Prophet said: 'I would give half a canister of water to the enemy and half to my brother. Let him get up and still do his harm if he wants to.'

God says: 'Love a stone for My sake. Love a flower for Me. Love your friends and relatives for Me.' Let us love an ant, a flower. You love for God too, so love.

---

7. The Buddhist *Dhammapada*.
8. *Desiderata II*.

Be a light. For humanity, not necessarily for Islam. Whoever is human is a Muslim already. *Aha!* Don't forget this. Whoever is human is a Muslim. But if a Muslim abandons humanity, that is shameful. When I come to think of it, the world of Islam is in this shape despite its deep adherence to God and our Prophet. What would have happened if it hadn't done even that? Be human, try to be human. Try to be human. If they go to the moon, Muslims should go to the sun.[9]

With me, everyone is the same. I love you – my brothers in religion – more, but everyone is the same. I love the cosmos. I love the universe with its animals, its plants, with all its particles. Down to an ant, down to a blade of grass, they're all my life and soul. I love my religion above all else, I love my Prophet above all else.

The best of times, the worst of times

The things God creates. The forests were finished, coal. Before coal was exhausted, petroleum. Before oil is ended, they're going to find solar energy, a boundless treasure! Now if the sun is finished too, that'll be the end of the Earth.

Now, when compared to history, thanks to our beloved Prophet, we're living in a villa of Paradise. Our eating, our drinking, our comings and goings are all a pavilion in Heaven. We'll have some sorrows, that's nothing.

Sultan Selim the Resolute[10] gathers his army, he goes east [from Istanbul] and from there to Egypt, always by candlelight at night! We're in such a boon [electricity] that not even sultans enjoyed this bounty.

There can't be a better life, the world of Islam and Turkey included. We lived through all that, eighty years ago. In these times, God has joined all human beings with physical and spiritual blessings. Selim the Resolute conquered the world, four hundred years ago he went to

---

9. When the Master said these words, I was immediately reminded of Ray Bradbury's science-fiction story, 'The Golden Apples of the Sun.' In it, a spaceship scoops up solar plasma, an unimaginably difficult task. The Master made this statement no later than 1987, yet it was only recently that the technologically most advanced nation on Earth even began to contemplate the possibility of going to the sun. NASA's Solar Probe Plus will be launched between 2015 and 2018, and will fly through the sun's corona (the edge of the sun). Apparently, then, the Master wished Muslims to be at least a quarter century ahead of the best in science and technology.

10. Selim the First, one of the greatest Ottoman sultans. He reigned in the early sixteenth century.

Egypt on horseback. He went there with his army in three years. Now they go to Egypt in two-and-a-half hours. And not just Selim, not any ruler, but so does a gipsy or [in the cargo] an ass.

God knows, ever since the world was founded, medicine and technology have now reached their peak. Nor was there anything like this before. It used to take a month to go to America. Now, with the telephone, it's right beside you. With a plane, right away. This is a good time, that is. But human beings are unable to use time. They may mean well, but they use it for ill.

Give thanks to God. You've come into the world in the best of times and you live in a good time. God didn't give this comfort you're in to those who went before you. And may He continue to give it from now on, but it's very difficult. Give thanks to God.

Our world is very sweet. But we don't know how to use it. We leave ourselves and the world in ruins. There's unrest in the world now. Why? Everyone is sundered from their Books. The Peoples of the Books are all enemies of one another. The Books say: 'Don't do it, don't kill one another,' but they don't listen, that's why they're at each other's throats. If the people of Moses were to adhere to the Torah, the people of Jesus to the Gospel and the people of Muhammad to the Quran, they would all come together and be brethren. Everything would be solved.

Material and spiritual

The material alone won't do. Spirituality alone won't do, either. There are two aspects: exoteric (outward), esoteric (inward). The exoteric is what is seen and known. The esoteric is the unseen. One must work to win that, too.

The outer comes from the inner. The tree grows out of the seed. Words emerge from within a person. The inward precedes the outward.[11]

Does materiality lead spirituality, or does spirituality lead materiality? The spiritual leads the material. We do the physical life, but spirituality falls behind. The material depends on the spiritual. If spirituality is present, the physical comes easily. Let your spirituality always be heavier than your physical side.

---

11. In ontological terms, Essence precedes existence.

Let material and spiritual advance together. Otherwise there will be those who complain. They should go forth together.[12]

If we were to blindfold one among us, and say: 'Bring us a drink of water,' he would be confused, he would stumble right and left. Now we ourselves are blindfolded as regards spirituality. Blindfolded towards the orders of God and His Prophet.

If you can advance materiality and spirituality side by side, things will be fine. The two must be at the same level, like the two pointers of a scale. Otherwise, one will complain of the other.

Spirituality cannot do without the physical. We have to advance them together. Our Prophet possessed the spiritual side from the start. But he always went by the physical. Why? Because it is through the physical that things get done.

The light of reason

Whatever our Prophet has called 'sin,' know that there's harm therein. Whatever he called 'merit,' there's well-being, there's life in it.

What does one who fears God do? He lives in Paradise, both here and there. What does one who doesn't fear God do? He lives in pain, in despair.

If you fear God, you obey His orders. When one obeys God's orders, the love of God blossoms in one's heart.

We're going to pass everything through the filter of reason, and accept it only then.

If someone were to hold the sun in his hand, we still wouldn't accept it if he said: 'I am God.' Don't forget your servanthood. Let us prove our servanthood to God. Let us be intelligent, let us live by intelligence.

God makes our dark days light. He spreads butter and honey on our stale bread.

1. God says: 'I love you very much, love Me in return. Invoke My name.'

Let us thank God profusely, let us prostrate, because He has made us into human beings. What would we do if He had placed us in the frame of some poor animal?

A waiter gives you some water, you thank him. Isn't there any thanks for God, who bestowed on us this entire universe? Do a thanksgiving Prayer. Say, 'What can we do for You? At least let's obey Your orders.'

12. Think of two horses running abreast, one slightly larger than the other.

2. 'I nvoke you very much, do the same for Me.'

3. 'I created the worlds for you. I placed the earth at your service so that you may live, obey Me and know Me. I created you for Myself.'

With this honor, may God fill us with light, knowledge and wisdom, inside and outside.

God and his Prophet aid those who accept them, may they help you. There is the yes-sayer, and then there is the nay-sayer. May they grant intelligence to nay-sayers so that they too say 'Yes.'

Thanksgiving

God created the eighteen thousand worlds. But He's not in love with the worlds, He's in love with man. Everything is for you, but who're *you* for? That's what needs to be understood.

God says, 'I do not turn down anyone's plea. Great is My glory, and I'm the Most Merciful of Mercifuls. But I give them their physical and spiritual requests when the time comes. When it's the right time. Also,' says He, 'I love them. But I wish they would love Me, too. I invoke them,' He says, 'I remember you. I desire that you remember/invoke Me, too, and very much. I created you, I love you very much. Try to love Me deeply in return.'

We don't say: 'God is Generous. He knows what is good for me better than I do myself. He is the master of my son, my daughter, my wife, and my food and drink. He knows better.' We don't take refuge in that, we fall into our own commotion right away. Yes, ours is a difficult case. Very difficult. A slight illness occurs with this body, we love this body more than we love God.

God loves us so much and we have such a great opportunity to love God. Yes! Starting from the sun to begin with, from the realm of space, angels, the peoples of the earth, animals, plants, He has loved human beings more than all the rest. They [the others] are His creation, too. He's loved man, sir. And then He's left us a terrific Book, a Book that unites its predecessors and successors, the esoteric and the exoteric: the Glorious Quran. A magnificent Book. And then again, He's made us the followers of a Prophet who combines all predecessors and successors within himself.

We're extremely lucky. His community is very lucky. Whoever loves him, wants him and follows his path is very lucky. And then He has created these divine blessings on earth and in heaven for us all.

Whatever is our share, let's take that, consume it and enjoy ourselves. Never mind the rest. Let's give thanks to God.

When you say 'Thanks be to God' with every word, God will pass you from everything. What does Ibrahim Hakki say, 'Your kindness is nice, Your hardship is nice.' If you say that, God will give you a *thousand*.

The sun we receive, the clothes we wear and everything else are giving thanks that they were created for us, for human beings. You and I – if we don't give thanks for every day we live, if we remain heedless ... it would be better if we gave thanks, too.

The school of wisdom

The other day [some people] were here, and I explained to them.

'Things aren't finished with Fasting, Prayer, Pilgrimage, Alms-tax and the Word of Witnessing,' I said. Yes! They're not finished, not by a long shot. Then I gave an example.

A person sends his child to elementary school. He educates him in primary school, but he doesn't stop there. 'Finish middle school too, my child!' That's what the times call for. He finishes middle school too, 'Now finish high school, come on, son.' He finishes high school too, 'Win the college entrance exams, go to that, too.'

Now, the way we are, child, it's very difficult to get a high grade and enter university. The kids study night and day, and they still can't win.

I told them this example. '*And we*,' I said, 'Prayer is the light of our eyes, the crown on our heads. Things aren't finished with Fasting, Prayer, Pilgrimage, Alms-tax and the Word of Witnessing. We need to enrol in a School of Wisdom. Yes! Let's enter and graduate from a school of wisdom. Let's see if we'll be able to succeed in that school of wisdom. Will we get passing grades? Time flies. Let's exert ourselves a little, pass our exam and enroll in the school of wisdom.'

If you meditate a little bit – you, young people, all our friends – 'What am I? Why did I come here?' Not just for food-drink-marriage. Animals do this, an elephant does it, a fish does it, an ant does it. Be righteous, God is with those who are straight. Right! As long as God is with those who are right in both motives and acts, what more do you seek? What more, child?

It is necessary to finish a university. It's necessary to graduate from it. What is that college, do you know? The school of wisdom. One has to enroll in our university, the school of wisdom. We should finish the school of wisdom in order that: why we came here, where we're going, what is the reason, what is Prayer, what is Fasting, these become clear a little bit.

My picture is my words. What you've received, don't leave at the door with us. Take the good and continue.

Our wish is a sound mind to all humanity, peace to all humankind. Whoever wants to go, whoever doesn't like it, let them leave. And whoever likes it, let them stay forever and not leave.

Now, we've laid the foundation. The base is reinforced concrete, that is, of steel. Having cast the foundation, we will now rise slowly, floor by floor.

Compassion and Mercy

(God is both Compassionate and Merciful. Compassion encompasses (a) this world and (b) all creatures in it. Mercy pertains (a) to both worlds and (b) to those who obey Him.

There is both wrath and bliss in Compassion. The attribute of Compassion does not exclude the attribute of Wrath, for all around us we see wrath occurring together with bliss. 'The Lord looking down in pity' at his subjects does not always intervene on their behalf. Such intervention is reserved for those who have agreed to follow certain guidelines, which, of course, first of all requires the admission that the Lord exists.

In Mercy/Grace, there is pure bliss. On those who have accepted this covenant and live by these terms, God showers His blessings. They become special recipients of His Mercy. This does not necessarily mean that they will be freed of hardships in this life. It does mean that they will be freed of them in the next. It is up to human beings to take the necessary precautions in this respect.

This world is the seedbed of the afterlife. What we sow here, we reap over there. Our future is dependent on what we do. Simply put, the division between Compassion and Mercy means that those who believe and do certain things are enabled to harvest results not available to those who don't.)

We enter the eighteen thousand worlds with the Naming: 'In the name of God, the Compassionate, the Merciful' – that is the key.

Ali says: 'If the seas were all ink and the trees were all pens, they still couldn't exhaust the meaning of the Naming.' The eighteen thousand worlds stand with the Compassionate. Surely the seas would end before that explanation was finished.

'He, the Compassionate, the Merciful.' There's a universe here. Find that, and you won't need anything else. Like the sun, the Naming encompasses everything.

A person boozes and walks in the sun. Another is a thief, so does he, another is a scientist, he walks, too. The sun does not discriminate, it warms them all. This is the attribute of Compassion. But the scientist and the drunkard are distinguished from each other. That is the attribute of Mercy.

God has allowed that which is beneficial. He has prohibited the harmful. He says: 'I love those who work, but I'm with the righteous.' If you hold on to what is prohibited, you will go with the prohibited. But: 'I am on the side of the righteous.'

There are six billion people on earth. They're all within the attribute of Compassion. A billion Muslims are within both the attributes of Compassion and Mercy. The rest are only within the attribute of Compassion.

Then are all human beings within the Prophet? They are. Because our Prophet came with human attributes, all human beings are not outside but rather, within him.

The eighteen thousand worlds are within the attribute of Compassion. Everyone can go to God. But they're unable to. The attribute of Mercy was set forth for their improvement.

The Name of Compassion pertains to this world. The Name of Mercy pertains to both this world and the next.

One can't pass into the attribute of Mercy unless one says: 'There is no god but God, and Muhammad is the Prophet of God.' Just as you have to go through the vice president in order to get to the president, one has to go through the Prophet in order to reach God. The most intelligent people have foundered at this point.

Everyone and everything – stones, animals, plants – are in the attribute of Compassion. There is no limit to the attribute of Compassion. There *is* a limit to the attribute of Mercy. The attribute of Mercy divides the attribute of Compassion in the middle: believers, nonbelievers. We [believers] are in both Compassion and Mercy.

Compassion and Mercy were given to all prophets in their time. They all received these attributes. Mercy belongs to all the prophets. Compassion is general, Mercy is the province of the prophets. But only our Prophet was able to realize both in their fullness. The others were unable to do this. Some were driven away, some were hanged, some were killed. Only our Prophet was able to succeed. This is why the Quran is not the book of Islam, it is the book of the whole *universe*. Our Prophet was able to fulfill both Compassion and Mercy.

Jesus took Moses as an example. Moses and Jesus brought a distinction with the attribute of Mercy. Muhammad applied this.

The other prophets are now in the domain of Compassion. Our Prophet is both Compassion and Mercy. Compassion belongs to the whole universe, Mercy belongs to Muhammad. It would be better if those in Compassion entered Mercy.

Because there is wrath in Compassion, our Prophet invites human beings to the zone of Mercy. Whoever enters the realm of Mercy becomes a member of the Prophet's community. Whoever does not enter, he is our brother, too, he remains within Compassion. God tells Azra'il [the angel of death] seventy times a day: 'Take the lives of my community with ease.' What mystery is this? There's a sign here.

(To get stuck with either Compassion or Mercy exclusively would be one-sided, as shown below.)

Compassion without Mercy

Comment: *Everything is fine.*

If you say that, you cancel the attribute of Mercy, you do away with the prophets, you remove the Base Self, you eliminate good and evil. Good and evil both become fine. Only the attribute of Compassion remains. But God says, 'Recognize good and evil.'

Comment: *We have to see the essence. We have to see the One.*

If you haven't trained the eye and the ear, saying it with the tongue won't do. If you say 'I've seen God,' you'll be lying.

Don't add the slightest thing to what the Prophet of God said. The Naming is three words: God, Compassionate, Merciful. Mansur al-Hallaj[1] wished for the salvation of all humanity. He remained with the attribute of Compassion. So don't consciously go a hair's-breadth further than the Prophet.

Mercy without Compassion

Shall we omit the attribute of Compassion [all-inclusiveness]? Shall we say: 'In the name of God, the Merciful'? We can't remove it. All prophets – and finally the Prophet – were given both attributes.

If we drive away the drunkard, if we send away the other, we remain in the attribute of Mercy [exclusiveness]. But all prophets came with the attribute of Compassion, and invited to the attribute of Mercy.

Both the attributes of Compassion and Mercy are in the Quran. You cannot say, 'Why is this person a Christian, an Armenian (Orthodox), or an infidel?' If you can convince them, do so. Otherwise, leave them alone. As far as we can, we are to invite the Jew, the Christian. What does the Prophet say? 'I was ordered to debate with people until they say "There is no god but God."' We're going to invite. But beyond that, there is to be no hate.

---

1. Famous Sufi who was martyred for saying, 'I am the Truth.'

Universality

The universal religion

All the world, the whole universe is Muslim, no-one's aware of the fact. If America or Russia were to say, 'The sun belongs to us,' you'd laugh, wouldn't you? In the same way, Islam belongs to everyone.

May God grant it to all human beings. May they become our brothers [in religion], too.

We're going to consider everyone, we're going to try to lead them forward – a garbage collector, a peasant. Then we should try to be beneficial to neighboring countries.

I've made all religious and all irreligious depend on two words: Don't eat an illicit bite, don't engage in illicit lust. I'm saying this to *all* humanity. But beyond that, I can't promise anything.

Before human beings were created, there was a command of prostration to all human spirits: 'Am I not your Lord?' They all said 'Yes' [7:172]. This means that because of this prostration command, *everyone* is born a Muslim. The meaning of a Saying goes, 'Every human being is born a Muslim.' Then they grow up, reach puberty, accept another religion and depart.

The Prophet

Everybody opposes those of another religion.

After a battle, our Prophet does not return to Medina, though he could have. If they return, they could reach Medina by midnight. But he doesn't. He stays there that night. In the morning, he visits the wounded. Then he asks:

'Your brother and an enemy soldier are wounded in war. You have a glass of water in your hand. Which one would you give it to?'

They all reply, 'To our brother, O Prophet.' 'Okay,' he says, 'they're both hungry, and you have a bite to eat in your hand. Who do you give it to?' They say, 'To our brother.'

'That's not the right answer,' he says.

Abu Bakr and Omar ask: 'What would you do, Messenger of God?'

'*Even if he had attacked me in person*, I would give a drop more than half a glass to the enemy soldier. He can get up and draw his sword again if he wants to.'

Now, Muslims think harshly of non-Muslims, but they don't do what the Prophet of God did. They don't think of the Messenger's [inclusive] attribute of Compassion, they just take refuge in his [exclusive] attribute of Mercy. And that's why it doesn't work.

I wish a Muhammadan knowledge, morality and wisdom upon all human beings. The universe is Muhammadan. The prophets are all brothers.

Is Muhammad the father of humanity, or is Adam? If you look at it esoterically, Muhammad is the father, the light. But in terms of external appearances, Adam is earlier.

'I came for all humanity.' That's what the Prophet says. 'I came as light.' Our Prophet is the master [teacher] of the *universe*, not just the master of Muslims. May God grant all the Muhammadan community his intercession, and may He admit all non-Muhammadans to the Muhammadan community.

The Book

The Quran is not just the basis of Islam. It is the basis of humanity, it is the basis of everything.

Just like our Prophet, the Quran bears both the attributes of Compassion and Mercy within itself. It encompasses the entire universe. Whoever says 'There is no god but God, and Muhammad is the Messenger of God' enters the zone of Mercy. Those who do not, remain in Compassion.

The Quran is not the book of Islam, it is the book of the entire *universe*. Whatever God has created, it is the constitution of them all. One needs to follow the path of the Quran, which God sent to an ant, a weed, to all the universe. 'I love those who work, I am with the righteous.' The Quran addresses everyone, not only Muslims.

The Torah is exactly the Quran, in part. The Gospel is exactly the Quran, in part. The Psalms are exactly the Quran, in part. The people of the Gospel are more than any of us. But there is no practice. The Quran is there, but there is no practice. Whenever practice ends, cruelty begins. [That's why] we're in wrath now.

After Moses and Jesus, Muhammad is the last president. There won't be any other.

Why not? That's very important, too. Because the Quran doesn't leave space for anyone else. It encompasses the past and the future. It is the final constitution. It's the constitution of all that God has created. That's why it's many Verses. If a prophet were to come, what more could he bring?

The Quran is the sun, water, earth. It is everything. The Quran is the constitution of the universe. Open the Quran if you want democracy. Democracy is the Quran in its entirety. The Torah, the Psalms, the Gospel, the Quran – these are democracy.

Islam is democracy. The Quran embodies democracy within itself. A president does his Prayer behind a pauper. This is democracy. The president arrives at a mosque, the ranks are crowded. Unless someone gives his place out of respect, the president will either squeeze in somewhere, or will remain outside. Democracy is *this*, not false democracy.

Democracy lies at the basis of the Quran, because it has given everyone their rights. Why doesn't a book come that supersedes the Quran? Because it's the most perfect.

The Ka'ba

The Ka'ba is not the property of Muslims alone. It is the property of all humanity. May God grant the sons of Saud the intelligence to open it to all the world a month before the Pilgrimage starts. It is the property of all humanity. It doesn't belong exclusively to Muslims.

The door of hope

(*God is All-forgiving. He says: 'My mercy encompasses My wrath.' He also says: 'I will forgive anything, except ascribing partners to Me.' Below, the Master points out the way by which the gates of grace will be flung wide open: a sincere repentance, together with the conscious resolve not to follow earlier paths of error again.*

If sinners repent, they will be forgiven. According to the Sufis, God's attribute of Forgiveness could not manifest itself if people did not sin. Thus, for the universe to be complete, sin and repentance too are necessary. This is supported by the Prophet's Saying to the effect that if a community did not sin, God would replace it with one that did. But without repentance, sin is only the occasion for regret.)

Let us work.

A student came to a hodja for a Quran course. But he was unsuccessful. Finally his teacher said, 'Son, go back to your father's house.'

The boy set out. He got tired at one point and took a rest. As he looked around, he saw that flowing water had worn away a rock. It had flowed and flowed and flowed, and hollowed out the rock.

'My God,' he said, 'is my head harder than this rock? This rock was softened and carved by this water. Is this head harder? My God, give me strength, save me from embarrassment towards my father, I can't do any less for them.' He went back.

The next day he came to class again. The teacher asked, 'What happened, Hassan, my child?' He explained, 'I went that far, to such a place. I did a Prayer, I looked at the rock, I thought to myself, I can't go to my father with this shame.'

The hodja thought. 'Bravo, son,' he said. 'God willing. Let's hurry.' He caught up with his friends before they graduated. He does better than his classmates, he puts them to shame. He recites in tears. He received his diploma, as he was going home he passed by that same rock again. He took an Ablution and did a Prayer. 'If it weren't for you, I couldn't have done it,' he told the rock.

Work like that, God willing. If you work, God will provide, both materially and spiritually.

Look at what Rumi says:[1] '*Come*. Whether a follower of Jesus, of Moses or of Islam, come again. [This door is not the doorway to despair.][2] If you break your repentance a hundred thousand times, still, come again.' The pearl of wisdom here is that, if you break your penitence a hundred thousand times, come to *repentance* again, *aha!*

You have a gold ring or bracelet. You drop it one day as you're washing your hands. To the bottom of the well, and from there it flows away. One day a jeweler finds it, washes it, it emerges spotless clean. The jeweler says, 'twenty-four-carat gold.' Again it is cleansed. And you do a repentance, you too are cleansed.

These are good similes. Thousands of books [are in] this single example.

---

1. Widely attributed to Rumi. Its real provenance is said to be Kashani and Abu Sa'id bin Abi al-Khayr.
2. The sentence in brackets is part of the quotation and completes it.

The audition

(We are invited to an audition in the presence of the Master. We enter the living room. It is crowded and perhaps a bit too hot. People are sitting around in reverence. Two pieces are to be read: the 'Peace Prayer' [on this, see also the Prologue] and 'O Humankind,' a piece by the Master from decades ago. I have included below all the comments on these pieces by the Master that appear in my records.)

Whoever reads 'Peace' should first of all make peace with himself. There is intelligence, there is thought, there's the body – let's first make peace within ourselves, and then in others. The Sound Mind, the Livelihood Mind. Let's have a Sound Mind.

The Peace Prayer – in this, there's humanity, there's morality, there's culture, all at once. Let's disseminate without discrimination, whether it be to a Muslim or a Christian. Democracy is this morality. Not the democracy you see [around you], though. The democracy that God and his Prophet have enjoined. This is democracy. It's all the meaning of Verse and Saying.

Read it and let's listen. Whoever prints and distributes a thousand copies of this is on the road to Paradise, God willing.

The Peace Prayer

My God, grant that we may sow peace wherever we go.

This is democracy. This, let it be this.

Let us be reconcilers and unifiers, not sowers of dissent.

They say 'democracy,' you know? This is democracy.

Allow us to disseminate love where there is hate, forgiveness where there is injury,

All Traditions, all sciences … It's enough for us if we practice this page.

faith where there is doubt, hope where there is despair, light where there is darkness,

'Light' is your reading. You're reading, and we're receiving light here.

'Light where there is darkness …' How beautiful! How beautiful. 'My God,' he says, as though he's embracing God. 'My God.' May God grant all of us that love. A Holy Tradition: 'The mountains, the rocks, the seas didn't accept Me. I entered the Heart of My servant who loves Me.' He wants to come in, we don't let Him in.

> *and joy where there is sorrow.*

Now, what they call 'democracy,' this is democracy, it's what you're reading. Otherwise, democracy is just a name without substance. This is Muhammadan ethics for us all.

> *Help us to be not of those who see the failings of others, but of those who hide them; not of those who seek consolation, but those who console; not of those who wish to be understood, but those who understand; not of those who crave to be loved, but those who love.*
>
> *Grant that we may become like the rain …*

Four poles. Rain, sun, earth, night. Four powers. If you can't find these in a human being it's terrible, you have to search and find it. These four poles are tremendous.

> *… like the rain, which bestows life without discrimination wherever it flows; like the sun, which enlightens all beings everywhere without distinction;*

See, the sun touches a rose garden and its fragrance comes. Beside it a sewer has burst, it's flowing away, the sun dries and edifies it. It protects in general. This is the attribute of Compassion.

> *like the earth which, though everything steps on it, withholds nothing and bestows its fruits on everyone; like the night, which hides all shames from view.*

Yes! Let's apply for one of these four poles, God willing. *Aha!* If we request just one, our eyes and ears will become our friends. These four poles are at the service of humankind, of animals, of plants.

> *Grant us the destiny to join the ranks of those who give rather than receive,*

Yes! To work. To work.

those who are forgiven because they forgive, those who are born in Truth, live in Truth, die in Truth; and those who are born again in eternal life. Amen.

The revelation that came to Muhammad is reflected to us. It's all Verse. It started with the Quran, it's the Quran right to the end. Revelation. This is democracy, this is ethics. The Glorious Quran is democracy. What manifests from this writing is the Quran and the Traditions. There are meanings of Verses in it, the rest are all Sayings.

This is democracy!

Now read the one above that. You know what the rivers of heaven are? To read these with desire, to feel sweetness, to shed a teardrop. Those are the rivers.

O humankind

The Divine Law (*shariʿa*), the Orders (*tariqa*), Gnosis (*maʿrifa*), Reality (*haqiqa*) all emerge from this. It's the foundation of them all.

In the name of God, the Compassionate, the Merciful.
There is no god but God, and Muhammad is His Messenger.
O sons of Adam, sons of Man, we have to obey the commandments of God, who has created us, very faithfully in order to prove our servanthood. We must pay very careful attention.

What is man? We have an owner. See, you act on your father's orders, you act on your mother's orders, when you go to college you will act on the orders of your instructor.

Consider the following dialogue:
'O sons of Adam, human beings, do you fear God, your Creator?'

No matter whom you ask here, all of them will say, 'We fear God.' Whether consciously or unconsciously.

'Yes, we have no refuge except Him.'
'Thank you for recognizing your Lord. God, who has created us, has many commandments for us human beings. How do you stand with respect to His orders?'

Ahem! Obedience to God! Obedience to the constitution! This is the constitution.

> 'We can't do them. We're unable to carry out His orders as we should.'
> 'Well then, do you love God, our Creator?'

I've tied it up in two points. All these volumes of books are in those two points.

> 'What else is there to love but God?'

Again, whoever you ask, whichever one of us, 'Do you love God?' 'Yes, I do.' Whatever nation you ask, they'll say 'We love God' in their own language.

> 'How are you with His orders?'
> 'We can't perform them like we're supposed to.'
> 'In that case, you're lying on both counts.'

That's all. Deluding themselves. 'Do you fear?' Everybody fears. 'Do you love?' Everybody loves. 'Do you follow His orders?' *Uh-uh*. You neither fear nor love.

He who fears God and loves God should prostrate himself to God.

To prostrate oneself to God means to follow His orders. To carry out His commandments. There *is*, that is – there *is* a Lord of this totality, *aha!*

> The faith and creed of a person who does not prostrate to God is weak. Can you comprehend the taste of a fruit without eating it, by imagination alone?

I eat an orange, you look at me and say, 'Yes, yes, I've eaten it.' But he's eaten nothing. He gives to his friends, he doesn't know its taste. She hasn't eaten an apple, she's seen it, she doesn't know.

> To know and understand God on an empty heart and dry words is a vain illusion.

An illusion, nothing else.

> To believe and have faith in God, to perform the Five Pillars of Islam and the Six Pillars of Faith, is a general requirement.

Right. That is, the basis of Islam, the Divine Law. They all have a basis.

> May God and God's Prophet, Muhammad, help you. Amen.
> From Adam – the first man and Prophet – to Muhammad, the last Prophet, a Prophet has been sent to every period and every society of humankind.

A prophet has come to every realm, to every time, to every society. One has to make the three organs [eyes, ears, tongue][1] one's friends. From Adam to Muhammad, they're all in this page. Every prophet has a constitution. But they're all connected to God.

> They are all commanded with Prayer. No prophet has come without Prayer.

I put that point there so that whichever prophet came without Prayer, let's go and join his community. There isn't any!

> In order to inform human beings He has created of His commandments, God Almighty has addressed them via His Prophets. He has made known the essence of these discourses and commands to His servants with Four Great Books and the Hundred Pages.

This is the knowledge that has come. Pages, that is, one sheet each. A sheet. To some prophets. But Four Books have come. The people of the Psalms are few today. The people of the Torah. The people of the Gospel are many. And the people of the Quran.

> Through the Prophets, it has become incumbent on every society to believe in God with a sincere heart and to carry out God's divine orders physically and spiritually.

---

1. See The Base Self/The three organs.

To be human, that is. To prove our humanity. We have a Creator, we have to prove to Him that we are human. Otherwise, God doesn't need our obedience or worship, child.

> God's commandments to humanity have been proclaimed in the Psalms [revealed to David], the Torah [to Moses], the Gospel [to Jesus] and the Glorious Quran [to Muhammad]. [Earlier prophets have received various divine pages that add up to a hundred.]

That is, those are all subsumed in the Quran. It is the final Book, the Glorious Quran.

> God Almighty has not concealed His material/spiritual Essence and Reality from His servants.

He hasn't concealed, He hasn't withheld anything in terms of the body, of worldly nourishment. The realm of space – starting with the sun, stars, air, snow – He hasn't withheld anything.

> It is necessary to live humanly, thoughtfully and attentively.

A human being, to live as a human being! To *abandon* bestial ethics. Human morality. To make friends out of the eye and the ear. Again, it all comes down to that.

Four poles, four elements

(The Master often spoke of four poles and four elements. The four [or sometimes five] poles are the Sun, Water, Earth, Night [and Air]. These are manifestations of God's attribute of Compassion, and anyone who takes on the characteristics of even one becomes a saint.

The four elements are the four classical elements of Antiquity – earth, water, air and fire. Yet the Master's use of them was radically different from what they usually conjure in our minds. It was novel and much more sensible. They were treated as symbols for various aspects of the human psyche. In this usage, fire corresponds to anger, air to caprice, water to tranquility and earth to humility. An alternative but analogous correspondence is described below.)

The four poles

Four, five poles: the sun, God created it first, billions of years ago. Earth, I'm stepping on it with my foot. Water, there's no life without it. We cleanse ourselves with it, it doesn't say, 'What are you doing?' Earth – you go somewhere, you obey the call of nature. You see a flower, a fruit, you pick it, earth doesn't object to you. Air, we can't live without air. Night – Kuddusi Baba calls it a 'Coverer,' a coverer of shames. If it were day all the time, humans and animals would all go crazy. If it were night all the time, nothing would get done.

These are attributes of Compassion. They belong to human beings, to animals, to everyone. If America were to say, 'The sun is ours,' it wouldn't do.

None of them could exist without the sun. It is totally different. When applied to human beings, the sun is the intellect. It is knowledge, it is life. Night is heedlessness. Water is reproduction: 'I created you from a drop of water.' The Divine Name of 'the Living' is upon it.[1] Earth is the body.

The sun, water and earth are three poles. Whoever takes on one of these enters the domain of the Perfect Human.[2] He becomes a giver, not a taker. All three are givers, they're not stealers! They're all givers.

---

1. God created all living things from water (21:30).
2. The concept of the Four Poles goes back a long way in Sufism: 'Like the sun, the sage shines on all the world; like the earth, he bears the good and evil of all; like water, he is the source of life for every heart; and like fire, he gives his warmth to all and sundry' (Sari (Sirri) Saqati, AD 769–867).

Water is a giver, earth is a giver, the sun is a giver. Life can't exist without any of them. Let us not protect ourselves. Let us give to the neighbor, to the government. To the stranger. He's shooting at us, but in his moment of need, let's give.

Be like the sun. Be like a river. Be like earth. Be like the night.

The earth bears the burden of the rest. It bears what nobody, no prophet, no pharaoh bore. You know what I call the earth? Perfect Human!

The four elements

The four elements of the inner life are as follows. Fire represents the devil, air the ego, water God's grace and bounty, and earth the Heart.

What pesters all humanity is fire and air. They're both in this body. When fire erupts in a city, a neighborhood, and the wind is blowing, it will crackle and burn. If you cut off the air, fire will be extinguished. Also, fire can't burn water. Water extinguishes fire. Earth, too, puts out fire, it smothers it.

When we're angry, whatever the cause of our anger, we immediately have to take refuge in morality, in Muhammadan ethics. That will snuff out our egotistical fire, God willing. What do we do? When something egotistical manifests, we get angry too. But one should intervene with water, with morality, with calmness, in order to put out that fire. If you intervene with the ego, with passion, you become inflamed too. The two fires come together, they'll burn down the house! This is the simile. Water is Muhammadan ethics.

These are the four elements. But who owns this factory, who makes them function? The spirit! Otherwise, air will be attracted to air, fire to fire, water to water and earth to earth.

God created Adam from earth. Then he was given fire, air and water. He was hemmed in from these four directions. We think that was there and then. But every baby is given fire, water, earth at birth. These four are in man, and there's an end to them.

Air is the most difficult – that is, the airs and caprices of the self. If air and wind blow, fire will flame up. Once you rein in air and fire, what remains is water and earth. Those two get along well together. The earth is very fertile, it blooms with water. It becomes a rose garden, one sits in a villa of diamonds and jewels in a corner of Paradise. We have to cut off air and fire, we have to give weight to water and earth.

Fire and air belong to the Base Self. Now the saints first cut off the air. Fire weakens. When fire dims, they start working on fire. When fire is done too, it's easy. Once you place them under the charge of the spirit, what remains is water and earth. One has reached the Tranquil Self. When air and fire are brought under control, Compassionate attributes begin – angels invade.

Next, try to rein in the earth. When that's done, water comes next. When that, too, is delivered to the command of the spirit, the mysteries of God begin. God says in the Quran, 'As long as My servants are pleased with Me, I'm pleased with them.' [The stages of the Pleased and Pleasing Self – 89:28.]

The self does not die, it surrenders. The Prophet of God said: 'I made my self surrender (i.e., a Muslim).' When the earth and so on come under the command of the spirit with the permission of God, that's when the divine mysteries begin. So it's very difficult to make the self a Muslim.

Let me give you another example. One works and works on the self, it becomes covered with ashes. One thinks the self is subdued. Until a time when, in a pinch, something egotistical comes up, you remove the ashes covering the cinders with tongs, and the fire springs back to life. One thinks one has reformed the self, but something comes from somewhere and it flares up immediately. As someone said, 'It's easy to become a servant of God, but hard to become a follower of Muhammad.'

Water, fire, air and earth are opposed to each other, that's why human beings can't get along. Without water it would be a disaster, without earth it would be a disaster. If a fire falls here and you pour fire on it, this place will burn. One has to go at fire with water.

What puts out fire? Water. Always try to be water, try to put out the other's fire. How do we do this? By tranquility, by beautiful ethics. If you become fire or gasoline yourself, it'll flame up even more. Always and everywhere, repress your self. Be water, be good-mannered. Don't work with fire, that's passion. Work with water. Do it light. In a normal way.

I see that all society, everyone included, is playing with fire and air. We haven't reined them in. How far can a condition like this take us? It's incendiary, egotistical and diabolical. Don't be a plaything of the self and the devil, make *them* your playthings. Please, let us get this fire and air out of this body, let us live in a Paradise in this world.

The tomb of the body

We will go from one tomb to another. We're all afraid of the other tomb. This tomb never crosses our minds.

Do whatever you do while this spirit is in the body. What good is it after the spirit leaves the body?

Verses and Sayings declare the punishment of the grave [prior to the Last Judgment and hell]. *It exists.* The People of Wisdom have mostly thought of that tomb, the last breath, that tomb. 'My God, let me go with a mature faith. And protect me from the pain of the tomb.' That's the prayer of us all. But humankind is in a tomb now: the body.[3] We don't see this tomb at all, we see only that tomb. *Aha!* We're all in a tomb now. There is a great spirit that God has bestowed on humanity. It is presently in a tomb. If we think about this tomb, if we can find health and salvation in this tomb, that tomb will go easily. The thing is this tomb! Whatever we do, whether good or terrible, we're going to take there with us the states and conditions we've achieved in this tomb. We're going to take *from here*, there's nothing over there. There's no pain there, we're going to take the pain there *ourselves*. This tomb is ours. But if you enter that tomb with an *enlightened Heart*, an enlightened life, the tomb will be pleased.

Yes, we're in a tomb, sir. Whatever you do, it's in this body, in this tomb. Whether good or bad, we're going to take over from this tomb. Our eyes are fixed on that tomb no matter what. What are you going to do with that? Look at this tomb. Here again, a Saying: 'In the grave, a window on heaven is opened to some, a window on hell to others.' One takes it there from this tomb, there's nothing over there. It all goes from here.

From the moment it enters this body, the spirit is in a tomb. We're in a tomb, this body. The point is what we take over to the other tomb. Good and bad, virtue and evil are all in this tomb. The crux is this tomb. We're going to carry over the fire and the rose from this tomb. Let us build this tomb as Muhammadans. We're going to supply the food of the afterworld tomb in this world.

Human beings are good, originally good. But they soil themselves like children. And the grownups? They cleanse them. Finally, humans become clean. Ali has a prayer: 'Peace be upon the prophets and messengers, upon the friends of God and the truthful, upon the people of faith and the people of wisdom.'

---

3. The ancient mystery religions, too, viewed the body as a tomb.

Yunus Emre says: 'I lie on the Bridge of the Path that is narrower than a hair and sharper than a sword.' The Bridge of the Path is the Divine Law. He worked well in this world. There are four elements in man. What disturbs the body, the spirit most is air and fire. If one restrains them, one will be in comfort. When you cut off fire and air, water and earth remain. It is a fertile soil, and when rain falls, it's done!

The spirit is not bound by the four elements, the four elements are bound by the spirit. The Base Self does not die, it is reformed. They work hard until they reform it. They put it in a bottle. If the bottle is not sealed properly, air will blow, the fire inside will flare. The fire boils over. Once they seal off the fire, they reform the air as well. It can't affect the fire. What remains is water and earth. When rain falls on fecund soil, a rosebed, a rose garden is produced.

It is then that the spirit begins to move. Then, the spirit begins to sing like a canary bird. Then we will have planted the flag, and the fortress stands conquered. Then we will have some peace. The other tomb, too, will become a rosebed, a rose garden. This is asceticism. One enters a forty-day period of asceticism[4] in order to harness the fire, the air. But if we promise God [about the Two Doors], if we reform the fire, the air, asceticism won't be necessary.

---

4. Compare Lent, the Christian fast of forty days. (Moses spent forty days on the mountain and Jesus spent forty days in the desert.)

Ethics

The First Pillar of Islam

Morality is the foundation. There are Five Pillars of Islam. There are Six Pillars, the first is ethics. Prayer, being a Muslim, and so on are things you do for yourselves. What I need is morality. To feed the hungry, to give to the poor.

Leave the fragrance of a rose behind you. Leave an appealing sound, leave a rose fragrance. There's a saying: 'One rose doesn't make spring.' To enjoy springtime, everyone should plant a rose in their own garden.

Leave a pleasant taste. If all this city were yours, it won't abide with you. It didn't to those before us.

The basis of knowledge is ethics. If there is no morality at the basis of a science, that science will rise and rise, but will fall in the end.

The basis of religion is also ethics. If one has morality, one can perform one's religion. Otherwise, one cannot.

If morality is beautiful, worship will be right. Without morality, there is no worship. Morality is the foundation of worship.

The big thing is morality. If one has no share of morality, of courtesy, one has neither reason nor faith. Reason, faith – one has to protect these. And that is possible only with courtesy.

Is invocation (*zikr*) better, or is morality better? Morality is better. Those are the orders of God, we're going to do them anyway. Without ethics, they'll all be in vain. You'll step on ice and slip – *swish!*

Good and evil

You are not to regard good and evil as the same. You're not to see them as equal. We're not going to merge them, we're going to distinguish between them. God says, 'Both good and evil are from Me.' But He further says, 'Follow the good.' He doesn't say: 'Follow the evil.'

God says, 'I created both good and evil. If you follow the good, you will come close to Me. If you follow the bad, you will obey the ego/ the Base Self. Don't hold Me responsible later on.' He distinguishes between the two, He doesn't hold them the same. God says, 'I've informed you of good and evil. If you obey the self and Satan, don't blame Me, because I've told you about good, evil and everything.'

The Prophet of God says: 'Be beautiful in morals, be beautiful in ethics.' If the foundation of a building is mud, water or a flood will sweep it away. But if it is iron and concrete, it'll bear everything. It is just the same with ethics.

The Prophet says, 'I was sent to perfect your ethics.' Not other things, only morality. He doesn't say 'your education, your medicine, your technology.' 'A mighty morality' [68:4], the Quran says regarding him. A billion Muslims agree on the proclamation of faith, on the Quran, on the Prophet, but the members of a family can't agree on ethics among themselves.

The big thing is ethics. You, too, be very careful about ethics. You could have a roomful of jewels, of books, and they could burn down to ashes in half an hour. Be very careful. Not just in Allowed [honestly earned] money, but in everything.

All existence is for you. Who are *you* for? A flower becomes honey and comes to you. Flesh becomes milk and cream and comes to you. To live mindful of these facts. They call this 'meditation' (*tafakkur*). We're going to give everything its rights, everything is going to be pleased with us, so that God will be pleased with us, too. Sun, star, tree ... all should be pleased with us. Give thanks to God. Don't be destructive to the globe, be beneficial.

This is a testing ground. We are responsible for what we see and hear, not for what we don't see and don't hear.

My last testament to you: always be on the side of the good.

Ethics and knowledge

Which is greater, morality or knowledege? Morality is very great. Knowledge is great, too. May God grant peace to humanity. Where does peace come from? It comes from ethics. Where does ethics come from? It comes from knowledge. May God leave no one without knowledge. May God leave no one without ethics.

The Prophet says: 'Seek knowledge, even if it be in China.' But he doesn't say 'I came to you to complete knowledge,' he says 'I came to complete ethics.' Knowledge is necessary, but *morality is important. Morality is important.*

Without ethics, what would knowledge do? Without knowledge, where would you find ethics? The two support each other. You sit here, we talk, you go out or go home, you strike your child, you break your wife's heart, or else you quarrel with someone in the street, our discourse here is ruined, it all goes down the drain there.

Prayer is a must. The Divine Law is a must. But things don't end with Prayer. First comes morality. Without ethics, Pray all night long [if you want to]. In the morning one goes and wrecks it.

Next, to help those around you. To visit the sick. Love one another, come to each other. Someone's business is going badly, collect among yourselves and give. Don't just watch. Someone has to go to his hometown, he doesn't have the money, give.

Ethics. Morality is the beginning of everything, child. You could invoke with your teacher all night, you go home in the morning, you scold – without cause – your wife or your father at home, it all goes to naught. If we fill this place with the riches of this world and you strike a match, they'll all become ashes.

Attitude to others

Try to do good to each other, to human beings, to all humanity, even to your enemy. Try to be beneficial to animals, to plants.

- Love one another. For God. Whether native or out-of-town, love one another, one and all. Stick to each other. Look after each other. Don't say, 'My Lord, it's all for me.' Protect humans, animals, everything. If someone is jobless, find him a job. Put the sick in a hospital. Don't lose love. This world came with love, may it also go with love, God willing.
- Be easygoing. Always sweet speech, smiling mien. Not when you're comfortable – actors can do that too. The thing is to do it when you're choking.
- Gentleness. Always with gentleness. Be meek and mild.
- Whoever gets along well with everyone is very close to God, very close to God's Messenger.
- The one who knows must bear the one who doesn't know. The one who knows must manage the one who doesn't.

A Holy Tradition says: 'There is a lump of flesh in the human body [the heart]. That's where I look at.' The important thing is intention. Let us set out with that intention. Even if we can't get there, it'll be as if we did.

What is necessary

To be normal in one's every move. Always to emulate the Prophet of God.

To be normal, to aim at the medium in all our comings and goings, in everything. If you go to extremes in worship, the body isn't used to it, the body is ruined. Not to go too far, nor fall too much behind in one's work, one's spirituality. Forget home when you leave home, forget work when you leave work. Go to work five or ten minutes earlier than everyone, leave five or ten minutes after everyone. Because your service is to the whole nation, the entire nation has a right over you. Don't trangress that right.

What is life, do you know? If you're distraught inwardly and outwardly, what use is it if you live in a palace? If you're happy inwardly and outwardly, what difference does it make if you live in a chicken coop?

Shabby clothes don't make a dervish. Wear a spotless silk shirt, wear a tie. Wear gold, wear it for God, don't wear it for your ego.

You want to do something, imagine there's a sheriff, a policeman beside you. Like this every moment. Don't forget the cop, and everything will work out fine.

'What did you do for God today?' If a president, a shepherd, a soldier thought about this every day, there would be no need for police or rangers.

Emulate the Names of God

One Name of God is 'the Just.' Let us love justice.
Another Name of God is 'the Truth.' Let us always be true.
Another Name is 'the Sublime.' Let us always be cheerful and good.
Another Name is 'the Healer.' Doctors are in this one.
Another Name is 'the Judge.' The judges are here.

The people of the West possess our ways. A bath in every home for cleanliness, hot water, cold water. If everyone sweeps his doorway, the whole city will be clean. If one takes an Ablution five times a day, one will have entered flowing water five times. They're doing what we ought to be doing.

If you benefit from a friend in terms of *intelligence – intelligence*, not profit – be good friends with them that you may benefit. You love the friend very much, you can't benefit, but nevertheless you love. Then be of benefit to *them*. I've told this to young people *thousands* of times. You see that you can't benefit, be beneficial yourself. You find that they can't receive, either. They can't benefit you and you can't benefit them. Even so, don't hurt their feelings.

Bold – one has to be brave and hopeful.

A child eats a hot pepper and begins crying. You put a candy, a chocolate in his mouth to ease his pain. Similarly, when someone says something bitter to you, respond with something sweet. Sweetness against bitterness. Settle the bitter with the sweet.

They say, 'The hand that gives is above the hand that receives.' Don't try to take, try to give. A hand-to-mouth existence won't do. You'll suffer the burden of your wife, your children. Earn honestly [i.e. 'Allowed' money], don't be afraid to get rich.

God is with you *everywhere*. Everywhere! And the greatest worship is to raise those children and see to it that they graduate. Marry them off. God willing, that is the highest worship, first-rate worship. If you turn away from them, one will be expelled from school, the other will have no allowance, the other won't have shoes, the blame is on you. If you were to invoke God's name night and day, you couldn't pay off that burden. First the *family*, then invocation, worship. If the family is left unsupported, if it isn't looked after, if it becomes destitute, and you repeat God's name twenty thousand, fifty thousand times a day, the responsibility for that family is there.

If there's a job that harms the interests of the nation, you're going to earn billions from it, stay out of it. If it's good for humanity, for country and nation, the profit is very small, that's okay. Don't go in on the side of loss. Whatever is useful for humankind, for animals and plants, do it perfectly well. Whatever is harmful, say: 'I'm sorry, I'm not the right person for this.'

Patience is good, patience.

Don't steal. Don't hurt anyone's feelings. Don't obstruct anyone's rights.

Stay on good terms with everyone. Be offended with nobody. That's my last testament to you.

Try to get along with your enemy. Don't be offended by [remain on speaking terms with] even your worst enemy. That's the thing. Don't see them as enemies, try to make friends with them. If you do this, you will succeed. A friend is a friend anyway, try to make your enemy a friend. We should try to make even your worst enemy smile. That's the way of the Sound Mind.

Work ethics

Don't be on the lookout for your salary. Try to make that company, that man rich.

What does God say? 'I love those who work. I help those who work.' That's all. To work, both materially and spiritually. What do we need? We need to persevere. To continue in every task. Not to abandon it. To be brave and hopeful – 'I'm going to succeed in this task!' If you do this, you will be successful. God says, 'If you want from Me, work. Be more hopeful.' Be hopeful physically and spiritually.

I've been talking to these people for twenty, twenty-five years. I just looked now, they're still at Square One. Why? Hopeless.

Work, employ lots of people, that's my last testament to you. But *righteously*.

To be superior, a sun, physically and spiritually.

Run, don't stop. God's first order to human beings is, 'Work night and day. Work straight, I'm with the righteous.' We work during the day, there's rest at night, He says: 'Meditate during the night.' Meditate on your worship, meditate on your job, you can prepare for it in the morning.

The Prophet's first duty to us is: 'Don't be beggars, be donators.' How can we do that? With work. With honest work. Work of the kind God and His Prophet desire, not the kind our ego desires.

Do your duty honestly, as a human being. Don't postpone today's work until tomorrow. If you do these and still lose your job, you'll be given a better one.

A cloud comes. A wind blows and sweeps the cloud away. The sun appears at once. That's how we're going to withstand difficulties. The cloud goes, the sun comes out. We have to be patient. Ibrahim Hakki says:

> *Suddenly a veil opens,*
> *The remedy for the ailment arrives.*

We have to patiently apply salve to the wound.

Whatever your job in the physical world, you should strive to find a better one. The same goes for spirituality. One should look further. One has to strive. Give thanks for what little there is, try to earn more.

To work hard at every task, whether physical or spiritual. To be hopeful and brave. If you have courage, you'll become a professor.

Hold your job higher than worship. Because God is forgiving, but His creatures are not.

We have to advance both this world and the afterworld together. If you turn only towards the other world, you'll become a madman of God (*majdhub/majzub*).

Work so hard that the place you work for has no rights over you, but you have rights over them. Visit a tree, a stone, for the sake of God. If it is for God, God will reimburse you. Visit people for Him, talk to them, try to wake them up.

The white stones

Rumi says in the *Mathnawi*, 'What seed is there that, once sown, doesn't sprout?' Sow wheat on the earth. Rumi says: 'What we say, what we sow, will one day sprout in Hearts.'

There was a wise man, and he had a neighbor. One day the neighbor said: 'Pray for me.' The wise man said: 'Only prayer is not enough, one has to be worthy.'

He goes off, brings a couple of white stones, he places one in his neighbor's garden and one in his own. The neighbor asks: 'What is this for?' 'It's a talisman. It'll ward off the Evil Eye of passers-by.' Summer comes, the garden blooms, he tells his friend: 'Look, plants have sprouted everywhere, except on this stone. *And you are a stone.* Nothing sprouted on the stone in my garden, either.'

'Is *this* why you wasted a year?' 'Yes!'

If it were soil, it would sprout. Sow a seed *somewhere*.

Be such that everybody is sure of you till the end of your life. The Prophet was known as 'Muhammad the Trustworthy.'

Work, work. Whether wise or ignorant, he who works, wins. Just as the one who works wins in the material world, it's the same with spirituality. God says, 'I give to those who work.'

Serve *all humanity*, both materially and spiritually. Obedience and worship are fine, but service is general. We're four people here, this lamp sheds light on us. If we were fifty thousand, it still would do so.

Don't meddle in other people's affairs. Don't trouble anyone, don't trouble even an ant, okay? We're going to disturb ourselves, we're not going to disturb others.

If you're good, everything will be good. Try to be good. Try to be useful to human beings, to animals, to plants, down to a piece of weed.

Serve humanity, especially when you're young. 'When you dress and feed the poor, when you visit a sick person, you do it to Me.' Your Fasting and Prayer belong to you. Don't step on an ant knowingly. Do not consciously step on a weed, that weed is your life and soul. Get along well with your children. Don't break anyone's heart. Whoever doesn't know, win their heart.

For example, a person has imbibed alcohol and has fallen by the roadside. If we too spit on him, that won't do. We're going to take him to his home, to a hospital if he's sick, and pray for him. If he's a Christian, we're going to invite him to God and his Prophet. But beyond that, there is no room for hatred.

If friends drive you away, say 'Okay' and approach them again.

Don't gossip. That's my last testament to you. A man of religion doesn't do bad things. Someone speaks against him, you join in, it'll be too bad for you. This is the greatest morality of being Muhammadan. Don't join in, don't be a party to slander.

If an imam (a Prayer-leader) is a thief, you should cover it. What for? For the sake of Islam. Say, 'He wouldn't do such a thing. If he really did, may God reform him.'

A man of religion leaves the mosque and goes to a bar. Shall we call all men of religion bad? A teacher has done something wrong. Shall we call all teachers bad?

We shouldn't be cruel to anyone, and we should forgive anyone who is cruel to us. That's how you have to be.

Step softly on the ground. Walk like an angel.

Towards one's spouse

Don't hurt each other's feelings. Live in your home like angels. If your husband [or wife] calls water 'yogurt drink (*ayran*),' say, 'It's *great* yogurt drink.'

Be a shepherd to your family. Otherwise a wolf will catch them, a thief will steal them.

We get along well with my wife. She has fire in her hand. A fight is ready at once! If I threw gas on it, we'd both burn. So I prepare water. Be a little hard of hearing, a little hard of seeing and cut from your tongue,[1] everything will become milk and honey. If your spouse is angry with you, make her/him a cup of coffee.

---

1. This is reminiscent of the three monkeys of the Chinese: 'See no evil, hear no evil,

If you're happy with your spouse, have children. Don't delay.

[To married couples:] You're lucky. You have two fathers and two mothers. Know this to be the truth. Act accordingly. The ego doesn't want it, apply pressure on the ego. When it gets angry at something, tell it: 'You're lying. They're my life and soul.' When the devil is gone, everything will be milk and honey. If you can use it properly, you'll be in comfort.

Don't call a relative of your spouse 'bad.' Even if they're bad, say they're good.

Towards children

Don't dive at a child, don't attack. Take them gently in your lap and explain nicely. Don't be parents to your children, be their *friends*.

You can find everything, but you can't find a father or mother. And you can find everything, but you can't find a child. So this is two-sided, don't give each other cause for worry.

Comment: *Young people are rebellious.*

Still, treat them with mildness. Young people are all like that.

Be friends to your children, both of you. Being parents is something different, don't be a mother or father to them. You'll ruin everything if you do. I tell this to everyone, they all succeed. I say, 'Don't tear that book,' the girls – they're children – tear it. I say 'Tear it,' they look at me like this. Let's not break when we're trying to mend.

Towards parents

Because parents are experienced, one should do everything after consulting with them. You're going to buy this lighter, 'Dad, should I buy this?' If he says 'Don't,' that's the end of it. You bought it, 'Dad, should I light this or not?'

She's your mother. If she calls a lighter 'A match,' say 'Okay.' After all, they're both fire.

---

speak no evil.'

If you oppose your father, you're in error in two respects. The first because you oppose, the second because he's your father. So you're spiritually at fault.

Even if your parents are separated, even if they drive you away, don't leave them. Be calm, be patient, you'll be the winner. Say 'Yes' to your parents, say 'Yes' to your spouse.

Don't deny. What I'm telling you is the face of Khidr. [Don't drive away salvation.] Don't tell Khidr: 'Begone!'

The prayer of your mother for you is worth a *thousand* prayers. Don't hurt your spouse's feelings, either. If you act in this way, God will love you.

A family was having supper. Their son came and brought something. 'What's this?' 'I brought this for you with the money I earned.' The mother and father were in tears. The boy says: 'That's when I understood what it means to be a father or mother.'

Don't eat the Forbidden, don't look at the Forbidden, be like an angel. Let everyone call you an angel. They call tea 'yogurt drink,' say: 'It's very good yogurt drink.' Both to your parents and to everyone.

May God save us all from the Base Self. If we're free of the Base Self, we'll come a little close to friends [saints], to spiritual states and things.

[In addressing someone about to embark on a long trip:] Sow a handful of wheat, beans, lentils in those places [you go] and come back. Did you understand what I'm saying? You didn't. Sow Unification, worship and so on in those places. God says, 'If you give thanks for little, I'll give you plenty.' This is both physical and spiritual. And spiritual more than the physical. If you do your duty, I'll give you more.

Consult with three people about a matter. If they all say the same thing, do it. If they say different things, postpone that matter until a later time. If two out of three give the same advice, you can still do it.

If you have a house, if you rent it out to a cruel tenant, that tenant may leave the house in a year or two, but the house will be ruined. He'll break its door and such like. Now I say, we are tenants in this body. Let us appreciate the worth of this house. To harm the house is the work of the Livelihood Mind. To know its worth is for the Sound Mind.[2]

Don't live in this house like a tenant, live in it like its owner. Don't damage the house.

---

2. See the next chapter: The mind and the heart/Kinds of minds.

Forbidden versus Allowed

This is a very delicate matter.

A governor comes to a very honest town. He can't find any way to corrupt it. Finally, he says: 'Everyone will bring an egg tomorrow.' They bring them. The next day he says, 'Everybody take their egg back.' The eggs all get mixed up, it's impossible to distinguish which belongs to whom, Forbidden mingles with Allowed. A month later, gossip starts. Five months later he announces: 'I'm leaving. But after me, you're going to take your dead out of the window instead of out the door.' He goes back, mission accomplished. [That is, even this little can result in confusion between Forbidden and Allowed.]

To love and give joy, that's the path of heaven. Gossip, that's the road to hell. We want heaven on the other side, He gives us heaven here too. To control oneself, nothing else.

'Let a dust particle alight, I'll brush it away.' No. Don't let dust land on you. All human beings are angels. Let's just not get ourselves dirty. This word is for all of you. If gold falls in the mud, it is still gold. Someone will wash it clean. You're all gold.

If one has fallen into the mud, one shouldn't remain there. One should get up, clean one's clothes with hope and with Sound Mind. On a holiday, a mother dresses up her child brand new, the child runs out and falls in the mud. The parents are annoyed, they give him a slap or two. They clean him up with difficulty, he goes out again.

You put on a white pair of trousers, a car splatters mud from the road. Or you enter a swamp. Are you going to remain like that? A cleanup, an ironing, you continue on your way. Get out of that swamp.

Don't get stuck in the mud. You're three people going your way, two get stuck in the mud. Try to save them. If you can't, don't get stuck yourself, too.

Suicide and murder are the same thing [4:29]. Our Prophet did everything right. He held the two the same. This is for the believer, of course. The unbeliever doesn't believe anyway. Euthanasia is considered suicide or murder in all Four Books and its punishment is accordingly. It is morally wrong.

Work, struggle so that your supper will be Allowed.

Don't fool anyone. Be honest. It's okay if you are fooled, but try not to be fooled, either. If you fool someone, you too will be fooled. Someone else will fool you. God knows everything. Don't act as if you don't know it, you'll fool only yourselves.

The mind and the heart

The mind and the heart make this body survive. But it is health that makes the body, the mind and the heart survive. May God grant a Sound Mind to us all, and then good health.

'My community,' says the Prophet, 'will not get sick if they listen to me.' We're going to do everything with reason.

What the eye sees, the ear cannot see. What the ear hears, the eye cannot hear. What both can't perceive, the mind does. They're all linked to each other.

I had an aunt [when I was a child]. I would do something wrong, she'd come and pull my ear: 'Son, son,' she'd say, 'don't act with the eye, act with the mind.'

Everything done with the intellect is auspicious. Nine-tenths of intellect was given to our Prophet, the rest to all humanity. Yet he still says: 'My Lord, increase my intellect.'

One has to be a Muslim in order to bring mind and goodwill together.

The computer – that emerges from the human mind, too. From human to human. 'I love man very much, I serve man by the hand of man.'

Kinds of minds

There are various kinds of minds. The most important are: the Livelihood Mind (*'aql al-ma'isha*), the Sound Mind (*'aql al-salim*), the Kingly Mind (*'aql al-sultani*), the Total Mind (the Universal Intellect, *'aql al-kull*).

The Total Mind is the highest. As a human being, our Prophet accepted it. The Universal Intellect gathers the Compassionate, the Merciful, everything within its span. Just as the sun belongs to nobody and everyone benefits from it, so too is the case with the Universal Intellect. In order to receive that mind, we all need training in Sufism and asceticism. There is seclusion in all the orders.

Now, there are many minds – compassionate, diabolical and so on. Basically, I have divided mind in two: the Livelihood Mind [which can also be called the Subsistence Mind] and the Sound Mind. The Subsistence Mind is mainly interested in food and drink, marriage, entertainment, wasting one's life and passing away. 'Let me fill my stomach, let me find comfort and live in comfort. Let me do and destroy as I please.' It satisfies the ego, it eats, drinks and sleeps. From a president down to a beggar. That is, the entire organization of the brain remains idle. This is the Subsistence Mind.

Then there is the Sound Mind. The Sound Mind begins to investigate. It's very rare in our time. To be safe and liberated in everything. With the Sound Mind, a human being becomes superior to the angels. It is spiritual. It is the mind bestowed by God on the spirit. It obeys God. It lives in accordance with God's orders. One both earns one's livelihood, eats and drinks, and submits to the Sound Mind. The Sound Mind keeps its promise immediately. Either it doesn't make a promise, or keeps it. The Sound Mind is not like the Subsistence Mind, it thinks of everything and everyone.

I once saw a book by [the Sufi master] Kenan Rifa'i. 'Sound Heart, Sound Mind' was written on almost every page. May God grant Sound Heart and Sound Mind to us all.

The Sound Mind is higher than miraculous feats. Sound Heart and Sound Mind are the highest miraculous deed. How is one going to find the miraculous without that mind?

Let us all work materially and spiritually with a Sound Mind, God willing. Let's not drift away from God. If we break with God, we'll fall into the claws of the Base Self, the devil. It makes everything appear fine to our eyes. And then, all of a sudden, *pow!*

They say, 'Don't act with the Subsistence Mind, with the eye, the ear and the tongue. Ask a (person possessing) Sound Mind first, then act.'

To utilize the Sound Mind. To plant the flag of unification on top of the head. To say 'God' and not turn back.

Let me give you an example. Think of a factory. There are millions, billions in its vaults. Everyone departs in the evening, only the night watchman is left. There are billions in the safe, but he doesn't know the combination. He just receives his pay every month.

Now God has given us all this treasure, this head. The Sound Mind. Let's not be a watchman to the treasure, let us own the treasure.

The captain and the engineer

Now, what would the mind do without the heart? And what would the heart do without the mind? An elephant has a heart, too. The two have to be kept in harmony.

The wise give the following example. They say, 'A ship sails out to sea. Hundreds, maybe thousands of people, animals, goods. The captain keeps watch, he is the mind. The heart is the chief engineer who moves the ship, [in charge of the engine room] three decks below.'

The body is a ship.[1] Our body is our vehicle, let us use it wisely. A Saying: 'I made the entire universe your vehicle, and I made you My vehicle.' The whole universe works for man. The wild weed you step on feeds the cow. The one to the other, that to the next, they all serve human beings.

'If the captain and the engineer are at odds,' they say, 'the captain maneuvers right or left, he either hits a rock with the ship or it runs ashore, the ship is wrecked. The engineer can't see him. What can the engineer do?' This is a very good simile.

They say: 'If the engineer doesn't heed the captain, he loosens a screw, the ship stops, what can the captain do?' They've given this example as regards the Sound Mind and the Sound Heart, sir. The two have to cooperate. If the mind pulls in one direction and the heart pulls in another, it parts at the middle and falls toward the Subsistence Mind. If they unite, they reach the goal, physically and spiritually. We have to unite the Sound Mind and the Sound Heart, otherwise the ship won't move.

The Subsistence Mind doesn't think of anything but the stomach, its pleasures and its children. The neighbor's house catches fire, his car is wrecked, there is danger – 'What of it to us?' There's a funeral, it doesn't go. It only thinks of its own comfort, and in that comfort it consumes and consumes, but is never sated. It is a friend of the belly. No matter how great one's wealth, it always seems insufficient in its eye.

And then the Sound Mind. It obeys God's orders, it follows the path of the Prophet and God, it thinks of its country, its nation, down to a handful of earth, an ant. That is, in the Sound Mind, the heart and the mind have reached agreement.

---

1. Another Sufic saying: 'The body is a ship. The mind is its rudder, thought is its sail. Make your ship swim, let me see you.'

If the Sound Mind is not achieved, a whale, an elephant, a mosquito, an ant all have hearts. They're alive, they can't function without a heart. If we unite the Sound Mind with the heart, things find their proper place. The ship moves off to sea, toward another shore.

Don't run your ship ashore. Harmonize your mind (the captain) and the heart (the engineer). Run your body with the Sound Mind. If the two join forces, it'll journey to the realm of space.

Faith

(*To recap, the Six Pillars of Faith are as follows: 'I believe 0. in God [and after that,] 1. in His Angels, 2. in His Books, 3. in His Messengers, 4. in the Day of Judgment, 5. that whatever destiny befalls us, good or ill, is from God, and 6. in the Resurrection after Death.'*)

Everyone has an idol. Some people's idol is money, other people's is their wife, their child. They worship the idol fashioned by their own hands, instead of God.

I bear witness that there is no god but God, and that Muhammad is His servant and Messenger – this is the first gift of the Prophet. You can repeat it thirty-three, fifty-one, or one-hundred-and-one times a day. Years ago, a lady told me: 'If divine effusion is cut off, repeat this a hundred times a day.'

In the Name of God, the Compassionate, the Merciful [the Naming] – this is the key. All Verses of the Quran are unlocked with it, the chapters recited in Prayer are opened with it.

I believe in God – I believe that God exists, that He is One. Whatever I do, inwardly or outwardly, God knows and sees. He sees, He knows, He is present everywhere. If we wink at someone, God knows about it.

Once we accept this, we can accept the rest.

The Six Pillars of Faith have an outer and an inner aspect.

In His Angels – God's angels exist. God alone knows their number. Angels don't get sick. They are in God's service. But do you possess the ethics of angels?

Angels exist. *So what?* What of it to us?

Can we take on their ethics? How many of their morals do you have? We fast for a month, that month is angelic morality. When one is separated from food, drink and lust, that is the morality of angels. What we need is their beautiful morals, do you have them?

In His Books – Books. Do you believe in the Quran? Do we believe in the Four Books and the Hundred Pages? We all say 'Yes.'

How are you with its conditions? Can you practice its precepts? Which of these Verses have you embodied? Have you taken on the morals of one or two, are you following them? Ethics. Character traits.

Remember what Aisha said: 'The Prophet's morality was the morality of the Quran.'

In His Messengers – All prophets plus the Prophet, who is the light of our eyes, the joy of our hearts. That Prophet whom you love very much, how do you stand with his ethics? How many of his morals do you possess?

This is the point: to moralize ourselves with the morals of the Messenger.

The Day of Judgment and the rest, you can keep.

[Psychoanalyst Jules Masserman, in stating his views on leadership (*Time* magazine, July 15, 1974), reached the following conclusion: 'The greatest leader of all time is Muhammad.']

This man is an American and Jewish. Does he go to heaven or hell? How do you know he's going to go to hell? Maybe he pronounced the Word of Witnessing!

Courtesy

Do you know what courtesy (*adab*) is? To wake up, to know, to make known. A courtesy towards God, towards the One who gave us this body.

Courtesy is not just the headscarf of women. The *universe* is within courtesy. To eat, to drink, going shopping, everything is within courtesy.

I sometimes think about courtesy ... From an oak tree, down to a piece of weed. Its roots, the branches of the roots, God has covered them with earth in order to hide them from man. In the case of animals, God hides the shame of *all* animals. Their private parts are all concealed. The most important among those covered are sheep. But the rest are covered, too. The goat [is the one exception], they associate the goat with the devil, its tail is upright. Even *animals*. But human beings have become worse than animals. Human beings don't have shame, but animals have shame. If only a morality, if only some good manners would come to the rescue.

True courtesy is to act under the control of the [internal] sheriff. To obey God's orders. Every moment – nowhere is one excluded from this.

'Who lacks courtesy has neither mind nor faith' – so say both Verse and Tradition. I read this in a book, the words aren't mine: 'Enter with courtesy, receive what you can and depart with wisdom.'

Do you know what courtesy is? To cover up and so on, but in actuality, courtesy encompasses *the universe*. We think it's about eating, drinking and covering. Take the Gospel in hand, take the Torah, whichever book we look at, they all say 'courtesy.' The Glorious Quran is entirely courtesy. Totality is in courtesy – it encompasses *the universe*.

Admirable conduct

The words of our Prophet: 'Be hopeful. Be patient.' How beautiful! We're going to be hopeful and patient, we're going to say, 'We will succeed.'

Be benevolent, tolerant. As you do this, you will become sweet. As you do [the opposite], you will become bitter.

Wherever you see a fire, douse it with water. If you too throw fire on it, *uh-uh*, things will be ruined. They swear at you, they hurl the greatest insults, speak nicely to them. When a dog barks, do you bark back? When a needle touches you, don't jump, be tolerant.

Be accommodating, be flexible. Be of one face, divide that face in ten. If they call tea 'yogurt drink' and yogurt drink 'tea,' accept and confirm them [as long as it doesn't impinge on essentials, like the Forbidden/Allowed distinction].

You work entirely for yourself. But one should work for others, too. Don't always expect healing from others. Give healing to others for a change. You're working for the world, know that the world is working for you. You should see it that way.

Affairs of the world and religious affairs should be on a par, like the two pointers of a scale. This is what the Divine Law says.

Connect the physical to spirituality. If you do the opposite, both will collapse. The stomach is for the spirit. If the spirit is for God, then everything's okay. Otherwise, one lives like an animal. One should link the body to spirit and the spirit to God. The body is connected to the spirit, the four elements pull it down. To obey God's orders, to escape egoism, to erect the flag of Muhammadanhood.

Keep your eyes open inwardly and outwardly. Be sharp. Dress the latest fashion, be with God inwardly.

Don't mess with shaky [illegal] business. Always be on firm ground. Let it be little, but let it be firm.

Eavesdropping is a very bad thing. That's God's door you're listening to.

The three things that are most hateful to God are: 1. [Being preoccupied with] earning money; 2. killing one another; 3. the spread of lust. Lust is the worst, it's very widespread now. And war.

This lighter won't light if it hasn't gas in it. The lighter has everything, someone lights its flame. This head has everything, as long as you work and study. Don't be lazy.

Be with God every instant. Be with God when you eat, drink, go to bed and get up. Does God see, hear, know? If we determine these three points, we can neither steal nor do any evil.

If someone gives you a present, a date, don't hurt their feelings, thank them. If you don't want it, give it to someone else.

Nowadays, both girls and boys have become hunters. They take one, take their fill and go on to another. Thousands of boys and girls are complaining. They seduce and abandon. Don't fall into this trap. Go straight to the marriage office. Say, 'I love you, I want you, if you're ready for marriage, let's go to the justice of the peace. Otherwise, don't waste my time.' If they say 'Next year,' say: 'I can't wait.' Quickly. A brief friendship. Say, 'I'm ready.' If they're interested, they'll say 'Okay.' Otherwise, they'll say 'No.' Don't fall for any tricks. They're not suitors, they're hunters, they're going to hunt rabbits. It's egotistical, diabolical.

Become engaged, but don't seduce the girl. Maybe you'll leave her one day, she'll be deflowered.

You're walking in your house, you see a breadcrumb. No harm in stepping on it, but there is one harm. You eat it, you consume it, why step on it? If it were a scorpion, a wasp, you couldn't step on it, you'd be scared.

- When you're going to curse someone, instead of cursing, say: 'May God give you intelligence.'
- Spend *good* days. But the good days are in our hands. If we do good, if we don't do evil, if we do good as strongly as we do evil, good days will be ours.
- If we call a bad person 'bad,' it'll only be worse. Let's hold their hand.
- Don't eat too much wherever you go. Stay hungry, come home, eat at home.
- The greatest thing is to discern one's error and not to repeat it. To be ashamed of one's error. That's very good.
- Don't be a burden to others, ease other people's burden. The intelligent are to raise the unintelligent to their own level. Whoever knows has to carry the one who doesn't know on his back.
- Our greatest loss is our wasted breath. The breaths we inhale and exhale for nothing.
- God doesn't do the least amount of injustice. An angel records whatever you speak. God distances from you things that aren't good for you via angels.
- Eat little, work much.
- People shouldn't do work they don't know.
- If one person says 'Yes' to a thing and another says 'No,' find their middle ground.
- A small evil and a great one are both evil.

Have you ever seen a scorpion? You want to do good to a snake. You want to give, give it milk, for example. You bring your hand near, it bites right away. Do good to those who know its worth. Those who don't won't understand. You'll do it, but they won't understand. Let's do good, but to human beings, to those who are good. Would you do good to a pickpocket, to a snake? One will beat you up, the other will bite you.

Help even an ant. Even if a drunkard, meet the needs of those in need. Whatever that need may be.

You're walking in the street. If someone collides with you while you're looking around, he's in the wrong. But if you collide with him, it's your fault. If you bump into a blind man with the sight you have, you'll get punished.

The greatest error and the greatest work is to deal with human beings. Right from the start, man has been repairing man.

Do you fear God? Then don't fear death. Would anyone who's relying on God and His Prophet fear anything?

'I did it myself and found it myself, then who's to blame?' On that count, 'If you do good, you do to yourself, if you do bad, you do to yourself. Whatever you do, you do to yourself' [17:7].

A new life is beginning for you. What does Ibrahim Hakki say? 'Forget the past, embrace the future.'

Animal rights

Do not consciously step on an ant. Don't step on it. They're all a gift from God. Don't cut the branch, the root of a living tree. They're all serving us. Be very careful.

You're passing by, a kitten, a puppy has fallen into the mud. Raise it out, put it aside. If you feel mercy for a kitten, a puppy, how can you fail to have mercy on human beings?

Don't throw stones at animals. Don't even tap them with your finger. Love them, fondle them. They're your life and soul.

My last testament to you, don't deal in living things. For feeding them, for killing them, don't deal in living things. Don't buy or sell animals, do some other job.

A colonel had a vow to keep. He asked me: 'What should I do?' I was crossing the Galata Bridge [in Istanbul] twenty years ago. They're frying fish alive on a fire. Bestial!

I said, 'Buy as many live fish as you can and throw them back in the sea.' He went, he couldn't find any there. He went to the other end of the bridge, he found some there, freshly caught but dead. He threw them in the sea. That's useful too, they'll be of use to the fish in the sea.

I told him: 'Don't go hunting,' he didn't listen. He had two fingers blown off, only then did he give up. Every kind of hunting is bad. It hurts the animal. What would you do if they killed one of your children? Well, these animals are your children, too.

Hunting is Forbidden. If one causes hurt, he himself will be hurt someday. Or else his child will be hurt. Hunting is banned. I was banned from it myself. Do you know for whom hunting is Allowed? The poor, they don't have anything to give their children. Hunting is Allowed for them. If he has a need, he can shoot one and feed his children. Otherwise, if you're going to follow your whim, then everything becomes Allowed.

Comment: *Ants devoured part of my harvest.*

The remaining crops are enough for you. I visited a brother of mine twenty years ago. He's finished his harvest, he's standing there like a statue. 'What are you waiting for?' I asked. He replied: 'For the wind to blow and winnow the wheat from the chaff.' The winds blow strong over there, and the next day a wind blew away everything – wheat, chaff and all.

I said, 'Of course, I can compensate this for you. But you're in error here. Can you guess what it is?'

He thought and thought, he finally discovered the reason. There are ant colonies surrounding the place of harvest. The ants haul wheat into their nests after the harvest is done. They gather other things, too, but this is their main food. I know because I too have done that kind of work. He had taken DDT [insecticide] from his house and poured it into the antholes. All the ants had perished. 'There,' I said, 'that's your fault.'

Whether good or bad, every responsibility depends on a cause. You can't escape that blame.

Political secularism (laicism)

(*Laicism – secularism in the political sphere – seems to have become a major bone of contention in recent times with regard to Islam. In an age when religion is increasingly being misused to secure political ends, the Master's approach in this respect comes as a gasp of oxygen. He never had anything against the secular state – what he was interested in was freedom of religion. Moreover, he based his views solidly on the Quran and the Traditions, as well as on Islamic history, in contrast to those who must resort to misinterpretation in order to bend truth.*

Two Verses: 'To you, your religion; to me, mine' [109:6] and 'There is no compulsion in religion' [2:256], together with one Saying: 'There is no clergy in religion,' ensure that a theocracy cannot exist in Islam. Every Muslim [whether scholar, preacher, jurist or saint] is a layperson – a veritable definition of the word 'laicism.' This is only to be expected from a religion renowned for its egalitarianism: as the Prophet said, 'All human beings are equal, like the teeth of a comb.'

But those who would harness religion to their political goals have always tried back-door methods, especially in recent decades. Some claim that the Verse on compulsion holds only within Islam but not without, a patent absurdity. Another Verse that has been abused in this way is 'Judgment belongs only to God' [6:57], where 'sovereignty' is substituted for 'judgment' in order to pave the way for a politico-religious ruling class. Needless to say, this goes against everything Islam stands for, including its opposition to distorting the meanings of holy texts.

In sum, laicism and secularism are nonproblems for a correctly oriented Islamic mentality. What matters is to avoid sin – a different problem altogether and a possibility under all conditions, including an 'Islamic' or 'shari'a' state. This is the main issue.

In what follows, questions addressed to the Master on this subject at various times and his replies are brought together. His comments on terrorist activities are also included in this section.)

The laicism in Islam has not been understood properly. 'To you, your religion ...' [109:6].

Aq Shamsuddin is the teacher of Sultan Mehmed the Conqueror [Mehmed II]. Istanbul is conquered, Mehmed says, 'Accept me among your dervishes. I want to enter the circle of Invocation.' Aq Shamsuddin replies: 'No.' He comes and settles in [a small, obscure village]. Mehmed tracks him down and writes him a letter. Aq Shamsuddin replies:

'You are a sultan. Carry out your office, your Prayer is accepted. Otherwise, the fortresses will be lost again. You are a ruler of the exoteric world. If you delve into these matters, the fortress will be destroyed.[1] You are responsible for protecting the fortress. Sultans and shaykhs cannot come together. But shaykhs can help sultans.' Many Ottoman sultans were aided by Sufi shaykhs.

Comment: *There are those who say laicism was taken from the West.*

No, no, no. It was taken from Verse and Saying, affairs of religion and affairs of state were separated, the religious organization was placed in the hands of the government.

Question: *Do you mean that laicism is in accord with Islam?*

It is in accord.

Comment: *Laicism is useless.*

That word is wrong, too.
 [In an attempt to force his Christian subjects to convert to Islam,] Selim the Resolute [Selim I] said, 'I shall kill all unbelievers.' His Shaykh of Islam, Zenbilli Ali Efendi, said 'No' twice, he knows that his head is going to roll on the third. While he was leading the Prayer, he recites the Opening Chapter out loud: *'Praise be to God, the Lord of the Muslims'* instead of *'Praise be to God, the Lord of the Worlds.'* [The Opening Chapter is recited at every Prayer cycle.] Once, twice, Selim understands, he gives up.

[To a prominent Turkish Islamist politician:]
 Don't mix religion and politics.

Question: *Can religion and politics coexist [separately] in a country?*

They can.

Comment: *Sovereignty belongs not to the nation, but to God.*

---

1. And so it was: towards the end, Sultan Abdul Hamid II was a Sufi dervish. According to the Master, he was too soft and lenient, he did not exercise the firmness required of rulers. That's how the Ottoman Empire collapsed.

You misunderstand that word. I'll cut it short: become prime minister yourself, then do what you want. You'll miss this present government.

Everything is free. What better Islam can there be? *Every religion exists freely in Turkey [in 1991].*

Comment: *I want to live in a shariʿa state.*

What kind of *shariʿa* do you want? This is not the way. If a friend of yours fell into the sea, and while there, started saying, 'Water, I want water,' what would you say? You're in water, what more do you want?

'Those in authority' [4:59] are good, we're bad. What has the government prohibited you from? It doesn't say, 'Don't do the Prayers.' If you went out on the kerb, spread out your Prayer-mat and started Prayer, everyone would turn and look, nobody would take you by the arm to the police. If you got on a car and went from here to [a distant neighborhood] shouting *La ilaha illallah* ('There is no god but God'), everyone would say, 'He's crazy,' but nobody would take you to the police station.

We say, 'If only a Muhammadan government would come.' This government is Muhammadan. There has never been a time like this. The mosques are free. If you were to shout *'There is no god but God and Muhammad is His Prophet'* while you're walking on the street, people would look, they'd say, 'He's overflowing,' but the police wouldn't arrest you, nor would anything else happen. What if there were some other government? What hardships our Prophet suffered! He had to do his Prayers in secret. The troubles he went through until he was able to gather an army. Now, the mosque is free, the bar is free, everything is free.

Whenever they prohibit your religion, your faith, then we'll do it secretly. Now, our rulers are good. We're living in outer space and don't even know it. We're in this grace for the sake of His Beloved Prophet.

Comment: *A hodja said, 'We'll bring in the shariʿa state when there's a majority.'*

That hodja has to be punished. There is *shariʿa* in our country, the mosques are open, everyone is free. [Turkey is a secular country. What is meant by the first part of the statement is that everyone is free to practice Islam, to follow the precepts of the Divine Law according to their conscience.]

What does that mean, '*Shari'a* is going to come, the president is going to do Prayers'? Has this happened? Will it happen? This is idiocy.

Comment: *There are young people who want a religious state.*

Ignorant youth, they would.

Question: *Is it necessary to conform to the social environment regarding headscarves?*

It's mandatory. Mandatory. Where there is permission, they can cover their heads. Where there isn't permission, at school, during exams, let them uncover their heads and go in. If they uncover their heads, it's a sin. But if they abandon university in order to cover their heads, that's murder. The simile is this. That's all, man. If there is a responsibility, blame it on the president.

One must 'obey those in authority' [4:59]. If you don't accept the constitution, you have to leave this country.

Comment: *What we want doesn't exist anywhere.*

Then you have to go to outer space. With this mentality, you'll soon find yourselves in jail.

They're followers of Khomeini. They're very dangerous. They don't go to mosque, they Pray separately. They must be from Iran.

Comment: *They want to establish the caliphal state. And they're going to be the caliph.*

What foolishness. What idiocy. All this is due to ignorance. Being a caliph requires morality. Without ethics, one becomes a pharaoh.

Comment: *Everyone wants to become caliph.*

This is all due to Forbidden food. They lose their God-given intelligence, they become possessors of diabolical intelligence.

No reformation in Islam

(Having stated his position in clear and uncompromising terms above, the Master was also adamant about another point:)

Is there reformation in Islam, or not? No!
Is there reform in religion, or not? There can be no reform of the Quran. The Quran is the Divine Law, the Divine Law is the Quran.

Democracy

Islam is democracy. Democracy is the Quran itself. The Torah, the Psalms, the Gospel, the Quran are all democracy. Let them look at the Torah and the Gospels, they'll see democracy there. Democracy is at the root of the Glorious Quran. Because it has given everyone their rights, it has apportioned them.

This comes down to us as an account from before the time of Sultan Abdul Hamid: the British took six Verses from the Quran. They didn't mention the Quran, they called it 'democracy.' The British discarded two of the Verses, retained four and named it democracy. I don't know which Verses they were, the British didn't say.

[It is even said that] fifty or a hundred years ago, the House of Lords was debating democracy. Is there democracy or isn't there, has it progressed? One lord stood up and said: 'England has embraced democracy. One more step, and democracy will embrace England: we have to become Muslims!'

The British teach us Islam, the French teach us Islam. They know it better than we do.

Terrorism

Terrorism does not emerge from Islam. Peace emerges from Islam, ethics emerges from Islam, culture emerges from Islam. These are the enemies of Islam. They've taken the label of Islam, they're wearing and bearing the label of Islam.[2] [In general, those who misinterpret

---

2. For a more detailed treatment of these issues, see the Appendix to my first published book, *The Station of No Station* (Berkeley, CA: North Atlantic Books, 2001): 'Fundamentalism and the Taliban,' pp. 211–18, and the Prologue to *The Secret of Islam*

the Quran] deduce these from the Quran, but they deduce what they prefer. They don't deduce what we prefer.

[Terrorism in Algeria, 1996–7:] No Muslim could perpetrate such brutality. They would kill men, but they would not slaughter women and children. America and Europe have to be alerted. If they don't stop this, terrorism will spread to all of them. [This statement was made nearly five years before September 11.]

(Berkeley, CA: North Atlantic Books, 2003): 'Rescuing Islam from the Hijackers,' pp. xxxiii–lix.

Knowledge/science, art

(*Although the Master has primarily the religious and spiritual sciences in mind, he by no means excludes the physical sciences. This cannot be done, because Hidden Knowledge, 'Knowledge from the side of God,' is a synthesis of both the physical sciences and the spiritual sciences.*)

Do you know what the worst thing is? The worst? Ignorance. To become the laughing stock of the devil, the Base Self. If we escape the dominion of the Base Self, the devil, knowledge will invade us.

[A saying of Ataturk, founder of modern Turkey:] 'Science is the truest master [teacher].' Right, very true. It's the meaning of both Verse and Saying.

Question: *Not just the physical sciences, right?*

Yes, both the exoteric and the esoteric sciences.
Study every science. Don't remain without knowledge. We content ourselves with what we know, vast treasures remain there, we're not aware of it.
God's Beloved Prophet said, 'Seek knowledge, even if it be in China.' Where are we, where's China? [Nowadays,] knowledge is at our feet [fingertips]. And Ali said: 'I'll be the slave – that is, the servant – of anyone who teaches me a letter of no matter what science.' The times require science. Learn every science. Study every science, learn every language. We all should learn, not just English but French, German ...
The first step of knowledge is 'Learn and teach.' The first word of our religion is 'Learn and teach.' [The first revealed word was 'Read.' (96:1)] If we exercised our minds a little bit, the fire of compassion would burn within us all. The best of human beings is one who learns and teaches on the good side. It's storm and darkness everywhere. If one were to light but a candle on a hill in that darkness, it would be seen from all around. People would flock to it.
Don't miss the time and the place – even if it's only a drop, take it. Study, wake up, awaken one another. We're going to learn until we die, regardless of whether one is a person of knowledge or of virtue.
Medicine and technology are very close to God, but there's faltering. The times have brought it about like that. A prophet came to each community and reformed them. Now, human beings have left the world behind and are trying to conquer the realm of space. Sticks and

stones have gone, now there are poison-gas bombs (weapons of mass destruction). At the pinnacle of medicine and technology, they're at each other's throats!

The world has filled and emptied many times. Never has it advanced so far in medicine and technology. But this too will fall. It's peaked, it's going to fall. It's begun to recede. From now on, advances in technology will burn themselves [be self-destructive]. They will burn the country, the nation and themselves. For medicine, there's still time.

All the technology of today cannot make a pepper, a tomato. Or a banana, a carrot.

Europe took medicine and technology from us. Ali Kushju, Ibn Sina, al-Farabi – Europe took away their knowledge. Europe took science from us, now we're taking it from Europe. A sign of the end-times: 'The sun will rise from the West.' It's a Saying. The sun is [i.e., it symbolizes] science. Now we receive science from the West.

God says: 'I take intellect from the human being and give him technology.'[1]

Religious/spiritual sciences

You've graduated from university, you've put the diploma in your pocket. There's a second diploma: to know God and make Him known, to love God and make Him loved, to see God and make Him seen.

The Schools [the Four Schools of Jurisprudence in Islam] are high school. We honor the Greatest Imam [Abu Hanifa], Imam Shafi'i, Imam Hanbal [and Imam Malik – 'imam' means leader]. But what are they for? For entering university. We're trying to study at the

---

1. This brings to mind the science-fiction story in which basic arithmetic was forgotten due to over-reliance on calculators. Every procedure, and every technological device based on such a procedure, involves a series of steps that are carried out automatically without exercising the intellect. The mind falls into disuse and atrophies as a result. It is a tradeoff of ease in exchange for intelligence. Norman Mailer has observed: 'Live in a technological environment long enough and you begin to feel as if your soul is frayed. A curious process has been going on in America for many years. You could term it the dumbing-down of Americans [due to technology].' (Interview with *The Sunday Times* on 9/11, September 8, 2002, see Mailer, *Why Are We At War?*, New York: Random House, 2003, p. 92.) As Marshall McLuhan noted in *Understanding Media* (1965), 'every media extension of man is an amputation.' William Irwin Thompson elaborates: 'If we have cars we don't walk to the corner store anymore. If we have artificial intelligence extending the central nervous system into cyberspace networks, we all get dumber ...' (www.integralage.org/docs/WITchap1.html, accessed 04/04/2003).

Muhammadan University. Can one go back to them? What is Shiism? We follow Abu Hanifa. But at the University of Muhammadanhood, this or that no longer remains. Only God and His Prophet remain.

Unless you strike this lighter, it won't burn. What good is gas without fire? Without spiritual science, physical science is no use. What good is body without spirit? Without spirituality, what use is it? See, they're all professors. What good is it?

Without the sun [e.g. during an eclipse], all humans are bewildered, they don't know what to do. Sacred texts are like that. [Without them, humans] are bewildered.

The Quran is the sun of knowledge for all human beings. Our Prophet has radiated the light of this knowledge to all human beings. All human beings are within that light. The earth is for all human beings. Water is for all human beings. The night is for all human beings. They belong to everyone. [And so does the Quran.] They're under the attribute of Compassion, they belong to all humanity. The attribute of Mercy divides: French, German, Muslim, Christian.

Is the Quran general or special? [That is, is it for all human beings, or only for Muslims?] It is general. It's given the knowledge. But if you don't study, the fault is not God's. If you're not applying that knowledge, the fault is yours, not God's.

Nothing works without knowledge. The Quran is the pinnacle. It's got everything, starting from Adam. We're only just beginning to understand the Quran. With medicine, with technology, the Americans, the Germans, the French are teaching us the Quran. They live the materiality, we live the spirituality. They'll turn to us in the end, because it's all in the Quran. There's no knowledge to come other than the Quran, don't wait for it. We think it's new, it comes from there, it's unraveled [and comes from] there.

Let's recognize the value of this clear religion, it's valuable. It's so valuable that this box-sized Quran holds the whole universe in place. In terms of knowledge, whether physical or spiritual, we cannot add anything. But we're being cut off from even what exists. If there were anything to be added, another prophet would have come by now. We cannot add to the Quran. We cannot add another sun on top of this sun. We cannot benefit it, we're going to benefit *from* it.

The Glorious Quran is from the esoteric to the exoteric. We're going to circle around from the outward to the inward. From the esoteric to the outward, from the exoteric back to the inward. If the esoteric and exoteric sciences are combined, one becomes two-winged, one can fly anywhere one wants. Otherwise, one is single-winged.

Whether externally or during sleep, certain manifestations occur. They call them 'states.' You see a dream, you hear a voice. Here, you are to rely on knowledge. Is it close to a Verse? A Saying – has the Prophet of God said such a thing, is it close to a Saying? There it is revealed. It's the touchstone. Obey that, go wherever you want.

When you go to the market, you can't buy everything. Knowledge is the same. Take what you need.

Practice makes perfect

We're not going to study and forget. We're going to study and apply it.

[Someone wanted to understand the Quran.] I said, 'Do you perform the Prayers?' He said 'No.' 'Well, look,' I said, 'take the Quran and hang it on that pine tree. Will the pine tree understand anything from that Quran?'

The largest living thing is a whale. Next, on land, an elephant. Place the Revelation that came to Muhammad on the back of a whale, place it on its belly, nothing will happen. You're a man of knowledge. You take the Quran, you mount an ass, you begin to recite. You're reciting as you ride. Would the ass understand anything? If you make a human out of the ass, then it'll understand.

The goal is not to study, the goal is to apply it. If you apply [your knowledge], your troubles will disappear. You study, but you don't practice. Drop a cat from four or five hundred yards, it'll land on its four feet. If you apply these, you too will always land on four feet.

How should you read a [religious/spiritual] book? You open the book, you read three pages. Then you stop. You check yourself. If the states you've read in those three pages are present in you, then you continue. You read three more pages.

[The Companions of the Prophet used to read a page of the Quran. They would not pass on to the next page until they had fully applied the instructions of the previous page. In a similar vein, Abdul Qadir Gilani has written: 'You won't understand what I say, you'll understand only when you've put it into practice.']

Distribute, don't fail to teach

[To a doctor with deep knowledge of religious matters:] You may have heard, in the old times we used to hear it like this from our grandfathers, our fathers. There are no banks, but [a person] has collected a lot of money, the children needed it, they'll need it again. They would place it in an earthenware jug, he himself – he doesn't even show his wife! – it'll be necessary someday, he got it from earth, he would pile [bury] it back into the earth. Gold, silver, whatever. But the time would come, because [death] has no definite time, [his life] would be drained suddenly, that would remain in the earth because it's buried, right?

And some have earned Licitly [honestly], they would indicate to their wives, their children: 'We have capital in such-and-such a place, survive on that.'

Whereas you have this treasure, are you going to take it and bury it in the earth one day? *Give it away*. Let's distribute the treasure, not everyone can take it anyway.

Teaching methods

As far as possible, answer with Verse and Saying. If you don't know, say 'God knows.'

In this time, you're going to explain to people with an example. First, find a fitting example. Give an example first, then state the Verse or Saying. Otherwise they won't understand. Also, [cite references]. This way, if there is an error, it will return to them. That's what the Prophet of God did, too: first he would give an example, then a Chapter, a Verse.

Useless knowledge

[This concerns the Saying of the Prophet: 'I take refuge in You from useless knowledge.']

Useless knowledge is widespread now. It's prevalent in all human beings.

'This happened, that happened ten billion years ago.' Let's try to save ourselves now, in the sea. Let's save ourselves so that we don't drown.

Intuitive knowledge in animals

God has placed the teacher of every creature within it. The one that grows and learns the hardest is the human.

I was young, I was going on a partridge hunt in the forest. I saw a mother partridge and fifteen or twenty offspring, they've been hatched either that day or the day before. When it saw me, the mother partridge gave a cry: '*K-h-a-k!*' and shot off. I looked, its young, too, had disappeared. When I looked closer, I saw that each one had tightly grabbed whatever was close to its feet, a stone or a twig, and rolled over on its back. It's lying as though lifeless. In an instant! Who taught you that?

I retreated to a distance, hid and began to watch. The mother partridge came over immediately. Its young got up, too, and gathered around it. They went away. I saw this with my own eyes.

There's a mountain bird, slightly larger than a sparrow. When winter comes, it takes ninety-nine stones and places them in its nest. Every day it puts one stone aside. When they're finished, snow has covered everywhere, it bores through the snow, comes forth and gives thanks to God. Where is the teacher of this, where?

Once, I was walking in the forest. I heard an unusual chirping of birds. I drew close, storks had built a nest on the branch of a tree. In the nest were the offspring of the storks, and a snake was trying to attack, to reach them. All the birds had gathered around and were chirping so that it wouldn't snatch the young. There's a relentless struggle going on between the parent storks and the snake.

Then, the father stork beat its wings and departed. A bit later it came back. It was holding a spider in its beak. It dropped the spider into the gaping mouth of the snake. The snake descended from the branch, it writhed and writhed until it died. The spider had been poisonous.

At which school did you study this, at which university did you learn it? Its university is within itself.[2]

---

2. This story also provides a clue regarding how to treat the Base Self, which is symbolized by a snake.

Science Fiction

These are all going to happen. They will happen in time. They're going to go to those places. 'This zone is mine, that zone is yours,' there will be wars up above. They're going to kill each other, not with weapons but with electricity.

[The movie of H. G. Wells's *The Time Machine* – the Eloi:] Paradise, that is. [The Time Traveler and Weena:] Adam and Eve.

[Arthur Clarke and Stanley Kubrick's *2001: A Space Odyssey*:] They're symbolizing the Kaʻba with this [the black monolith].

Music, art

Question: *Is music prohibited in Islam?*

No. A Saying of the Prophet: 'Three things have been made lovable to me: beautiful sound' – that is, music – 'scent' – not the smell of musk, the smell of cleanliness – 'and greenery.'

Large brooks should flow, you should listen to them like this. Water produces the sound of music. So does the wind. So do birds. The important thing is not to listen to music with alcohol and women, not to put that in one's Heart.

Comment: *Then music isn't prohibited in Islam.*

Of course not. There are hymns. There is the Quran, it is recited with tune and mode. I like music, I like music very much. I like the violin, the oud. I like the nay [the reed flute].

All art is permissible as long as it does not mislead people [towards the Unclean/Illicit].

Closing the Two Doors

(Of all the subjects the Master spoke of, this was in his eyes by far the most important. In order to do justice to his emphasis, the Two Doors would have to be repeated on almost every page of this book. Since that can't be done, the following should be read with this fact in mind.)

Watch [protect] your tongue, your loins, your hand against the Illicit.

From Adam onwards, humanity has had two obstacles. Unclean gain, unclean lust. These two tricks have seized humanity: egotistical, diabolical tricks. These are the two points that are the devil's great trick. All sainthood, all friendship of God, are *after* one leaves these two points behind.

Illicit gain, illicit lust will destroy the world. Lust ruins both the individual and society. Fornication is the most terrible thing. It ruins a person, it ruins a society, it ruins a nation. Don't ever approach fornication: that is the commandment of the Four Books, of the Torah, the Psalms, the Gospel and the Quran. Together with Illicit Lust, we shall dispel illnesses like AIDS. 'So you approach it, eh?' The disease appeared and spread everywhere.

A family that consumes what is illicit – you know that the father, the mother, the child cannot be redeemed. If your father's bite is Prohibited, don't eat it. You know that my tea is Unclean, don't drink it. Do not stray into gain on the Forbidden side. 'God is enough for me,' as they say. The Prophet is enough for everyone. Those who go to them will not go lacking. They will lack neither in knowledge nor in anything else.

The three prerequisites of the path are a job, a spouse and faith. I ask those who come and go, 'How are you with faith in God, with your spouse, with your job?' To those who say, 'All's well,' I say, 'You're in Paradise, don't disturb your palace in heaven.'

These three points, in turn, depend on two points. The first is: if you know that the tea I offer you is bought with illicit earnings, don't drink it.

Don't touch what is prohibited. If you fall victim to hunger and thirst, and there is money by the thousands strewn on the street when you go out, and you're hungry, still don't take it.

The second is very dangerous. It is worse than the first. Lust is such a powerful drive that it can destroy a human being if not used properly. I call this 'the two fire channels' (in man and woman).

You're single. Until you get married, until you marry a suitable woman [or vice versa], everything is ruled out. She can come and sit on your leg, she can arouse your lust beyond endurance, yet you should still see her as your mother or your sister. She is your mother, your sister. One does not engage in lust with one's mother or sister. Even an animal doesn't do it. Don't even eye her. It shouldn't even pass through your mind. She is your sister [or he is your brother].

Use this, okay? Use this.

Don't touch what is forbidden even if you were to die of hunger.

The second is more dangerous. Those who can curb the first can't contain the second. If, outside of marriage, a woman were to come and sit in your lap, if your lust were to boil up, she's your mother, your sister. Don't glance with your eye. Don't even pass it through your mind.

These are the points that really wreck. Own up to these two points. [Saints like] Hajji Bayram Wali, Rumi, were called saints only when they were able to master these two points to perfection. [The same applies to] all of them.

You can't find this in books. You won't find *any* of this in any book. This is the crux, these two points. One is, don't look at what is forbidden [in terms of gain or profit], the other is, don't incline towards [illicit] lust. When you promise, come, and the crown of sainthood is yours. But whichever of these you do, it's no use if you were to perform the Formal Prayer or chant Invocations day in and day out.

Whoever pulls in these two brakes – in terms of illicit eating and drinking, and lust – Sainthood will be yours immediately. You might say: 'Uncle, are you crazy?' I'm crazy. Be crazy yourselves, and you'll be the winners.

Now to summarize, it boils down to the two points I've been telling you. When you're established in these two points, when you do your Five Daily Prayers, when you're with God every instant, that's it.

Don't eat what is forbidden, don't look at what is forbidden, perform the Formal Prayer. The path consists of these three.

Formal Prayer is the chief of all worship. The chief.

Don't give up the Formal Prayer. This is my last will and testament to you.

Taking the Permanent Ablution

You know what that Ablution is? To promise God, to promise God's Prophet, not to eat the Illicit, not to look at the Illicit. One goes to God with that Ablution. One should promise God and the Prophet of God, that Ablution mustn't be broken. That's the real Ablution. The Ablution for Prayer can be broken, but not this one.

One should believe, take an Ablution and not break that Ablution to the end of one's life. Okay? That Ablution is not like this one. Break it and take another, it's not like that. One who believes in God promises God, follows the Beloved Prophet's path, protects himself from the Unclean, denies it to his self and enters the grave with that morality.

Now the external Ablution, we eat and drink, there will be need (to relieve ourselves), we're going to break our Ablution, one has to take an Ablution again after the previous one is broken.

Then there is the Ablution of the spirit. Of the spirit, including the body. Whatever God has prohibited in the Quran, has declared Illicit for ourselves, our family, our children. Whatever the Prophet of God has forbidden to us via Sayings regarding egoism, speech, going to bed, getting up, it's all included.

We're going to think like, 'My God, with Your permission, with Your strength and power, whatever there is that is egotistical, help me.' Abandon it. Repeat three times: *I bear witness that there is no god but God, and I bear witness that Muhammad is the servant and Messenger of God.* 'My God, do not separate me from the path of Your Beloved, I have given my promise.' This is an instant. It is an end. One should not break that Ablution till the grave, whether one's corpse is washed or not.

You know that in our hometown, there are God's bounties and commands, mulberries, apricots, apples. They are planted along the road, in the orchard of their owner. Without the owner, we're not going to take one and put it in our mouth. Do not eat a single apricot without the consent of its owner. It'll break the Ablution immediately, *snap!* – like that. You can eat if you request it from the owner. Or else you pay for it and eat.

Saying 'Hi' to each other repeatedly, we'll learn something from one another, God willing. In terms of the spirit. Not in terms of the body, but in terms of the spirit.

Now let's come to the two points. For example, you want to come here from Malatya, either you have business, or to see someone. Whatever. But you don't have money. You don't have a hundred Liras to buy bread for your children, let alone come here. But you step outside, you're going to go to your uncle, you're going to borrow a hundred, five hundred, a thousand Liras from him and provide that day's food for your children. This is very important.

As you go, as you pass through field or garden, you see thousand-Lira, five hundred thousand-Lira banknotes spread out. You're in so much need. You want to take the hundreds, the thousands. You glance around like this, there's nobody. What you want is strewn out. Money by the thousands. This is the essential point.

You see it, 'Yes, there's nobody, and I need it, but it's not mine.' God sees, right? He sees the earth and the sky, right? That's the real Ablution. You're going to leave it there and pass it by. You're still going to go, borrow a hundred, five hundred Liras from him and buy food for the evening for your children. Yes! This is very important.

And what else is there?

Whether married or single. If you're single, if you're unmarried, until you choose one for having children with, even if you stay together for months, one is the betrothed and brethren of the other. Single. If married, all the universe is your mother, your sister. We're not even going to think about it, let alone eyeing, looking at this one or that one. This is the second. One is material means, not to take even in hunger, and then this one. If the eye strays, 'Whoa, stop it.' If the ear strays, 'Stop.' Whoever does this, promises God, I will immediately pin the certificate of sainthood to his lapel. That person is a saint. If we cut this out, we cut off the seven Base Selves [the effects of the Base Self that manifest themselves at all seven levels of selfhood].

Question: *I want a shortcut.*

Do you know what a shortcut is? Let me tell you. The first: not to eat an Unclean bite. The second: not to look at the Unclean. When you take these two steps, you'll reach God at the third. Without distressing them the slightest, I tell those who come here these two points. 'Let's think about it, we'll come later.' They don't come back.

As long as you don't pass these two points, there can be neither prophethood, nor masterhood, nor sainthood. If you give up these two points, you're dead, your Base Self is dead. Illicit lust, illicit gain. Once you close these Two Doors, you're a master, God willing. Worship day and night, climb mountains, go into caves, it all boils down to these two points. Then, it's enough to say a hundred Invocations per day. But if you don't heed these two points, it's no use if you repeat a hundred thousand Invocations till daybreak. For there can be no Prayer without Ablution. Even thinking about it voids the Ablution. Human beings live, but they live as dead people. Lust, gain. To observe these two points, to die before death. When you quit the Illicit, there, you're dead. You've died before you die. When the gates of hell are closed, you've entered heaven. In the presence of God, God sees, how can you commit an Illicit act? When you observe this, a hundred Invocations is enough. If you don't do it, a hundred thousand Invocations a day is no use. You have to promise God. But if you invert that promise, you'll be a liar. You can't escape punishment.

A Saying: A young man comes, he says, 'Messenger of God, I'm sixteen-seventeen years old. I don't have money to marry. My eye strays. Isn't there a solution?'

'The first solution: in our religion, one should marry as soon as one reaches puberty. The second solution: if you can't get married, hunger is necessary.' 'I can't get married' – 'Fast.' If you want to live, don't fill the stomach. The heart now survives a hundred years.

Islam has five pillars: Fasting, Prayer, Pilgrimage, Alms, the Word of Witnessing. There's another pillar: To marry a pious girl [or man]. Because it won't work without that. One: Forbidden gain and Two: Forbidden lust. If you close those Two Doors, the Eye of the Heart will open.

The Prophet says, 'There is prosperity in marriage.' Family life is very sweet. It became a custom from Adam to Muhammad and afterwards: a *clean* engagement, followed by a *clean* wedding. So that we may see the happiness of our children, our grandchildren. To marry and to have children are the duties of the body, the duties of being human. Carry these out.

A self-made wedding is not possible. It should be among an *assembly*. There should be witnesses. Just a [religious] wedding ordained by an imam isn't enough, either. There is the official marriage. A child is born, under whose name will it be? I like the official marriage very much. Outside *marriage*, everything is prohibited. When you observe this, everything is yours. Angels surround you.

Today, things are easy. Ibrahim Adham[1] abandoned his crown and his throne to set out on his quest. Today, let us erect these two walls, that's enough. Presto! We will be saints.

---

1. See below, The saints/Ibrahim Adham.

The Base Self

Other schools, universities have many subjects, exams. As for the school of wisdom, the University of Muhammadanhood, it has only one exam: to control the self. A human being is at this test every instant. The greatest enemies for us are the Seven Base Selves [the Base Self manifestations that confront us at all seven levels of selfhood].

The greatest thing is to control the self. The second greatest thing is to feel compassion towards all creatures. The third greatest thing is to fulfill the principles of Islam to the letter. You should be *l-i-k-e* the *d-e-a-d*: external events should have no effect on you.

Whether male or female, your enemy is within. Your friend is within, too. Our self is our enemy until the time it becomes our friend. When it becomes a friend, it becomes a friend of the Friend as well. The Friend says: 'Be careful, don't eat the unclean, don't do anything unclean, your return shall be to Me' [2:156].

In old times – they still have it – foxes, their fur is worth money, they set traps. It can't give up, just as it wants to grab it, *snap!* it gets caught. Let's not get caught too. If it can't set a trap from the outside, it starts anxiety within. It's very formidable. Let us protect ourselves from the trap of the ego, from its fire. Everything else is already our friend.

Don't feed the enemy in your bosom. Don't give this self a moment's respite. Don't eat three meals a day, reduce it to one or two. If the stomach is full, it won't do Invocation. We've submitted to it till this day. Let's corner the ego, let it submit to us for a change. Say, 'Let's squeeze the self a little bit.' Tomorrow we're going to become a handful of dust. The insects will be pleased, the earth will be pleased. Let's do a thing such that God is pleased.

We're still partners. The ego is a partner, a very formidable partner. It steals, it doesn't let on that it steals. It knows how to make itself loved. This partner eats and eats and eats away at us, it finally buries us in the ground.

Step on the self.[1] Step on it so that you may become a human being. I need people like you, but you have to listen to me. These are all affairs of the Base Self. I'm seeking you, you're not seeking me.

May God not leave us to our selves. May He not chastise us with our selves. May He train us with His grace and pleasure, with Muhammadan morality.

---

1. Or 'press down your ego' (Isaiah 58:3, 5. Trans. Rabbi Arthur Waskow).

We tell a child who goes near the stove: 'Don't touch it, you'll get burned,' he touches it in spite of that and even though he feels pain, he later tries to touch it again. We're just the same.

The Base Self says, 'Do this, do that.' It says, 'I like this, I don't like that.' The ego doesn't want anyone. You have that state on you: you don't like anybody.

The self doesn't like disease. If we consider, disease is necessary, too. The hardships of the world are necessary, too. These are going to mature us.

The great ones all controlled their selves. They did the opposite of what the self told them to do, they reined it in. Even in the greatest of them, the Base Self continues its influence.

I treat my self like a child. I say 'No' to whatever it wants, only I give a little of what it wants in order to shut it up. This is how I put an end to its impulses such as 'You're hungry, you haven't eaten,' which would otherwise never end.

Nothing is possible before the self is calmed and pacified. A seeker went to a teacher, 'Put me in shape,' he said. But because the self ceaselessly vibrated, shook and attacked right and left, it was possible to do nothing. The teacher can stop this vibration, but the responsibility to stop it belongs to the disciple. The same seeker went back to his teacher after bringing his self to a quiescent state, and this time he saw that everything proceeded smoothly.

Nothing can be done before the self is stopped, because the rampant self also prevents the principles of Islam from being applied. The tiniest opportunity is enough for the self to wreck everything.

As the seeker trusses up his self, as he reins in and controls its every onslaught, he must think that his master is actually doing this from within. He must not ascribe it to himself.

What is requested of you is not service. Are you going to be a waiter? More than that, what is requested is that you control your self. Before quieting his self, the seeker cannot clothe himself in his teacher's morality, cannot adorn himself with his state and cannot ethicize himself with his ethics.

Opposition to the self is necessary, my child. There's no sin in that, child. Because it's for God, because training the self is for God. In order to take a step forward towards God, training of the self is necessary.

There is a saying: 'Smiling mien, sweet speech, entice a snake from its hole.' Do you know what that snake is? That snake is our self. If we throw it out, everything will be accomplished. A smiling face, a sweet tongue make that self a Muslim. It gets the snake out of the person facing you. One should use this with everybody. Through patience your self becomes a Muslim, and nothing is left after that. If you leave the entourage of the Base Self, you enter [become endowed with] the Attribute of Compassion.

[The devil finds his natural ally in the Base Self, which is everybody's inner demon. In the Master's vocabulary, 'Satan' and 'Base Self' were sometimes synonymous and sometimes distinct.]

There are two enemies: One is that which we call Satan, the other is the Base Self. Now everybody is in their hands.

The self is the greatest angel. God created man and told the angels: 'Prostrate to him.' It said, 'You created me of fire and the human of clay,' and didn't prostrate.

There are two enemies. One: the self inside. Two: Satan outside. Satan pesters one until the stage of Fusion.

We now recognize the Base Self, don't we? Once we train it, there is neither ego nor the devil. The self, Satan, they're all in us. The greatest fire is not hellfire. That exists. The greatest fire is the fire of our ego. If we extinguish that, we won't suffer hellfire, either.

Levels of selfhood

There are seven or nine selves: 1. The Base Self, 2. the Critical Self, 3. the Inspired Self, 4. the Tranquil Self, 5. the Pleased Self, 6. the Pleasing Self, 7. the Pure Self. [To these are sometimes added:]
    8. The Perfect Self or   8. The self of the Teacher,
    9. The Total Self or   9. The self of Muhammad.
[Otherwise, the last two are telescoped into the seventh.]

It doesn't work, it stinks. The vinegar oozes out. Sixty years ago, a young man recognized me, he came over. The smell of intestines is coming from him. 'Where do you work?' I asked. He said, 'At the slaughterhouse.' Let's throw away those odors, let us take on a Muhammadan fragrance. Let us be freed from that slaughterhouse stench, let us take on a fragrance of immortal life, let us step out the door.

God has given man everything. Eating, drinking, sleeping. If he reins in two things, the air and the fire – that is, the self and Satan – he becomes superior to the angels. Look at what God has given man, and look at the human condition.

The pet snake

A man found a baby snake in the forest. He brought it home, he gave it milk with a spoon, he fed it. The snake grew.

One day a friend came to visit him. He saw the snake roaming around the house. 'What's this?' 'Well, it all happened like this ...' 'This will kill you, it's a snake, an animal.' 'No,' he said, 'it protects me, it's jealous of me.'

A week later, the man was sleeping. His mouth was open. The snake flowed from the mouth of the man into his stomach. The man awoke, he put his hand to his mouth, he found that only the tail of the snake was still outside. If he were to pull, it's going to tear apart his stomach, he's going to die. In the end, he died in any case.

They came. They slit the belly of the man, they killed the snake. They both died, all for nothing.

The beggar of God

I call some people 'beggars,' they get angry, they don't understand. Those who understand are pleased.

There's the money beggar, the physical beggar. These are beggars of the belly. Then there's God's beggar. In God's way. 'Let me do extra worship, let me please someone, let me visit someone.' That's a beggar, too. One should be the beggar of the spirit, the spirit! One should seek out the Friend, one should find the Friend.

Comment: *I can't fast every day*.

Fast on some days. Be both the beggar of the belly and the beggar of God. Strum on both strings.

The three fears of the self

The self fears three things: hunger, Prayer, death. It fears nothing else. And the person who knows God, who fulfills God's commandments, fears the self and nothing else. The person who fulfills the orders of God and His Prophet is afraid: 'Oh, is my self going to commit an error?'

One who worships the self serves the three orifices [the mouth plus the front and rear exits/orifices]. Human beings recognize neither God nor prophet. All the universe works for these three orifices. Ingests from one, expels from the other two. All asceticism has been ordained for these three orifices. All prophets came for these three orifices. Who subdues the three orifices becomes the lord of the orifices, that is, of the self.

Whatever is done should be done for God, not for your self. Prayer and death are two great bounties. God has given human beings many bounties. The greatest boon is to obey God's commandment, that is, prostration. The other is death. We're going to do one, and we're going to be ready for the other.

God has two bounties for human beings, but they shun both. Prayer, s/he doesn't go near it. And death? 'Oh no,' s/he says, 'don't come at all!' S/he doesn't even look toward that side. Yes!

I tell everyone who comes: 'God has spread all His bounties before human beings, there are two divine bounties above them all. What are they?' Some say 'The mind,' others say this or that.

One is Prayer, the light of our eyes. And the other is death. These are the highest bounties. What would we do if there weren't death? Yes! What would we do if there weren't Prayer? We who believe in God and His Prophet, we run away from both bounties. We flee the highest boon, we flee Prayer. Death? We don't even look in that direction. It stands before our eyes every day. 'Oh, let's live!' Well, these are the greatest divine bounties. One is Prayer, worshiping God, the other is to be ready for God's commandment every instant. 'I've come, I shall go.' Not to run – *Aha*. Not to run away.

We do one, thank God. We do Prayer. But we run away from death. How long are you going to flee? Accept it! Accept it.

Question: *Do you mean dying before death, sir?*

No. What I'm saying is true death. The one you're saying, an end to the physical/spiritual, selfish/diabolical Forbidden things – including Lust. That's that death. Whoever ends that, takes an Ablution for God, that's dying before death. And the final death, for all of us, that's the greatest bounty. What would we do without it?

One should contemplate death every day, every hour. Death.

As for death before dying, it's to avoid what is Forbidden. Egotistical, diabolical. There, he's dead. And the last death will come, too. To train the self. When the self is trained, that means death before dying. They take [the corpse] and place it in the grave, but the spirit is mobile, both in this world and in the next. May God grant that kind of spirit. It's mobile, it sees everything, but we can't see it. It happens when one's alive, too. Spacefolding.[2] The man's talking to you here, they see him lecturing at a mosque in Istanbul. He did his Spacefolding here. The spirit evolves, but it doesn't come and go. It's a spiritual evolution, not a physical one.

Death is Attainment. Some people come and ask for Attainment. I say: 'How are you with death?' They don't want it. But then, Attainment won't come. Don't fear death, let death fear you.

Say, 'Let's live as God wants, let's not want death.' Nobody wants to die. Don't be afraid of death, love it. What fears death is the self you bear.

What did Yunus Emre say? 'Give your life, you cannot find the Beloved without giving up your life.' *Aha*, that's what's necessary at this point. 'You can't find the Beloved without giving your life.' Let alone our life, we can't sacrifice even a hair! To surrender, to surrender. To surrender *spiritually*. Now in Yunus' words, if you find a life *after* giving your life, that's death before dying.

There was another couplet [by Niyazi Misri], I like it but I don't know. People of the Path, People of the Law, whoever it may be. It says, 'Don't come to this arena' – there's wrestling, you know? arena, platform – 'Don't come to this arena, many heads are cut off in this arena, no questions asked.' You know? That's all I know.

It rains in the winter or in summer, right? God has created Muhammadanhood, His blessings are showering like that on us. It has continued from Adam to this day and will go on till the end of time. But they unfurl an umbrella and run, so that it won't touch them! Because our self doesn't want it, the self doesn't want blessings to touch us.

We say *In the Name of God, the Compassonate, the Merciful* with every word, don't we? We say it at every step, at every word, when lying down, when drinking, without knowing it. This is the blessing, it's the blessing itself. But the self contrives that it doesn't even occur to us. *Aha!* It opens the umbrella, it doesn't allow it even to occur to us.

---

2. See The secret and the sublime/Spacefolding for more details.

Never mind Paradise

May sorrows depart and blessings remain. The great ones worked a lot, they were left a soul and a body, at that point they said: 'His chastisement is nice, and so is His bounty.' Concerning that, Yunus Emre has a saying. May God bestow Paradise on us all. That is, to escape the devil's side and to attain heaven. But now, at that point, Yunus says: 'That Paradise, those palaces and kiosks underneath which rivers flow, that food and drink, those houris and servants, all those pleasures – give them,' he says, 'to whoever wants them.' *Aha*. That's what we're all after. Look what he says at the end: 'I need *You* and You alone, what business have I with all those pleasures?'

The two guards

Now, looking at what Yunus says, those pleasures of Paradise, we're going to go there and live with those pleasures, God willing. But if the Base Self is there, humans can't have peace. Now the Base Self has a remedy.

Suppose you had – God protect you – a terrible enemy who would kill you, murder your children and pillage your property. An external enemy. And suppose you had two friends who caught him somewhere, tied him up, brought and placed him in front of you. What are you going to do? He wants to kill you – this is for all of you, fellows! – but your two friends tied him up and placed him in front of you.

Now, if we take refuge in God and His Prophet in every detail, struggle with that enemy day and night, God and His Prophet, with their permission, will prepare the ties of that enemy and *place* him in your hands. Then what will you say? 'Have you surrendered?' 'Yes, I have.' 'Okay, I forgive you, don't do it again.' Your self requires the same.

Here again I rely on a Tradition. During a discussion, the Companions said: 'Prophet of God, do you have a self too?' A self. 'Yes,' he said, 'I'm human. I have a self too, but it's not like yours, it's very malicious, it has a very evil disposition. Satan is busy with me all the time. If he can vanquish me, you're all lost anyway.'

'Prophet of God,' they said, 'even though your self is so malicious, we can't see anything egotistical or diabolical in you.' 'Oh,' he said, 'with the permission of God, I've made it a Muslim/made it surrender. Its evil can't touch me.' Yes! Its hands and feet are tied.

The meaning of a second Saying is again on this subject: 'He who knows his self knows his Lord.' To surrender. Then the path will be opened. Pay attention to these, okay?

'Who knows his self knows his Lord.' After one has suppressed the self, after one has made it a Muslim [i.e., made it surrender] one goes to one's Lord, the path to the Lord opens. But if one doesn't struggle with the self – if one doesn't make the self prostrate to Him, can one see the Lord? One cannot.

One does not kill the self. One trains [and purifies] the self. Our duty is to inscribe the Naming on the Heart. Once we do that, the self does not disappear, but it becomes a Muslim. Say, 'I'm dead, but I'm dead towards my self.' Say, 'I'm alive towards God, God's Prophet, all human beings, my job and my work.' Say to your self, 'You like *baklava* sweets, I like spinach. You like meat, I like rice.' You're dead! A dead person can't do anything. Don't forget this word of mine. If there's a slip to one side, say, 'I'm dead, God,' take refuge in Him. Nothing Illicit.

The Base Self lashes out at us no matter what we do. I'm dead, yet it still bothers me. Don't surrender to the Base Self. There has to be internal war, war with the Base Self.

One who does not love his world, cannot love his next world. We're going to love the world as God, our Creator, wants us to. We're not going to love it for our self.

The three organs

God says, 'I have given you a pen of divine power. Use it well.' It's this tongue of ours. 'I imprisoned man's tongue within two fortresses.' One is the teeth, looking like a fortress battlement. It tears that, then comes the lip. It tears that too, it burns and bores through. God says, 'I placed it in a sealed place.' If someone makes a mistake, he says: 'If my tongue had stood still, I wouldn't have done it.' The tongue doesn't stand still. The eye! The eye acts on what it sees. The ear acts on what it hears. The tongue is a translator, it doesn't err. The tongue has no power. The eye and ear are what inflame the tongue. The eye and the ear are enemies of the spirit, until they become its friends. After that, they are its helpers. If the eye and ear are reformed, the tongue too will be gentle. Don't trust the eye, the ear, the tongue. Trust in the mind.

Three organs are important: ear, eye, tongue. The ear begins to heed the mind at thirty years of age, the eye at thirty-five, the tongue at forty. The purpose is to control the air and fire in the human being. The self does not die, it is controlled. What remains is water and earth, and this is what we are taught in the Quran. You read the Quran, but you don't understand it. There, I've summarized the Quran for you in two words.

The fast of the mind, the eye, the ear, the tongue. Someone is consuming illicitly, you see it, if you say 'Oh, I wish I could do it, too,' it means the fast, the Ablution is broken.

In the brain, in the mind, there are two dams. Two dams built by God. One is bitter, the other sweet. The bitter one lets bitter water flow. It forgets and burns away. The egotistical dam.

Once you turn off the faucet of the selfish dam, your tongue, it comes very differently then. It's the water of life, it gives joy, it thinks of everything, down to an ant, a frog, a bumblebee. And that's a wellspring.

Now all these people operate with bitter water, with the bitter dam. They can't find the spring. Because that spring exists, whenever the bitter faucet is turned off, the springwater starts, the water of life starts.

Madmen of the belly

I've divided the mind in two. On that point, some people are friends of the belly, some people are friends of the spirit. Now if one is a friend of the spirit, training the self is necessary. In that case, the friend of the belly is abolished. Opposition to the self is necessary, child. Training the self is necessary because training the self is for God, because it is necessary to take a step forth toward God.

Take refuge in God, take refuge in God very emphatically. Don't break away from God.

It is because people *break away* from God that they suffer these troubles, they quarrel with each other. They're worried about the belly, nothing else occurs to them. 'Let me be president, let me be prime minister, let me be the party leader' – the whole world is like that. The belly. These are friends of the belly. The friend of God is not like that. S/he fulfills God's commandments, takes refuge in God and knows that everything is from God.

There are two kinds of friends: Friends of the spirit, friends of the belly. Don't offend the friend of the belly, say 'Hi.' And befriend the friend of the spirit. One has to be friends for a while in order to understand. If you observe a solitude, a courtesy toward animals and plants in a person, be friends with that person.

A Saying states: 'The friend of the belly takes offense.' You give and give and give, you don't give one day, he's offended. As for the friend of the spirit, he doesn't take offense. He isn't offended if he's driven away or beaten. Now there are only friends of the belly, no spiritual friends.

Love one another for God. If you love one another for the belly, you'll take offense. If you love one another for God, you won't break apart. If you're friends of the belly, love will end. If you're friends of the spirit, it will go on forever. Because we have no friendship with the spirit, we're unaware of the spirit. Affection, love are now all predicated on the belly. If there's money there's everything, if there's money there's love, it's all predicated on the belly. We give thanks for the belly. We haven't been able to arrive at giving thanks for the spirit yet.

We're all still in love with the belly. Where is love, where are we? What we all have is belly-love. I don't see the love of God in anyone yet. Everyone loves his own self. I haven't seen anyone who loves me in fifty years. We're all at the Base Self. Not one of you has made it to the Tranquil Self yet. There's honey and there's trash. We alight on both honey and trash, just like a dung fly.

The wrath of God versus the wrath of the self

Somebody shoots somebody, somebody kills somebody. You're not going to count those as the wrath of God, you're to count them as the wrath of the self. If they view the wrath of God as the wrath of the self, it'll be a pity. They will have sinned. God's attribute of wrath works with justice, with divine judgment, with Quranic judgment. The wrath of the self is different. To take revenge. To insult, to beat up, to strike and break. You have to understand these matters.

Food for the spirit

The spirit wants three things from the [material] world: 1. water, 2. greenery, 3. beautiful sound – the Quran. But the body wants everything.

Prayer, the Quran, the good side are food for the spirit. Food and drink are food for the body. Water. Forests, greenery. And then beautiful sound, music. These three are food for the spirit, for the ear, for the eye. The others are food for the body.

The food of the body, the food of the spirit. Don't deprive them. The food of the spirit is worship, obedience, a smiling face, sweet tongue, patience, submission to everything. This is food for the spirit. Then there's the food of the body. To earn and eat honestly. If one eats, drinks, earns, works honestly, it will benefit the spirit. It will fortify the spirit. If one remains selfish in worship and prayer, in food and drink, in this and that, this will be an obstacle to the spirit, it will prevent the spirit from going to God.

Worries come to us from selfishness. If we connect our all to God, worries will depart. One falls, 'God, you made me fall.' One gets up, 'God, you made me get up.' If it's like this, worries will depart. Troubles do not leave one. One leaves troubles behind.

In a Holy Tradition, God says: 'I do not take back what I've given someone. Because it would not be worthy of Me.' The Most Merciful of Mercifuls. He says, 'They lose it themselves and think I did it.' Lose. Themselves, whether physically or spiritually. 'I don't remove it from them, they lose it themselves.'

Whenever pride overcomes you, think of how you were formed from filthy semen fluid and menstrual blood. Don't allow yourself to be degraded, but don't be overcome by pride, either. Don't let others treat you as inferior, because you are a bearer of God's trust. View yourself as great in terms of spirit. View yourself as an ant in terms of the ego.

There are two magnets. One is egotistical, diabolical. The other has honey. The human being stands like a pointer in between. If the selfish is dominant, *smack*, one hits that side. It's impossible to escape. But if one works on the Compassionate side, one will hit that side. By talking, by reading ... read, but it's really by working that you will hit the Compassionate side.

If they ask: 'What's the most difficult thing?' Say: 'To obey a prophet and his Book.' 'And what's the easiest thing?' 'To obey the ego, the devil, and to fool people.'

If it's for God's sake, everything will happen. If it's for our self, it'll be ruined. If it's for God, it'll be permanent, it won't face ruin.

'God is witness.' If a person knows he's in God's presence all the time, what can his self do? There's no self in that, nor the devil. God knows everything, sees everything.

You're trying to advance both the diabolical and Compassion together. That won't work. If you add milk to this tea, they call it tea with milk, one can drink it. But there's something that's obtained from milk: yogurt drink. If you add yogurt or yogurt drink to this tea, you will be able to drink neither the tea nor the yogurt drink. Don't try to be both things at once. Cleave to one side, hold tight to it.

If you mix the Allowed with the Forbidden, the Clean with the Unclean, it'll be a soup. If you mix the two, it won't be Compassionate, it'll be egotistical. The diabolical will be there.

The fly that defeated the eagle

Yunus Emre says:

> *A fly hurled an eagle to the ground*
> *[It's true and not a lie,] I too saw the dust it raised.*

The self is a fly. An eagle has the strength of fifty thousand flies. It can knock a big man down. A clean man of religion, a dung fly can ruin him. A dung fly hurls a great man of knowledge to the ground. Although God has granted us all this, we can't give up a fly. Our self is a fly, wherever it sees dung, that's where it'll dive. We don't give up a fly.

Trees have bugs. The bug of the human is his self. It gnaws and gnaws and gnaws, it turns one into a shell.

We're all sick. Our greatest sickness is the sickness of the self. We become the plaything of the self. The spirit does not get sick. There are two kinds of illness: one is physical illness, the other is selfish illness. Be careful, don't fall ill. It's worse than cancer. The greatest cancer is selfish cancer. Once we vanquish that, there's no fear, nothing. Egotistical cancer holds the whole cosmos in thrall.

You're going to be Compassionate, not selfish. How? By stepping on your self. You're going to say, 'I'm dead in every respect. *In the Name of God, the Compassionate, the Merciful. There is no strength or power other than God's.*' You're going to begin. Gain and Lust. If you watch out for these two points, the deed is done. If you've passed these two points, you're dead, your self is dead. The self is dead. Once you close these Two Doors, you're a master, God willing.

Let's not lose the Muhammadan morality. We're all united in the Five Pillars of Islam and the Six Pillars of Faith. 'Whoever is unable to vanquish his self, let him continue to recite the Word of Witnessing.' So the one inside hasn't believed yet. We're all united in the Word of Witnessing and the Word of Unity. The rest is local color. Imam Ghazali says: 'Whoever can't take care of his self, of the devil, let him recite the Word of Witnessing a hundred times a day.' The self can't prevail, the devil can't draw near. Continue for a week, a month, you'll find that you're liberated. Good news for you!

The seven orifices

[Here's another way to understand] the seven egos. The eye, the two eyes are the wildest among them. The eye sees but the ear hears, that's four. The tongue, five. Two orifices below, seven. The wildest of them all are the two orifices. The Prophet of God is the one who bridles them, puts them in their place, dissuades them from wildness and informs them of God. Without the Quran, without the Way (of the Prophet), we would be like animals. We would still eat and drink, but we would live as in a jungle. We still see it: at the pinnacle of medicine and technology, they live like animals.

See only if it's in accordance with the orders of God and His Prophet. Hear only if it's in accordance. But if it belongs to the eye, the ear, 'Wait a minute, what are you doing?' Then one seeks a Licit bite. Then the desires below. 'What are you doing, one [spouse] is enough for you. What're you going to do with more? They're all your mother, your sister.' Until that happens, all move according to their lights. When that happens, the Sound Mind plants the flag of unification there.

The spirit

Don't fall prey to your self. Become the president of your body. After you become president, would you search for another president? Don't become fodder to your self, make *your self* your fodder. Don't be a root to your self, make the self your root. That's the thing. Don't be the servant of your ego, make the ego your servant. You can't separate the spirit from the body. They're together now. When they're separated, you die. The body should be subservient to the spirit. You can't make the spirit subservient to the body. Everything ends, is mortal, the spirit is everlasting.

Comment: *The spirit and the body are created together. The spirit is not pre-eternal.*

You mean the spirit is formed with the body? No, that's wrong. The spirit exists from pre-eternity. The body is born later. They're all one, they're all milk, in cups of different colors. That is, the spirit of us all is one.

Question: *Why can't we see spirits?*

Can you see the wind? The wind exists, but you can't see it.

The vain peacock

As the peacock struts in the field, it says, 'Is there anyone more beautiful than me?' It goes near a body of water, it's going to drink, it sees its feet. 'Is there anyone uglier than me?' All its pomp is deflated. In the same way, we are beautiful with our spirit but ugly with our self. Only God is superior to man, nothing else. But if a human being submits to the ego, there is nothing uglier, like the peacock. If s/he obeys God's orders, there is nothing more beautiful. The Six Pillars of Faith, the Five Pillars of Islam, the basic stepping stones of the Divine Law are the ornaments of the peacock.

The body is the palace of the Compassionate. We've made it the palace of the ego. We've made a palace of the ego out of the palace of the Compassionate, which God is supposed to enter and occupy. What a pity. In the palace of the Heart, we've installed the Base Self, we act according to its whims. [The poet Shem'i says:] 'The sultan does not alight in the palace until the place is magnificent.' Where the king is supposed to sit, either a cat or a dog has come and is sitting. My God, forgive us, Lord.

The eight gates

I have just one thing to say. Whether old or young, God has made humans very precious. He loved them very much and created them. A lion, a fox – you may like its fur, but it's an animal. Let us own up to the label of 'human being,' God willing. Let us use that label in a clean way.

If you were to sell your clothing and then see it again later on, and the man says, 'Yes, I bought it from you,' 'Give it back to me!' How can that be? For you sold it and received the money. Similarly, this vehicle [the body] belongs to God. Don't say, 'It's mine.' If a friend were to give you a white handkerchief: 'Keep it, but I'm going to take it back some day.' A year, two years pass, you use it, you wipe your nose. While it's *dirty*, he asks for it. That shame is enough for you.

What I've just said is between two friends. But the other is God. He's given a spirit. Now there are eight gates there that make the handkerchief live in joy. They're enough for you, your children, for all of you. The Four Books, the Hundred Sheets are all within these eight issues.

[The eight gates are the eight gates of heaven, or the eight heavens: 1. Compassion/kindness/affection; 2. Righteousness; 3. Loyalty; 4. Generosity; 5. Patience; 6. Discretion; 7. Knowing one's poverty and weakness; 8. Giving thanks to God. To these are opposed the seven hells: 1. Pride; 2. Covetousness; 3. Jealousy; 4. Discord; 5. Backbiting; 6. Lust; 7. Anger.]

Eight heavens, seven hells – even here there is privilege. The gates of good are one greater. Who has the key? You have the key. Heaven is there, but you don't open its gates, you go and open the gates of hell.

The worst of the seven hells are lust and anger. The most dangerous for us are illicit anger and lust. To throw away those seven, to die before death. Let us find the immortal life. Shaykh Hamid Wali[3] says, 'We are the Living, we do not die.'

We're all thieves. Here is the garden, we're trying to steal a gold coin.

Satan

When we break away from God, when we forget God, we fall into the lap of the devil. It's over and done with. Your self will become the servant of the devil. You'll think you're the smartest, the most beautiful in the world.

Satan says to the self, 'Come, brother, let's wreck this building, you from the inside, I from the outside.' When a person wants to turn to God, Satan tells the self, 'Friend, it's passing from me. If you can do something from within, do it.' That is, he leaves matters to the ego.

The devil is a good worker. If we worked half as hard as the devil, we'd be rid of him long ago.

3. This refers to Somuncu Baba/Shaykh Hamid Aksarayi (1331–1412).

The reason God allows Satan to pester us is to set man apart from the plants and animals. Because the human being is an animal. He becomes human if he knows his God. Without the devil, we couldn't find the Straight Path [we couldn't tell right from wrong or good from evil].

He created good and evil, but He says, 'Know good and evil, avoid the evil.' Otherwise, the angels were already doing everything. But there is a value in the human being. Against that worth, He created the devil. Let man find it. Satan is a creature, too. The Pharaohs, the Nimrods all strayed with Satan. But Satan says, 'I'm a creature.'

There's a point the devil trusts in. Satan has learned the 'prayer of the Greatest Name.' He says, 'Because I've learned the prayer of the Greatest Name, I'm going to recite it at my last breath and still go with faith.' But there, he doesn't say: 'My God, *if You destine it for me*, I'll recite it and go in faith.' If he *said* that, he'd still be off the hook. *He can't say it.* 'I'm going to recite the prayer of the Greatest Name in my last breath and still go in faith.' That is, 'You're You and I'm me.'

Now in carrying out divine orders, Muhammadan orders, a creature is not as intelligent as the devil. Our task is difficult. To ease things is better. Make it easy as much as you're able to. Satan is the most intelligent. It's very difficult to escape him, because he's *very* intelligent.

As you all know, Satan disobeyed only a single commandment of God. He disobeyed the order to prostrate to Adam. What will happen if a human disobeys God's order to perform the Five Daily Prayers? God has thousands of commandments for us in the Quran. What's going to befall us?

Satan [was] an angel, smarter than them all. He was the most knowledgeable of angels, he slipped with one error. And this is good for humanity, for those who know. For those who don't know, it's an occasion for regret.

According to one account, he was a teacher of the angels for forty thousand years. God creates Adam, Adam stands up, he says: 'Praise be to God, the Lord of the worlds.' The angels are astonished. 'Where did you learn *that*?' they remark among themselves. Satan doesn't prostrate to him. 'You created me from fire. Fire is light, clay is earth.' [Satan was banished because of his disrespect for the human being. So whoever shows no respect for human beings is reduced to the status of the devil.] Azazil,[4] the angel, trusted his knowledge and wisdom.

---

4. This is original name of Iblis/Satan, the fallen angel.

He said, 'I won't prostrate, that's how it's going to be.' He abandoned courtesy. And God said, 'You've found your place. I need you, too.'

The devil can't approach angels. If he does, they drive him away. Let's drive away the devil and be host to angels.

Is the devil useful or harmful? If you submit to him, he's harmful. If you don't submit to him but make him a Muslim [make him surrender], he's beneficial. He can take you to the Empyrean, to the highest heaven. [The devil is being equated with the self here.]

The Divine Law

Religion is a sun. Religion rules over everything. Over medicine, technology, science, the world. Nothing can happen without religion. Humanity is bewildered, it's looking for a religion. So are the Christians.

What is it that best brings forth a human being? It is *religion*. Because without that, a person lives like an animal. Second, it is Islam. We don't find Islam by being human, we find our true humanity through Islam. Earlier religions are two-floor houses, Islam is a five-floor apartment.

The Five Pillars of Islam, the Six Pillars of Faith are the basis of the Divine Law. The Divine Law is the Quran and the regulations of the Quran. What we call the Law is the Glorious Quran. But the Quran has come for all humanity, it has not come for the House of Islam alone. It has come to the human, the sea, the mountain, the soil. Let me say this in two words: Religion = Quran.

Without fear, without this heaven and hell in the Quran, nobody would perform the Prayer. 'Fear those who don't fear God.' That's why both fear and love are necessary.

My last will and testament to you: don't stray from Muhammadanhood, don't stray from the Divine Law. No matter what you are, don't abandon these. Never abandon the Law. Whoever abandons the Divine Law is not one of us. Knowledge – that is, the Law – is the most trustworthy friend.

A path to God cannot be found without the Divine Law. And there is no Prophet without the Law. I desire easiness for you. Now if this child were to win a place at university without going through primary school, middle school and high school, they wouldn't do his registration. If he persisted, they would drive him away. That's why all these are necessary.

A university professor can teach in elementary school, but a primary school teacher can't perform as a university professor.

A person against the Law is entirely against the Paths/Orders, doesn't understand Gnosis and Reality anyway, and thus becomes a wretch. A child gives the money he finds to the police. That's the Law. Now that person revokes the Law, there is no Path anyway, he doesn't know Gnosis to be able to do anything. The Law is elementary school, the Paths are middle school, Gnosis is high school, Reality is graduation from university. But Reality cannot be reached without the Law.

Law, Schools, Gnosis, Reality. Primary school, middle school, high school, university. Now they want to eliminate primary school, how are you going to study the rest? The road goes from here to there. How will you go when you cut off the road? In England, in France, in America, everywhere things start from the foundation. The *road* goes from here.

Question: *Can one abandon the Divine Law if one graduates?*

No. One cannot. Because if one does, one doesn't understand. It is necessary in order to provide an example for the people. If you abandon it, you will have won it only for yourself, others will be deprived. Why did the Prophet serve as an example to the Qurayshites? There's a Saying: 'If I told the truth about everything, all human beings would burn.' But he continued to explain the Law to the people. If he hadn't, he would have been dismissed from prophethood.

The Divine Law. Someone kills somebody, they mete out the punishment. Is this within the Divine Law, or outside it? Someone claims ownership although the deed isn't in his name, it's refused. Is this in the Divine Law or out of it? A robber steals millions. They punish him. Is this the Divine Law or not? The Divine Law is spread over America, Russia, England, all nations. The entire universe is within the Divine Law. Is there a law, a legal system? That is the Divine Law. Just as the earth cannot be without the sun, man cannot be without the Divine Law. Wherever they separate the rightful from the wrongful, there is the Divine Law. The Divine Law isn't just covering one's head and performing the Prayer, like you say. The universe is within the Divine Law, and the Divine Law is within the universe. Who is its judge? God.

The Divine Law is the constitution. It is the law established by the Prophet, it won't do if you don't enact it. In medicine, in technology, laws are in force everywhere. The Divine Law of all the prophets has continued. From Adam to Muhammad, the Divine Law of each is different. But all have been placed in the Quran. Leave aside the Quran, did our Prophet perform the Five Daily Prayers or didn't he? That's the important thing. If the Divine Law is missing, if Prayer and Fasting are missing, even if one performs miraculous feats, I'll strike him down. If you see a man flying in the air without the Divine Law, throw a stone and knock him down. There are many Orders now, they say, 'We've left the Divine Law behind.' There can be no Order/School/Path without the Divine Law and no Divine Law without Orders. The bridge of the Path is the Divine Law.

Don't belittle the Divine Law. Everything happens with the Divine Law. Without the Divine Law, you'll fall into the sea, you'll become fodder for fish. The Divine Law is a lifesaver, it's a piece of driftwood. Sufism is a sea. The first prevents you from being drowned in the second.

Whatever is not good for human beings, that has been prohibited by the Quran. Whatever is beneficial, that has been placed in the Quran. Whatever is harmful to the body, they've called it a sin. Whatever is useless to human beings, they've named it sin. And there are Sayings, [the most important and authentic of which are] about twice the number of Verses.

There is something we still haven't understood. Gabriel brings the Quran, but the Quran issues from the two lips of the Prophet. But the Sayings come from the same place. I don't tell this to anyone, I tell it to those who will understand: Did the Sayings emerge from his ear, his eye? They, too, came from that tongue, from between those two lips. Did a word emerge from our Prophet's mouth, or didn't it? That's what you have to look at.

If he had called them all Sayings, we wouldn't have been able to bear it. If he had called them all Verses, again we couldn't succeed. How did he manage this task in twenty-three years among all those battles? We talk for five minutes and get tired.

Question: *Have they altered the Quran?*

No, no, they can't corrupt the Quran. Then again, some come here, they say, 'It was like that then.' I say, 'I don't know then or now, I know only one time.' They ask, 'What is that?' I reply, 'Whatever our Prophet said, whatever he did, that's the time I know.'

The Verses are fixed. Read them. That time and the times to come will find themselves in those Verses.

All animals possess beauty, the most beauteous is sheep. Go out to the garden, tie one up, set the other free. Lie down yourself. You get up half an hour later. Which of those sheep gets beaten? The one that isn't tied eats the tomatoes, it ruins the garden. The owner throws a stone or two and drives it from the garden. The other wants them too, but it's tied up, it doesn't get beaten. It is always the vagabond which gets beaten.

Comment: *According to the Prophet, benevolence (ihsan) is to worship God as if you see Him.*

That's the important point. For instance, a policeman catches a thief, he takes him to the police station, the thief's eye sees but his hands and feet are bound. He can't do anything. When we're about to do something egotistical, to be under the control of a guard every instant.

Comment: *Male and female brethren are kissing each other's cheeks.*

In an environment of strangers, it's prohibited for brother to kiss sister and for the child to kiss the mother. Because how will strangers know that she's his mother? Our Prophet didn't [even] shake hands with females. These things corrupt religion, they distort the Law. While doing this, it can slide over to the other side (to fornication).

Comment: *They say that to call the Prophet the founder of the Law is polytheistic ['associationism'].*

The Prophet didn't establish it himself, he communicated God's commandments to human beings. I give this book to you, you go and give it to someone else. Tell them, 'If there is any blame, it belongs to our Prophet.'

Comment: *Being a Muslim is very difficult.*

It's very easy, girl! Promise God, that's all. And the angels will be witnesses, you're done.

Overflow

This is my last will and testament to you all: don't open the veil of the Divine Law. Don't add the smallest thing other than what the Prophet of God said.

Mansur al-Hallaj, Bayazid of Bistam, there are many like this: 'I am the Truth.' Still, you're not.

Whoever strayed beyond the Path received the slap. Only two persons didn't overflow, that is, there wasn't any gossip. One is Ghazali, the other is the Grand Shaykh [Abdul Qadir Gilani]. Why? Because they didn't overstep the line of God and His Prophet.

Mercy versus justice

(If the innocent and the guilty are both treated with mercy, this is to reward the guilty and punish the innocent. Unfounded mercy removes justice, it is a transgression and contradicts the Law. The healthy attitude is to maintain a balanced judgment.)

Do prophets behead people? They do.[1] Do prophets sin? They don't. They are innocent, they act under [divine] orders. Some friends come to me and say, 'We wouldn't even hurt a fly.' I say, 'You're more compassionate than the Prophet.' They pause. That is necessary, the other is necessary, too.

When a fly or a mosquito bothers me, I kill it, but when I see a fly that's fallen into water, I save it. Because that's what's necessary in that case.

Some important Verses

(Bear in mind that the quotation marks do not always represent a literal quote but rather, the meaning that the Verses are trying to communicate. Sometimes, it may be a deduction based on a combination of Verses.)

'God does not corrupt the faith, the holy book of a nation, the nation corrupts its own faith, its own holy book' [13:11]. The meaning of a Sacred Tradition depends on this Verse. No matter what nation, whether Christian, Muslim or Jewish. If they are cruel to each other, if they deceive one another, for instance if they buy for five and sell for ten, if they kill one another, if they gossip – 'If people in a nation live egotistically, treat one another unjustly, I unleash a cruel nation upon them, the cruel destroy each other.' The cruel are corrected with the cruel. It's like that everywhere now, in Europe, in America. Also: 'I have given knowledge to human beings. If they abandon that knowledge and pursue other knowledge, I preoccupy their minds with livelihood, again they destroy each other.' Now the age is that age. Be good so that someone good will come to you.

---

1. Compare 'I have come not to bring peace, but the sword. For I have come to set son against father and daughter against mother' (Matthew 10:34–5) and 'The sage is not kind. He treats the people like artificial straw dogs' (*Tao Te Ching*, Chapter 5).

God says, 'I invoke you much, you too, invoke Me much' [8:45]. 'They invoke God while standing, sitting, or lying on their sides' [3:191]. See, it says 'on their sides,' not 'on their backs.' So you can invoke lying on your side until you fall asleep. The Prophet always used to sleep lying on his right side. He told the truth in every regard: 'Don't lie face down.' The stomach will come under pressure. Don't lie on your left side, the heart and the stomach will be compressed. Lie on your right side, everything works in balance and harmony.[2]

It says in the Glorious Quran: 'If I revealed this Quran to a mountain, it would shatter' [33:72]. The human being is weak, foolish and precious. Man has them all.

The interpretation of a Verse: 'One who knows and one who does not know – how can they be the same?' [39:9]. The one who knows is going to bear the burden of the one who doesn't know – up to a point. Beyond that, he's going to let go.

'I test your patience. I test your rebellion. Be patient, do not complain.'

God has given the rights of the rightful and the wrongful in the Glorious Quran. He says, 'I punish the wrongful either here or over there.' He punishes many in this world.

We're unable to manage a family here. He manages totality.

God says in the Quran, 'I have completed religion over you' [5:3]. I have completed other religions [with Islam]. After that, to go to the Torah, the Psalms, the Gospel won't do. He's explained everything.

'Hold tight to God's rope' [3:103]. What is the rope? God's servants are ropes to each other. Superior men say, 'The good are very good.' They don't say, 'I am good.' Also, 'Hand to hand, [that] hand to God.' Human beings are means to each other. God says, 'I serve you with your own hands.' That is, a person becomes close to God, God serves other people by the hand of that person.

---

2. The Master then demonstrated this: the right hand under the head, legs drawn up, the left hand extended towards the left foot. When one lies on one's left side, one is prone to bad dreams. Sleeping on one's left side with a full stomach is also a serious cause of nighttime heart attacks.

Charity

(According to the Master, wealth is a good thing – for philanthropic purposes, for ridding the world of its poverty and ills. Anyone who earns honestly and fulfills this requirement has the right to wear clothing made of gold, should one so desire.)

The three hoarders

It's been sixty years now. One day, I performed the Friday Prayer in a mosque across the street from [a hospital in Ankara]. It's winter, I began to walk uphill. A man was coming towards me, he slipped and fell twice. I held his hand and helped him up. He said, 'I'm a hodja with the Directorate of Religious Affairs. I gave a sermon at the mosque up there, I'm returning.' At that time, the Directorate was at the bottom of the hill. We began to walk downhill.

'In the sermon,' said he, 'I talked about the three hoarders. Man is a hoarder. He puts aside. The bee is a hoarder [but humans take away its honey]. The ant is a hoarder, and when rainwater comes and flows in through the entrance of the nest, both the warehouse and the ant perish.

'Let's not be stockpilers, God willing. God will provide. On a day when we have in excess, let's distribute it to others, God will give again.'

'Thank you,' I said, 'you've given me a present.' By that time, we had arrived at the Directorate.

Hoarding isn't good. Grabbing from one another isn't good.

It's from a Saying: 'Among living things, there are three hoarders. One is man, the next is the ant, the last is the honeybee. The others don't worry, I deliver their sustenance to their feet when they want it.'

Man takes the honey of bees in the wild, they die. The ones he cultivates, he leaves them too little, they die too. They call these three stockpilers. We're going to work for God's sake, wear for God's sake. We're not going to love stockpiling.

The road to Paradise

The meaning of a Saying: 'Three cauldrons, the one in the middle is empty. As one boils, it throws to the one at the other end, nothing enters the empty cauldron.' These are all symbols. That is, the rich give to the rich, nothing's left for the poor. Whereas the poor are shareholders in the property of the rich [via the Alms-tax]. What does God say: 'Who helps the poor has helped Me.' The upper class should approach the middle class and draw the lower class towards the middle. They should all unite in the middle.

Be intelligent. Earn Licitly, don't deviate from the path of God and the Prophet of God. Wear gold, play with gold, it's Allowed to you. Become rich the Licit way. Your Alms-tax will be proportionate, you can give to the poor.

Money is necessary, money is necessary for the sake of God. One enters Paradise with money. An acquaintance who comes here gave the following account:

One day when he was going somewhere, he saw a woman rummaging through a garbage can. The woman took away a putrid chicken she removed from the garbage can. He began following her to see what she would do with it. She went to a shantytown and entered one of the hovels. The man covertly began to watch what would happen from a window.

The woman cooked the chicken, then fed her children with it. After waiting a while longer, the man knocked on the door. The woman opened the door and said, 'Yes, uncle?' Without mentioning that he had followed her, the man said that he was passing by and wondered who lived there. He thus certified the woman's poverty in this way as well.

After he left, he went straight home. He took the five hundred thousand Liras he had been saving for Pilgrimage in the near future and returned to the woman's home. He didn't speak of the difficulties with which he had saved the money. He said, 'I'm very rich. Take this money, I have lots more.' He placed it in the woman's hand.

That night he saw the Prophet of God in his dream. Our Prophet thanked him and gave him great news: 'You've won the merit of a *thousand* Pilgrimages,' he said.

Prayer, worship is God's commandment anyway. But in order to enter Paradise, one has to help others, and that can only be done with money. Instead of spending the four or five hundred thousand you have on the Lesser Pilgrimage, give a hundred thousand to the poor, God will accept it.

The Alms-tax

The rich come and ask me: 'We give the Alms-tax,[1] let's not pay taxes.' I tell them: 'The Alms-tax is the right of the poor, taxes are the right of the Ministry of Finance. Take your money from the pocket of your jacket and put it in your trouser pocket. The money is still your money. How is the state going to pursue these tasks, these investments? The money will return to you again as services.' They're convinced, they leave. 'We want to count taxes as Alms-tax.' You're going to give both.[2]

If Muslims gave their Alms-tax in full, no poor would remain.

Out of a [world] population of five billion, one or two hundred million may go hungry. But if they receive help from outside, they won't remain hungry either.

If you have debts, the Alms-tax doesn't apply to you. In Islam, if there are hungry within, one does not give to the outside. Your parents, your relatives, if you live separately and they're hungry, you don't give to anyone else.

Comment: *If the Alms-tax were given, no poor would be left.*

Yes, sir, none would be left. Factories would be built for the poor as well.

Comment: *The debts of poor countries are going to be canceled.*

That would count as Alms-tax.

Question: *What if every nation gave a fortieth (the Alms-tax proportion) of its national income?*

For that to happen, the nations of the world would have to become Muslim.

---

1. Giving a fixed portion of one's wealth to the poor every year. One of the Five Pillars of Islam.
2. 'Give unto Caesar what is Caesar's and unto God what is God's' (Matthew 22:21, Mark 12:17, Luke 20:25).

Alms-tax as charity

The most loyal person collects throughout the year, pays the exact amount at year's end – okay. May God accept it. But if one distributes that Alms-tax to the needy *before* a year is over, that's better.[3] *Aha!* And at the end of the year, calculate what is in your hand and give its Alms-tax, God will give ten times that amount. We're talking the truth here. The meaning of a Saying: 'Give charity to the needy, it will return to you tenfold, a hundredfold.'

[A master told his disciple, 'Someone is going to come. Give him the ten eggs we have.' When the man came, however, the disciple gave him nine eggs, thinking to save the last egg for supper. In the evening, a basket arrived full of eggs. The disciple counted them, there were ninety. He went and told his master. 'There should have been a hundred,' said the sage. 'Since there are ninety, you must have withheld the last egg.']

Someone gives Alms-tax once a year. Well, is he going to give Alms-tax *once* a year? Give Alms-tax *every day!* Give Alms-tax as you find the opportunity. That's in the month of Ramadan. For instance, it's New Year, the Alms-tax of the New Year. Whatever is in your hands at that time, give. Let us give what God has given.

As you walk on the road, a glass is broken, a bottle is broken, it'll puncture someone's foot or someone's tire. If we bend over, if we pick it up, if we throw it in a trash can, that's the greatest Alms-tax. A stone – it's going to collide with somebody's foot. Someone has spat, someone has vomited in the street, if we find some soil and reform it so that no one else sees it, it would be the greatest Alms-tax.

Someone was paid a million Liras for a service. He didn't accept it, saying 'It was my duty anyway.' If I were in his place, I would take those million Liras in my hand. Recognizing God and the Prophet of God. I would give it to the needy. *Ahh!* Yes! Because he [the payer himself] won't take it and give it to others! You've performed his job. Because you did it quickly, he may have further business with you, he pays you a million. Say, 'Thank you. I wouldn't take this, but I'm going to give it to needy people.' To his face. To yourself: 'God is my witness.' Give a hundred thousand each to five or ten families. Cool!

---

3. In other words, to give the Alms-tax portion of one's savings several times a year or whenever the opportunity presents itself to help needy people, instead of paying it out as a lump sum once a year.

Furthermore, that man was offended because he didn't take the money. Now he's doing business with others.

Live longer by charity

Charity increases one's life span. We have accepted this, thank God. And we've done the experiment. You're going to die today. You give in charity, that moment passes. There have been such experiences, sir.

Someone committed an offense. They decided to hang him. As they were taking him to the gallows, let's say at dawn, fresh bread was being baked at the bakery. He says, 'I desire to eat some bread.' He borrows a loaf from the baker. 'I'll pay you later,' he says, 'or the guards will pay you.' He takes it under his armpit. A little further on, someone has spread out a handkerchief and is awaiting a handout. He tells the guard, 'Give this bread to that man.' And the man who spread the handkerchief says, 'May God save you.' 'Amen,' he says.

They go, the judge and prosecutor are there. One person's been hanged already, it's his turn. 'Take another look [at his case],' says the judge. 'Let there be no mistake.' They decide on his acquittal. The judge says, 'pray for the government.' 'Thanks,' he says, 'I have others to pray for.' He prays first for the baker and then for the pauper. This is a true story. For all of you.

A dervish requests money from a rich man. He hits him with the back of his hand. He had a chain in his hand, it strikes the lip of the dervish. The next day, the rich man's son is stabbed when he tries to break up a fight. That night in his dream, he sees the dervish aiming at him with a bow and arrow.

The next day he looks him up. He finds the dervish in a café. 'This is what happened,' he says. 'My entire fortune is yours.' He brings out a lot of gold and sets it before him.

The dervish says: 'This isn't from me, it's from my Owner. May God forgive you. Don't worry, nothing will happen.' He doesn't take the money, he leaves.

So don't shy away from giving. Whatever comes to your hand. Both you and your friends.

I've told this to maybe a hundred people: in order to avoid embarrassing his child, a father deposited money in the bank. He gave the account book to his son, saying: 'Spend as you please.'[4] I'm telling this because I liked it very much.

It's a Saying of the Prophet: 'The hand that gives is superior to the hand that receives.' May God grant that all human beings be givers. When they have. When they haven't, what can we do.

Those above have, and yet they can't give thanks, they can't give. Those below want to give, but can't because they have not. There's also the saying of the Prophet: 'My God, I take refuge in You from meanness and poverty.' The miser, his hand doesn't go to his pocket. And the pauper wants to give, but can't.

[To a restaurant owner:] You see a hungry person come, you understand, say 'I've seen you somewhere' and take them in. Say, 'I've missed you, how have you been?' and feed them.

When we say 'charity,' we immediately think of money. But all these organs have their charity. How? With ethics, with character traits. The hand has its charity, the eye has its charity, the tongue has its charity, they all have their charity. To lie down for God, to get up for God, to sit for God, to talk for God. Then we can give that charity.

You see a stone on the road, you put it aside so that no one will strike his foot. You see spittle, you remove it so nobody will be disgusted. These are all charity. You do it with your hand, that's the charity of the hand. You do it with the foot, that's the charity of the foot.

Don't kill even a fly. But if the fly is going to kill you, kill it first. Something is going to harm you, act first. Be intelligent, give the charity of intelligence.

Question: *What about fake beggars?*

Give, give. I've given, you give, too. If you give two to the other, give one to them. What does Yunus Emre say, 'Be a lover of society, not a burden to it.'

Comment: *The animals sacrificed during the Sacrificial Feast possess the gift of life, too.*

Our Prophet has ordered what is useful to human beings and prohibited what is harmful. He wouldn't have ordered it if it weren't beneficial

---

4. This is reminiscent of the 'charity stones' (*sadaka tashi*) once existing throughout the Ottoman Empire and Central Asia, which I have dealt with in an earlier book, *The Black Pearl: Spiritual Illumination in Sufism and East Asian Philosophies* (2005).

somehow. Its real origin is in the episode of Abraham and Ishmael. Its benefit is that it increases the lifespan of human beings, and also repels accidents and misfortune. It's both God's commandment and a charitable act. [The meat is distributed to the poor and needy.] People are affluent now. In those times, the need was greater. The poor used to eat meat one day a year [thanks to this Feast]. The Bedouins would come, take it and leave. [Now, even if there's no poor to give it, it still] extends the lifespan and averts accidents.

A Robin Hood example

[The Prophet told Ali:] Someone lives in a neighborhood. His neighbor is hungry and thirsty, but he doesn't have anything to give. He robs the store of a rich man who doesn't give, he sells it, he calls out: 'Hey, neighbor, take this money and eat!' Intention, it's the intention again! Again he succeeds.

Destiny

God does not curtail anyone's sustenance or right. And God *does not seal off anyone's fate*. Because it's not worthy of His glory. Man shuts it off himself and puts the blame on God. 'My fate is sealed.' God doesn't seal anyone's fate, one seals one's fate oneself. And then there's the saying: 'I did it myself and found it myself, what of it to anyone?' Whatever one does, one does to oneself [17:7, 41:46, 45:15].

If everything were predetermined, fixed from the start, what need would there be for prophets? What need would there be for them to invite people to God?

Some Sayings of the Prophet: 'As you sow, so shall you reap.' Both physically and spiritually. ['What you give with your hand goes with you in the end.'] 'Don't do something, it will happen to you.' 'Don't speak ill of someone, it'll happen to you someday.'

Man shapes his destiny with his own hands. God doesn't cut off anybody's sustenance. He sits in a café, he pays for the tea, he's jobless, he says 'This is my fate.'

If these properties [of sainthood] have manifested in me, they can manifest in them, too [in any human being]. Except that there's also the issue of fate in this. The hen scratches the cow dung and begins to eat. Let's not attribute it to fate, let's put it down to the Base Self, because the Quran has been sent to us.

Don't be a burden to anyone. Work physically and spiritually, earn. All you need is to embrace God and God's commandments, both physically and spiritually. Don't lose hope. As long as you're human, you're higher than the angels, don't sink to the level of animals. You're superior, you're human, man has intelligence. God's commandments have been communicated to man by the prophets. Whoever obeys the commands advances on the path. He is stripped and cleansed of egotistical states and circumstances, of this and that. He becomes higher than the angels. But [to say:] 'This is what destiny has allotted for me' – that is indolence.

Question: *If I don't perform Prayer or obey in this world, won't I still have my lot in the next world?*

You have your lot, but it's here. If your father didn't go to the office, didn't take a case, didn't take this, didn't retire, would he receive a retirement pension? If he didn't go in there, if he didn't work, didn't participate in a court case, would anyone come and place money in your father's hand? Whoever says 'This is my fate,' just sits. There is a commandment. There are commands from God to human beings.

You have business tomorrow in the Parliament. You sit at home, you play with your children, that day passes. When you go the next day, won't anybody ask you anything? Where's destiny now? If you work, your manager will admire you, if you don't work, you'll get fired.

Comment: *If there is fate, we are not responsible.*

Wrong. We accept fate. But we're going to perform our duties of servanthood. Fate exists, we have to work.

Question: *One person goes to a saint, another can't see him. Is this fate?*

No. One goes to the mosque, the other goes to the bar. One has to exercise the Partial Will [one's own personal will].[1] There is both good and evil. If you abandon the good and choose the evil, you will be in error.

Good and evil are from God. He's left all doors open for the good. For the evil, He says, 'Close the doors. I am able not to create evil. I created evil so that you may look at evil and choose the good, may obey the prophets. I could have created you without evil, without sin. But you would be like angels. You would lack the honor of being human, the honor of being Muslim. I have created good and evil. If you desire evil, that belongs to you, don't hold Me responsible. I gave you evil, but I also gave you the information: 'This is evil, don't do it.' Don't hold Me responsible later on.' Be wary of Sufism. 'That's from Him, that's from Him, too' – no. You are to open the gates of good and close the gates of evil.

Question: *What about one's lot?*

One has to seek out one's lot. You want an apple. If you sit here, the apple won't come, you have to go and buy it from the grocer.

---

1. There are two kinds of will: the Total Will, namely the will of God, and the Partial Will, or the wills of individual human beings. These are components of the overall Total Will, but they have been distributed to human beings for their own use. We must, however, exercise our personal will responsibly.

Question: *Can't destiny be changed?*

First: A Saying of the Prophet – 'All human beings are born as Muslims, they enter the religion of their parents and so on when they reach puberty.' Destiny is changed here.

Second: Our Prophet was born into the tribe of Quraysh fourteen hundred years ago, the fate of *all* humanity was changed.

Total Will, Partial Will

Total Will: the wide circle. Partial Will: the narrow circle. They don't exercise precaution, they blame it on predestination. Some great persons have renounced precaution and left everything to foreordination. I object to all of this. You have to take your precaution, if it still happens, only then is it predestination. This tobacco is here, and so is the rolling paper, but the cigarette won't get wrapped up by itself.

Is there a Partial Will, or not? There is. We're going to obtain the Total Will with the Partial Will. We cannot obtain the Partial Will with the Total Will [i.e., we must work to obtain the consent of God so that a result we desire may come about].

Comment: *The Prophet's teeth were broken during battle, he didn't give up.*

What are these, the Partial Will. The Total Will isn't present, the Partial Will is. The Prophet of God did everything with the Partial Will. He always acted using the Partial Will.

Precaution versus predestination

Precaution (*tadbir*) is important, too, but the main thing is predestination (*taqdir*). If foreordinaton is like this, what can we accomplish with measures? Predestination annuls precaution.

Destiny is not for the likes of you. You have to act with precaution, not with fate. Destiny applies to people like us. A man knows that he's going to have a traffic accident somewhere, he consciously goes there, stands in that location and the accident happens. This is not for those like you, it is for those like us.

The Prophet of God took precautions. After our Prophet, the caliphs, too, walked with precaution. Abu Bakr and Omar acted with precaution. So did Othman, so did Ali.

Precaution is the child of predestination. In Yugoslavia, [the Sufi saint] Muhammad Nur al-Arabi said: 'Precautions have no importance, the main thing is predestination.' This saying is true. [He was summoned to Istanbul, the seat of the Ottoman Empire, to explain himself.] Sultan Abdul Hamid [II] listened to the disputes from behind a wooden grating. Nur al-Arabi said: 'Under normal circumstances, we act according to our own minds, this is precaution. But if we are in the presence of the Sultan, we can't act without orders, and that's predestination.' Sultan Hamid liked this very much.

First, we err in precaution. Second, we call the results predestination and delegate it to God. Some come and say, 'Sir, this was my lot.' We're going to take measures, but we're going to leave the decision to God. If it works, fine. If it doesn't, that too is from God. But if we err in precaution, we will also err in predestination. If you walk in the middle of the highway, those who come from the front and back will honk their horns. If you walk on the sidewalk, there's nothing to worry about. But if you walk on the highway, a driver will come up and say, 'You've already assured your own destruction, are you going to be the cause of mine, too?'

Question: *Precaution can't change predestination, right?*

If we take measures, if we apply every means and still don't get results, that's from God. But if we don't take precautions and blame God for the outcome, we'll be doubly guilty.

If our Prophet had desired, couldn't he have performed Spacefolding,[2] like Moses and Khidr, instead of hiding in a cave [during his Emigration]? Of course he could. But he didn't, he always acted by taking measures like ordinary human beings. Gabriel had said to him, 'On your order, I shall destroy the tribe of Quraysh.' In spite of that, he acted with lenience for eleven years. He performed the Emigration normally: he took measures. First precaution, then predestination. He placed Ali in his bed [when the assassins of all the clans came to murder him]. Together with Abu Bakr the Truthful, they hid in the cave for three days.

---

2. See The secret and the sublime/Spacefolding for more details.

But he could have performed Spacefolding. He could have told Abu Bakr: 'Shut your eyes,' and when he opened them, they would have been in Medina. He didn't. He didn't do things by performing miraculous feats or miracles. Study the period from his birth to his Emigration to Medina, you'll see that he always acted with precaution. He didn't leave matters to predestination. Only once, during the Battle of Badr, he said, 'My God, there are three hundred Muslims, what will I do if you take them away?' Gabriel came: 'Messenger of God, take a handful of sand and throw it toward the enemy.' A storm blew up, it became pitch dark. A Verse was revealed about it: 'It was not you who threw when you threw, but it was God who threw' [8:17].

Death, afterlife, the Apocalypse

Earthly retribution

Sometimes, God settles one's account in this world, too.

God exacts (avenges) the wail of an ant from a sultan. Remember the story of Abu Hanifa and the sparrow.[1]

Omar [the second caliph, who buried his daughter alive according to the Arab custom before Islam], possessor of justice, died by the sword of a servant. Ali [the fourth caliph] died by the sword of a servant. Ali sent [his sons] Hassan and Hussein to protect Othman [the third caliph]. While those were protecting the front, they pierced the wall in the back. Othman said, 'If anything can save me, the Quran will, otherwise let me die over it,' and did not rise from reading the Quran. To the firstcomer, he said, 'I've done much good to your father, don't be the one to kill me.' That one went away. The second carved Othman in two. What mysteries these are.

Selim the Resolute was going to return from Egypt and conquer Europe. He said, 'Draw me a map of the world.' They drew it to the best of their knowledge. He lay down on it to the full extent of his body, and said: 'This world is not enough for me.' A cancerous boil formed, he passed away.

Hitler declared war on the world. The day the German flag was hoisted at the French Consulate, I heard him on the radio: 'Either I rule this world, or I'll burn the world down and deliver it to God.' He was ruined by the Russians, killed himself and passed out of history.

The Ottomans had many faults. They strangled babes in their cradles and killed them.[2] They spent time with Armenian and Greek women.[3]

That is, God never treats anyone unjustly or cruelly. It's always, 'I did it myself and found it myself, so who's to blame?'

---

1. For details, see The scholars/Abu Hanifa/His death.
2. It was a policy after Mehmed II for sultans to eliminate all possible successors to the throne except one. This was done for reasons of state, so that contenders would not arise and make challenging claims, resulting in the weakening or disintegration of the Ottoman Empire.
3. In their harems.

Death and resurrection

Let's open our eyes. Not over there, but here. If I take off this jacket and walk, do I die? It's the same thing [with the spirit abandoning the body].

Human beings are going to be reborn. But no food, no drink, no sex, nothing. In spirit. The spirits are going to resurrect – no body. No eating or drinking. They will resurrect not with a material body, but a body that resembles matter.

Question: *Will human beings be resurrected with this body?*

They will find the same state as spirits. God's Prophet knows, this body will rot, but the same state. I give the following example. You go to a photographer, you have a full-view picture or a portrait taken, you bring it and hang it in your room. But you're not the photo. When the spirit is removed, it's the same thing. The spirit of the deceased rises to the [spiritual] sky, the body remains in the grave. The spirit does not remain in the body.

Whatever has been stated in the Quran, in true Sayings, will all come to pass. Let no one doubt it.

The throes of death are very difficult. The separation of life, of the spirit, from the body is very difficult. The truth is seen, but one can't tell [anyone].

You're going to have an exam tomorrow. If you succeed you'll be happy, that's Heaven. If you fail you'll be sad, that's Hell. That is, in reality we're at the door of Heaven and Hell every instant.

You return to Heaven with three things: your family, your friends [they'll come to see you off] and your deeds. You'll be left alone with your deeds. The others will go away. [This is a Saying of the Prophet.]

Let's enter Heaven all together, God willing. Together with the ants, with the turtles, with the flowers.

Whoever one loves, one goes to their side [at the Resurrection]. God knows the one who loves and the one who is beloved.

Prayer continues after one is transferred to the spiritual realm.

God will ask those in Heaven, 'Is there anything you want?' Some will say, 'No, we're content.' And some will say, 'We wish for Your Visage.' We're going to see the Visage *after* we go to Heaven. No Visage before going to Heaven. There's no such easy stuff.

The Mahdi

There's still a long time until the *Mahdi*,[4] your children won't see him either.

The community of the Faithful never lacks a savior. Every time is the time of a savior, but then a final Mahdi is going to come, and then no other. When the Mahdi comes, sainthood will be ended. Your children won't see it yet. God knows the exact time.

'As long as there's one person left who says *"There is no god but God,"* the world will not end.' That is, the stream of sainthood. Otherwise, there are millions who say *'There is no god but God,'* the end of the world can come. Know this as the truth: whenever sainthood is terminated, that's when the world will end.

[Besides being the last saint, there is a second meaning to 'the Mahdi.'] The coming of the Mahdi during the end-times, the descent [Second Coming] of Jesus, these will occur not as stated, but in another way.

Question: *Are they symbols?*

They're symbols. The Coming of Jesus, the reign of Jesus – a great Western nation is going to accept Islam. That's what is meant by Jesus becoming a Muslim. After that, the signs of the Mahdi Messenger are going to start. The Mahdi is not going to come in [human] form. A divine technology is going to come that's in accord with the people of faith. That's the Mahdi. It's still to come, that is. No one but I will tell you this. Maybe it will still come from the computer. Everyone expects the Mahdi to come, but everyone expects a person. No. It's going to emerge as a technology. But the pious don't think like that, they think he's really going to come.

Question: *Is the descent of Jesus from Heaven a cipher like this?*

Yes, it's a cipher. That is, a Christian nation, a nation that accepts the Bible, is going to accept Muhammadanhood.

---

4. Rightly guided one (or redeemer) who will come during the end-times.

Doomsday

Whatever has emerged from the mouth of the Prophet, those are all going to happen. 'Human beings will end the world with their own hands' – a Saying. It's going to happen. The Apocalypse is going to happen. Everything that emerged from the two lips of the Prophet is going to take place.

I heard it somewhere when I was seven or eight years old: 'In time the Mahdi Messenger will come, Islam will continue for a while. But gunpowder won't burn against the Mahdi Messenger.' I've remembered this. When we heard about the atom, the atomic bomb [in 1945], I recalled that. Gunpowder will burn, but will have no effect, what can it do? *Aha!* Gunpowder will burn when fire is applied to it, but its rule will be over. This is one.

The other is, when they started out on space, I thought of Noah's Ark. If there's something like that someday, a nuclear war, they're going to escape into space. After the term of the atom, the rage of the atom is over on Earth, they're going to come back and land on Earth. The Third Adam, that is.[5] The First Adam [is the Adam we know from religious tradition as Adam]. The Second Adam is Noah, he was created with the Flood. I recalled that. *Aha!* Now these rascals are looking for a place in space. If, someday, something like this happens, after the fury of the atom – so many years – has passed, they're going to return to Earth. But they can't find a place in the realm of space, among the stars. They won't be able to find a planet like Earth. In *Invitation to Peace* [1987],[6] I gave the maximum period humans can withstand space as five years. It's actually one year, I'm overstating it. If you go to Mars, you can live there for five years at most, how are you going to survive?

A Doomsday is going to come in any case. The atom – *whoosh!* It happens such that the divine sciences are terminated. Humanity approaches oblivion. Faith departs from humankind. Illicit gain, illicit lust become dominant. Satan says, 'You're like Pharaoh, you're like Nimrod.' Then, such a generation is going to come that mercy, loving-

---

5. See 'Noah's Ark plan from top Moon man' for ESA chief scientist Bernard Foing's views on establishing a DNA library on the moon (accessed 09/16/2004): http://newsvote.bbc.co.uk/mpapps/pagetools/print/news.bbc.co.uk/1/hi/sci/tech/3635972.stm. See also: http://www.space.com/scienceastronomy/noahs_ark_040913.html.

6. The Master was always very concerned about world peace. He directed the preparation of four pamphlets dealing with the subject. One of these, written in 1987, was acclaimed at the time by the presidents and prime ministers of various countries, and by the Vatican.

kindness, is going to vanish. That generation is going to do it. The three Adams – they don't study history, they don't know. I say 'the Third Adam.' Nobody studies history, how are they going to know who the Second Adam is? One has to study the history of Islam, the history of the prophets.

Noah's deluge occurred with water. The mountains and rocks didn't burn, fire didn't burn. With the atom, the mountains burn, *wheeoow!* The fire of the atom is more intense than hellfire. Hellfire doesn't consume mountains, the atom does. There's only one weapon more powerful than the atom – the human [the Perfect Human] who enlightens, who leads.

The last resort is to unite over a holy book, to unite on the Quran. And that, they can't do. It wouldn't even occur to them. So that's how it's going to happen.

Archangel Gabriel told the Prophet: 'No further prophets will come. Only, I'm going to come down to earth three times, and three things will be removed. [First] I will remove the mind, [next] I will remove courtesy and shame, [then] I will remove the abundance of the earth. The Quran will remain on the shelf. Then I will come [for the last time].'

The rules of the Four Books have been abolished. They exist, but nobody looks at them.

They're going to destroy the earth with their own hands. There are many Sayings about the end of the world, one from Medina states: 'Your world will not end, except that human beings will destroy their world with their own hands.' The end!

Another Saying: after the Battle of Uhud, they're going towards Medina. 'Do you see those mountains?' says the Prophet of God. 'The time will come when those mountains are carded like cotton.' Softer than soil, he says 'cotton.' What's going to end the world? The atom. What's going to tease [mountains] like cotton? The atom. Mercy will depart from human beings. Not yet [though].

Democracy, multiple parties and their children: illicit gain and illicit lust. The world will go down with these. I'm telling you the back and the front of it. Write these down in your books.

The atom will become so powerful that even peasants will possess it. By that time, Turkey will have the atom [bomb], too.

Obedience to the Torah, the Gospel, the Quran will be abolished. Human beings will be much more merciless than they are today. God will remove mercy from human beings. After that, Heaven forbid, a human being won't be worth as much as a cat. People will murder each other.

The Apocalypse is going to take place at the time of the Dusk Prayer. That's why the Obligatory (*fard*) part of the Evening Prayer is before the customary (*sunna*) part: for the sake of that last generation. This is a secret and a symbol.

America will bomb, let's say, England with the atom. England will bomb America. America will bomb China. China will bomb France. And thus everyone will bomb everybody else.

There's another Saying: 'An egg stood on end in the west [in Africa] will be seen from the east [in Egypt, and *vice versa*].' It's going to be that flat, that is.

The bombs of today destroy only living things. Those will burn both the living and the nonliving, will turn them to ashes. The seas will invade the land surface, creating mud from the ashes, *quiver quiver quiver*. And what will happen then? God forbid, America, Russia, Europe will all become as flat as can be. I answered this [in 1987]: outer space. Whoever has a spaceship will rush out to space. The longest survivors will last five years.

Doomsday will come in a hundred or two hundred years. As long as sainthood lasts, it won't come. God and God's Prophet know, *Doomsday will come with the atom*, let me tell you that.

The Third Adam

The astronaut who returns to earth after nuclear war will be the Third Adam. But he won't return in an ordinary way. He will come back with a new justice, he will establish God's justice on earth.

The Third Adam will establish justice. He will bring [God's] mercy even if he had been a sworn communist. This cannot be any other way. He will come with the spirituality and maturity of the Prophet of God. I've said this before. Because the Quran is final. Nothing else comes after it.

Question: *So the Quran will be preserved?*

Yes. And if God wills, He won't burn the Ka'ba or the place of our Prophet in Medina.

The pen is mightier than the sword

Thirty years ago, I decided that all humankind should abandon war and fight with the pen. Things are slowly going in that direction. Thirty years ago [in 1962, the year of the Cuban Missile Crisis]. We don't want the sword now either, enough of the sword. Let them all be filled with belief, with faith. Let all weaponry end, let them all return to the Quran. What need is there for weapons when there's the Quran? Without deviating from our Prophet, fight with the pen.

The form of combat has changed now. Not the sword, the pen. Sound judgment.

The Turks, the Seljuks, the Ottomans – may they all rest in peace – came with the sword and went with the sword. They gave their heads and seized, it left their hands without taking any heads. They took possession of so many lands. Where are those now? The Quran is favorable, God's command permits it. [The Prophet said:] 'I take pride in the numbers of my community.' So the sword doesn't work, it's more the pen that works.

The way out

America has come to the top now. But can it maintain it? They have to issue a decree from the United Nations. Whichever government manufactures weapons, they have to pounce on it and destroy it. Not with weapons, but with the pen. If they do this, maybe the world will have some peace and quiet. Weapons, aircraft, tanks – may God destroy them all, for the sake of His Beloved Prophet.

The United Nations has to do it. Weapons are prohibited. The government that manufactures them is to be removed from power. There is no other solution.

In order to avoid this, the *United* Nations has to dwell on it. It has to take things under its jurisdiction. It has to remove conditions that violate the Torah, the Gospel and the Quran. Only the United Nations can take care of this. There's God's blessing, but no work. If God and God's Prophet guide to the right way, if the United Nations take it in hand, *only* that way can they solve this problem. Otherwise it's impossible.

Of the nearly two hundred nations now extant, one person who is wisest, most cultured and who loves his country and nation should be chosen from each. Those chosen should love humanity and other nations as much as their own. From among these, the most intelligent seven should again be selected by examination, plus twenty or thirty members. These should compose the United Nations.

Then, all kinds of weapons and all war should be prohibited. When war erupts anywhere, the representatives of the parties concerned should first try to resolve differences between themselves. If they can't resolve it, the rest (the UN) should intervene to stop it.

Next, hunger. After war, hunger too should be eradicated. Whatever it takes should be done to achieve this. Without weapons and hunger, humanity will be able to maintain peace for a while. In time, smaller countries would join bigger nations [in regional alliances, somewhat in the manner of the European Union]. Small states would give way to large states, and in the absence of weapons the latter would live in peace. This means not just toxic (NBC) weapons, but all weapons. This is the only solution. There is no other way.

Someone has to follow this through. Humanity is going. Let's unite it, let's bring it together while we still have the chance.

May God's Prophet guide to the right way, may it bud from the United Nations. Otherwise it's going, the snake will pour out its venom. Humankind is going to oblivion. Do Prayers and pray a lot. Not just for yourself, for all humanity. May this fire be extinguished. May fire be replaced by love.

Miscellaneous topics

Politics

(The Master was not against the participation of individuals in political life for the good of society, as the following statements demonstrate.)

Politics is necessary. Don't be straight as a poplar tree. Bend a little this way, a little that way.

A saying of Moses: 'You go to a town, a city, they're all one-eyed. Then take out one of your eyes, because it won't fit them.' Another way of expressing it: 'In the country of the blind, you too should shut one eye and go about.'

In administration, both firmness and lenience are necessary. A little fighting, a bit of toughness is necessary. Whoever remains on the defensive all the time always gets beaten up.

Honest people come to me, they ask: 'Should we enter politics at this age?' I say, 'Enter right away. If you don't, some pest will enter instead of you, you'll suffer the consequences of his deeds.' Let me give another example: a dark room [parliament]. If you place a lantern, a lover in there, would that be bad?

There was a colonel in Kayseri, he became a doctor, he came to me: 'They want me to become a member of parliament. I won't do it without consulting you.' It was time for the Night Prayer. The light was on. I got up and turned it off. 'Do you see me?' 'No.' I turned on the light and came back. 'Did you understand anything?' 'No.' 'You're righteous. You'll say a true word in parliament, you'll be a light in the darkness. I want you to be an MP.' 'Now I understand,' he said.

'Let's not enter politics.' If thieves were to invade parliament, could you possibly be comfortable? One has to be useful to one's country, one's nation. In the way of God, not in the way of evil.

A lesson in politics

A seeker had served his master for twenty years. He was wondering, 'Why doesn't the Master give me anything?' His master said, 'Come.' They went to a nearby brook. Bees and flies had fallen into the water and were struggling to get out. His master said, 'Let's save a few bees together.' But every bee the seeker grasped at stung him. His hand swelled up. His master said, 'Stop.' He took a piece of branch and held it near them. The bees climbed onto it and were saved.

'You see?' the master said. 'You can't even save a bee from water yet. Be patient, work. God willing, your wish will come true in time.' The disciple said: 'Forgive me, Master, I'm very impatient.'

The science of politics requires that you hold fire with tongs, not with your hand.

Being chief

Be a leader. Leadership is important. In order to get things done everywhere, be a leader. If you are a member, you prepare milk for everyone to drink, a fly comes and falls into it, nobody can drink it. But if you're the leader, you can shoo that fly away, too.

Timing

What you say is all true. But you have to bide your time. Everyone is going to oppose you, you're going to say 'Yes' to all of them. Our Prophet received prophethood before he was born, yet he waited until he was forty years old.

You have a glassful of water and a glassful of fire. We can put the water anywhere, leave it anywhere. But we can't leave the fire anywhere. If you meet with something that burns, use it slowly.

In order to take the pigeon in your hand, you have to bring the birdfeed close slowly.

When you walk on snow, don't leave tracks.

If you urinate or defecate, it stinks. But if you go three or four days later, it doesn't smell, the sun dries it up and covers it. But if you take a stick and stir it up, the bad odor will spread again. This is a saying of Ghazali.

Economics

If human beings valued spiritual instead of material wealth, they would achieve everything they desired by material wealth. There would be no wars, there would be brotherhood, there would be happiness, they would win everything.

Wealth is necessary. Human beings should be wealthy, with faith, with belief, with good morals. If these are present, wealth is good. Otherwise it's not worth a penny.

Wealth is good. Spiritual wealth is even better. The patience demanded by wealth is more difficult than that required by poverty, because the Base Self has all kinds of desires.

Eat and drink what is Allowed. Eat as God commands, wear gold if you want. Enough to hold body and soul together, to be reticent – I say 'No.' Work. But give it its due. A golden suit, there isn't such a thing, but if there were it'd be worth a million. You'd pay the Alms-tax of that, the poor would be happy. Don't be afraid to be rich. Try to be rich physically and spiritually. Work hard, be very rich. Even wear shoes of gold.

Be rich, be rich for God. Spend for God's sake.

Wealth, money, these are our vehicles. 'Let me be rich,' that's a needless burden.

Question: *So gold isn't Forbidden?*

How can it be Forbidden? Put it in your pocket, not in your heart. I didn't see it, they told me, [a famous man of religion] used to wear two or three gold and diamond rings and sometimes bracelets, they would jangle when he slammed his hand on the table. The hodjas say 'Give the Alms-tax of gold,' but they don't call gold Forbidden. Money isn't Satan, don't call money Satan. One who uses it for good is the owner of good works, one who uses it for bad is the owner of bad works.

To a man whose business was failing

1. If you don't put the liver in the fridge, the cats will get it.
2. God doesn't practice cruelty on human beings, He doesn't cut off their sustenance, a person makes errors himself.
3. Jonah remained in the belly of the whale for forty days, it couldn't digest him and threw him up. Continue with Jonah's prayer that he recited while he was in the whale's belly: *'There is no god but You. Glory be to You. Surely I have been of the wrongdoers'* [21:87 – see Appendix].

Sustenances are separate. Some don't work, God brings and places it in their bosom. Others work and take their sustenance from God by force. Ours is by working. We're going to get our sustenance by work.

The stock exchange isn't gambling, but it's corrupt. [I prefer government bonds and papers.] It's [similar to] gambling, and they also lose money there.

1. Don't lose your Muslim culture.
2. Don't fool anyone, they'll fool you, too.
3. Even if it's a million, don't touch it if it's Forbidden.

'I've found a job, should I take it or not?' You've found a job, what are you waiting for? Don't miss the partridge today, look for the rabbit tomorrow. If you lose your job, God will give you another job. God won't let you starve.

The greatest wealth is to believe in God and His Prophet. Further down, to work and earn, to spend for God's sake.

Money, let it come only if it bodes well. Somebody wins four hundred million in the lottery. The little son starts throwing it in the stove. He realizes at the last packet. He cleaves the child in two by the legs.

Interest

They've invented something called 'interest-free banking,' it accumulates the greatest interest.

Young people working in banks come to me: 'We're going to resign.' I tell them: 'Do your job. Wherever you go, you're going to receive bank money. The banks pay the salary. Only, don't take a paper, an envelope from the bank.' Some have resigned and lived in misery, some have continued and received their retirement.

Question: *Sir, is interest prohibited, or only its extreme form called usury?*

Actually, all forms of interest are prohibited. [And not only in Islam, but in Judaism and Christianity also.] But I'm the most pious among you, interest permeates the banks, even I receive my salary from the bank. What's really objectionable is exorbitant interest [usury]. It exists today too, outside banks. But actually, every kind is prohibited.

Question: *You mean even one percent interest is prohibited?*

Yes. I find it Unclean. Our Prophet said, 'Blood feuds, fornication and interest are beneath my feet.' Those who take it and use it lose in the end.

Question: *What if I distribute the interest to others?*

I find it very beneficial. I receive interest from the bank and distribute it to others. Do the same. But I can't give a religious ruling (*fatwa*) on this. They've said that interest is Forbidden. We can't pass a ruling that it's Allowed.

If people buy a book with money, they'll read it. If they don't buy it with money, they won't read it.

If you go downstairs, if you say: 'I want to go to [another neighborhood], I don't have any money,' maybe one car, one taxi out of a hundred will take you there, if that. So everything is with money.

Just one word to you: (1) Don't fool, don't be fooled. If we fool, we'll *definitely* be fooled, no matter how clever we are. (2) Don't deliver on credit. (3) You bought it for five, you're going to sell it for six, the customer is offering four – sell it, don't miss out. Another will offer eight, you'll make up for it.

(1) Fire those who aren't useful. Increase the salary a little bit of those who work. (2) Don't fool, don't be fooled.

[Someone had just opened a new business.] Tell him he shouldn't leave the money to anybody. He shouldn't leave the cash register to anyone. If he sees a poor person looking around, let him call him/her over immediately: 'Friend, I know you.' Let him wrap up something and give it to him/her. If he does it like that, his earnings will multiply a thousandfold.

Sell the house, sell the lot, but don't pay off debts with that. Make that money your capital, use it, use what you earn from it to pay off debts. This, what's gone [what you've lost], is a slap in the face.

This world can feed fifty billion. If they do what we tell them, it's enough for fifty or sixty billion.

This world can feed twenty billion. It can even feed a hundred billion, as long as there's sound judgment. Do you know what I rely on in this? 'I give them their sustenance before I create them.' Yes, We widen the globe. Just by looking, half the world is empty, brother. Half of Turkey is empty. Nobody's there. No villages, no cities. There are five billion, this house, this globe can carry another hundred billion.

They went to Australia, they ruined that, too. Wherever man goes, he ruins it.

[A hotel merchant: 'My father used to say that fifteen percent net real profits[1] are Allowed, a greater margin is Forbidden.'] True. The meaning of a Saying.

Question: *Can black (laundered) money be borrowed?*

Yes. How it's earned is not important. Because *you* didn't earn it that way.

Christianity

There is no god but God, Jesus is the Prophet of God.
There is no god but God, Jesus is the Apostle of God.
There is no god but God, Jesus is the Messenger of God.

There are two billion Christians. They don't say 'There is no god but God, Muhammad is the Prophet of God,' but they've taken all of the

---

1. Corrected for inflation.

Quran from us, they're practicing it on the good side. Christendom doesn't abandon *'In the name of God, the Compassionate, the Merciful.'* They always say it in their own languages.

In terms of cleanliness, industriousness, honesty, Europe owes a lot to the House of Islam. In general, Christendom took from Islam, both materially and spiritually [especially in the late Middle Ages]. Christendom owes a lot to the Quran. There are several European professors who are saying this.

Comment: *But they're more advanced.*

Yes, they've taken it and taken it further. Also, they've applied it.

The House of Islam is very lazy now. We're very indolent. Non-Muslims are lazy in spirituality, but very hardworking in physical matters.

We cross ourselves too, but we cross ourselves with 'There is no god but God, Muhammad is the Prophet of God.' [Here he demonstrates an esoteric Sufi meditation technique.]

(Regarding the Eucharist:)

How can one eat the flesh and drink the blood of one's beloved?

Prayers (supplication)

Everything isn't accomplished by prayer, work is needed too. How can anything happen by praying? Things come about by working for them. One has to struggle. Work first, pray afterwards. I first place the aspirin in my mouth, and then pray for a cure. First a doctor, medication, then prayer. It'll pass without doctor or medicine with prayer, too, but you'll pass from yourself. Our Prophet did it, but he was the Prophet. First a doctor, medicine, then prayer. Tell this to everyone. First one needs work, a doctor, technology, medicine. If everything could be accomplished by prayer, there would be no need for technology, medicine and so on. If things could be done by prayer, God wouldn't have created doctors. What need would there be for them? Things don't end with 'God willing.'

One shouldn't seek the solutions provided by medicine in religion. They were taking a patient to and fro, from hodja to hodja. I said: 'This is a matter for medicine, for a doctor. What can a hodja do?'

If prayer was enough, our Prophet would have accomplished everything from where he sat in his house. What need would there have been for those battles and other things? Prayer is dependent on work. The Prophet is the greatest, he worked the hardest. You, too, work ceaselessly. Many languish, few work. The poor thing has come all the way from America, thinking that prayers will solve everything.

Mecca is high and clean. Medina was marshland. The Emigrants became ill. They said to our Prophet, 'Pray for us with your blessed mouth.' He said, 'Bring picks and shovels tomorrow.' The swamps were dried up. 'Now I'll pray,' he said. First take precautions, then pray.

Mehmet, who was praying in Kurdish, asked my Master, 'I wonder if God knows Kurdish?' 'Whichever language you know, pray in that language. God knows every language,' he said, 'don't worry.'

If everyone got everything they wanted immediately, it wouldn't do. Who would pray to God? Nobody would. Because what one wants is realized instantly.

Women

Man and woman are equal, only men have the edge in physical strength and intelligence. Before Islam, they used women like a piece of throwaway cloth, like a rag. Our Prophet exalted woman and gave her rights. He valued her highly, almost more than man. 'Paradise is beneath the feet of mothers.' He gave women's rights fourteen hundred years ago.

You women are of very high worth. You are blessed. Know your own worth. Women have been created very sacred. There are thousands of female saints. It is women who have given birth to all the prophets and saints. Yes, women are sacred!

Aisha taught the Quran to the Community after the Prophet. [The following applies to all other women:] From my viewpoint, a woman cannot be a spiritual teacher to men. She can be and do everything else.

Question: *What do you think about women who work?*

My child, what should she do? She has to win bread, so she works. Now what you say is true. The man should earn, whether little or much, and the woman should stay at home and look after her children. But the time for this is past. Now is a different time.

Question: *(A lady:) I'm not working. Should I work?*

It would be very good if you did. God and His Prophet love those who work. Find a job that's appropriate for you.

[To a girl:] Why don't you work?
 'My father won't let me.'
 Wrong, very wrong. Find a job and work.
 [To the girl's father, concerning her mother:] Find a job for her, too.

The Prophet has tolerance for everything. *Everything*. But he doesn't tolerate fornication, filthy things like that. He cuts it off immediately.

Leavening of humanity

One thousand four hundred and seventeen years ago,[2] the Prophet of God was nicely planting seedlings in hardened hearts. Those who lived then couldn't eat fruit, he was trying to make them eat. Now they eat sweetly. The Quran will continue until Doomsday, this is how it will continue.

At that time, fourteen hundred years ago, they couldn't eat. Now let's eat with flavor. Now we can eat. That day, he was throwing the Verses you read on rock. He was watering so they could grow. But today, praise God, they bear fruit.

We enjoy the fruits of others' labors, without staying sleepless at night, without doing the Ascension.[3] The things he suffered to do the Ascension. The things that happened.

Superstition

(*Truly great Sufis like the Master and the Grand Saint have nothing to do with amulets. Belief in their efficacy is a matter of vulgar folklore. To those who requested such things of him, the Master used to say: 'I don't know*

---

2. Statement made in 1997.
3. See below, The Prophet/The meaning of the Ascension.

such things, they're not my specialty. Go to someone else if you want to.' The Master's general views on superstitious activities were as follows:)

Knowledge of magic, casting spells, writing amulets and so on are again very pervasive. Mediumship (channeling), moving tables, moving teacups and such are all within the knowledge of magic. Fortune-telling and so forth all have their source in the past. They've started again, let's see what they will do. But the Quran does not allow any of them, it bans them all, they're all empty. Our Prophet prohibited all of these – fortune-telling, mediumship, spiritualism, writing amulets – right from that very day.

Try it yourself

For one week, don't mention God's name at all. And for one week, check out the Naming [recite *In the Name of God, the Compassionate, the Merciful*]. Whichever week passes more auspiciously, advance on that. Continue for a week with the Naming and for another week without it. Whichever week you like better, continue on that.[4]

For every task – children entering school, illness and so on – repeat the Naming a hundred times. And also pray for [the success of] that task.

It is stated in a Saying: 'If a person going to bed enters the bed right foot first, turns onto his right side, places his hand like this, recites the Throne Verse [2:255] three times, goes to sleep while repeating the Naming, gets up in the morning right foot first' – when leaving, open the door with your right hand, [extend it] as if they're giving a small flag into your right hand, step out with your right foot. Live like this for a day, for a week. Next, do the opposite. Then, whichever you find more beneficial, continue with that. One always experiences an accident or mishap. If nothing happens, one [still] doesn't have peace of mind. The other one is protected by angels until evening.

---

4. This is the empirical or experimental method, one of the three foundations of modern science (together with reason and inspiration). This is why Sufism is held to be a science, and why one can speak of 'the spiritual sciences.'

II

The Inward Path: Sufism

Sufism

> If stone touches hand
> The hand is glad
> If hand touches stone
> The stone becomes amber[1]

Introduction to Sufism

You can't enter Sufism without the Divine Law. You'll get drowned in the sea. You'll become birdseed for birds. If you revert to the Divine Law at once, you'll be saved from being drowned.

First lay the foundation with [exoteric] knowledge, then pass on to Sufism. Right now, the building can't stand it. Don't be subject to Sufism, hold the light, the lantern, of Sufism. Enter Sufism through the Five Pillars of Islam and the Six Pillars of Faith. That is, enter it with the Divine Law. If you don't enter it that way, you'll go straight to the bottom of the sea. You'll be fodder for fish. You'll think, 'I'm doing a good thing.' No, that's not the case.

Getting drowned in a glass of water – Sufism isn't that. There's everything, even Hidden Knowledge, in it. Sufism is a sun. Our Prophet is a sun. The Quran is a sun.

Respect, reverence – these are the essence of Sufism. When your mother gets mad at you, you're going to embrace your father. When your father gets angry, you're going to embrace your brothers and sisters. But if you get angry at this one and get mad at the other, you can do neither the Divine Law nor Sufism.

If you seek out the good, the good will come and find you. In order to learn esoteric science, one has to practice the exoteric science of Muhammadanhood. Then, someone will pop out from here or there and grab your ear: 'Did you wish for the esoteric?' Practice Muhammadanhood to the letter, and the possessor of esoteric knowledge will [find you, will] come and grab you by the ear.

I'm trying to do everything the Muhammadan way, but everyone runs away. Don't deviate a hairbreadth from the Divine Law. Sufism and philosophy continued, entered some dead-ends, exploded and stopped there. But the Divine Law stands tall and continues after more than fourteen hundred years. Become real with the Real, attain Reality, the

---

1. Hand: Teacher, Stone: Seeker, Amber: Gold.

Divine Law is still necessary. Even there, even at the stage of Reality, it has to be maintained. It shouldn't be distorted, or they'll throw stones at you. You'll have corrupted others, *aha!* So don't abandon the Divine Law.

Having two wings

[Human beings are in basically] three states. The first shakes off the dust, it's gold. The second dusts it off, it's silver. The third, that's us/me/you, things are tough. One works to make it silver, and then gold.

Knowledge comes first. If one finds Sufism with [exoteric] knowledge, one will be Two-Winged. If one finds Sufism without knowledge, that's One-Winged. The highest scholar, if he can't find Sufism, he's also One-Winged.

The blind men and the elephant

A hodja is instructing the blind. Every day, he's describing something different. Then one day, he describes an elephant. He takes them to the zoo on a Sunday. One of the blind men feels the ear of the elephant, he says, 'It could be a nice pillow.' Another feels its trunk, he says 'It's a nice hose.' Another feels its legs, 'Four columns.' Another feels its tail, 'A nice broom.' 'Yes,' he says, 'your words are all true, they're all a single life form.'[2] Each chooses a preference according to his opinion.

We're the same, we enter a discourse. All these are true, they're circling around it. 'Can we stick a name on it?'

The chicks and ducklings

Another man is raising chickens by a lake. One day, as he's taking five eggs, he replaces them with five duck eggs, they're fifteen again. The time comes, chicks and ducklings emerge from the eggs.

One day they go to the shore of the lake. The ducklings jump into the water. The mother hen is agitated, 'My babies are going to die!' Its owner is amused.

---

2. A variant of Rumi's famous tale (*Mathnawi*, III, 1259–69).

The greatest scholar or Quran-memorizer is hesitant when it comes to the Divine Names. They can't go in the water. The 'duck,' the Sufi, can both go in the water and wander on land. He's Two-Winged. The scholars, the pious are Single-Winged. And they can't find a common ground. The Sufi, the esoteric scientist, accepts the exoteric. The exoteric scientist can't accept the esoteric. But if one passes beyond them both, Hidden Knowledge is there, they both disappear.

Wisdom

One can be *in* wisdom, but one cannot be the *owner* of wisdom.

There are those who are in wisdom. Elementary school, middle school, high school, it's very difficult to go to college now. In college, one slowly begins to understand. When the school of Gnosis ends, wisdom begins. Some things can be explained in Gnosis, too, but when wisdom begins, there tongues fall silent. That's why books stop there. The Grand Saint Abdul Qadir Gilani wrote many books, too, but none of them crosses the line. He says 'Here be wisdom' when he comes to that subject, and leaves it at that.

Balance

You go to a grocer, you buy two or three kilos of rice, you set down the money. The grocer has three or four sacks of rice, but when he's measuring it, you both keep your eyes on the scales. You wouldn't be reconciled to a violation of rights. In the same way, I tell those who come to me, 'The rights of neither the physical nor the spiritual should be violated.' Neither one nor the other. One side of me is physical, my other side is spiritual. I don't want one to exceed the other. I want them to progress together.

Read my mind

One day a lady came to me. We began to talk. 'Where are you from, who are you?' I asked. 'You should know!' she said. 'What does that mean?' I asked. She said, 'We've heard about you, you're supposed to know everything. My friends told me, "Ahmet Efendi knows everything."'

I asked her, 'What's your profession?' She said, 'I'm a doctor.' I asked, 'Have you ever examined patients?' 'I examine five, ten, twenty patients a day. I work under a professor, I examine them.'

'What do you say to the patients?' I asked. 'Do you tell them anything?' 'I first ask them about their father, mother, birthplace and gender,' she said. 'Then I ask, "What's ailing you?" Then I tell them' – a shot if necessary, hospitalization if that's necessary and so on.

I said, 'See? You yourself have answered the question you asked me. Tell me what your illness is. Tell me what's on your mind so I can answer it. I don't know anything of that sort.' 'Okay,' she said. 'Thanks, I've learned what I came for.' 'Goodbye,' I said.

The garbage collectors

One day I was coming home, at the bus-stop I saw two young men. They had leaned their brooms against the wall and were having a sweet discussion: 'If I were prime minister, I'd do this, I'd do that.'

I said, 'Children, don't be offended. Just sweep this street, do your job, that's enough for you.' I walked away and came over.

They say, 'If a person doesn't have [any] sins [but just] gossips about the government, that's enough for him [as a sin].' 'One who knows and one who doesn't know – how can they be the same?' [39:9]. Two garbage collectors don't approve of the prime minister! These things are like that, both physically and spiritually.

Enlightened by beans

God made human beings superior to all creatures, but at the same time He left man face to face with a very great trial. A human being undergoes that test every instant, at every breath. If God hadn't made man superior, man would have become an angel, or an animal or a plant. He placed that test inside man. At every instant, man is with his self. If he obeys the self, he fails the exam.

A little bit of fire will burn down everything. But when you throw it in water, that fire is extinguished. Let's throw the devil and our ego in water. They're all fire, let's extinguish them. That water is God.

These talks are resolved by thinking, by meditation (*tafakkur*). What does God say: 'Meditate for an hour, it's like worshiping for a year.' A Tradition of the Prophet: 'One hour's meditation is better than a thousand hours of worship.' Just as you smell when you eat garlic, the smell of egotism still comes if one performs Prayer for a thousand hours.

One day, a disciple went to a master. He said, 'Master, enlighten me. I want to surrender to you, but I have many errors. One, I tell many lies. Two, I steal a lot. Three, I harm human beings and don't benefit them. Would you still accept me?' The teacher said, 'The good are good already, you're the one I need: Do you know *I believe in God?*' 'I have faith in God.' He asked, 'How are you with His commandments? *And His angels.* Have you adopted the morality of angels? *And His prophets?*' 'I love His Prophet, I do a tenth of His commandments.' '*And His Books.* The commandments in His Book?' 'I do what I see fit, I ignore what I don't.'

The master said, 'Fix yourself and come back.' Two months passed, the disciple came back. 'Master, I did as much as I could.' The master tells his servant: 'Bring me a handful of dry beans.' When he brings it, he gives it to the student. 'Throw one out of your pocket every day, and with each one throw away an immoral habit.' One or two months later he comes back, 'Master, I did it.' The Master says: 'You've become a human being. Go.'

He enlightened him with beans. He used to say, 'A hodja made me a Muslim with beans.'

We love, we listen, we want, but we don't throw away one bean. The furniture at home – you throw away what you don't need and keep what you need. If you throw away God's commandments, how are you going to walk the path to God?

The secret of the fragrance

Fifty or fifty-five years ago, a young preacher came to Ankara. A story he told is still in my mind.

There was a man in Damascus, he went to the Bayjan public baths. Now there wasn't soap in those days, they used to rub clay on their skin to clean themselves. This young man, too, begins to rub clay on himself. A wonderful fragrance comes from the clay.

The youth asks the clay: 'Where did you get this wonderful scent from?' The clay answers in the language of its state: 'This fragrance doesn't belong to me. I was on such-and-such a hilltop, human beings come and take us from there to use us for cleaning up. A saint sat and rested under a tree for ten minutes, his smell permeated me. That's where they took me from. And what about you?'

The youth says, 'In that case, I would be ashamed to rub you on myself.' He poured some water on himself and came out. He was crying as he went along. Someone asks why, he tells him. It came down to us.

[Those who come in contact with a Perfect Human] all bear that fragrance. When someone comes who has seen and talked to the masters, after they talk a little bit I feel as though I'm talking to the Master. Tell everyone that I took the fragrance from there (Malatya).

The best thing

You know what is the truest? To live as a human being, to live as a Muhammadan. And then? Together with Prayer, to practice a little asceticism on one's self. Not to take one's self so seriously. The Two Doors of Defilement. To shut the doors of unclean gain and unclean sex. You're drinking tea, you know it's unclean, say: 'I'm sick, I can't drink it.' If they insist, drink the tea but pay for it yourself. [Or else, donate its worth to the poor or to charity.]

The basis is unclean sex. If the most beautiful girl in the world were to come and sit in your lap, to take refuge in God without hurting her feelings. That's the basis. 'You're my sister,' send her off without beating or swearing. If you recited a thousand Invocations, what good would it do if you viewed another lady with lust? If you said ten thousand, what good would it do if you violated someone's rights? It boils down to the two points I mentioned.

If that's in place, that fragrance begins to come from you. Otherwise it's all in vain. These are difficult matters. It's not like being a village headman. All saints became saints after they passed these two points. Do it yourselves, and I'll pin the promotion to sainthood on you. Don't stray from the Divine Law. Don't deviate from Muhammadanhood. You can go to any Invocation gathering you want. Don't dive into Sufism. It's sweet, but there's poison in it, you'll die. There are hundreds of would-be masters in Ankara. *I bear witness that there is no god but God, and I bear witness that Muhammad is His servant and Messenger.* This subdues the ego, recite it a hundred times (a day) if you're unable to cope.

A Sacred Saying states: 'I did not fit anywhere except in the Heart of My faithful servant.' He says, 'the Heart of one servant,' He doesn't say 'all.' Yunus Emre says, 'You can't find the Beloved without giving up your life.'[3] How can you have the first without the second? One has to

---

3. Compare Matthew 16:25 and corresponding verses in the other Gospels.

give up one or the other. If you want to do both, it'll work only so far. But for anyone who's *serious*, one has to give up the world.

Stages in Sufism

[One classification of stages in Sufism is] the Knowledge of Certainty, the Eye of Certainty and the Truth of Certainty.[4]

The Eye (or Sight) of Certainty manifests itself at the fourth level of selfhood: the Tranquil Self. 1. The Base Self, 2. the Critical Self, 3. the Inspired Self – at the level of 4. the Tranquil (Serene) Self, the Sight of Certainty comes close like this.

The level of Absolute Unity (*Ahadiyya*) is the third level of faith [and roughly corresponds to the Truth of Certainty]. To pass from duality to the One. That's the last step, at the seventh station [of selfhood]. It's the station of Abraham.

One who is at the stage of Unity can give instruction to all the Twelve Sufi Orders. At that stage, you can't pick a rose, you can't step on an ant. You sit here and talk to your friend in Istanbul, in America, in Erzurum. Television! They [scientists] took all these inventions from man [from latent human potentials which are realized in the Perfect Human Being].

A drop in the sea

A man went to the seashore, he filled a bottle with seawater and brought it. He asked, 'Is what's in this bottle the sea, or not?' Now we are not – perish the thought – God. But neither are we entirely separated from God. We're a drop from the sea.

Niyazi Misri said: 'From every particle comes the call: "*I am the Real.*"' All particles are from the Real, but the Real isn't from these particles. God exists in each particle, but each particle is not God. Just as something is in the sun, but it is not the sun. Okay, He's in everything, He's in this, He's in that. But let's do our duty, let's not be He.

Question: *Do you like X's ideas? And why?*

---

4. The Knowledge, Eye and Truth of Certainty are mentioned in verses 102:5, 102:7, and 56:95 and 69:51, respectively (in a different context).

No, because he calls everything 'God.'

The essence of Sufism is the meaning of the Verse, 'I'm closer to you than your jugular vein' [50:16]. I'm closer to you than your thought. But then some say, 'If God is so close to me, then I'm God and God is me.' Heaven forbid, don't say that. Be very careful, don't say 'I'm God.' Now if you asked me, 'Ahmet Efendi, are you the sun?' and if I said, 'I am,' I would be lying. I'm not the sun – however, I *benefit* from the sun.

During the Ascension, God said to the Prophet: 'Wish for your heart's desire, and it is yours.' He answered, 'You are my Lord and I am Your servant. I take pride in being a servant. What more can I want, when You've already made me Your servant?'

Many people with superior intelligence read Niyazi Misri, they think they've become Niyazi, they don't do any of the things Niyazi did. Read Niyazi, but be careful, don't say: 'I'm Niyazi.' Don't say, 'I'm in that space.'

After reading Niyazi's *Diwan*, many friends abandoned the Divine Law, they abandoned Prayer, they abandoned Fasting. 'I'm finished with Prayer.' Repent! That's why I lay the greatest emphasis on studying the Divine Law. Accept it together with the Divine Law. Gilani's *Divine Bestowal* (*Fath ar-Rabbani*) is heavy going, it's as heavy as Niyazi's *Diwan*. Kiss the place where your forehead touches the Prayer-mat, shed a tear, don't fall under that influence. Bring me to your mind and get out of that space.

Ali's saying: 'I'm the dot under the Arabic letter *B*,' that's one, and Niyazi's *Diwan*, that's the other, these two cause many people to end up with zero on the bottom line. He hears that, he says, 'I'm Ali.' He reads Niyazi, he says 'I'm Niyazi.' Until you've become a dot, don't say 'I'm Ali.' Say, 'I'm going to become a dot like Ali, I'm going to become like Niyazi.'

The nightingale is in love with the rose, the crow is in love with filth, with scum. Don't hold these two the same. Speak carefully and understand fully during discussions. Don't equate the nightingale and the crow.

There are thousands of friends, they all slipped at this point. Some say, 'I'm Rumi,' others say 'I'm Niyazi.' If you claim: 'I'm the president,' 'I'm the prime minister,' pretty soon you'll be found out. Some were swept away by fame, others became absorbed in Sufism. Just in Ankara, I myself know fifty masters like that who went astray. It won't do without the Divine Law. There's a Quran. There are the Prophet's Sayings. In everything, one should act according to them.

[Ibn 'Arabi's doctrine on the Unity of Being:] Is this hand yours? Is this foot yours? But they're all one body. That's where he's going.

Now top scientists in the West are working on these matters. They're looking for that core. What is the essence of the universe?

There's a father, he's very wealthy, his children can't judge the worth of his legacy when he dies, they squander it and go bankrupt in the end. We, too, can't judge the worth of this religion because we inherited it. But the West knows its worth and uses it in various ways.

I'm not the sun, I'm *in* the sun

The sun is taken as an example on these points. If America said, 'The sun belongs to us,' they'd be a laughing stock. If the World of Islam said, 'The sun belongs to us,' they'd be a laughing stock. The sun is general. It shines on the flower, it shines on the dung. But are these the sun? No!

There was a lady, an English teacher, who thought she was at the *I-am-the-Real* stage, at the 'Fusion-of-the-Fusion' [i.e., highest] station. She came here again one day, we're talking, she's saying things of this sort. 'You,' I said, 'walk around through the kitchen, go out on the balcony, stay there a while, then come back.' 'Okay,' she said, she went out through there and stayed in the sun, then she came back when I tapped on the window from inside.

'What did you understand?' I asked. 'I went out,' she said.

'You were in the sun all that while.' 'Yes,' she said.

'Are you the sun?' I asked. 'No,' she said, 'how can I be the sun?' 'But you *were* in the sun, weren't you?' 'Yes, I was.' 'Are *you* the sun?' 'No.'

'Well then, what is all this?' I asked. 'I don't want to offend you with this,' I said, 'I want to train you.' She took offense and didn't come for three months. But where's she going to go, poor thing, she came back again.

Tell the Sufis: 'You're in the sun, but you're not the sun.' I've checkmated many Sufis that way.

The fish in the sea

There's a Sufic saying: 'You're a fish, you're in water, you can't swallow the water. You're in Attainment, you're looking for Attainment.' You're a child, that is. They're in water, they're searching for water. They're in the middle of the water, they can't quench their thirst. And some live all their lives in a field without ever knowing about the sea. Don't be a fish, be the sea. If it comes from the inside, God will make them find it. If it doesn't come from the inside, they couldn't find it if they had ten addresses. It's been said: 'Become, become! Wherever you are, still, become.' We can't eat it, brother, we can't eat it.

Miscellaneous

- From the Sufic viewpoint, they've called Gabriel 'Intelligence,' Michael 'Eye,' Israfil 'Ear,' and Azra'il 'tongue.' These are all related to the head.

- 'He hears the tread of the black ant seven levels beneath the earth.' The ant is the one who hears! [God hears through the ant's hearing.] What wonders these are, sir.

- Imitation won't do, Stabilization is necessary. Imitation is a paint, it can be erased, it can be removed. Stabilization is a permanent paint. We all drink from the same cup, the same glass. May God not separate us from this Muhammadan sun, and may He bestow it on those who don't have it, too. There's an ode that says:

    Wake up, skull, wake up
    Come and be painted in our color
    Wake up, heedless one, wake up
    If you don't like us, be painted in the Muhammadan color.

- The driver and the watchmaker are the professions closest to Sufism. Your driver is beside you, but you don't listen.

- The wise say, 'Hand to hand, that hand to God.' So there's neither you nor me, what there *is* is God.

- The 'Forty' [the period of asceticism and seclusion] is forty days. With my Master's permission, I've reduced that to two days.

The beginning

A new life is starting for you. That's what Ibrahim Hakki of Erzurum says: 'Forget the past, embrace the future.' Climb slowly. Climb the first step.

The three prerequisites

I ask those who come to me: 'How do you stand as regards a spouse, a job and faith?' To be dependent on no one. 'When these three are present,' I say, 'you can go on the Path. You can travel the course.'

A person has faith, his job is fine, but his relationship with his spouse is impaired. Then he still can't travel the Path. This is danger, great danger. He's fine with his faith and spouse, but his financial situation is bad – again, it won't work. It has to be there. But if this tripod is in place, that person can enter the Path. Because he has peace of mind. There's nothing to disturb his peace. May God bestow it on us all.

Be careful about these three fronts. I tell it to everyone. In time there'll be those who apply to you, tell them the same thing. 'How are you with faith? Can you fulfill God's commandments?' 'Yes.' 'How are you with your spouse?' 'Fine.' 'And with your job?' 'That's okay, too.' Tell them: 'Come to my side.' 'Everything's fine, but not with my spouse.' 'Put that in order, then come.' Spouse and faith are in order, but business is bad: 'Find yourself a job, earn a bite to eat, then come.' Three phases – this is important, this. No matter which one is missing, a person can't enter the Path. He can't travel the course.

With one's faith, job and spouse. When these three come together, *aah*, a person can fly. One can fly, physically and spiritually. If you have all three, you're in Paradise, you're in an earthly villa of Paradise, don't disturb this peace.

The three enemies, the three friends

We're very comfortable. God has created everything in its proper place. But man has three enemies and three friends. What are the three enemies? The eye, the ear, the tongue. These are very great enemies. But if we make friends out of them, they become very good friends. They become good friends in every respect, in work, in living. These three friends take everything in hand. And this is explained only in the Four Books: the Torah, the Psalms, the Gospel and the Quran. These books teach how to make friends with these three enemies. Don't forget these words of Grandpa.

What drives humanity to a frenzy, especially in youth after puberty, are this enemy – the eye – and this enemy – the ear. There are no others. The ages fifteen to thirty are the most dangerous. But if we make these our friends with the aid of that commandment, the whole universe is under their command. They know being, good and evil. The eye strays to one side, it says 'Stop.' The ear hears something wrong, it says, 'I didn't hear that.' Once these two, the eye and the ear, are mastered, the tongue calms down.

God says: 'Because your tongue is so blessed, so worthy, I placed it behind two fortress battlements.' See, the teeth look like battlements. And second, the lips. 'I placed it within two great fortress battlements so that it won't be ill-tempered, won't speak ill.'

You know and everyone knows that the error of the eye and the error of the ear are blamed on the tongue. If our tongue stays put, we find solace. If our eye stops, our tongue stops. But the tongue is within two fortresses. This translator – the eye – and this translator – the ear – tear down these two fortress battlements – teeth and lips – and let the tongue out. When these eyes and these ears are reformed, when they come under the rule of sound judgment, this tongue, too, finds peace. The three houses unite under the commandment of God. Then, someone swears, one tolerates, someone strikes, one tolerates, because it's all in vain. One prepares oneself accordingly. Yes, if we all make friends of those three enemies, it is the essence of Unification, it is the essence of being human. If one makes friends with these three organs, everywhere is good. But if the three organs are enemies like this, everything is bad. Don't forget this. Try to be friends.

The most mature state of humanity, Rumi and Hajji Bayram Wali are among our saints, it's after they become friends with these three organs that they call them saints, call them enlightened. They become saints after you bring those three organs under the rule of the intellect and the spirit. Starting from childhood, whenever you're able to accomplish it, make friends with these three, then you become a Friend of God. And in order to be friends with these three organs, this morality is necessary.

Practice makes perfect

Read a lot. And practice a bit. Don't read useless books. Practice, practice. Not reading, but practice. Practice is necessary in any case. If there is practice, one will succeed.

Suppose I sent you to work with a jeweler. If I came two days later and you told me, 'Uncle Ahmet, I've become a jeweler,' is that possible? But you go, a week later you come back and say, 'I'm a jeweler.' 'How?' 'Well, I'm working at a jewelry shop.'

How many years do you have to serve in order to comprehend that? At least five years. A jeweler, what we all know – a craft, that is, a craft. An ironsmith, a carpenter, these are all crafts to be learned. But brother, [you've gone] from one place to another, you haven't come across a jeweler, you haven't worked under one, you haven't mastered the craft – this won't do. One has to work somewhere, one has to learn the craft.

Niyazi Misri says, 'Take a step and come to the school of wisdom.' Prayer, Fasting, the Pilgrimage, the Alms-tax are the commandments of God in any case. But when you look at a bird, a tree, to extract meaning from these, to be able to interpret [read the signs] – that is wisdom.[1] We're trying to earn the Hereafter with Fasting, with Prayer. This is like trying to earn a hundred million with a lottery ticket worth fifty Liras. Can one really win?

To believe with faith. *I bear witness that there is no deity but God, and I bear witness that Muhammad is His servant and Messenger.* The Prophet of God says, 'I am but God's servant and Messenger.' Then, in the Word of Unification, *There is no god but God, Muhammad is His Messenger.* May God grant us constancy, may He grant his [the Prophet's] intercession. Beyond that, recite whatever you recite, invoke whatever you invoke, but don't abandon Prayer. Invocation, worship, obedience, they're all within Prayer.

---

1. This means that when you see a cloud in the sky, for example, you do not know why it is there or what its meaning is, what it signifies. But a sage knows. Within the flow of the universe at any moment in spacetime, there are local and global indicators which point to the general direction of flow. These signs may be correctly read and interpreted by those who are able to do so.

You're the traveler

Now look: You came and applied, you said: 'Uncle Ahmet, I'm going to buy a car.' You pay the money, we put it in the bank, you get in the car, the brakes are yours, now *move!* You own it, you bought it with your money. But the brakes and all belong to you, if you go and hit a rock, if you run over a man, what can I do?

They long for it, they take the book, they read it, they can't control the brakes, the brakes of the Base Self.

[To a person who says 'I've come to be filled,' but doesn't listen to advice:]

This cup of tea is full to the brim. If you put any more in it, it can't take it. It has to be emptied a little bit so that we can put in more. Now the topic is about knowledge. You're full. Give a little to make room.

Learn and teach. That's the first [revealed] page of the Glorious Quran. And it's the situation of the Quran now, too. It doesn't give unless you give.

Here's an example. You're going on the road in a bus. There's a hill, then another hill, then a hill after that. Spiritual fields are inexhaustible. They continue to unfold.

God in search of man

Do we seek God, or does God seek us? While we seek Him, He embraces us, otherwise we can't do it. He seeks me, what more need I seek? But no. If you prayed and blew upon a bottle of raki[2] for fifty days, it's still raki. These people are like that. I pity them. They've fallen into a zone of darkness, and only there do they travel. They're used to tea, I say 'Here's milk, it's beneficial,' they don't give up tea.

It happens by being trained gradually. If you fed lamb chops to a baby it would die, if you gave it a fruit it would die. It's used to milk. God says, 'Eat little, drink little, sleep little, talk little. Invoke God often.' Humanity does the opposite of this. They eat, drink, expend through the two orifices and then: 'We're Muslims.' Thank God you're Muslims! You do whatever you desire.

---

2. Ouzo, schnapps. The blowing is intended to transfer the spiritual power generated by prayer to a recipient.

I'm thinking of gold. Out of a ton of ore, at most a few grams of gold are obtained. It is melted in fire, then [refined] again. Finally, it becomes pure gold.

Another example: let's be clean. You dress a child of six or seven in an outfit you like. The child likes it, too. A week, ten days pass, there's another outfit you like, you want the child to put it on, but because she's become accustomed to what she's wearing, she says, 'Mommy, don't put it on me,' and cries.

For sixty years, I've been wanting to dress everyone in new clothing. Everyone says, 'Oh, don't touch what's on me, don't take it off.' The Base Self. Let's put on new clothing. The new outfit is, well, the Five Daily Prayers as He's ordered, the Five Pillars of Islam, living according to Muhammadan ethics. Let's change the apparel and depart that way. With a clean suit, with a Muhammadan morality, that is. Let's part with our Base Self, for heaven's sake! They'll be questioning you about these later on. Let's all leave the clothing of the Base Self and put on Muhammadan clothing.

Now, you left this place, your foot slipped, you fell in the mud. What are you going to do? You're going to get out of there, go home, clean your clothes and take a bath yourself. You've fallen, but you're not going to stay there. As long as we're on the Path.

A child fell into the mud with his holiday clothes. His parents fussed over him. He said, 'Mom, Dad, look at yourselves. My mom will wash it, it'll be clean. But how are you and Mom going to cleanse your dirt? The dirt of the Heart?'

Don't soil this tomb. Don't soil your Heart. These are all meanings of Verse and Saying, but we're talking in the language of states here. We say, 'My God, protect us from the Suffering of the Tomb.' But which tomb? *This* tomb! Not in that cave, in this cave [pointing to his body]. Let's repair *this* cave.

God-ish: the language of the Quran

Question: *We don't understand the meaning of the Quran. Why do we read it from the Arabic?*

Why shouldn't we read it just because we don't understand its meaning? Here's an example for you: a fruit like an apple, an orange, a banana. But we don't know its name. They bring it, we eat it, but we don't know its name. Let's eat that fruit, girl! Let's 'eat' the Quran. Say, 'This fruit is delicious, I eat it even if I don't know its name.'

[The Quran can be read in every language.] Everyone reads the Quran in English, in Arabic. Why shouldn't it be read in Turkish?

Now to read the Quran, one first has to know good Arabic. And then we still don't understand it, we have to go to someone who understands and learn from him.

It has been said: 'The Quran was revealed in Arabic, but its meaning is God-ish.' The Quran is not Arabic. If it had been, every Arab who read it would have become a saint. [So even if you know perfect Arabic, you don't really understand the Quran.] The Quran is Lord-ish (*Rabb*-ic).

If one starts reading the Quran without an Ablution, the Quran will become a newspaper. The Quran won't cease to be the Quran, but a human being will cease to be a Muslim.

The Glorious Quran is our magnet. As long as it remains on our shelves, even if we don't read it, don't worry, we'll survive. Neither rise above the Quran, nor descend below it. Don't deviate from the Quran. Whatever the Prophet says, don't deviate from the Prophet. The first step is the Five Pillars of Islam. No one can go to God without the Prayer. If you perform your Prayer, you can go to God. Trickery will get you nowhere. Study for a hundred years, learn knowledge, the Quran, the Sayings, I'm giving all you will learn in five minutes. Go to a hundred hodjas, read the Quran ten times from cover to cover, go to a hundred masters, go to ten founders of Orders, and study for a hundred years, that's what I'm giving you. Give thanks to God. Give thanks that He has bestowed this universe, this Book, this Prophet.

The first light is the Glorious Quran. They found it with the Quran. The second is knowledge. That light is actually everywhere in the Quran. It was unveiled to Ahmet Yasawi from the Verse, 'We have granted you a clear victory' [48:1]. To another, it can open from elsewhere in the Quran.

Sainthood

The afterworld is Forbidden to worldly people, and this world is Forbidden to otherworldly people. This world and the afterworld are Forbidden to saintly people. You have to give up both, then what remains is the Real.

They are the class that doesn't sleep. When they fall asleep, lose consciousness a little bit, they get up and take a Bodily Ablution instead of an Ablution. Eat, drink, sleep, speak sparingly. The great ones always emphasize this. That's how they succeeded. May God grant it to us, too.

I've tied the level of sainthood to three things: (1) quit Unclean lust, (2) quit Unclean gain, (3) perform the Five Daily Prayers. I've proclaimed this to everyone, I've said: 'Whoever fulfills these, come and I'll pin the promotion to sainthood on you.' Nobody's come yet.

In order to become an influential, cultured, great person, a saint: don't beg from anyone. Work, earn, place in other people's hands yourself.

Run from the Unclean and from fornication as you would from a lion you encountered in a forest. You can escape from the lion's claw with one dash, you can't escape from that. Let's fulfill God's commandments in this tomb, this body, let's be comfortable in the other tomb.

Let's be wealthy. Let's be rich materially and spiritually, not just in this world.

It's difficult until one becomes a saint. It's easy afterwards.

The essence of man

In order to be an 'honored human being' [17:70], one has to speak to honored human beings, to fulfill the duties of the Law to the letter, to clothe oneself in Muhammadan morals, to love the Folk of Truth very much materially and spiritually. To meditate and act with great care in order to find the Truth. It will be incomplete as long as one doesn't practice with body and spirit meticulously from a Book.

A person who has accepted Islam, our Prophet and the Glorious Quran, has put on pure white clothing. You've dressed yourself in that, and then you've stuck red on it, you've pasted black on your pants. Everybody's looking at you, and you think that they're looking because they like what they see. They're looking at your failing. I'm telling this to all of you. To anyone with sense, that's quite enough.

Niyazi Misri came a bit close during his later years, he said:

> *Know that the Essence of Truth is your essence*
> *And His Attributes are all your attributes*
> *Self-knowledge is the treasure of wisdom[1] and your liberation*

'Know that the Essence of the Real is your essence.' A Sacred Saying: 'I did not fit in anyone's Heart but the Heart of the Perfect Faithful.' Nobody says 'Don't do it,' He says, 'Work and become,' for heaven's sake! Work. Yes! Let's work and do it. Don't wait for God from afar, bring Him close.

Now let's be very careful here – God cannot be man and man cannot be God. But He's given a clue: 'I'm closer to you than you, than your jugular vein' – both Verse [50:16] and Saying. Man is close to God and God is close to man. Don't wait for God from afar, train your Heart accordingly. If we were to invite the president here, there's no place to sit. One has to make preparations. 'I wished to be a guest to the moon, the sun, to mountains. But none of them accepted Me. I was only able to enter the Heart of a human being.'[2] I became a guest to man, that is.

---

1. 'Treasure of wisdom' is the Master's addition. It does not exist in Niyazi's original verse.
2. The combination of a Verse and a Sacred Saying: 'We offered the Trust to the heavens and the earth and the mountains, but they shrank from bearing it and were afraid of it' (33:72). 'The heavens and the earth do not contain Me, but the Heart of my faithful servant does.'

Now, here's what occurs to me. Beginning with the Perfect Human, the Prophets: someone who says 'God' – he knows nothing – who says '*Say, He is God*' [112:1], God is his visitor. Niyazi says, 'Who says "*God, He*" is my guest in the Heart.' That is, He's a guest to anyone who utters *There is no god* ... [the Word of Unity] and *I bear witness* ... [the Word of Witnessing].

Two people were invoking. Both are saying *God*, the Name of Majesty.[3] When it was uttered fifty or a hundred times, one of them said: 'Beautiful God, God my life, my spirit, my God who makes me say *God*.' 'What're you doing?' 'If He didn't make me say it, what could I do?' 'You're right.'

Again, Niyazi says:

> *I used to seek a remedy for my worries,*
> *My worries were the remedy*

Worries are the ailment, remedy is the medicine.

> *I used to look right and left to see the visage of the Friend*
> *While I was seeking outside, I realized He was the Beloved*
>   *within my life*[4]

Seek and find, all these are the meanings of Sayings. Everything is exhausted, but God's kindness, bounty, abundance are not exhausted. Carry these words outside, too. Tell them, for heaven's sake! Awaken them too.

A dervish said: 'You are my Creator. And I am the one who proves You with You. I am Your servant.' 'I made the universe a vehicle for man, and I made man a vehicle for Myself.'[5] He created everything, everything is for Himself. Only the Prophet of God understands this point. The saints have caught an atom of this.

This world, this worldly eye doesn't leave us alone, because we're used to it. Whereas there are such wonders, such worlds behind it. To rise, to study, then to come of age at fifteen or twenty, to have a job. To marry, to have children, to be a government employee, craftsman, or worker. Then the children start off, then their children, it just goes on and on like that. We think that's all, we think there's nothing else.

---

3. Allah.
4. Niyazi's original verse reads 'was life within my life.'
5. From *The Treatise on Divine Aid*, God's inspiration to Abdul Qadir Gilani.

Man is so exalted, yet so debased. What is going to become of us? Look at that sacredness, look at that profanity. Niyazi says, if you desire the Real, if you want to learn:

> *If you want the Real, go and look at the image of the human being*
> ...
> *The Essence of the Compassionate has made His image human*[6]

All the universe finds its Attainment in Man. The soil, the stones are in love with the human being. Animals love to watch humans. Especially the snake. I've seen it often. It comes and watches, like this. But because we fear it, we throw a stone and kill it. The snake is the enemy of all animals, and all animals are the enemy of the snake.

'I created Man in the fairest stature' [95:4. But when] Man strikes and kills, he is so ugly. They call one among them a prophet. When he begins to teach, they kill him, saying: 'How dare you interfere with our affairs?'

Attainment, culmination. Shem'i[7] said:

> *Nobody attains the Truth until one is distant from all ...*
> *The king does not enter this palace of the Compassionate,*
>   *till it is magnificent*[8]

You open your hands, you invite God, He'll come and sit – if it's clean. But you invite a president to a hovel. He becomes curious and comes one day, he sees that there's no place to sit even for yourself. Make a place worthy of him so that he may come and sit someday.

The master

Let's eat and drink, let's study, let's get married, okay. But things don't end there.

The road to God passes through the saint. Books and reading won't do it. One needs a guide, a teacher.

---

6. The first and last verses of two consecutive Misri couplets. A reference to the Saying: 'The Compassionate created Man in His own image.' Cf. Genesis, 1:26–7.

7. Commentator on the *Mathnawi*, d. AD 1600.

8. The first and last verses of two consecutive Shem'i couplets. 'The Compassionate' is added by the Master.

You go on a trip, you're going to Konya, you come to a crossroads. You don't know which one leads there. There are animals around, but you can't ask any of them. But if you see a shepherd, a human, you can ask him. If you're the right person and look for the fragrance of a rose, in this land you'll find a rose at once.

A person needs a master at every stage. Even at the highest stage, one needs a master, one still needs Gabriel [the archangel who was the Prophet's guide]. A person's eyes are opened, he attains the stage of Absolute Unity (*Ahadiyya*), a master is necessary even at that point. Indeed, that's the most dangerous point, he's more necessary there than anywhere else. So one should tell everything one sees and experiences to the master.

We need spiritual teachers, good spiritual teachers. The externalist hodjas can't do this.

[A relative of the Master explained:

There was an Ahmet Hodja, he tried to go by the Book, but finally he got mixed up.[9] He delved too deeply into the science of the Quran and went mad. He began to swear at his loved ones and talk to flowers and walls. [The Master] said, 'One has to leave those places behind. What a pity.'

I asked him about this. He inquired, 'Did he study only the Quran, or is he connected to an Order, does he have a master?' He didn't.

'Then his situation is difficult,' he said. 'If they work, everyone can arrive at a certain point. One begins to see the genies, stations are offered him. If he has a master, he will see him through those stages. Otherwise, he'll get entangled with them and won't be able to progress.']

False masters

Now there are lots of masters too, you understand? Some give honey, others give poison. That's like the saying of Imam Ali: 'Falsehood appears as Truth.' Someone finds a master, both he and the master are in danger. Niyazi Misri has a saying: 'Don't give your Heart to every master, they'll make your path difficult.' There was a man who was forced to go to the toilet frequently as a result of wrong training.

---

9. With the genies. On the latter, see the footnote in The prophets/Solomon.

There are many masters, they give you honey, you're poisoned. They give a candy, it's like pepper.

Those without a master

What about those without a master? They know God, they know His Prophet. Those who remain outside, they're all mine. They're all under the ruling of the Word of Unity. So are all masters, and so is the world of Islam. The masters don't have a separate Word. I too learn from the Quran.

Is our Prophet the master of the Faithful, or is he the master [teacher] of the universe? Is the Quran the book of masters or the book of the universe? You wear black, I wear white, these are just names. Nobody can interpret the Quran according to their own lights.

My Master is a very great man. But in everything and every state, he takes our Prophet as the goal. My master, whom I love more than my own life, and I have submitted to the Prophet.

Each one of us is a flower, not the owner of the garden. Be intelligent!

The master is the Quran. Its vehicle is the Sayings. When a person serves his family, acts morally and controls his self, everyone is a master. My philosophy is to do one's worship, love one's country and not to look at the Unclean. Such a person I call a master, and one who does the opposite of these, I call ignorant.

What does Ibrahim Hakki of Erzurum say?

> *Go, search, a wise sage find*
> *If you can't find one, a pious wife find*
> *If you can't find that either, a desert spot find.*

If you can't find a sage, find a pious woman and marry her, she'll train you. If you can't find that either, retire to a deserted place and train yourself.

The requirements for a master

A master is necessary, but there can be no master without the Prophet. To abandon all wrong ways – egotistical, diabolical. To obey the Quran. To obey the Prophet.

Sometimes we tell the Prophet of God, 'As long as there's God, you remain over there.' This is wrong. We should say, 'We're going to find God *with you*.' First we're going to go to him, then we're going to go to God. Yes, we can't go to God without him. We can't go directly to a minister, an usher has to take us to him.

Who is your master? He is Yunus Emre. Who is your true master? He is Muhammad. We're in between. The true master is Muhammad. He is the master [i.e., the teacher] of the universe.

There isn't a master or an Order without the Divine Law. If a master has Muhammadan ethics, don't abandon him. Courtesy, courtesy. Otherwise, say Hello, don't hurt them. Don't cause gossip among the brethren.

Whoever knocks on this door, whoever climbs these stairs is not turned back. If s/he is, s/he is either in deep error or very lazy. We do not abandon those we hold. One of the disciples of Sayyid Taha, a descendant of the Prophet, was led astray by the devil. He left the master's circle. Some years passed. One day, as Sayyid Taha was giving the call for an Obligatory Prayer, he suddenly began to shout: 'Accursed! Begone! Begone!' Later, he explained his action: 'Satan was about to remove the faith of that disciple in his last breath. We do not abandon those who join our discourse even for a little while.'

Prayerless masters[10]

A master must know the Five Pillars of Islam and the Six Pillars of Faith, and should obey them to the letter. Otherwise he will receive a slap.

I know fifty masters who say, 'I've passed beyond Prayer and Fasting, I've become free-and-easy with God. What's the Divine Law? Are you still dealing with Prayer? We've passed beyond all that, we're dealing with Sufism.' Yes, they say that!

The Fusion of the Fusion [*jam' al-jam'*, Unitive Integration] is the last station. They say, 'We're at the station of Fusion of the Fusion.' That is, they fool themselves.

Some Sufis from Erzurum, Izmir and Istanbul say, 'Fasting and Prayer have fallen away from us. The Divine Law is left behind. We've arrived at a station greater than Muhammad's.'

---

10. This term belongs to the Master.

This is a great mistake. A station greater than Muhammad can be none other than God. There they put the shackles on their necks. May God reform our egos. May He never separate us from servanthood. During the Ascension, He said, 'Muhammad, wish, and it shall be yours!' 'My Community.' 'I've given that, what else!' 'I wish for your servanthood.' He's at the highest station. God has given man everything, but you should say, 'Give us as much as Muhammad has allowed.'

According to one account, the angel that became Satan was a teacher to the angels for forty thousand years. He said, 'You created me from fire and Adam from earth, excuse me when I don't prostrate to him.' With the pride of knowledge – listen to this carefully – the pride of knowledge. So God said, 'I was going to appoint someone to a position, you be the devil.'

Similarly, whoever says 'higher than the Prophet,' say 'No.' Above the Prophet, above everything, there is only God. The place for one who says 'higher than him' is the insane asylum. Object to him, hit him on the head. It's no use even if he flies in the air, throw a stone and knock him down. The highest station is the station of prostration, of servanthood. Some say, 'The Divine Law is for beginners, we've left that behind' – let's get out of that station, God forbid.

Don't look down on Prayer. If there is a prophet who came without Prayer, I'll go there too, I'll abandon Prayer at this age. There isn't.

The guidance of the master

Every master wishes to leave a hundred people when he leaves. At least a hundred. Never mind a thousand, a hundred. It's because few people respond to training. Otherwise they're generous, they don't hold back. We give, but for this tea one needs a teacup, a saucer, a spoon. If one doesn't have these, where are we going to put the tea?

The true child of a master is 'The one who comes from our path, not the one who comes from our loins.' They say, 'Hand to hand, hand to God.' [The disciple's hand links with the master's hand and the master's other hand connects to God.]

You, I, anyone. When we're in filth, we hesitate to go to a master – 'How am I going to face him?' You go, he lifts you out of that dirt and cleanses you. *Aha* – when we're *in* filth, we're still going to go. With God's permission, he will clean us. That's how you should act.

In order to plant a flower, one should soften rock, one should make soil of it. Everything cannot be given at once. A parent may want to feed lamb chops to a child. A human being wants to feed something he likes to his companion. But if they were to feed them, it would get stuck in their throats. Slowly, slowly, one has to get them accustomed.

If anything happens, you're going to know it from us. If someone wrongs you, if they act wrongly, you're going to spare them for us. Then it won't bother you at all. As Luqman said to his teacher regarding the bitter melon, 'From your hand, it wouldn't matter if it were the poison of poisons.' For that patience, he had a year more to go, he graduated him right there and then.

[One day, another master came to visit the Master. He told his visitor: 'You're a Noah, too. How many people are on your ship?'

He answered, 'They're all running away. And like Noah's son, some of them say, "I don't need a ship, I'll climb on top of yonder mountain."']

From Adam to Muhammad, whoever enters their religion boards Noah's Ark. May God bestow a Muhammadan Ascension on all of us.

The flying frog

There was a frog, it was jumping this way and that. It saw some pigeons arrive. They bathed and cleansed themselves. 'This is my home,' it said, 'I can't fly like these birds.' It asked the birds, they said, 'We have wings.'

'Let me fly, too,' it said. 'You don't have wings,' they replied. 'Let me give you an idea,' it said. 'How?' 'I'll hold on to a piece of wood with my mouth, two of you take hold of the ends of the stick with your beaks, and you can take me for a ride.' They took it, one of them said, 'Better not speak or say anything.' It looked down, it was pleased.

Then they came upon another flock of birds. 'What's this?' they asked. 'Well, we're taking this frog sightseeing.' 'Why,' they said, 'what a wonderful idea this is! Who thought of it?'

As soon as the frog said '*I!*'...

The responsibilities of the disciple

(Those who expect much – and from whom much is expected – have to work hard. The training of the promising seeker is more strenuous and serious than that of the ordinary follower. Such students must experience every pitfall of

the way, so that they will know exactly how to handle each situation when they themselves become teachers in the future.)

Opening the veils falls to the servant of God. The responsibility belongs to us. The master has eyes and ears [i.e., is human], and so have you. Let's work and become masters ourselves.

A disciple asked a master about finding God. The master said, 'Two-thirds of the Work is to break the desires of the self, one-third is to obey your teacher.' We could spend a third of the day with worldly affairs, a third sleeping and a third with God. We don't busy ourselves with God for even an hour! Even the angels would laugh at us.

A man went to a mosque, did the Prayer with the congregation and began to pray. The Prayer-caller is going to shut the mosque and leave. He waited for half an hour, the man's prayer didn't end. He brought the man's shoes over and dropped them in his open palms. 'You did a five-minute Prayer, you've been supplicating for two hours. What did you give, what do you expect in return? The shoes are enough for you! Get up and leave,' he said.[11]

God says, 'I placed *twelve million* sciences within your cells.' Twelve million, we can't live with even a hundred.

If one has contempt for Prayer, if Prayer is missing, everything is missing. If Prayer is complete, everything is complete.

Not everyone can be a master. You take a twenty-five-kilogram load, you can come up the stairs. When you take on a hundred kilos, you can't carry it. There's a selection between human beings. It doesn't manifest in everybody. There is the sun, but there are all kinds of states under the sun.

A disciple visited his sick master. 'Master, let me die in your place.' 'Why?' 'You're useful to all humankind, I'm useful only to my children and myself.'

A disciple was advancing in the dark, holding a light for his master. When he tried to hold it for himself for an instant, he stumbled and fell. You too, always hold your light to others, even when it's a master.

'I found a friend, evening came quickly' [from a Turkish song]. This is between the master and disciple. Just when one comes to one's senses, one is going to benefit, either the one goes or the other. Those who found have always found by separation. Rumi, Yunus, Shams,

---

11. The Master also used this in another context, ending it with the words: 'Do everything in summary. In brief. The summary.'

Hajji Bektash ... When together, one is too intimate, too familiar. But in separation, burning begins.

One performs the Ascension through the master

We can't do the Ascension, we're going to do our Ascension with the one we love. Two people came, 'Your Ascension is very soon,' I said. 'You're going to do it with your master.'

Someone Attained, 'I found it, I found it!' 'What did you find?' He doesn't say what he found: 'You wouldn't understand.' Someone pulled him aside: 'Son, what did you find?' 'I found from God's master.' 'Go, may it do you good!' he says.

We do neither the Ascension of the Prophet nor the Ascension of the master, but the Ascension of the Base Self.[12] To work. The sport of lovers is Invocation. If we do the sport of the spirit like the sport of the body, we will succeed.

The graft

The self is like a tree. You cut off the branches, the trunk remains. You cut off the trunk, the root remains. I tore out the root and faced the Perfect Human.

Then there's grafting, that's good, too. You make a graft, it penetrates down toward the roots. It transforms. The Muhammadan graft. But grafting is very difficult.

---

12. That is, from our own self to our own self. If one is able to achieve extinction in the master's spirituality (*fana' fi al-shaykh*), one is able to make the Ascension of the master, and if one is able to achieve extinction in the Prophet's spirituality (*fana' fi ar-rasul*), one is able to make the Ascension of the Prophet. The latter is the highest stage of Realization.

The Prophet's Ascension consisted of two legs: first the horizontal (geographical) trip from Mecca to the Farthest Mosque (the Temple of Jerusalem), and then the vertical (spiritual) ascent to God. In the same way, the seeker's journey must consist of two parts: first, a horizontal or ramped transfer to the selfhood of the master (*nafs al-murshid*), followed by a further horizontal or ramp transition to the selfhood of the Prophet (*nafs al-Muhammadi*). Second, once this takeoff point is reached, a vertical spiritual ascent. Before the initial steps are done, the last stage should not even be contemplated, otherwise one makes the ascent with one's little local self. The result is about as different as a puddle is from an ocean.

Someone came, he was a good horticulturist. I asked him, 'Did you ever eat grapes from an oak tree?' 'Not possible.' 'And from a poplar?' 'No.'

I said, 'I did.' 'Where?' 'At Çirmikli, Malatya. They plant a grape vine beside an oak tree, in a year they fuse. You can eat grapes from an oak.' The man was astounded.

Also, they pour earth on a rock. They plant a vine. In two years, it places roots in the rock. So does the fig, so does the olive. Olives grow on rocks, too.

The jeweler's apprentice

Someone came to me one day. He took out a bracelet from his pocket and asked, 'Is this gold or fake?' I said, 'I don't know, ask a goldsmith.' They can't understand you, they'll understand whenever they become goldsmiths. You see that someone doesn't understand, accept his word. As time passes and his understanding increases, he'll come around to your word. Stop being a petty government official.

Here's an example: You can't be a goldsmith. But if we could stay with a goldsmith, withstand his hardships and even his expulsions, and learn the carats a little bit? We can't be a goldsmith. We can't collect that amount of capital. At least the carats. How much to buy it with, how much to sell it for, one has to learn those things. I don't see that in anyone who comes here. They just come here for the scenery.

Open your eyes and your hearts a little bit. It'll be a pity for you. What you see in your dreams is a blessing, so that you should know and understand the goldsmith a little bit. But everything stays the same.

A jeweler told his apprentice, 'I'm going over there, tend to the customers.' A minute or two after he leaves, a customer comes in. 'How much is this, son?' 'I don't know.' 'How about this?' 'I don't know.' But if he attempted to speak as if he knew, things would be ruined.

Gossip and men of religion

Everyone in Ankara complains about their master. I tell them all the same thing, even though I know none of them. 'No human is without error, go and learn,' I say. What do they give that they should receive anything? Whether materially or spiritually. My testament to you all: whoever is a man of religion – for example, a Prayer-leader at a mosque, a master, a Prayer-caller. You know for certain that he is a thief. They come to you and complain about the same. Say, 'No. He is a man of religion. He wouldn't do such a thing.' 'I saw it.' 'You saw wrong.' Cover it.

Why? Because it touches religion, it touches the Prophet. When there is no one around, send a message to that person. This is true worship. Monitor each other. Invocation, you do for yourself. True worship is outside. Don't gossip about religion. Speak of religion on the good side. Whoever is a man of religion, don't speak of his bad side even when you know it. Say, 'He's a good man.' The Prayer-leader of that mosque – say, 'No, you've misunderstood.' Pray, 'My God, let him give, don't let him take.'

The Paths (Orders)

Spiritual schools

I call them 'spiritual schools.' Schools of spiritual Unification.

There can be no Order without the Divine Law and no Divine Law without an Order. There can be no Path without Prayer. I am a follower of the Divine Law, but I also have an Order, we belong to a Path. Prayer, to say 'God,' to sound the Prayer-call – these are all the Divine Law.

If a Path has no Divine Law, it will perish. If it has, it will move forward.

Tie up one of two sheep and leave the other free. One eats the greenery in the garden – it both eats and gets beaten. The other remains secured. This is the difference between the Divine Law and the Orders: one is attached to a master, the other is not. There is no other difference. The Divine Law is the Path and the Path is the Divine Law. The Path recites more Divine Names a bit more, there's no harm in that.

Unity in diversity

There are many kinds of Paths. What brings us all together, the Naqshi, the Qadiri, is the Word of Witnessing. They all come together in the Word of Witnessing, then they separate. Each has a different Invocation, a different attribute. The whole world of Islam comes together, first in the Word of Witnessing,[1] second in the Naming, and third in the Word of Unity. After that, 'You're wearing black, I'm wearing white,' there we diverge.

Don't follow groups. Follow God and His Prophet, don't follow groups.

All Orders are true. They all belong to our Prophet, they all say the same Word: *I bear witness that there is no god but God, and I bear witness that Muhammad is his Messenger.* They all do their Prayers, right. That's why all Paths are true. There's nothing rotten in them. If a person

---

1. This means the *kalima al-shahada*.

becomes attached to an Order but can't do his duty, it's he who is rotten and not the path.

The Orders and the followers of the Prophet's Way [Sunnis] – one has entered an Order, the other hasn't – they're two brothers. There is no difference between them. One does his Prayer, says his beads, protects himself from the Illicit. The people of the Paths do the same, only their name is different. The [exotericists] also have Extra Prayers. But they don't do them, what can we do? The Orders also have one or two bead lessons [Invocation]. But the other doesn't do that. If a person does his Five Daily Prayers, he's telling five hundred beads a day, he isn't aware of it. So why are the followers of the exoteric and the esoteric at odds with each other? Because they don't tell each other what they're doing. They don't communicate.

There are Orders, there are names. Qadiri, Naqshi, Rifa'i, Mevlevi, Melami and so on. That is, there are a thousand Orders. They're separate. There is no difference between them, the names are different. [Bob, Charles, Richard, John] and so on.

I make some yogurt drink (*ayran*), I say, 'Here, it's delicious,' the other says, 'No thanks, I'm going to have tea.' It's not possible for everyone to get the same taste from the same Order. Some like apples, others like pears, still others like quinces. Some like cherries, some like apricots. A variety of colors, each is a different color. We're all united in the Glorious Quran. Then it differentiates into colors. Some wear white and some wear black.

But all of these practice the orders of God. There is no difference between them, because they all say the Word of Witnessing, the Word of Unity, do the Five Daily Prayers and protect themselves from the Unclean. They're all the same. We're all Islam, the Divine Law and the Paths. The Qadiri is a brother, the Rifa'i is a brother, the Naqshi is a brother [or sister]. They're all brothers in the Quran, the Sayings, the Messenger. It's a difference of names. We're all brethren, praise be to God.

Now all the worlds – the eighteen thousand worlds on earth and in heaven are mentioned in the Quran – are created by *One* God. God is not two nor three. Okay. [This is one point.]

Next, let's turn to the world of Islam. Now the Glorious Quran is the Book of all the world, not simply the Book of Muslims. It is the book of the ant on the ground, of the stars, moons and suns. Of angels! Yes! It is the Book of Totality. That's two.

Our Prophet, the light of our eyes, the joy of our hearts, our life, our soul – yes, that's how we should love him! – he is the Prophet of all existence, not just the Prophet of Islam. [This is three.]

Whoever says *There is no god but God, Muhammad is the Messenger of God* becomes part of his Community. Those who don't say *There is no god but God*, don't repeat the Word of Witnessing, have not become members of his Community, but are still his accessories. Those who don't *say* these are still in the company of Muhammad, they just don't recognize him – either because they're stubborn or because they don't know. But they still belong to him, they're his property.

Now the rest – the People of the Prophet's Way, the Paths, Sufism, Qadiris, Naqshis, Mevlevis, Melamis, Ushakis, there are many – all of them, when they sit down to do Invocation, what do they say at the first step? They definitely say *In the name of God, the Compassionate, the Merciful*. They repent to God. They say *There is no god but God*. They pronounce Blessings on the Prophet. All the Orders do that. The saints are attached to that, the Friends of God are attached to that. So where is the difference?

The difference is in name. The difference is not in Unification, but in the names. God is One, Unification is one. Your names are all different, the names of the Orders are all different. That's where the difference is.

Melami is purification, to abandon everything. True Melami is to follow the orders of the Prophet. Bektashi is the essence of Sufism. It always takes from Verse and Saying. Hajji Bektash was a student of Ahmet Yasawi. [All Orders share these characteristics.]

Comment: *The Melamis say, 'The only doer is God. I don't do anything, whatever I do, God does.'*

Tell them, 'So all the prophets, all the books that were sent, God sent in vain.'

All human beings, animals, plants, stars, the moon, the sun, they're all on the Path, nobody's aware of it. Do you know where the Path of the whole universe is attached to? To the Quran, to Muhammad. Can you escape the sun? Go to America and it's there, go to Africa and it's there, go to the Poles and it's there. That is, you don't have a night. The night passes, the sun is there.

Discussions

If you do something for God, even if you do it in Imitation, God will grant its Realization. God will put it in its place. Yes, do something. Only, if you feel something egotistical, diabolical in a gathering, prevent it immediately. Tell a Verse, a Tradition, something from Hajji Bayram, from Rumi. You see that you can't stop it, it's mushrooming, leave that gathering at once.

Meetings are forests. Forests attract God's rain. And if the Quran is recited a lot somewhere, it attracts God's Grace. That's why you should read the Quran a lot.

There are two kinds of bee. One is the honeybee, the other is the bumblebee. Did you have a discussion with honeybees or bumblebees? If you can make that distinction, congratulations to you. If you want a discussion every instant, be with God's commandments all the time.

You go to a gathering, there's gossip and so on, say 'God!' out loud from the heart as you sit down. They'll pull themselves together and make room for you. This is like heating iron in fire. When you strike it with a hammer, sparks fly in all directions, everyone protects themselves from the fire.

My yoke is light

Some of the worship of the Orders is a bit more. They do their Extra Prayers when they find the chance. But the People of the Prophet's Way [Sunnis following the Divine Law] can do it too, it's not important if they don't.

Then the master, their teacher, gives them a hundred, two hundred Invocations a day – up to five thousand, ten thousand, I hear. Starting from a hundred, they give five thousand, twenty thousand repetitions. What are those people going to do? They can't recite them, they can't recite five thousand [Invocations] in twenty-four hours. They couldn't do it even if they didn't go to work.

I don't want to burden them. Recite a hundred Magnifications a day, don't look at the Unclean, don't reach out for the Unclean. The Naqshi, the Qadiri, the Mevlevi, they're all contained in this.

God

Everything is from God. If a fly moves its wing, it's from God. Someone's lack of interest – that's from God, too.

'I know what you don't know,' says God, 'a leaf doesn't fall from its branch without My command.' But this Partial Will we have, this eye, this ear, don't let go – they break the rope at that point. 'Without My command, an atom does not move from its place.' If we approach this with complete trust, everything will be all right, regardless of whether we're hungry, remain poor, or become rich.

One of the Qadiri masters, Kuddusi Baba, one of the Transformed,[2] is begging. He closed the distance a little bit in his later days. He says, 'My God, Kuddusi Baba's every state is known to You. There is no need to inform You.' Certainly. He's come a bit close. As for us, we open our hands and pray for an hour. Without loving for the sake of God, physically and spiritually, we can't find an atom [of this]. Someone says Hello to another person and says, 'God is witness, this event happened like this.' *Aha!* If one is with this point, with God every instant, if one holds God witness as God has commanded, if one relies on God, one won't fall. One will never fall.

Another says, '*God is my deputy.*' They both make Him their deputy and do all sorts of outlandish things. May God forgive our errors.

Let's devote at least a third of twenty-four hours to God. Let's get up at three or four o'clock at night, until the Dawn Prayer.

You ask for water, they don't bring it, two or three times, you're offended. God's commandments are like that.

No matter how bad a thief or anything else a believer in God might be, two policemen are with him every instant. What can you do? You can't do anything except good.

God says, 'I serve humans by the hand of humans.' God serves us. It all comes to that. God is the one who bestows on us. [Our hands are God's hands.] To one by the hand of another. Because they see each other's hands, they forget God.

'Don't spend two days equal.' We're always in shame. He says, 'I'm pleased with my servant, as long as my servant is pleased with Me.' Don't be ashamed by that, if you're able to!

We're all forlorn. Why? Because we've broken up with God. We're all forlorn until we connect again. God tries to catch us, we always flee Him, like a child.

---

2. *Ar. abdal.* See p. 227, n.6.

How should one give thanks to God? 'Thanks for placing us in a human frame, not an animal frame. Thanks be to You for making us the followers of a Prophet who combines his predecessors and successors. Thanks for making us obey a Book that gathers the universe within itself. Thank goodness for making us of those who love Your Beloved Prophet and Your Book.' Both married and unmarried: 'Thanks for giving us such a husband [or wife]. Our father and mother are pleased with us, we're pleased with them. Thanks for not creating us crippled or blind, our organs are in place. Thanks for giving our sustenance, for not leaving us hungry for two-three days.' Especially in these times, they're eating both through their mouths and noses. Good appetite! Then, two cycles of Thanksgiving Prayer. That's it.

Object to injustice. Pray for goodness. 'I've put a bird in your cage.' What is that bird? Knowledge, wisdom, Sayings, [the love of] good people placed by God in our Hearts. What are you going to do with an empty birdcage?

Love

The love of God is greater than anything else. When you press this cigarette to your hand, all being becomes concentrated there. One forgets everything else. Love, too, is like that. Your life becomes concentrated there. If you can concentrate on God like that, everything is stripped away. Human attributes are uprooted, none are left.

A Sufi lover of God, Yunus Emre, says: 'My God, Paradise, with its rivers of honey and sugar, its houris and servants, is a fact. But give them to whoever wants them. It's You I need, and You alone.' What business have I with beans? It's You I need. Our love is nothing. That love should last until the grave. We love here and forget over there.

Now, there are a thousand kinds of love, spiritual love is the love that leads to God. The love that goes to God with the spirit. When divine love enters a Heart, it burns away everything like the sun, only God remains.

Many people have found divine love through metaphorical [human] love. If physical love doesn't find culmination, it is transformed into divine love. 'Let me know God, see God, hear God,' one goes on that path. For instance, one falls in love with money, or with a girl, a woman, but can't attain her. Like Layla and Majnun.[3] Layla and

---

3. Layla is the Juliet and Majnun is the Romeo of the Middle East. Another such pair

Majnun are very sacred. They find divine love through metaphorical love. They couldn't obtain the metaphorical, they switched over to the divine. There are many like that. May God convert our work, our love – which is metaphorical – to the spiritual.

The other day, a colonel came from Bursa. 'How did you become like this, how did you obtain these manners?' I asked. He said, 'You'd laugh if I told you. I was seven or eight years old, I came home. My mother was reading a book and weeping. "Son, you wouldn't understand." Layla and Majnun. I read it, I cried more than my mother.'

Some turn to God with that love and earn quickly. Others don't understand, their lives are frittered away. Pity the elderly. What use is it if one doesn't see one's Beloved? It's worthless. Don't lose your faith. Rumi, Yunus Emre and his teacher Tapduk Emre all went by the path of love. They're at the level of the Compassionate. That is, in the end they arrived at *In the name of God, the Compassionate, the Merciful*.

A person is stripped from the world, but the *world* doesn't let go of that person. To burn for God. Weeping for God is a bit difficult. We don't have water in our bucket. This is very important. When our father dies or our child dies, we shed tears. Can't we shed tears like that for God? Compassionate tears, not egotistical.

Comment: *I love all things*.

No. The love of everything is different. You can't love the good and the evil in the same degree. Otherwise you'll lose your love.

A child, a dog, a cat. The love of these three can't be equal. To love them is different, but you can't make them the same. The child will grow up to be a human. Cats and dogs eat if I give, otherwise they claw.

Let's say you're deeply in love, or very horny, hungry or thirsty. But if someone were to come and press fire on your hand, you'd forget them all. They all vanish, because you're burning. Now the love of God is like that. That's the essence of Invocation.

An apple, a banana is nice on its branch: look, watch, look. But one should pick and eat it. If one *swallows*, then there's no need to look.

If He didn't desire to give, He wouldn't give the desire.

---

is Farhad (Romeo) and Shirin (Juliet).

Work

Question: *Sir, does this love come about with Invocation?*

With work, with work. Only to work, to work seriously. There isn't anything else. I think of Rumi and Salahuddin, the goldsmith.[4] What does the Saying state? 'Hold *tight* to the rope of God.'

Question: *Can't love be a gift?*

That's very difficult. Some favored saints did come, but even they went through the process. They, too, found by working for it. See, six or seven hundred years, eight hundred years, a thousand years have passed. We're still following in the tracks of Rumi, of Hajji Bayram Wali, of Yunus Emre. But hundreds of years have gone by. That means it's so difficult that no one was trained, there's no one to replace them. We visit them, we wish for their spiritual aid for the sake of God. It's difficult. With work. To work with Sound Mind. If it's the Livelihood Mind, it will again get caught on a hook, get impaled on a fishing rod. So, Sound Mind.

Great effort, great struggle, great work is necessary. We're unable to do our duty. Do your duty, then leave matters to God.

It's not easy, one has to work hard. I ask some of those who come, 'How long did it take you to finish school, university?' Well, you want to learn in five minutes.

Which tree bears fruit the fastest? One is the grape vine, the other is the peach tree. And that takes three years. Now that you've caught it, you want instant fruit. Work for at least three months, a year, then maybe you'll be able to give or receive fruit. I have trees forty, fifty years old, not one flower has budded yet.

To be the servant of a Perfect Human – it's very difficult!

Comment: *A master says, 'Step here and here.'*

That's right, but it's hard to step.

There used to be cobblers. The cobbler mends shoes, hammers those iron nails until evening, he gets tired. He quits work, he's going

---

4. Salahuddin was shaping gold with a small hammer in the marketplace. Rumi began to whirl to the rhythmic sound of the hammer. Inspired by Rumi's whirling, Salahuddin began to whirl, too.

to go home to his family. If he were to collect the nails by hand one by one, it would take all night. They had a large magnet like this, they would move it around among the leather rubble, the nails would cling to it. The leather fragments go in the garbage can. It's done.

Now we are to speak, to struggle for God as we believe. Finally, if it's iron, if it's close to the magnet, it will cling. And if it's a piece of leather, it will drop away. The nail is iron – wooden pegs won't stick, leather pieces won't stick. Take a magnet, it will only attract pieces of iron. We're going to take measures, if it is iron amenable to a magnet, it will stick. But a piece of leather, a wooden peg, those go in the trash can. That is, let's do our job for God here.

You haven't become magnets yet. Take the reed pipe in your hand, they'll play through you. Continue with earnest intent. You're reed pipes, the player is different.

Seek, find. One has to knock on the door. You came here. You knocked on the door, that's why it was opened. If you hadn't knocked, you'd still be waiting outside. Who knocks on the door succeeds. Whoever rings the bell, the door is opened.

The path is long, life is short. It'll happen. With courage, with work, to be hopeful. 'With God's permission, I'm going to succeed.' *Aha!* Together with work, to be hopeful. Not to be lazy.

Comment: *May God give your burden to us.*

If you can abolish the Base Self, maybe you can bear some of it. There are fifty thousand who know me, but they're all marking time. The night's sleep is too sweet. They say to themselves, 'What do you need it for? You've matured.' Thus are they deceived and drop away.

Now let me give an example: the lottery. They buy a ticket for ten thousand, fifty thousand Liras, they want to win a hundred million. Very difficult! How can that be? One has to work. It's been fifty years, I'm still ashamed of my Master.

Our Prophet departs from the love and lap of [his wife] Khadija and is enlightened in a cave among scorpions and snakes. Even the most favored have to do it with the sweat of their brow. Even though he's a Prophet, Moses remains on the mountain without food or water for forty days. We, with a master, among all these pleasures … This is childish. I laugh at you. One can't win it in bed.

They hand you a weapon, they say, 'Hit this target.' You're going to shoot, but before you do, you avert your face. How will you hit it? One shouldn't deviate, one shouldn't avert the eye.

Bayazid of Bistam is a great man, he's seeking. He was on his way to a friend. He's passing by an empty lot. He saw a cat about to pounce. It waited for half an hour. A mouse came. Just as the cat is about to jump, the mouse retreats. Again it lies in wait. Finally, it seizes the mouse. Bayazid says, '*Ah!* A cat has enlightened me.'

Turtles lay eggs. Until the young emerge from the shells, it waits there without food or water. And then it guides them.

All I see is work. The favored saints all worked hard. How Muhyiddin Ibn 'Arabi worked, how the Great Saint [Gilani] worked! It's not in our destiny, nor are we favored, we're going to work and seize it by force. One says, 'Don't side with your Base Self, tear the veil by force.'[5] Yes, the servant is going to open it. We're going to open the veils.

Work. If we lie on our backs over here and ask for water, that tap is full of water. But if we don't go, we can't drink. To force by work, to catch it. No one can win anything with comfort.

One has to seek. As an example, you want a flower, I give you one, but if you really want a flower you have to go to the florist or to meadows. Flowers are there every day. Nothing comes to us of itself. We have to run after everything.

The effort falls to you. You can't turn back and look, and if you stop, you remain there [arrested growth]. I give you the address. You're the one who is going to go, you're the one who is going to find.

The shepherd who was enlightened by a thorn

A village becomes attached to a master. There was a young shepherd, he begged them: 'Take me with you when you go,' but they didn't take him. They say 'We will,' years pass. A milk thistle. It's a brittle thorn with blue flowers. He envied its blue flower. 'Why don't *you* be my Master?' he says. 'They won't take me, you be my master.' He goes on like that for two or three months.

Autumn comes, the thorn dries up, the thistle breaks off. The wind drags it away. 'Oh, Master, are you going to abandon me, too? Why did you leave me? What's wrong with me?' He goes after it. The thistle comes and snags at the entrance of a cave. The shepherd is right behind it. He sees five or six people inside. 'Give me my Master,' he says. 'My Master came in here.' The thorn! One says, 'There is your Master.'

---

5. See the footnote on Nietzsche in The Chain/Mahmud Samini.

Now these happened to be The Seven.[6] 'Go,' they say, 'go to your flock.' Yes, the material is necessary, too. 'Bid farewell to your villagers and come back.' He goes back. He kisses the place of the thorn. To his people he says, 'Forgive me, I'm tired.' He weeps. He goes, he tells the village chief: 'Forgive me, please excuse me.' 'Is there anything you want?' 'I don't want anything.'

One of the sheepskins [places] was empty, one of the Seven had died. He goes straight back to the cave. 'Bravo,' they say, 'you've done what we told you.' He returns, they've lit a candle, there's a tanned skin to sit on, they say, 'Come, Master Hassan, sit down.' They point to one among them, 'This is your Master from now on.'

Yes! It happens like this with a thorn. One is edified by a thorn, can't you be edified with a human being? Faith, faith! Belief! God unites you with the Seven by a thistle. The milk thistle [stands for] faith, sincerity.

This is enough for you. I've given you the address. It's up to you to work. Ask me questions. Throw a stone, eat the fruit. When are you going to improve? If you had any sense, you wouldn't leave, you'd stay here. A thousand people run from God to the people, only one person runs from the people to God. My prayer is like rain in April. Open your chest, let it drip there. Be loyal. Pray, put me too in that prayer.

Question: *What if one doesn't feel the taste?*

Work is still necessary. There is a Verse of God: 'If you do an atom's weight of good, it won't be wasted, and if you do an atom's weight of evil, it won't be wasted' [99:7–8].

You know how they place codes on government vaults, the one who knows the combination opens it. Those who don't know it either break the safe or leave. And we have to discover the code between God and ourselves. *In the name of God, the Compassionate, the Merciful. There is no strength and power except by God, the Exalted, the Great.* Both physical and spiritual code.

I'm speaking both physically and spiritually. Someone graduates from law school, they give him as apprentice to a judge so that he may learn. They give him as apprentice to a governor. A mayor administers

---

6. 'The Seven' would be the Seven Transformed Ones. According to a view first suggested by Hakim Tirmidhi and elaborated by Ibn 'Arabi, the saints constitute an Invisible Royalty (*rijal al-ghayb*). Topmost is the One Pole (*qutb*). Then follow the Two Leaders (*imamayn*), the Four Pillars (*awtad*), the Seven Transformed (*abdal*), the Forty Nobles (*nujaba*) and the Three-Hundred Chiefs (*nuqaba*).

a region. A district attorney becomes the head of the Supreme Court if he works. If he doesn't work, he subsists like that. The same is true of spirituality. If you work, you become a mayor. If you don't work, you'll remain the governor of a small town. Everything is upwards. Don't remain undecided.

If one wants a little asceticism, to fast two or three days a week, to go about with an intact Ablution, to perform Extra Prayers. If we put in labor, God does not waste anyone's labor, they receive while lying down. But if you want to find without labor, you can't find it anywhere.

When weighing two pounds of rice, both your and the storetender's eyes are on the scales. Let no right be infringed. It's the same here. The ancients divided the day into three: eight hours work, eight hours worship, eight hours rest. If we can devote two hours to worship today, it's worth ten hours. So let none infringe the other's rights. What's destined for you will happen anyway. I look at the circumstances of the ancients and feel ashamed. What laziness has overcome us? If we worked one-tenth their amount, what wouldn't we accomplish?

Patience

If there is patience, everything will happen. Patience, patience, patience. If one is patient, one drinks one's tea with sugar, otherwise one drinks it bitter. Whoever does not suffer trials cannot enjoy comfort.

Turn to yourself, seek things, okay? It's enough that you've wandered up to now.

Now you, brother, you want something ready-made. A free lunch! You say, 'Make this iron, this steel wood.' Or else, 'Turn this wood into steel.' Well, seek that too. You'll find someone, I promise.

If you have no discomfort, it's a blessing. If a thorn pricks us, we're sad. What do they say? 'His kindness and His distress are one.' 'Your kindness is sweet, Your distress is sweet, too.' That's the best. Both are from Him.

We're going to give thanks for the physical and spiritual bounties of God. Thanksgiving, thanksgiving whether sweet or sour. That's where the matter ends.

Patience is meditation. Drop by drop, a lake is formed. If we're patient, an ocean is formed. But we're impatient. One said, 'I'm neither in heaven nor on earth, I'm with Him all the time.'

Spirituality is not distant from us, we're distant from spirituality. We're going to work and try to catch it. Be patient, work, you'll find. They'll give you what you want.

Worship

[The simile of bread:] Wheat grows, it's harvested, it's broken up in a mill, it's pounded to separate it from its husk, it goes back to the mill, its bran is separated, it's baked twice, finally it becomes edible. I'm giving this as an analogy for worship.

A person without worship is like a barren tree, a tree without fruit, a dried-up tree. Let's make the following analogy. A river. You own the river, you're in the river. And a crowd has come from outside, the knowers and the ignorant, acquaintances and strangers. 'Oh, give us some water, too!' You fill the glass and give them, fill it and give them. You? You're in the water already. Worship is like that. You do it, you donate it, to all of them, but it emerges from your mouth. It comes from that river.

Comment: *I haven't been getting any taste from worship for a week.*

Did you drink an Unclean tea, or what?

Ablution

Thank God, water is plentiful in our country. After you relieve yourself, take an Ablution immediately. If you go around with an Ablution, you'll perform the Prayer with ease. Someone doesn't perform the Prayer, say: 'Go around with an Ablution.' Ablution is that valuable. If a person goes with a clean Ablution, the angels bestowed on us by God will be with him. If he doesn't, the angels on duty are again with him, but they don't come near him. They hate it.

The great ones go with an Ablution and lie down with an Ablution. The greater ones, when a little sleep enters their eyes, they stand up at once, say the Word of Repentance and take a Bodily Ablution [ritual bath]. They consider sleep impure. See, and you say you want to be a saint. These things are difficult! Do the Wakeup Prayer, that's enough for you. To eat and drink a lot, to sleep a lot. These two are the enemies of God and the Prophet of God. When one eats a lot, the stomach is comfortable, then sleep comes. These things are difficult.

I don't eat or drink anything without an Ablution. If I do, I feel soiled. You, too, don't eat or drink anything without Ablution. It's useful to have an intact Ablution at all times. What if you're together with your wife? If you don't have an Ablution, the resulting child will be your devil. The foundation here is weak – not just in Turkey but everywhere. One must have an Ablution when one is together with one's wife. The mother may not have an Ablution, but at least the father should have it.

While taking the Ablution, one should devote one's whole intelligence to the Ablution and not bring anything egotistical to mind. To take the Ablution carefully. You have an intact Ablution, you're going to do Prayer, but you have the urge 'to go.' Do so, then refresh your Ablution. Otherwise you'll be distracted during Prayer.

Prayer

Don't abandon Prayer. This is my last will and testament to you. To those who want a master – the Five Pillars of Islam. Your master is the Prayer. The Five Daily Prayers. Everything is in that.

Islam has only one name: Prayer. If somebody's going on the road, and if you call out: 'Fatima,' she won't turn and look if her name isn't Fatima. But if it is, she'll turn and say, 'Yes?' Islam is like that, too.

From the first prophet to Muhammad, whichever prophet came without Prayer, let's go and follow that prophet – that is, so as to avoid doing the Prayer. But there isn't any. Moses and Jesus' Prayer was in excess of our own.[1] But the original could not be maintained. They fragmented the Gospel. They fragmented the Torah, its essence wasn't around anyway. The Quran is all that's left in humankind's hands.

Of the Four Law Schools – Hanafi, Shafi'i, Maliki, Hanbali – whichever has the larger congregation, the more Prayer-leaders, you can do the Prayer behind them.

The importance of Prayer

If I told you, 'Do two cycles of Prayer, place your forehead on the ground, don't rise for twenty-four hours, and you'll win a billion,' you'd accept at once, and everyone would perform it. As for one who

---

1. Rabbi Hayim Halevy Donin, *To Pray As a Jew*, New York: Basic Books, 1991 [1980]. See also http://jews-for-allah.org/Jews-and-Muslims-agree/Jews-prayed-like-Muslims.htm (03/16/2002). The postures shown in these sources are almost identical with those in Islamic Prayer.

knows the value of Prayer, s/he says, 'My God, because I was able to do this Prayer, I should give a hundred million to the poor.'

If they ask you, 'Shall we give you the city of Istanbul, or will you do a two-cycle Prayer?' say, 'You can keep Istanbul, give me two cycles of Prayer.' Seven or eight hundred years ago, Yunus Emre described Paradise in detail. He said, 'Give them to those who want them. I need You, and You alone.' Give them to whoever wants them, I don't want any of that. You see? He's a lover of Truth. If they ask you, 'Shall we give you the world, or shall we give you Prayer?' say: 'Give me Prayer first and the world afterwards.' Because without Prayer, what are you going to do with the world?

If they ask me, 'What is the greatest pleasure, the greatest food, drink, and rest, material or spiritual?' It's Prayer. Prayer is what brings together the material and the spiritual, the worldly and the otherworldly. Those who don't do Prayer cling to the physical side, they lack spirituality. We have spirituality. We've come from God. If we leave our own parents and cling to other parents, we won't get any taste out of that.

God commands you and I implore you, don't abandon your Prayer. Beseech others just as I beseech you: they shouldn't abandon their Prayers.

For the comfort of all human beings, prostration is needed. Whoever doesn't prostrate can't find solace. He thinks he will, but he can't. He obeys the ego. Satan disobeyed only one commandment of God. What was that? The commandment to prostrate. If we disobey God's orders, we will have obeyed the devil.

Adam and Eve, too, disobeyed just one commandment of God, and became like this. He said, 'Eat, drink, but don't go near that tree.' You place it in your mouth thinking it's honey, it's poison, you [tumble down and] fall somewhere. Be very careful as to whether honey or poison is in it.

You've done a Prayer. Your Ablution is intact. You join an argument. Don't join it at all, take another Ablution, you have no missing Prayers to make up for either, do a two-cycle Extra Prayer. When there's an argument, do Prayer at once.

You've entered a dispute. You're hurting one another, immediately: Prayer.

You're angry with God, you've left Prayer aside. When you do that, the devil enters your home. If you abandon Prayer, you'll fall into the clutches of the devil. He'll vanquish you. The devil has many wiles. Don't depart from the Five Pillars of Islam and the Six Pillars of Faith.

Listen to this carefully: whoever performs the Prayer, starting with the angels, all humanity, the heavens, the animal, vegetable and mineral kingdoms, down to a blade of grass, all these become his congregation. They become his congregation, he becomes their Prayer-leader. This armchair, this table that you see, whatever there is, all prostrate to God, all in their own ways. You're human. But they're all *for* the human.

There is no Ascension[2] without Prayer. Prayer is a ladder [*mi'raj*, Ascension]. There is no elevation, no progress, without Prayer.

Without Prayer, everything is Unclean. What you earn honestly is Unclean, too.

Question: *Is every Prayer an Ascension?*

Whether one knows it or not, even if it's egotistical, God accepts every Prayer. The Five Pillars of Islam and the Six Pillars of Faith are mandatory.

Perform a two-cycle Thanksgiving Prayer to God every day. First, for having created you human. Second, for making us the Community of such a Prophet. And third, for having made known His existence and Unity.

There are three paths: God, the Prophet, the master. Whoever abandons Prayer becomes the property of the devil. There is no prophet without Prayer whom we could go to. Nor is there a master without Prayer whom we could go to.

If one becomes Realized, Prayer is still necessary. Nobody can be greater than the Prophet, the Prophet performed Prayer until his last breath.

There can be no prophet without Prayer, and there can be no master without Prayer. *There is no sainthood without Prayer.* If I saw you flying in the air without Prayer, I'd throw a stone at you and knock you down.

There is no dervishhood without Prayer, child. If someone flies in the air, commands miraculous feats, gives you news from East and West, but doesn't do Prayer, throw a stone and knock him down so he won't deceive anybody.

---

2. See The Prophet/The meaning of the Ascension.

The man who found a master

There was a man. He went to this master and that, he was looking for an easy way. Finally, he went to a Naqshi (i.e. Naqshbandi) master. The master said, 'Come in, son. I was looking for someone myself.' Then he began:

'*First*,' he said, '*diabolical, illicit lust, food, drink – that's over. Finished.*'

The man's a bit clean, he said, 'I accept that. Good. I refrain from those things anyway. I'm a guy like an angel.' 'Okay,' he said.

'*The Five Daily Prayers are mandatory*,' he said. 'I'm doing those too, thank God,' he said.

'Good, bravo,' he said. 'Then there are the Extra (Supererogatory) Prayers.'

'I've heard of those, but I'm not doing them,' he said. 'Can you tell me what they are?'

'Let me explain,' he said. 'First, there is the Wakeup Prayer. It's six cycles. An hour or two before dawn, you perform it like the Dawn Prayer. Afterwards, you pray, you say your beads (invoke), the Dawn Prayer-call is issued, you do the Dawn Prayer.

'After the sun has risen a little bit, there's the Daylight Prayer, four cycles Extra. You perform that. An hour later, there's the Forenoon Prayer, six cycles. You do that. The Noon Prayer arrives, the last two Customary cycles [of the Noon Prayer] you perform as four.

'The Afternoon Prayer, the Dusk Prayer, after the latter there's a six-cycle Piety Prayer. By the time you've finished that, the Night Prayer arrives. And after that we're back with the Wakeup Prayer again.'

'Is this how Naqshis are?' 'Yes.'

'Why, the ones I visited before were all easier than this!' he said. 'I have a family, I have children, I have to work, I have to sleep, I have to talk, am I supposed to deal with Prayer all the time? Goodbye.'

'Goodbye, son,' he said.

You fill your belly, you go to sleep. Is this the way Naqshis are? They sleep neither day nor night, because there isn't *time* left from Prayer to sleep! Yes, things aren't easy. There's no time from Prayer for you to sleep or eat or go somewhere. A Naqshi's Prayer is never done. Prayer without cease!

Either leave the Naqshis, or pull yourself together a little bit. The Naqshi has no *time*. S/he's always in the Presence! There's no such laziness in the Naqshi.

Everything is in Prayer. *Everything. Everything.*

The master without prayer

A man was looking for a master who did not perform Prayer. Someone told him: 'I've found your master,' he said. 'It's yourself. If you had faith, you'd perform the Prayer. You don't do it, you're your own master.'

For Kuddusi Baba, that was an Ascension. From the Night Prayer to the Dawn Prayer. God doesn't give us what we want unless we disturb Him. Let us disturb Him with worship. Let's knock on God's door, let's be beggars.

Prayer under adverse circumstances

Don't force the body. Because you're going to worship with that body. If you're sick, do it while you sit. If you're too ill to sit, you lie down on your right side, you can perform it there with eyebrow and eye gestures. You can do Prayer in an armchair without getting up at all. Don't hesitate, you can tell this everywhere.

The universe is a mosque. You're on the road, stop wherever you want and do the Prayer, you're in a mosque. If you don't know the orientation of Mecca, turn this way, turn that way, it's accepted. No matter which way you're facing, you intend toward Mecca, you perform it. Stand towards whichever direction you become convinced of. Even if it's wrong, God will accept it.

If one can't hold one's urine, one should take an Ablution and perform the Prayer while urinating all along. If one's legs were to be cut off, one still has to do the Prayer. Salvation is in Prayer. Liberation is in Prayer.

Prayer: the pinnacle of worship

Without Prayer, there can be no meditation. Meditation without Prayer weighs in on the side of the egotistical. It tends to the side of the devil. A person relies on his knowledge, all knowledge is in Prayer. All the keys of Truth are in Prayer, the keys of the diabolical side are in the ego.

All spiritual orders are united in *There is no god but God, Muhammad is the Prophet of God.* Prayer is the main thing. The others – ceremonies, whirling dances, motions – are beneficial, too. One says 'God,' one invokes.

Prayer is the pinnacle of all worship. The chief of all worship. But there are things yet to be done in Prayer, *aha!* To fulfill its requirements.

There are Prayers within Prayer! We should see the great Yunus and become Yunus.

Form [posture] is the requirement of Prayer. Standing, bending, prostration, [sitting].

One should recite the Opening Chapter [while standing] and *All worship is to God* [while sitting] with such concentration that nothing else is left in the mind. In those, we are saluting each other face to face – with God, that is. This is a *very important* point. They're all important, but these two are most important. The salutation in the Opening Chapter occurs in the Verse: *You alone we worship, and You alone we ask for help* [1:5]. During the Five Daily Prayers, in at least one cycle, repeat this five or seven times and then continue. When you pass on to the next Verse, *ah*, it's as if you're in another world. We greet God and God greets us, in the Opening Chapter and in *All worship is to God*.

After *All worship is to God*, we recite *Send Your Blessings* and *Send Your Grace*. There, 'the Family of Abraham' is mentioned. We pray for both Ishmael and Isaac, that is, for the Jews [and Christians] as well. This summarizes the Quran. [And we pray for 'the Family of Muhammad,' that is, for the People of the Prophet's Household and for the Twelve Imams.]

There, I've given you the whole of the Quran.

The prostration

Let me tell you something very valuable: Prostration to God. This is my last will to you. Don't be fooled. There is no other salvation.

There is much good in the prostration. God says, 'I am closer to you than you. But I am even closer in prostration.' Love prostration. Do it frequently. Pray during prostration.

The Prophet is going one day with his daughter, Fatima. 'Be careful, daughter,' he says. 'Don't trust your father, do your prostration.' Her father is God's Beloved, he still says, 'Don't trust even your father.' It's a Saying. Whenever you get up, do a prostration.

Effusion is obtained during this prostration. Effusion, abundance, is not obtained anywhere else. To love God and fear God without prostration is an illusion. Without doing one's duty as a servant, it's an illusion.

In Prayer, the first prostration is the prostration of the Compassionate, it encompasses the whole universe. The second prostration is the prostration of the Merciful, it encompasses only Muhammadans.

Concentration and breath control

Everyone finds Prayer difficult. I've been in it for seventy years, even I find it difficult. Nevertheless, it is the most important observance. Ramadan, the month of Fasting, comes once a year, the Alms-tax comes once a year. The Pilgrimage is once in a lifetime. The Word of Witnessing is every day, Prayer is every day. Prayer is the most important among them. If we abandon that, too, we're finished. We have only the Prayer left among the Pillars of Islam. Nothing can happen without that.

[Mental distractions:] We stand in Prayer but we wander elsewhere. We steal in Prayer. We leave our frame and go around somewhere else. They call this theft. When I start Prayer, I have fifty partners. One comes from here, the other from there. I say 'Stop,' but they say 'No, we have an account with you.'

You should disregard all unwanted thoughts that flood the mind and continue on your course. A method that is ninety percent successful against this is to squeeze the abdomen with the arms during standing and sitting. *I take refuge in God from the accursed Satan. In the name of God, the Compassionate, the Merciful.* We enter Prayer with our right foot. To squeeze slightly when you clasp the hands. There's a ten percent margin of danger here.

Then there is a method that will yield one hundred percent success. We take a deep breath and recite the Opening Chapter without exhaling. You should recite the Opening Chapter in one breath, the additional chapter in one breath. One breath, *God Most Great* [to bend over], three to seven times *Glory to God the Great* [during genuflection] without exhaling, up to *Glory to God the Exalted* [during prostration: also three to seven times]. Then, *All worship is to God* [prayer recited during sitting] in one breath. The *Blessings* and the *Grace* [also recited while sitting] in one breath.

If you do this, you'll be one hundred percent successful, you won't even remember your hands and feet. Since you're occupied with your breath, nobody can approach you. Because you're occupied with yourself. Don't bother with the outside. Tell this to everyone, mention it frequently in the mosque where you're Prayer-leader. This is the first.

During Prayer, you have to look at where you prostrate while standing, at your right toe during bending, again at your right toe from between your two legs in prostration, and at your right index finger while sitting. This is the second.

If you have time, do the Prayer slowly. If there's no time, do it quickly. When you have no pressing business, say your beads after Prayer as three times one hundred instead of three times thirty-three. [The usual is to recite the following three: *Glory to God*, *Thanks to God* and *God Most Great*, each thirty-three times.]

In telling your beads [after Prayer is done], the purpose is to bring worship down to the Heart by breath retention. Like, 'Let's see if I can finish this in one breath.' I could do one full rosary [three sections, total: ninety-nine] all in one breath. Don't forget this.

Suppose that in Prayer or elsewhere, you can't free yourself from egoism. Bring your loved one [the perfect master] to mind and you'll be freed.

When the Prayer performs you

They told someone, 'You Pray too much.' He replied, 'I'm going to do it until Prayer performs me. Then I can't leave it, anyway.'

Prayer is God's gift to us, don't abandon it until you come to the point where it doesn't abandon you. I ask people: 'Do you perform Prayer, or does it perform you?' If they say, 'I do it,' I say, 'That won't do.'

Whenever the Prayer performs us, that's when things will be solved. When you Pray eighty cycles a day [twice the amount of the usual Five Daily Prayers], the ego is left powerless. When you do Prayer eighty to eighty-five cycles a day, then Prayer won't abandon you.

Extra Prayers

The hodjas do a lot of harm. They say, 'Anyone who first has to do Makeup Prayers[3] can't do the Extra Prayers.' They can't do the Makeup Prayers anyway, they've accumulated. That's where the real illness is. A person has too many Makeups accumulated already, they tell him, 'Don't do the Extras, either,' and that's the end of that. If someone asks, be daring, say, 'My Makeups are finished, I'm doing the Extras.'

The Extras are twenty-two cycles per day.[4] The last Customary (*sunna*) Prayers of Noon and Night Prayers each have two Extra cycles

---

3. Makeup Prayers are those performed in place of earlier Prayers that were missed.
4. Wakeup: six, Daylight: four, Forenoon: six, Piety: six cycles.

added on them [making them four each]. The Obligatory Prayers of the day are seventeen cycles.[5]

When you're bored, blue, or angry, take an Ablution with cold water and do a two-cycle Prayer. Everywhere will be filled with good cheer. All your troubles will be blown away. An Ablution, a two-cycle Prayer, everywhere will become a rose garden.

Don't forget the Extra Prayers, don't miss them, at least two cycles a day. And especially, don't miss the Wakeup Prayer.

The Wakeup Prayer

Don't miss the Wakeup Prayer even if you can't do the others. Whoever works, wins. An hour or two before the Dawn Prayer, the pre-dawn period, is a different domain entirely. Prophets and lovers also speak of the pre-dawn period. To become. Sometimes, if there's an excuse, that's possible, too. Sleep is a nuisance. The disease of heedlessness. But the Heart should be there. Keep it between 5 and 6 a.m., then sleep twenty-four hours if you want to. If you're awakened at that hour, say 'God' and grab hold of a faucet. This is an order, a Muhammadan order.

Get up at 4, 5, or 5:30 a.m., the basic form is six cycles. Do it like you perform the Dawn Prayer, saluting right and left at every two cycles. The Wakeup Prayer can be performed between two and twelve cycles. The Prophet says, 'I was made to love Prayer. I perform all the Prayers. Among Extra Prayers, the one I love most is the Wakeup Prayer.' You'll be alone with God. No noise, no interruption.

Don't miss this Prayer. That's the harvest time. That's where you reap the fruits. You may do it one day and miss out two days, or do it five days and miss two days. That's the thing. After it you can tell your beads, do the Dawn Prayer, and that's it. Even if you get up at the Dawn Prayer-call, do the Wakeup first and the Dawn Prayer afterwards.

Let's light the candle, child. The candle is here, the match is here, wait until morning. One has to light the candle.

Question: *A person may do the Prayer externally but not love God in his heart. Isn't the sincere love of God the important thing?*

One fulfills the order, but he's corrupted inside. The other doesn't do any of them – Ablution, Prayer, this or that – but says, 'My Heart is pure, it's with God.' Which of these is better?

---

5. Dawn: two, Noon: four, Afternoon: four, Dusk: three, Night: four cycles.

The second is egotistical. Suppose I told you to bring me a glass of water. You say, 'Okay, sir,' and go outside. I'm waiting for the water. The second time, 'Daughter, bring me a glass of water.' 'Okay, sir, I'm bringing it.' The third time around, I'll go and get the glass of water myself, what will I do with you? Alternatively, you say 'Right away, sir,' and bring it the first time around. Which of these is better?

Let me tell you another example. You've come to the door, you ring the bell or knock on it. If the door didn't open, if you couldn't see the person you visited, wouldn't you be sad? Is it better to return empty-handed?

I've told you two examples, everything is in them. If a person is immoral, he should still fulfill the commandment. Let me tell you another example. All animals, from a whale or elephant to an ant, have hearts. If one says 'My heart is pure' but does not fulfill the commandment, one is either an ant or an elephant. All animals are pure, the purest animal is the sheep. It has a heart, too, but it's still an animal. *To fear God, to love God.* How do you stand with His *orders*?

One Prays, but steals, one Prays, but drinks – we don't go into those matters. But a proper Prayer is mandatory. I wish this from God for all of you.

The effect of alcohol on Prayer

It leads to the postponement of Prayer. According to our sciences of Divine Law, if a drop of raki or wine falls into a well, that well has to be emptied and washed out before its water can be drinkable again. That is if a drop falls into a well. Now if a drop falls into *this* well [the mouth], it'll ruin Prayer and everything else. Until you get it out of there ... Be careful, don't put anything in this well. Because it is this well that postpones Prayer. We eat something somewhere, we do something consciously at work or at a neighbor's house – it's this well that postpones Prayer. But if one has the willpower, one can still wash one's mouth, take an Ablution and do the Prayer.

If a drop of urine falls into a well, it'll contaminate the whole well. If a drop of Uncleanness falls into this well [the mouth, the stomach, the body], the same thing happens. It's very difficult to clean.

Prayer in other languages

Question: *Suppose an American, a German, a Frenchman, that is a Westerner, came to you and said: 'I am going to accept – or have accepted – Islam. And I want to perform its worship. But I find it difficult to memorize Arabic prayers. Can I perform the Prayer in my own language?' What would be your reply?*

All right. Okay. They translate the Quran into their own languages and read it, why shouldn't this be? The hodjas wouldn't accept it, but we do.

Question: *Well, in those prayers there is 'Allah,' can they use its equivalents in their own languages in place of that?*

That's okay, too. It would be better if they said '*Allah*.' If they can't do it, let them say it in their own language. For example, what do they say in English?

Comment: *They say 'God.' The Germans say 'Gott,' which is also from the same root. The French say 'Dieu.'*

Let them say it that way. Later they will understand, and pass on to the other.[6]

Prayer and Invocation

It's been twenty years. A few Qadiris came, they're of the Qadiri Order. One of them said, 'We do the Friday Prayer at a mosque.' There was a man called Hamdi, he's dead now, may he rest in peace, he had knowledge, he was a scholar. His house was close by, he used to preach at that mosque *gratis* every Friday.

He continued: 'This man [Hamdi] takes the pulpit, he recites a Verse or Saying, he passes on to the interpretation, he says: "Those followers of the Orders"' – right there, at the very beginning – '"I hear them all night long, they chant until morning, no sleep, they disturb themselves, they disturb their neighbors."' The man spoke about this

---

6. A two-cycle Prayer in English is described in H. Bayman, *The Black Pearl: Spiritual Illumination in Sufism and East Asian Philosophies*, Rhinebeck, New York: Monkfish, 2005, pp. 208–16.

every Friday, he went on for a year, they couldn't stand it any more. They came to me on a Sunday.

Well, I know that man, too. I said, 'God willing, with God's permission, I'm going to come with you to that mosque next Friday.' They were pleased.

I went the next Friday. He shouldn't see me, we sat behind a pillar. There's still forty minutes until the Prayer service. He came, took the pulpit, and sure enough, before a Saying was over he's on to the Orders again. With my own ears. I saw it, that is. They might have misunderstood. He started, I didn't make a sound.

He did a lot of mud-slinging. He's pouring it on real thick.

We finished the Friday Prayer, I sat outside on a bench, Hamdi saw me as he was coming out.

'Well, well, so you *do* come here?' His house is across the street, he invited me. I said, 'Sit down.' I rolled a cigarette and gave him one, too. He smoked, I smoked.

I said, 'I have nothing to say against your knowledge, your scholarship. May they increase. I'm going to tell you something, I want you to answer me.'

I hadn't read this anywhere, it was an inspiration of the moment. I didn't say 'You're doing this' or anything like that.

'God has made Five Daily Prayers obligatory for us,' I said. 'And after every Prayer, we tell ninety-nine beads, right?' 'Yes,' he said, he's listening now.

'At every cycle we recite six Magnifications – *God, He is Greatest*, at every cycle. For the whole day, forty cycles, that's two hundred and forty Magnifications.' And I continued along this line: At each Prayer time, there are three times thirty-three or ninety-nine beads (glorifications: *tasbih*), for five Prayer times that's five times ninety-nine or approximately five hundred glorifications. In the Magnification, two Divine Names, *God (Allah)* and *He (Hu)* are mentioned together, twice two hundred and forty is four hundred and eighty. Also, there are the calls for Obligatory Prayers.

'Hence,' I went on, 'during the Five Daily Prayers, the Divine Names of God are repeated at least a *thousand* times.

'I hear that you're speaking out against the followers of Orders. You're saying that they recite Divine Names. Aren't these Divine Names, too?' I asked.

'Now, you recite five hundred with the beads, and you recite five hundred Unifications [Magnifications], who recites the Unification more than you do?' I asked.

He stood up at once, 'Ahmet Efendi,' he grabbed my hands, 'Forgive me,' he said. 'You won't hear of it again.'

Then we went to his house and had some coffee. Later, he too joined an Order.

I've told maybe fifty hodjas in Ankara about this since then. We should avoid schisms. The members of Orders (esotericists) and the followers of the Divine Law (exotericists) are branches of one tree. That's how we're going to answer them.

Now if I were to tell you, 'Repeat the Divine Name *He* two hundred and forty times, say *God, He is Greatest* two hundred and forty times,' you'd find that difficult. But we do it in Prayer. Yes! In addition to that, we have three times *Glory be to our Lord the Great* at every bending, or a hundred and twenty per day. We have three times *Glory be to our Lord the Exalted* at every prostration, or two hundred and forty per day (there are two prostrations in each cycle). Then we have God's Names mentioned in the Opening Chapter. There are forty of those, plus five at the end of the Prayer times. The same number of *In the name of 'God,' the 'Compassionate,' the 'Merciful'* – three times forty-five Divine Names there alone. Then we have Divine Names in the additional chapter [recited after the Opening Chapter at every Prayer cycle]. By the time you reckon them all, it's past two thousand.

Can there be any Invocation (*zikr*) greater than that? They say, 'We didn't know about this.' Who invokes God's name more than you do?

Be very careful about Prayer, there are so many things in it! May you be moralized with the ethics of the Quran.

Invocation

They produce fire by rubbing two moist pieces of wood together. And we're going to produce fire within by invoking enough. *Whoosh!*

Whoever invokes God frequently, God loves that person. On this point, it is written in the Quran: 'Invoke Me' [e.g. 8:45, 20:34, 33:41]. 'I, in turn, invoke/remember you *very* much.' Just as a forest attracts rain, the Invocation of God attracts His mercy. Continue frequently. Let's recite [the Word of Unity] often, by day and by night, let's invoke it without counting. You're in Paradise. You're all in Paradise. There's the command of Invocation on every particle. Everything in the universe invokes God in its own language [17:44]. The sun works for us, the whole world works for us. As for us, let's not work for our Base Self, let's work for God.

Say 'God' in your own language, in English.

Some receive a lesson of five hundred, one thousand Invocations, they recite in a hurry in order to finish quickly. Instead of doing that, let's recite a hundred but do it fully. Then there are those who come and say, 'Is it okay to invoke while watching TV?' [I laugh at them.] I say, 'Okay, do it.'

Comment: *I lose my sleep at night.*

Recite an Invocation from where you're lying, or get up, take an Ablution, and perform a Prayer, sleep will come immediately. Because the Base Self, the devil won't let you! Those who know struggled hard to overcome sleep. And you want to sleep!

A man sought a good man. He went to a lot of masters, they all said, 'Do this, do that, repent.' No one accepted him, he was a bit wild. His watch was broken, he went to a watchmaker, *tick-tock*, he bought a clock and took it home. He said, 'You be my Master.' He put it over his heart [and repeated with it]: 'Oh, God, Oh, God' (*Al-lah, Al-lah*). In three months, God manifested Himself.

How to bring Invocation down into the Heart

Hold your breath, recite *There is no god but God* fifty or a hundred times, take another breath and recite again. Then it'll descend to the Heart. The Base Self can't occupy itself with anything else, because it's preoccupied with itself during that time. Also, during Prayer, recite the Opening Chapter in one breath, recite the additional chapter in one breath – a short one, such as the Abundance [Chapter 108] or Sincerity [Chapter 112]. In genuflection, watch the big toe of your right foot. These are all gifts from me to you. You've come to this age, you didn't know these until now, I'm telling you. There are many exalted things you don't know. If you abandon your own knowledge, the Prophet of God will give you that knowledge. But you don't abandon what you know.

Recite the lesson – the Invocation you've received from a master – after performing Prayer. 'God' (*Allah*), the Name of Majesty, addresses the spirit directly. *There is no god* purifies the Heart, at *God* He hears Himself. Hold your breath, recite the Name of Majesty thirty-three times in one breath.

In Prayer, we're going to recite the Opening Chapter in one breath. Let's take a breath, the additional chapter in one breath. Genuflection in one breath, prostration in one breath. *All worship is to God* [the first sitting prayer], again in one breath. There's restriction of breath, nothing is able to come to mind because our Base Self is preoccupied with the breath. Again, hold your breath in order to bring it down into the Heart. Let's not overdo it, we'll constrict the heart. Only in this way can we make it descend to the Heart, we begin to recite the Name of Majesty from the Heart.[7]

In one branch of the Naqshi, they hold their breath and push the tongue against the palate so that Invocation will descend to the Heart. I was doing my military service, there were four or five friends [from the Qadiri Order] in Adiyaman, they had marks on their foreheads. 'Our master made a stick so that we wouldn't fall asleep. [The stick is placed in a vertical position, the sharpened end resting against the center of the forehead.] Whenever we doze off, *pang*, it pricks.' The things they've done in order to awaken!

Never overdo it

(*In Invocation, quality is much more important than quantity. Intensive concentration during the Invocation of a small number of formulas takes precedence over great numbers.*)

Question: *Can there be a danger in Invocation?*

Yes. Yes. How can Invocation have a danger? Let me give an example. Either a pot of food you're going to cook, or Turkish coffee, or tea. You place it on the fire, you light the fire. If you don't pay attention to it, if you don't watch it, if you busy yourself with something else, both the coffee and the tea will overflow, the pot will pop its lid. I was making coffee, I bent over to put the box back, it boiled over in the meantime. That's the danger. Properly, child. To do Invocation properly. To do worship in its place. If the fire is too high, it'll burst its lid. This is a small simile, that is. If you see that the fire is too high, you must reduce it a bit.

Another such analogy: we place a cup of tea here, it's full, we're going to drink. Okay? But because of your love for me, you have some milk in your hand, if you say, 'Uncle, let's add a little milk,' it'll spill

---

7. The Heart, or the spiritual psychic center that corresponds to the physical heart, does not coincide with it anatomically but is located two finger-breadths beneath the left nipple.

over. That is, to avoid this. But you're going to drink half of the tea, then you can add milk on top of it, you can drink both. Not to spill it over, to avoid overflow. 'I'm going to dedicate myself to Invocation, no matter what' – the head will flip its lid. A tiny hair twitches in one's head, it's over. You can do neither this nor that. You'll become a madman of God, that'll be the end of it. God preserve us all.

You know why this happens? 'Everybody sees things, why don't I?' One exerts oneself, one devotes oneself to reciting prayer beads. If a hair's-breadth shift occurs in the mind, the Order is lost, the Invocation is lost, everything is lost. A hair snaps in the head, one becomes paralyzed. When Divine Attraction comes, leave it and get up. Stop. Don't get caught in the electric current. Calm down and then continue. One hundred Namings, one hundred Unifications [per day] in place of all those. If you heed me, go downwards. You'll benefit, you won't lose.

Someone was under the influence of Divine Attraction.[8] I told him, 'Your wife, your child will flee from you. Restrain yourself.' Slowly, very slowly, he applied the brakes.

What did I tell you, don't play with electricity. You go to an electrician, you become his apprentice, you learn the methods, you don't get electrocuted. You say 'I'm going to fly,' you open the window, straight down! You board a plane, the pilot will take you. But if you say, 'Let me fly, too,' you go straight down!

Don't hurry to become a saint. One finds oneself in the insane asylum one day. Why don't they teach middle school, high school immediately? Why does primary school exist? Why doesn't one start university right away?

Consider two cases. One is a university professor. His work is interrupted, he has to teach at an elementary school. He'll be sad, and he'll reflect. Now consider the exact opposite. A primary-school teacher teaches at a university. Before he's talked much, the kids stand up: 'Whoa, Teacher! That won't work!' Because they've studied at the university. Everything in its place.

Two friends climb a mountain. They see a partridge. 'I'm going to catch it.' 'You can't do it, don't go.' He goes, just as he's about to catch it, the partridge flies off. 'If it can fly, why can't I?' He falls and breaks his back. His friend summons help from the village.

---

8. Under Divine Attraction, a person can shake and quake involuntarily, like the Shakers and the Quakers.

Ten thousand Names. *Whew!* One falls off the rock and is smashed to pieces. Do your Prayer, don't consume the Unclean, don't offend your parents, that's it!

Some masters give their disciples ten thousand, thirty thousand, *one hundred thousand* Invocations per day. This is very risky. When is that man going to eat, when is he going to drink? He can't do it in time, he can't accomplish it. He'll become a madman of God.

You're going to recite a thousand? Recite a hundred, do it properly, a hundred Magnifications. If you throw a thousand beans, you can't hit the target. Throw one.

My Master Ahmet Efendi asked me one day: 'How are things in Ankara, isn't there a friend or something?' 'There are. Qadiris, Naqshis. They recite five thousand, ten thousand Invocations per day.'

He said: 'Shall I tell you something? Were you a soldier, did you do target practice, did you hit the bull's-eye? Bravo. If you had taken a crateful of bullets and hit only once, they would have punished you. Tell you what: shoot just one, hit bull's-eye, take refuge in God.'

Ten thousand isn't necessary. Shoot once, hit the bull's-eye. Recite one hundred, at most five hundred daily, that's enough for you.

Comment: *Someone has invoked too much, it was as if her eyes were flaming.*

Uh-uh! Tell her Grandpa said, 'Let her perform the Prayer quickly and discontinue Invocation.' Let her do only the Daily Prayers, not any Extra Prayers. I tell everyone about Illicit Gain and Illicit Lust. Don't glance sideways, do the Prayer, that's enough, you're a saint. Whoever does this, I'll pin the promotion to sainthood on him right away. So many people have become sick due to excessive Invocation. Fulfill these three points, that's enough for us. If you don't do that, recite like a nightingale until sunset, then go at night and commit an outrage, what good will it do? What did the great ones say: 'To control one's hand, one's loins, one's tongue.' If you were a thief by profession, and there were two policemen beside you, you couldn't do a thing. Similarly, one should be with God all the time.

The secret and the sublime

Die before you die[1]

There was a touchy man, even a flea would disturb him, he died. His neighbor called the hodja. The hodja washed the corpse, his neighbor watched. The hodja turns him this way and that, he inserts his finger. 'See?' the neighbor said, 'you were disturbed by a flea while you were alive. Now the hodja is doing all these things, you don't make a sound.'

Try and become like this [like a corpse in the hands of the corpse-washer]. Be like the dead so you may be liberated.

Yunus Emre says, they all say two words: 'Die before you die.' Nobody died, that they should be resurrected. I tell you only one word: 'Die!'

Unveiling

If we come to that state, dreams will vanish. We'll see with these eyes what we're going to see in dreams.

They come to complain about their master, I give them an example. Children now start school at six years of age. First finish primary school, middle school, high school. It's very difficult to obtain grades to enter university. If you can obtain, you'll come.

Don't long for 'seeing' much. You'll be lost, no one will inquire. 'Don't enter this arena, many heads are cut off, no one inquires,' says Niyazi. Everything should be normal. You'll get the dues of your work, don't worry. Don't dive deep. 'You're a fish, you're in water, you can't swim.' Fish are in water, they don't know water. What we see, what we live are all miraculous.

Continue with life. Without health, nothing is possible. With health, everything is possible. Slowly, gently, we're in no hurry. First let him finish primary school, then middle school. If he starts university [now], he won't know what to do.

Don't ask for Unveiling. When it's opened, it won't close. Then you'll beg. Those who were Unveiled prematurely all went insane. There was a woman who worked hard to get Unveiled. Now she sees a violet spot

---

1. A Saying of the Prophet.

wherever she looks. Medical doctors are unable to help, because this is a spiritual condition.

Miraculous deeds and asceticism

Question: *What is the Eye of the Heart?*

Hanging in front of a person's face like a veil, the past, future and everything about that person is seen. Or else, again in front of a person's face, or where you're looking at, the Afghan War and so on is seen.

Comment: *God gave to the Prophet freely, he didn't earn it.*

He polishes, he is cleansed of human attributes, divine attributes remain. This is where intense asceticism is necessary: in erasing human attributes.

You know what is truest? To live humanly, to live as a Muhammadan. And afterwards? Together with the Formal Prayer, to apply some asceticism to the Base Self. Not to attach so much importance to the Base Self. 'I did what my Base Self didn't like.' Asceticism, that is.

If you want Unveiling, miraculous deeds, 'I want to see something,' [this calls for] hunger, asceticism. Formal Prayer won't do it. The role of Formal Prayer is different. If you performed Prayer to the end of your life, the Base Self [still] has to be bowed by hunger. When the stomach is hungry, that's when the love of God increases.

Eating much, drinking much, sleeping much. And the beginning of sleeping much is eating much. Why did the Prophet of God leave the bosom of the ravishing beauty Khadija and spend forty days on the mountain without food or drink? All prophets found it through hunger.

'I want to possess miraculous deeds.' In that case, asceticism is necessary. Asceticism, much worship, hunger are necessary. And that happens only with hunger, not otherwise. You can do the Formal Prayer, you can be like an angel, but it won't work without hunger. You stay hungry for three or four days, a week, that'll do it.

Asceticism is good, but don't weaken the body, for it is [your] vehicle. We're going to give the body, eating, sleeping their due, but not in excess.

I knew [a master]. He would tell his disciples to fast for twelve days, to break their fast on the thirteenth day. Many of his disciples couldn't stand it, they fell ill. Only one in a hundred, one in a thousand were able to do it. Finally, [that master] decided to fast the twelve days himself, but he couldn't stand it, either. That illness came to him from asceticism.

Spacefolding

(What is spacefolding [tayy al-makan]? In a nutshell, it is the annihilation of distance. Take a blank sheet of paper and mark two distinct points on it, A and B, towards opposite ends. The shortest distance between A and B is a straight line. But if you fold the paper through a higher [third] dimension, you will be able to bring the two points right on top of each other – they will coincide. This is what scientists mean when they speak about 'wormholes,' 'spacewarps,' and 'teleportation.'

By the same token, one can speak about timewarps or timefolding [tayy al-zaman], in which temporal intervals are annihilated. Since we have learned from Minkowski and Einstein that space and time are not really separate, we can also speak about spacetime warps.

The folding of space is a concept well-known among Sufis, as the Master's following explanations illustrate. In the past, it would seem, some Sufis have had the ability to collapse distance and/or spacetime intervals – improbable as this may appear.)

We speak by phone from the South Pole to America. This is spacefolding: to bring near what is distant. The telephone is spacefolding. I call the phone, TV and airplanes 'spacefolding.'

[Fax:] It's mind-boggling. In the old times, trained saints used to do these things. The hardships they went through to do it! They [scientists] took everything from the human.

The great saints of God used this in their time. He sits in Malatya, from Heart to Heart, 'Ahmet, how are you [in Ankara]?' Now, the miraculous deeds of the saints are all manifesting [in the guise of physical science]. Niyazi Misri says, 'You're the ore of the universe's manifestation, Prophet of God.' It emerges today.

There is a secret, an essence of man. With that, a human being can see Britain, Germany, those countries, as he speaks to them. But these are hidden. Muhammadanhood unveils these. You know the speed of light? It's faster than light. Every human has it, it's opened only by those who exercise it.

The Heart in which God has installed His Throne of manifestation, watches the realm of space, let alone the Earth. How many suns are there, how many stars? There's no need for the newspaper or TV, he watches everything. The Prophet of God dwelt on these a little bit, he attached more importance to the Earth. Now we read these, we imitate the [Perfect] Human. Because God hasn't established His Throne [in us].

Question: *How can one speak with another's voice?*

He answers him with that person's voice. Spacefolding. Hearing his master's voice – yes, sir, that too is spacefolding.

Although Satan is the enemy of God, he can go from one end of the world to the other in an instant. If he can do that, why should it be inconceivable that a Friend of God can go to Mecca in the blink of an eye?

There are three kinds of spacefolding. The first is to get up and go to Kayseri [using supernormal means]. The second, to be both here and in Kayseri. The third, to be everywhere. Four or five places at once. The cheapest of these is to shorten the path a bit in going to Kayseri. And the cheapest, easiest miraculous feat is to talk to the dead. I saw two people in my life [like that]: One in Ankara, the other in Malatya. They spoke to the dead in the graveyard. I don't see the dead, they do. I talked to one, he said 'God willing, in time you, too, will see.' I never saw him again.

You all perform a kind of spacefolding. To be able to do the real thing, one has to work very hard. Hunger is necessary, much worship is needed, one has to die before dying. In terms of imitation: You're reading a book here, your mind is in Ankara. You're Praying here, in a second you're in Britain. This isn't spacefolding, but it's the precursor of spacefolding. You all have this. Nobody's aware of it. You lie on your back here in Ayvalik, you speak with Faruk in Ankara. Tell your self: 'With God's permission, you're doing spacefolding for me, you're not aware of it.'

Spacefolding is such that there is nothing faster. It doesn't take a second. You can reach this place with a *great* worship, a *great* hunger. They can't obtain it any other way.

[Shaykh Shihabuddin's story of timefolding:[2]] They attribute this to the Grand Saint Gilani. [The seeker stabs the knife into the pot.[3]] Maybe he [Shihabuddin] did it, too.

They can't accomplish [teleportation] by science. They can only do it with the permission of God and His Prophet, under the guidance of a master, with asceticism and hunger. Otherwise, they can't do it with science. The phone is enough, the satellite is enough. It is Hidden Knowledge. They're talking to America, talking to Britain. What greater spacefolding can there be?

Who discovered America? [Columbus.] And one went from us [Piri Reis], he made the map without going, from where he sat. The other makes it by traveling. He made it without seeing. God brought the world in front of his eye. Just as he showed our Prophet the Farthest Mosque in Jerusalem. Ibrahim Hakki was like that too. God brought it in front of his eye.

[After the Master performed spacefolding in a car with a disciple, he told the disciple:] Don't remain with such things, these are for children.

The child of the spirit

[*Tifl al-ma'na*, the spirit-child:] This is very delicate, this. It is a spiritual child that is fatherless, like Jesus. Everyone wants without effort. Be the possessor of the child of the spirit. If you were to retire to a cave for forty years, maybe you'd understand what this means. May God forgive my error, I'm telling you: the spirit becomes pregnant.

[*Walad al-qalb*, the child of the Heart:] The Heart has a child. The Heart becomes pregnant to it. Whatever you do, try not to abort that child. It's actually the child of the spirit, not the child of the Heart. Worship and good works [doing things that please God] yield a baby, the baby of spirituality. Then there's the baby of materiality: you get married, you have a child. May you have a baby of spirituality. As one continues to act on one's knowledge of the Divine Law, the Heart is finally awakened. [The child of the Heart] is born after all of these. It is born in the last station, the Station of Absolute Unity [*Ahadiyya*, nonmultiplicity, nonduality]. That is, there's no place for the Base Self

---

2. From 'The sultan who became an exile,' in Idries Shah, *Tales of the Dervishes*, New York: E.P. Dutton, 1969, pp. 36-37.

3. See below, The Chain/Abdul Qadir Gilani/The right time.

here. If we come to that state, dreams will vanish. We'll see with these eyes what we're going to see in dreams.

'Unless one is born again, one cannot enter the heavenly Angelic Realm.' [Abdul Qadir Gilani in the *Mystery of Mysteries* – compare John 3:3.] Correct. The child of the Heart. This grows, develops, rises to the heavens, you see everything. Those are the ones they call the People of Miraculous Feats.

How to see the world

A man, a peasant, lost his ox. He searched for it until midnight and was coming back. He saw three people talking.

'When I look into this [cup], I see the world.'

'When I look in this [mirror], I see the world.'

'And when I look through this ring, I see the world.'

He comes up: 'I heard what you were saying. Find me my ox!' They can't get rid of him.

'We're going to place its ear in your hand, hold tight.' Towards dawn a man comes along with the ox. One of them says, 'Is this yours that you should take it?' The man runs away, they place its ear in his hand.

Those men could do this, why can't we?

No one wants to leave their shell. Some are the size of a walnut shell, some of an egg, some of a pear, some of a quince. If we could go up to the realm of space? The realm of space is so wide, it could hold a hundred thousand Earths.[4] But everyone likes their own mind. Get out of that eggshell, for heaven's sake!

Food, drink, work, these are normal. But decline, decline, decline, we're going to go tomorrow or the day after. A handful of brains is going to become soil. Let's wake up a little bit.

If we work, both the eyes of our head and the Eye of our Heart will be opened here. If we don't work, it'll be opened over there, but it's better if it's opened while here. If you can open that, with your mind, you can see the entire universe. [Jamshid's Wineglass.[5]] This eye's vision is limited. They say, 'The eye that can't see itself is blind' [Gilani].

---

4. A symbolic rather than an exact number.
5. According to legend, the Persian sultan Jamshid had a wineglass through which he could view the entire universe.

A person whose Eye of the Heart is opened dies at once. If the Eye of the Heart is opened, there's no you, there's no son, there's no husband.

To walk on the sea is difficult. You walk on land. If you work a little bit, you'll walk on sea. If you work a bit more, you'll go to the realm of space. This word is for all of you.

The minds of us all haven't entered here yet, we can't comprehend. Can it be? Yes, it can. You take a drawing to a carpenter, he can't do it, he gives it to his master. You take a ring to a jeweler, the novice gives it to his master.

The Prophet of God knows best, 'the breath of the Compassionate' comes from [the Prophet] himself. So there's definitely a cipher. For example, he says, 'I saw my Lord in the form of a beardless, handsome youth (*shabb al-amrad*).' The youth is himself.

Question: *You mean the spirit-child?*

It's himself.

[A granddaughter of the Master saw two Ahmet Efendis and a beautiful baby in a dream. The Master said that one of them was his own Master, the First Ahmet Efendi, adding:] He and that baby finished me off, they rule everything.

[Seeing a child and a pool in one's dream:] That child is the child of the Heart. The pool is your labor. These are all [from] the Name of 'the Living.' Repeat *The Living, the Everlasting* thirty-three times a day.

Hidden Knowledge

What we call Hidden Knowledge is the ethics of our Prophet, materially and spiritually. The important thing is to live like the Prophet of God, with his morality, to finish one's time on earth and go.

In Sufism, in the esoteric sciences, this is called Hidden Knowledge. Now the discoveries of modern science are all Hidden Knowledge, that's how you're going to see it.

You said esoteric science, its name is Hidden Knowledge. Have you heard of Moses? He's a great prophet, very great. But what did God say? 'Go and wait at such-and-such a place. Meet Khidr. He's going to teach you Hidden Knowledge.' He's a great prophet, yet he needs Hidden Knowledge.

Question: *What are the 'two beings'?*

Two worlds. One's that world and one's this world.[6]

[As a book was being read, when the word 'hypothalamus' occurred, he pointed to his head and said:] The nucleus of the two worlds [physical and spiritual] is here. Whichever world you operate, it's here. One has to operate this.

Hidden Knowledge is university. Primary school, middle school, high school, university. A person studies hard at exoteric knowledge, that's primary school. If one follows the path of the saints, one can get there.

Friends, we're looking for university before we study primary school. First, let's give this primary school its due. You get up and look for a university. It won't work, it just won't. You should say, 'Master, you're telling us about university. But without the foundation of primary school, it isn't entering our heads.'

[An example of Hidden Knowledge:] There are as many human dispositions as there are kinds of animals in the world.

The flight of the gryphon

There was a gryphon[7] bird. The gryphon lays two eggs a year. Intact. One day, as a gryphon was returning to its nest, its claw touched an egg. The shell cracked slightly. The mother saw that one offspring is about to be lost.

Animals have a knowledge of their own. That bird knew where the Fountain of Eternal Life was. It flew over there. It took a mouthful in its beak, it's going back. Ten miles, twenty miles, it got tired close to the nest. It alighted at the bottom of a plane tree. But it uttered a snort because it was tired, just as a person snorts in disgust. As it did so, two or three drops of the Water of Life fell from its beak.

It resumed its journey. It arrived at its nest. It administered it in droplets to the crack on the shell. The offspring was healed. It'll emerge.

There's a lot in this story: Hidden Knowledge, Sufism, Divine Law.

---

6. The Master has explained that the 'two wests and two easts,' which occur in a Verse in the Quran, also pertain to this world and the Afterworld.

7. Orig. *Anqa*, a mythical bird like the gryphon, Simurgh or phoenix.

We now go back to the tree it landed on. Those drops that fell from its mouth, one fell on the plane tree. Another fell on the vine, the grape vine, wrapped around the plane tree. And a drop fell on a snake, a boa constrictor in search of prey.

This is why these three – the plane, the vine, the snake – change their skin [are renewed] every year.

Now, we said Hidden Knowledge. This [body] is the plane tree. The vine that enwraps it: the troubles of the world that entwine human beings. And the snake is the Base Self of a human. It bites. One has to tame that snake.

I've been doing this for sixty years. I explain openly, 'This is paper, it's made from wood,' not one person has been able to drink the Water of Life yet.

That the sun will rise in the west and head toward the east is in the Quran [in a way we can't understand]. I'm going to give you two examples, but you couldn't bear it. Still, let me give one. Our Prophet says, 'Seek knowledge, even if it be in China.' He doesn't say, 'Go to China.' He's saying, 'That knowledge exists in Islam, in the Quran, seek and find it.' But you can't understand this, you can't bear it.

Subtleties (*lata'if*)

I didn't enter that field, I don't know about those. I never did them. Unification of Actions, of Attributes, of Essence: I didn't go into that, either. Why? Because the foundation is two points. Without those two points, whatever you do is in vain. If the eye, the ear, the tongue, the mind in the head stray, if they aren't trained, you have to train them. The heart is below the neck. You have to unite it with the mind. If the heart is quiet after you stop silent Invocation, it hasn't awakened yet. And if you want miraculous feats – asceticism, hunger, spare sleep. One will get nowhere with such eating, drinking and sleeping.

The human body maps the universe

The Quran says, 'Cover your ornaments.' The ornaments are below the belly.

The lower half of the body belongs to the world, to the earth, to lust. The part between the belly and the heart encompasses the whole universe. As for the part between the heart and the top of the head, it is the location of incomprehensible mysteries.

'There is a lump of flesh in your body the size of an egg. If that is good, everything is good. If that's dirty, everything is dirty.' To avoid the unclean, to let the heart live nicely. If you don't want heart disease, stay hungry. Leave the table while you're hungry. Eat little in the evening. The channels of the head work well, they work with hunger. The Prophet said, 'Don't fill the stomach too much, don't disturb the heart. Instead of two servings, eat one.' When the stomach is comfortable, so is the heart, and when the heart is comfortable, so is the liver.

Above the neck is a realm. Between the neck and the belly is a realm, below the belly is a realm. To cleanse all realms from the Illicit. When you've done the head it's finished anyway, you've taken the situation in hand. One will have the body of an angel. Fasting every instant, at worship every instant, just like the angels. One won't be an angel, one will have the body of an angel. Later, one will be superior even to angels.

The realm of space is all above the neck. There isn't anything below.

Don't be overcome by the Base Self. Above the neck and above the eyebrows are different. The first is good, but the second is better. [Indicating a vertical line at the center of the forehead:] Rise here, take refuge in the mind. Hold in your imagination a man of religion you love, or if you can't do that, someone you love. You'll be safe that way.

The Guarded Tablet

The Guarded Tablet exists. Let's bring it close. Above the head is the station of Ascension to which the Prophet journeyed. What comes close? God's existence and Unity. Now when that comes, the Guarded Tablet comes and enters the head. What I'm saying is not wrong, it's the meaning of Verse and Saying, God willing. We've brought the Guarded Tablet close, the Ascension comes close, too.

Those who bring the Guarded Tablet close: Yunus Emre says, 'Within a mountain, I beheld / The eighteen thousand worlds.' How do the sun and moon fit in there? Is there anyone who has seen this mountain, this Mount Sinai? Show me this mountain. Here is that mountain [the head], it's this, this.

Hajji Bayram Wali: 'On two pillars [two legs] I beheld a wondrous city [the head].' I went to a city. I climbed up its hotel, I looked out through two windows [the eyes], whatever I looked at, I saw one.

We have business with a minister. But we need a leader. We need someone who knows that minister. Let's make all our applications to the Prophet of God and, God willing, he'll take us to God. He made the Ascension for all of us. God willing, he's the one who will solve the mystery of the head. Let's not forget the Guarded Tablet [pointing to his head].

There's another thing, let's bring that close too. May all partake of it, those who say *There is no god but God, Muhammad is the Prophet of God*, and those who don't. All of them, the whole of creation, are our brethren.

According to Yunus Emre, there is a dome in Paradise. Out of it flow four rivers, rivers of milk and honey, none mixing with the other.

Now what is necessary for us is the head. Four rivers, let's bring them close. Let's count the four. One is teardrops. One is the ear, bitter. One comes from the nose, it's sweet. And the river of *Kawsar*, nectar, is this mouth. They all emerge from this dome [the head].

We've brought that dome of Paradise and placed it in the heads of all. We've brought it closer than everything. We've placed the Guarded Tablet in the head. Let's not mix tea with yogurt drink, it'll all be ruined.

The value of above-the-neck is different, the value of above-the-belly is different. As for below-the-belly, it's things-other-than-God. Filth emerges from it, lust emerges from it, but everything enters here [from the head]. When we go to bed at night, let's not sleep for an hour, let's think about these things, let's write it here [in our minds], God willing.

Two eyes and two ears, four. Two nostrils, six. And one mouth, seven. Let's open these seven doors with the Naming and the Opening Chapter.

My God, thank you for giving these seven organs. This [the head] is the Mount Sinai of Moses. From the neck upwards, there are seven visible organs. There are a thousand, a million, invisible organs.

Let's not live like animals. This food, drink, recreation God has given you, He didn't give to prophets, He didn't give to saints. Fulfill their thanksgiving.

God says, 'The head from the neck upwards belongs to Me.' Take good care of God's property.

Without the brain, none of the organs are of any use. Without the heart, what would the brain do? Yes!

A tiny lentil sees fifty miles, a hundred miles. Medicine, technology dissect every day and search, they still can't fathom the building. Know the value of this head. Medicine, technology haven't been able to discover it yet.

The eye sees in front. The ear follows it. The nose says, 'The food is burning.' All these organs are working, but the one who operates them is heedless. Radio and TV are with the eye and the ear. The ear is an antenna. They took radio and television from this head.

Let's work on this mountain a little bit, okay? This head is the antenna of the eighteen thousand worlds, it's the antenna of the Torah, the Psalms, the Gospel and the Quran. We're going to take it and bury it in soil tomorrow or the day after, it'll be a pity. They're going to ask us, 'Which keys [locks] did you unlock?'

Here's good news for you. There are two keys that will unlock the treasures of the brain. Be careful not to allow an Unclean bite through these two lips. This channel [the eye] sees a hundred miles, control the eye channel. Same with the ear. Don't eat the Unclean, don't look at the Unclean. Don't approach Unclean lust. Fornication is the same as murder. If there's anything illicit, nobody will call you a saint.

Above the neck is the realm of space. As a simile, that is. From the neck to the belly, the earth, that is, the world we live in. Now, below the belly: if you use it as God commands, on the good side, saints will descend from you. If you use it on the bad side, you asked for it, hellfire is ready immediately. Be very careful with that channel, use it with great care.

Uniting the heart and the mind

In the Divine Realm, stripped of the world, of everything, united mind and heart, sound mind, sound heart. Without the mind, what would the heart do? An elephant has a heart, too, and so does an ant.

Do you know what is the most valuable part of the human body? The heart. The name of God is inscribed in the heart. It is inscribed at birth, it is there until one goes to the grave. But one must do what that entails. Until the Eye of the Heart is opened, nobody knows anything about anyone else. The curtain is raised *after the union* of the heart and the spirit under the Sound Mind. This is very important.

The 'Meeting of Two Bows' [*Qaba Qawsayn*, 53:9] is the highest station. It's the highest station of the Ascension. The station of the Grand Saint [Gilani]. Do you know where the 'Meeting of Two Bows' is? It's here [in the head]. The 'Lote-tree of the Boundary' is here, too. Closer [*aw adna*, 53:9, he shows a distance between thumb and forefinger], even closer. Becomes himself, that is. May God grant his intercession.

They've built the rockets, they've gone to the moon, to Mars, they're going to go to the stars, but we can't link the mind with the heart or the heart with the mind down here. The distance between the two is one foot. Yet we can neither lower the mind to the heart, nor can we raise the heart to the mind. The mind is separate, the heart is separate, the spirit atrophies. If you don't water a flower, what happens? It deteriorates. Let us join either one with the other, or *vice versa*. Such a short distance! They travel thousands of miles, they give up at such a short distance.

They send so many rockets into space, so many spaceships at so much expense. But they haven't been able to build the rocket of the shortest distance:

> They haven't built the spaceship
> between the mind and the heart.

III

Descent of the Light (Who's who in Islam)

The prophets

Introduction

The reason God sent religions is to awaken, and to wake others up.

All great prophets came to reconcile God with people. We are weakly constituted, the prophets' constitutions are expansive and strong. The Divine Law, the Prayer, the worship of every prophet is different. But they are all united in Unification [monotheism, nonduality].

Every prophet came to his community with [the discrimination between] good and evil. He sees that it's bad, he says, 'This'll ruin you even in this life, let alone in the afterlife. Abandon this.' 'Who're you?' 'The son of so-and-so.' It doesn't suit them, they strike and kill [him].

The prophets are all givers. Pharaoh and so on are all takers. It started with the children of Adam [Cain and Abel], wrath and bliss continue. Wrath is always greater. However, God says, 'My bliss – My loving-kindness, My mercy – is so great, it encompasses My wrath.' It begins there: all prophets come with the attribute of Bliss, a pharaoh stands up against each with the attribute of Wrath. And so it goes. In each society, a wrathful one opposed them. The prophets overcame them, again with wrath. It's incomprehensible. There's a great trial here, a great trial. May God [bring] us, our children and all humanity within the attribute of Bliss.

Many prophets exercised their office through dreams. Many did it through inspiration. Revelation [via angels] is rare. That is, those who exercised their office through revelation are few. Moses, Jesus, Muhammad, these came with revelation. That is, they heard it.

What mysteries are these? Adam's grandchildren came together and tried to hang him. The same with Seth, the same with Idris [Enoch]. Moses ran away from his country. God demolished the world for Noah, he became the Second Adam. Jesus was crucified. Our Prophet, all the power is in his hands, the things he withstood. What mysteries these are!

Every prophet is single. Idris did not come again as Elias. He was not born again.

Many prophets cursed their communities. Noah destroyed his community. Only the Prophet of God came for the liberation of all humankind.

Unarmed prophets were all unsuccessful. Our Prophet, too, was unsuccessful until he took up arms. Jonah ran away from his people, he invoked God in the belly of the whale. But because he was unarmed, he was defeated by the people again when he came out.[1]

Noah was armed. His weapon was the Ark he built. Because Jesus was unarmed, he was nailed to the cross.[2] Many other prophets were killed in a similar way.

Again, God has given the greatest trials to the prophets. They have suffered the worst hardships. Job suffered illness. Those who follow prophets, God has given them the second hardest trials. The followers of those, He's given the third hardest. In this manner, by degrees.

There's a difficulty here. It used to bother me a lot. They murdered the prophets. God created these creatures, God is able to take care of them. Thirty or forty years ago, I read somewhere: 'I gave the greatest hardships to the prophets. Whoever loves the prophets, they suffer those tribulations too.' I was so sorry. 'Why did You inflict this punishment on them?' This continued in my mind for twenty years.

One day, I was again reading a book and came upon a similar Tradition. *Donng!* An inspiration came. 'I' – I'm telling it exactly as it was – 'I did not give prophets hardship. And I did not give their followers hardship. They only suffer the hardships of the *people*.'[3]

I got up, I performed two cycles of Thanksgiving Prayer.

'How can the knower and the ignorant be the same?' He comes with knowledge, with *divine* knowledge. He comes with the knowledge of *God's* commandments, he finds the people astray. He suffers their hardships. That's where the trials come from. Otherwise, it's nothing. There's trouble in every home, in every family, among every couple of friends. To bear their burden. As far as we can. We see that we can't stand it, we're going to drop it.

There is emigration in all prophets – for example, Abraham. A [bright] star appeared at the time of our Prophet, of Jesus and of Abraham.

---

1. See the next chapter, The Prophet.
2. At least in appearance. For the Master's take on this, see below, The prophets/Jesus.
3. This ties in with 'he died for our sins.' The sense meant here is that because the prophets and their followers obey God, they do not fall into error. But since people in general fail to obey God's commandments, they bring down calamity on society at large, and then the prophet, too, is forced to suffer the consequences of other people's mistakes. Moses says to God: 'Will you destroy us [the whole community] for what the fools among us have done?' (7:155). On this point, see also The prophets/Moses/Moses and the ants.

They slaughtered children in the time of Abraham, Moses and Jesus. Seventy thousand each for Abraham and Moses.

Magic was widespread in the time of Moses. They say Pharaoh used to keep track of Moses via magic. God gave Moses a staff to remove magic.

Jesus healed the sick with his hand and his mouth. He would pray for someone, a blind man, caress his eyes, and he would begin to see. Even leprosy: he would pray, and leprosy would vanish. Herbal remedies were widespread in his time.

In the time of Muhammad, demonic possession was widespread. People would become possessed by genies (Tr. *jinni*) and *peri*.[4] Before the Prophet, genies, spirits would come to a man, and he would come forth saying, 'I'm a prophet.' These all ended with the Quran. God gave the Book, the Quran, to Muhammad. God says: 'I sent down the Quran to him. I put all knowledge – Moses, Jesus – all sciences in the Quran. I forbade all those things.'

There is a saying about King Solomon. There were three paths [before Muhammad]. 'King Solomon commanded by his seal, Moses commanded with his staff, Jesus commanded with his hand, and Muhammad commanded with the Quran.' The last encompassed the rest.

From Adam's time to Muhammad's, all peoples, all nations raised their children in the hope that they would become prophets. There's a poet contemporary with the Prophet, he says: 'They bury children in caves on Mount Sawr' so that they might become prophets. As the Torah and the Gospel mention, prophets were expected. Those with strong children placed their children in caves, accompanied by guardians. 'But,' he says, 'the bird of fortune landed on the head of Abdul Muttalib's grandson [Muhammad].' Everybody, and especially the Jews, tried a lot. They raised their children in caves, in order that a prophet might come from their line.

---

4. The word 'genie' derives from the Arabic *jinn*, which in turn derives from *jann*, 'hidden.' In the folklore of all people of all continents (even the Eskimos!), mention is made of sentient beings inhabiting a parallel continuum or alternate universe which impinges on our own.

These nonphysical intelligent entities remain invisible to all but those endowed with second sight, and are able to interact with human consciousness in such a way as to appear in a variety of forms. They can be both good and bad in nature. In England, the better ones have been called the 'good people' or 'fair people,' whence the term 'fairy' (Persian *peri*).

After that, after our Prophet, during the time of the Four Caliphs and after the fourth caliph, Ali, everyone desired their children to become saints. That's what they all strove for. They came pure into this world, and all worked in that direction.

Now the Seljuks and the Ottomans, *they* wished, 'Let our child become a sultan.' *Aha*, a sultan. 'Let him own a treasure, let him be a ruler.' And in the [recent Turkish] Republican period, 'Let our child become a doctor, let him be rich.' It changes, sir, it changes like that. That's why nobody reads *books* nowadays. There's no *curiosity*. I've distributed the same [reading materials] to *everyone*. Know this: nobody read a page. Or if they did, they didn't practice it.

Adam

Adam ('man, human') is like spirit, the universe is like body.

God gave all the secrets to Adam. Whatever secrets there are, he gave *all of them* to Adam.

Gabriel asked God: 'Did you create anything more beautiful than Gabriel?' 'I'm going to create a human being, its spirituality is going to be more beautiful than yours.' 'Has anyone of us seen it?' '[No.] You're going to be its teacher.' 'Of what kind is its beauty?' 'It doesn't know what beauty is, its beauty will be with Me, it will be beautiful with Spirit.'

[After he was created] Adam got up and said, 'Thanks be to God, the Lord of the worlds.' The angels were amazed: 'Where did you learn that?'

God commanded all the angels to prostrate to Adam. Azazil, the smartest angel, objected. He trusted his knowledge. 'You created me of fire, but he's of mud. I will not prostrate myself to him.' He's the angel who knows best. [Now he's] the one who leads saints astray. He couldn't trick the prophets, though. God said, 'I need you, too,' and he became Satan. He violated *just one* of God's orders, look what happened to him. But what are *we* going to do?

Property

Adam was lying idly, doing nothing. God said to Azra'il (the angel of death), 'Go and construct a building near where he is, let him see it, so that he'll begin to work, too.'

Azra'il was just about to start, Adam said: 'That's my property!' They came to grips with each other. Adam was trying to get the best of Azra'il, while at the same time trying to push his marking-stone a little farther with his foot.

Adam and courtesy

There's such a game of chess here ... Who comes, who goes, who gives, who takes? The Real manifests in Adam, manifests in Azazil [the fallen angel], manifests here, manifests there ... If we meditate a bit, certain things will become clear.

The spirit entered through Adam's nose. It spread throughout his body. Three times he cleared his throat – like a baby, it would die if it didn't. Where did you learn that? He got up, there's nobody there. He's a statue. A mudcake of clay. Adam knows nothing. What is needed? To teach him.

He said, 'Thank God,' but someone is making him say it, he's not saying it himself. The angels are watching him, he knew all their names. They said, 'Where did he get that knowledge?' God said, 'I gave it to him.'

God said to Gabriel, 'Let's give him something.' He sent three presents: Mind, Faith, Courtesy. He said, 'Whichever one he chooses, bring back the other two.'

Adam thought. He has no mind, no ideas, he's a mudcake. Again this isn't Adam's work, it's God's. There's a Giver. He said, 'I'll take Mind.' Gabriel said, 'You chose the best.' He said to Faith and Courtesy: 'Come on, let's go.' Faith said: 'Without me, Mind can't manage.' He turned to Courtesy, 'Let's go.' Courtesy said, 'I'm the garment of these two. Without me, neither of them can manage by themselves. I stay, too.' So they all remained with Adam.

Gabriel conferred with God. 'What shall I do?' God said, 'Everything's found its proper place, if he can use them. The trust has found its place. Come back.'

Adam is in the hands of Eve. Courtesy got disoriented. Eve removed courtesy from Adam. Similarly, when Satan [Azazil] rebelled against God's order to prostrate before Adam, [clever though he was], he lost his mind. If he'd had courtesy, he still would have obeyed. But he lacked that, too.

Now, don't we possess these three? We do. It's the very same hour, the same moment. As with Adam and Eve, so with us all. This word is valid every hour. They read this, they hear it, but they don't understand.

This is very important. Starting with Adam, it's valid for every human being. They think it belongs fifteen thousand years ago. But it's the same. It's oneself.

When courtesy departs, they both go. Whoever lacks courtesy, know that he has no faith. Whoever lacks faith, know that he has no mind. That is, without courtesy there is no mind. Without courtesy, the greatest scientist/scholar has no knowledge. Ibn 'Arabi, the Greatest Shaykh, says: 'Whoever lacks these three is an animal who speaks.' When the three are present, that is the Perfect Human. Everyone can harm him, he will harm nobody. Now, all three exist in Adam – that is, in us. If we can use them, they're all there.

Is prostration to Adam or to God?

Question: *Is the prostration to Adam actually to God?*

It's to Himself! Prostration is to God, and to no one else. Satan couldn't understand that the word was not from Adam, it was from God. Prostration is to God, not to Adam. Otherwise, as humans, we'd all be prostrating to each other. Prostration is to God. That is, [in that moment] the Absolute Unity (*Ahadiyya*) of God evolved to Adam.

Is prostration to Adam, or to the Real? *Prostration is to the Real.*

According to one account, the human spirit prostrated to Adam, too. It says, 'I came into this world in order to do the second prostration.' It did the first one over there.

Hud

Ad, the people of the prophet Hud, were very strong. They would strike a stone with their fists, they would stick their hands into stone just as we sink our hands into mud. God created a wind [called Salsal] that razed both them and the stones. They held on to boulders, it wrenched off boulders. It rained sand. The city of Ubar [the city of the Ad, discovered in Oman in 1992] is very ancient. It's older than Moses, older than Abraham. There's no treasure there.

Abraham

The story of Abraham resembles that of Moses. Pharaoh and Nimrod both slaughtered seventy thousand babies in order to prevent a prophet's arrival. Nimrod killed them all, but his prime minister approached his wife. That's how his wife became pregnant with Abraham. Our Prophet had great respect for Abraham. He always spoke of him as 'Abraham, my ancestor.'

Prophets descended from Abraham via two lines. The one is from Isaac to Jesus, the prophets of the sons of Israel. The other is from Ishmael to Muhammad. There aren't any prophets between these two, there are forty-five generations. There were many prophets in the other line.

For the sake of Abraham, Nimrod's people suffered the lightest 'deluge.' God created killer mosquitos. They killed everyone they bit. People hid under the ground from the mosquitos, to no avail. Nothing worked against them.

Early events

Abraham's father is Nimrod's prime minister. One day the astrologers say: 'A child will be born within a year, he will displace you.' Nimrod kills seventy thousand one-year-old babies. He has the ladies separated to tents in a different place. One day, his father goes to fetch a book, goes to bed with his mother and brings back the book.

Abraham's father is both prime minister and a maker of idols. 'My child, we deceive the people with these idols. Nimrod told me so.' As a child, he drags the biggest idol by its foot to the richest neighborhood. 'Why are you doing this?' 'You don't have to buy it. I'll just do it again.' A jeweler buys it, he sells the idol worth five Liras for a hundred thousand Liras. 'Father, this is what I did.' 'Son, they're going to hang me because of you.'

The fire and the rosebed

He's seventeen or eighteen. It's a big holiday. They all leave on an excursion. His father has the key to the temple of the idols. He says, 'Father, I'm sick,' and stays behind. He's the only one left in town. He smashes all the idols in the temple with an axe. Only the largest remains. He hangs the axe on its neck.

They search for the culprit for weeks, finally they come to Abraham. He says, 'The biggest one must have done it. It probably couldn't stand the lesser idols being worshiped.' They say, 'It's lifeless.' He replies, 'Then why are you worshiping it?'

They take him to Nimrod. 'Did you smash the idols?' 'No, I didn't. But I know the criminal who did it. Let me show you.' He takes them to the temple, he shows them the largest idol. They say: 'This can't do it.' 'Really?' he says. 'This can't eat, drink or smash.' He says, 'Then why are you prostrating to it?'

We have faith, but let's still not make any idols. God's name is in us, not in a piece of wood. Let's not make idols.[5]

That's when they threw him in jail. They light a bonfire that burns for a year, they throw Abraham right into its center. Gabriel comes, 'Let me raze this city to the ground.' Abraham says: 'I've spoken with your Creator and mine. He is enough for me.' This is Abraham's Trial by Fire. Gabriel comes three times to ask. He says, 'No, I trust in my Lord, He knows better.' He rejects all creaturely interventions. God says: 'Since you took refuge in Me, I won't burn you.'

All prophets have passed through this trial. The saints, those who wish to be close to God, have passed it, too. There, he passes all the stages of selfhood from the Base Self to the Pleased Self. Fire is his own self, his ego.

As a reward, God turns the fire into a rose garden for him. A water springs from the middle of the fire. It's still there, fish swim in it.[6] A rosebush sprouts. There Abraham prostrates himself to God.

The ram and the reason for the Islamic sacrificial feast

Abraham traveled a lot. He went to Egypt, where the pharaoh set his sights on Sarah, Abraham's wife. [However, just as the pharaoh was about to lunge at her, his lower half became paralyzed. Appalled, he

---

5. When a tree in Africa was being cut into planks in 1990, its cross section revealed *In the name of God, the Compassionate, the Merciful* in Arabic script on one plank. Some people tended to view this as miraculous and were almost minded to venerate the plank. This comment was made concerning that.

6. In Urfa, southeastern Turkey. Although Sir Leonard Woolley popularized Ur (in southern Iraq) as the hometown of Abraham, Cyrus Gordon has disputed this, and the locals of Urfa – which is close to Haran, another Abrahamic site – have a longstanding tradition of Abraham and major events in his life. See also *Biblical Archaeology Review*, Jan./Feb. 2000, pp. 16*ff.*

let her go free and back to Abraham, after which he regained the use of his legs.]

You've come upon a harvest! You're celebrating the Holiday of the Sacrifice, but you don't know why you're celebrating it.

When Abraham was ninety years old, he wished for a child, a boy, from God. 'My Lord, prophethood will be terminated. Give me a male child, I'll sacrifice to you what I love most.' Yes! We have to be very careful what we say [pray for]. God didn't oppress Abraham, Abraham asked for it himself. God gave Abraham what he wanted. But Abraham forgot his vow.

When Ishmael was nine or twelve years old, Abraham had a dream. He was reminded of his promise. But the problem is, what Abraham loved most was his son, Ishmael. He sacrifices sheep, to no avail. He sacrifices a hundred camels, to no avail. He distributes the flesh to bird and beast, it's just no use. God tells Abraham: 'You were supposed to sacrifice the one you love most. Were all those camels the one you love most?'

He placed his forehead on the ground. 'What do you love most? Ishmael!'

Yes, we should know very well what we're praying for. He took Ishmael. 'Son, we're going to collect firewood.' They went as far as Mina, Mount Arafat.

They go to Arafat together, Abraham does a Thanksgiving Prayer, he ties Ishmael's hands and feet. He wants to blindfold his eyes, too. His hands are shaking, he's a father and this is his son. How can you kill your own child? He's trembling, he's agitated. Among the prophets, Abraham went through the greatest trials.

'Father, what is this? You're tying my hands, you're very agitated. Why are you trembling?'

Abraham let forth a groan full of longing and flames. 'Son, this is the situation. I have to sacrifice you for the love of God. I sacrificed all my sheep in your stead, it was no use. I want to blindfold you so that I don't see your eyes, and you don't see the knife.'

'Father,' he said, 'You're a hundred years old. You're about to retire from prophethood. I'm your only son.' Isaac hasn't been born yet. 'I'm your *only* son. How can you sacrifice me? How much you must love God.' 'What can I do, son?' he says. 'This is obligatory for me.'

'*How did you receive this order?*' Ishmael asks. This is the crux of the matter, so pay attention. 'I saw it in a *dream*,' he says. 'I'm doing this on the basis of a *dream*.'

'Okay, Father, may fifty Ishmaels be sacrificed for your sake. Only, I have a question: in the presence of God, whom you love *so much*, how is it that you fell asleep and had a dream?'

Yes! Here Ishmael becomes the father, and Abraham the son. You know how we wish to see the Prophet in our dreams. What a great mistake!

Three times Abraham struck his neck with the knife, three times it didn't cut. He struck a rock with the knife, the rock shattered to pieces. At that moment the Magnification [see Appendix] is heard, a ram descends from a hill. Abraham and Ishmael also recite the Magnification. Abraham sacrifices the ram.

He prostrated to God. He took Ishmael and returned. Because Muhammad is going to descend from Ishmael. Abraham went through the greatest trials, Muhammad went through the greatest suffering.

So you see, if Abraham had sacrificed Ishmael, we too would have had to sacrifice our most beloved. But instead of that, we sacrifice a ram. And with that we feed the poor. That's the basis of the matter. Write this down, don't forget. You know the Night of Power, better than a thousand months? These festivities are like that.

The Ka'ba and the Black Stone

The Black Stone descended to Earth together with Adam. After Adam's punishment was over, he was told: 'Circumambulate this place with your wife.' The Ka'ba was four walls, it was wrecked during Noah's Deluge. All trace of it was gone, it was covered with sand.

Abraham had a dream. He saw an ant-hole. 'Dig here,' he was told. In the dream he was shown the shape of the Ka'ba. He went and dug, the foundations of the Ka'ba were revealed. He dug the ant-hole, first he found a golden stag and then the *Zamzam* water. [Later, Hagar and Ishmael would rediscover it.]

Lot

Our Prophet forbade fornication with both Verse and Saying. That's where humanity is headed now.

The people of Lot were so depraved that they abandoned even women and ran after young boys. Worse than animals. Lot prayed to God, two youths came. So handsome were they, you couldn't bear to look at them. One was [Archangel] Gabriel, the other was Michael.

His people were hot on their trail. That evening they gathered at Lot's door: 'You're going to give them to us.' 'Don't. I have three grown daughters, let me give them.' 'No.' Lot says, 'You'll have to kill me first.' This goes on till daybreak. That morning, Gabriel says: 'We're angels, we've come to save you. Leave, don't look back.' A mile outside [Sodom], his wife can't resist it, she turns back and looks. The city is enveloped in pitch-black darkness. She herself turns into a pillar of stone.

And now, humanity is headed in the same direction again. There used to be the prophets. Now there are the Torah, the Gospel and the Quran. But nobody's obeying them.

Moses

In the time of Moses, spiritual sciences were very advanced. Moses threw a glass of water, it became a sea. He threw his staff, it became a serpent. Pharaoh made the river flow in reverse. The Samaritan took some sand from Gabriel's footprint, he put it in the mouth of the golden calf, the calf began to moo. None of these can be done today.[7]

The way I imagine Moses, he's tall with a salt-and-pepper beard. A saying of Moses: 'If you're in the country of the blind, you too shut one eye.'[8]

The gold and the fire

The Nile is very fertile. According to one account, it even contains the Elixir of Life. So does the Euphrates River.

There are many important things in Moses. It's all there. The orange crate [i.e., the basket of bulrushes]. There's a lot right there – just look at history. But nobody studies history, how should they know? Take a history of Islam, buy a Quran and put it in your home.

Moses' mother put on a wide skirt so that the neighbors wouldn't understand she was pregnant. [When the child was born, she placed it in a basket or crate and put it in the Nile. It drifted right to the doorstep of Pharaoh.]

Asiya, Pharaoh's wife, said: 'If it contains a living thing, it's mine. I have no children. If it's lifeless, you can have it. You're always hoarding

---

7. In connection with Moses, see also The saints/Khidr/Moses and Khidr.
8. That is: 'When in Rome, do as the Romans.'

anyway.' Pharaoh is very upset when he sees Moses, but he can't go back on his promise. So you killed all those children, eh? God made him raise Moses on his lap! Pharaoh says, 'This is the one who's going to kill me' – intelligence.

One day, mercy overcomes him, he takes the child in his lap and fondles it lovingly. But ...

But Pharaoh's beard had grown too long. He grabbed him by the beard and pulled. He pulled out a part of his beard. God gave him that strength. Tears came from Pharaoh's eyes. He said, 'Didn't I tell you, he's going to be the cause? Kill him right now.'

A wise man who was present said: 'Sir, this is a child. Let's make a test. Let's put gold in one pot and fire in another. If he goes for the gold, he's able to comprehend, then we can kill him.'

Gabriel veiled the gold from his sight. He went for the fire, grabbed a cinder and put it in his mouth. Both his hand and tongue were burned, and that's why Moses had a lisp for the rest of his life. Pharaoh's vizier got up and said, 'We forgive him, you forgave him.'

When you take up a task, don't let go. Hold on tight, just like Moses did.

The burning bush

[After Moses escaped from Egypt, the daughters of Jethro found Moses.] He served Shu'ayb [*Hebr.* Hobab, Jethro] as a shepherd for seven years. [Then Shu'ayb married one of his daughters to Moses, and Moses returned to Egypt.] The entrusted objects included a staff, the girl [Zipporah, *Ar.* Safura, the wife of Moses] brought it. It pokes a person in distress, a staff.

[At first, Jethro did not want to give this trust to Moses, because it had been the staff of the ancient prophets. He told his daughter to fetch another staff. But no matter what she did, out of a bundle of staffs, this was the one that always came to her hand. Finally, Jethro was forced to give the staff of the prophets of old to Moses. This is how the 'staff of Moses' came to belong to him.]

On his way to Egypt, a storm breaks. His wife is pregnant. [On the mountain he sees a light.] He runs to the light – 'Perhaps some help?' There he sees the fire of God. A burning bush, or a pine or oak, a manifestation of light. 'O Moses, take off your sandals and then come.' The fire disappears. 'O Moses, fear not, I am your Lord.' He comes back to find that his wife has given birth, the storm has abated, everything is back to normal.

The storm is inside us. If a person is patient, distress is followed by relief. The storm is distress. If we take refuge in God when in trouble, He will grant relief.

The fire is God's helping hand, the fire of faith, that is, knowledge. [He says to God so many times,] 'Let me see You, let me see You.' 'Take off your sandals' – the sandals are his self.

The staff and the serpent

The contest between Pharaoh and Moses – Pharaoh says, 'Let's draw up our forces tomorrow, go to an open space, whichever side wins is the victor.' 'Okay,' says Moses.

Pharaoh went early. They made him a throne on a plain in Egypt. He gathered the audience. One [of the magicians] utters an incantation on water, it becomes a vast sea. One mutters on a piece of thread – it's magic!⁹ – it becomes a serpent. All kinds of spells. One recites on fire and casts it down, it becomes a great bonfire.

Moses goes, he sees these things, Moses is afraid. From the fire! 'My God, what am I going to do against these?' He appeals to God.

'O Moses, I gave you a staff. Say *In the name of God, the Compassionate, the Merciful*, stroke the staff and set it on the ground.'

He did as he was told. He set down the staff. The staff of Moses became a serpent, it grew and grew, it became a dragon as big as a mountain. First it approched the fire, *whoosh*, it blew out the fire. It approached the water, *slurp*, it swallowed it. The dragon swallowed all the serpents on the plain. It alone remained, it swallowed them all.

Then it began to move towards Pharaoh. Pharaoh is on a wooden stand, he got off, he fled for the city with the rest of the people!

Now Moses is afraid, too, he can't come close. No one's left, they've all fled. He appealed to God. 'O Moses, approach it, say *In the name of God, the Compassionate, the Merciful*, stroke it with your hand.' He approached it fearfully because it had swallowed them all. He recited it, stroked and it became a staff again. He took it in his hand.

That serpent is our self.

---

9. Real magic, not the sleight-of-hand used by stage magicians to con the gullible.

The contest on the Nile

Pharaoh is intelligent, but he doesn't believe in God. And he said, 'I am God.' He sent a message to Moses: 'Tomorrow we meet by the Nile. Whichever of us is able to make the river flow backwards, he has the last word.'

Moses was pleased, he said 'Yes.' He trusted himself. He pulled up his blanket and went to sleep.

Pharaoh had himself suspended by the feet [from the ceiling], he begged: 'Lord of Moses, don't put me to shame!' Upside down, he labored until morning. Saliva, mucus, they all came out. Moses slept all night.

The next day Moses begged and implored, to no avail. [Then it was Pharaoh's turn.] Pharaoh said with great wrath: 'Turn!' – and the river Nile began to flow backwards.

Moses prostrated himself: 'My Lord, why did it happen like this? I am Your prophet.'

'O Moses, he took refuge in Me. He worked, you slept. But don't worry, I shall make you victorious.' That night Moses gathered his people and escaped. They go to the Red Sea, it parts.

Everyone is asleep, that's why I remembered this.

The Red Sea

Moses takes his people and sets off. Pharaoh is in hot pursuit. Moses strikes the Red Sea with his staff, it parts. Pharaoh catches up, but just as he is about to make it to the other shore, the sea closes over. Three times he goes down and resurfaces.

There's a delicate point here. Pharaoh, on his white steed, takes refuge in Moses three times: 'Moses, I acknowledge your Lord. Save me!' Moses is annoyed. He's suffered so much. He says, 'Begone!'

Later, the following statement comes from God in an inspiration: 'You weren't able to fulfill your servanthood. He asked for mercy three times. Whether good or evil, you should have saved him and taken refuge in Me. O Moses, if he had asked Me for help even once, I would have saved him and set him up against you again. I would still have saved him if he had taken refuge in Me.'

The golden calf

Moses leaves his brother Aaron behind and goes up Mount Sinai. He told Aaron, 'You take care of the faithful, I'll be back after a while,' and departed.

A jeweler, a goldsmith. He understood a few things, he listened, he did a few things. A month or two after Moses had retired [to the mountain], he tells the wealthy, the ladies, everyone: 'I'm going to do something – on Moses' orders, of course!'

What does this goldsmith do, he gathers all the gold. He casts a golden calf. He goes to the place where Gabriel landed, he scoops up a handful of soil, brings it and pours it down the calf's throat. That heap of gold begins to bellow! Those who believe in Moses and those who don't, he gathers them all to his side.

This commotion goes on for quite some time.

Meanwhile, Moses has retired to Mount Sinai. He's telling God, 'Come, let me talk to you, let me play with you. Do this, give me that.' God replies: 'O Moses, be still. I've given you what you need. I have loved you very much. Be smart, stay where you are. I've given you everything, but I haven't given my Godhood – neither to you nor to anyone else.' And it is not given.

He received his due during that final period of asceticism. Mount Sinai is mentioned in the Torah, but it's not a mountain – it's Moses' 'mountain'! Moses' Mount Sinai is his head. [The 'mountain' was shattered – 7:143.][10]

Coming down, Moses communicates with his brother Aaron. 'What's new?' asks Moses.

Aaron explains: 'Such-and-such a thing happened.'

'I left you as my deputy!' He strikes Aaron's face with a resounding slap. 'How could you let such a thing happen?' Then he regrets it. He says, 'What can we do? I know where this play is coming from, but you received the slap.' He sets off with his brother in front.

'What did you do?' 'Well, sir,' one says, 'a mass of gold is roaring. We strayed from the path.' His own people! As soon as the goldsmith hears this, he runs away. They go, the calf is bellowing and sounding away like that, he wraps his staff around its neck like so, he says: 'Begone!'

They all swarm around Moses, saying: 'We gave our gold, we gave our bracelets, we gave this and that.' Moses says, 'To whom are we going to return them?' He takes the calf and throws it in the sea. The West is still looking for it.

---

10. According to the account of this Verse, Moses implored God, 'Let me see you.' God replied, 'You cannot see me. But I shall manifest Myself to this mountain and if it can stand it, then you can see Me.' But the mountain shattered and Moses was knocked unconscious. On this point, see also Exodus 33:20.

The tablets

Moses smashes the tablets of the Ten Commandments. That doesn't mean he broke them. God first gave Moses one law, one order. His people were unable to act on it. Then He sent the tablets with the Ten Commandments inscribed on them. When Moses came down from Mount Sinai and saw his people worshiping the golden calf, he smashed the tablets to smithereens. That is, since they couldn't act on the basis of the Ten Commandments, God said, 'If they can't run, let them walk. If they can't walk, let them use crutches,' and sent down the Jewish Divine Law [with its 613 precepts].[11]

The poor and destitute

God asks Moses: 'O Moses, what have you done for Me?'

Moses replies: 'I Prayed, I worshiped.'

'O Moses, those are for you. Did you visit a sick person for Me? Did you heal the sick? Did you feed the hungry? Did you clothe the poor, the naked, the shivering? Did you alleviate anyone's sorrow for My sake? Did you reconcile people offended with each other? Did you keep vigil all night and invoke? Those are for Me, worship is for you.'

One should walk on both sides. One should be with the Creator inwardly and with humanity outwardly.

Moses asked God: 'Can I be the distributor of sustenance?' God replied: 'Break that stone.' He broke it, inside that hard rock was a worm with a piece of greenery in its mouth.

'Can you do that?' 'Oh Lord, forgive me,' he says, and prostrates himself.[12] God is All-powerful. *He is able to do all things.*

Moses and the ants

What do the wise say? 'Talk about everything, don't meddle in mysteries.'

---

11. More precisely, 248 'positive laws' plus 365 'negative laws,' yielding a total of 613. Traditionally, 248 is the number of columns in the Torah or the number of bones in the body, while 365 is the number of days in a year, or the number of blood vessels and nerves in the body.

12. Another such story from Sufi lore: Moses said to God, 'Let me rule the winds.' 'You can't do it.' 'Please?' 'Oh, all right,' God says, and grants him his wish. Moses is unable to control it, storms and typhoons ravage the earth, ships sink. 'Dear God, forgive me, please take it back.' God says, 'I told you so.'

God says to Moses: 'O Moses, this city is going to be razed.' Moses warns them, its citizens flee, Moses flees. 'My Lord, that town has faith in You. Seventy thousand people in that town do their Wakeup Prayers [before Dawn Prayers]. Spare it for their sake.' No matter how much he implores, 'O Moses, don't meddle in My affairs. The command shall take place.' Moses prostrates himself to save the city.

[At that instant,] God creates an ant colony beneath his feet. Red ants, you know, the kind that bites? Thousands of ants begin climbing up his legs. One of them bites a delicate spot. He jumps up and tries to brush them off. Hundreds of ants perish. God says: 'O Moses, only one ant bit you. What was the crime of the others? One person did a terrible thing. Someone in that town bit me.'

He understands his error, he says, 'My God, forgive me.'

It happens like that. Because of one person, ten persons, millions go.

Let us be careful. Let's not bite. 'The wet [wood] burns together with the dry' [8:25]. One person does it, a thousand people suffer. Terrible.

Moses and the barber

Again, a city is going to be destroyed. Moses meets a barber and tells him, 'Gather the people on the mountain at eight or nine o'clock in the morning.' 'Don't hurry,' says the barber. In the morning, 'Come on.' The barber: 'O Moses, we have faith in you. What you say is true. [But] I won't alert anyone, I'm going to meet my fate together with all the rest. Gather a hundred people and leave.'

1 p.m., 2 p.m., still nothing happens. Moses says, 'My Lord, what mystery is this?' God replies: 'The barber. I spared the city for the sake of that barber.'

Like the barber in the story, let a person come forth and let the nation be spared.

Moses and the ass

Again, God says to Moses: 'There will be no rainfall this year.' Moses: 'My God, what shall we do?' 'Don't meddle in My affairs.'

Everyone plants squash on rooftops, they draw water from wells. Then God's mercy runs over, a cloud comes, it rains for weeks. Moses asks, 'They call me a liar. What mystery is this?' God says: 'There's a donkey outside the city nearby, go and see it.'

Moses finds the donkey. In the language of states, it says:

'For ten years my owner didn't give me food, he didn't give me water, he made my burden heavy. My back is broken, see, I can't carry weight. I wandered and wandered, I came to this tree. I gnawed at it with my teeth. I took refuge in God. I said, 'You gave me to the lowliest tyrant, I was patient.' I prayed like that while I was gnawing with my teeth.'

God said: 'O Moses, you see? I've spared those people for the sake of that poor animal.'

Divine justice

[The following story is included in this section because in Sufic literature, its hero is reported to be Moses:[13]

A man was very pious, but found the events of the world incomprehensible. He was always arguing with God that things should be done differently.

One day he heard a voice. 'Enough!' said the voice. 'Crouch behind that bush and watch what's about to happen.'

As the man watched, a horseman came to the nearby watering place, took off his gem-studded sword, set it aside, drank some water and watered his horse. Then he got on it and departed. But he had forgotten to take his sword.

Next, a small child came along, drank some water. Seeing the sword, he admired it and took off with it.

Then an old man came along. Just as he was drinking water, the horseman came back in a flurry. He had remembered about the sword. When he couldn't find it, he was suspicious of the old man. 'Where did you hide it?' he asked threateningly. When the old man protested his innocence, the horseman killed him, searched for the sword but couldn't find it and rode off.

The man jumped to his feet. 'This is exactly the kind of senseless murder I've always been protesting!' he said.

'Shut up and listen!' the voice said. 'The old man killed the horseman's father, so he owed the horseman a life. And that horseman once robbed that boy's family, so he owed the boy property. Don't ascribe injustice to the Divine just because you're ignorant of the full facts.']

This is not a story, it happened. It happened.

---

13. www.zaman.com.tr/2003/04/10/yazarlar/ahmetsahin.htm. Details filled in from very brief outline in notes.

Moses and the tent owner

Again, Moses is wandering in the middle of winter, he sees a tent as big as a neighborhood on a mountain. 'Let's see who this is.' He visits him. The tent is punctured on one side, they've made a separation. He says to the tent-owner, 'What are you doing here when you're so rich? Why don't you go down to a town, build a house and come up to your tent in the summer?'

The rich man smiled. 'In the Torah, the Book of Moses, it is written that God has granted us a life of five hundred years. I've lived for three hundred years. I have two hundred left. It's not worth bothering for two hundred years.'

Moses says: 'It'd be nice if you did. After us and after Jesus, a latter-day prophet is going to come, his community will live a hundred years at most. But they'll be like the dead after sixty. Those people will construct buildings the likes of which you've never seen. They're going to forget about the afterlife for the sake of this world.'

The rich tent-owner: 'Oh, those poor things. If I were in their place, I would take an Ablution, prostrate myself for a hundred years, finish my time and go.'

Moses likes that. He stays there for a week, he introduces himself. 'Would you heed a prophet?' he says. 'It would still be nice if you did it.' The man is of Sound Mind. 'I'll build the house,' he says, 'But I'll build it only one storey high.'

The community

Moses reaches a town, the houses are all the same, the men wear the same outfit, the ladies wear the same dress, the children are like that too. He stays for a visit, everyone brings a glass of water. If food were to come, it would be too much. They still take back the remaining water.

Moses asks: 'What is this, your situation?' They reply: 'We love Moses. We obey the Torah. We do these things, otherwise there would be jealousy.'

'I'm Moses. Tomorrow I'm going to address you.'

Moses is filled with admiration. 'May God's mercy be upon you,' he says.

May you too be like this.

The feast

Moses says to God, 'My Lord, I would like to give a feast in your honor.' God says: 'Leave such things be. You'll make a mess of it.' But Moses insists. 'Okay okay, I'll come, next Friday after two o'clock.'

Moses tells his people, they make great preparations. The day arrives. A dishevelled, sick man comes by, leaning on a staff.

'Who's the leader of this tribe? What're all these people assembled here for?'

'God is going to come.'

'I'm hungry and have far to go, take care of me and let me be off.'

He repeats it three times. Moses is annoyed. 'We're waiting for God so that the feast can start. Fill this jug from over there while we're waiting, He'll come by then,' he says. The old man fills the jug and leaves.

God doesn't come. Two o'clock, three o'clock, the people are outraged. Moses prostrates himself: 'My God, don't shame me.' 'O Moses, I came. Not only did you fail to feed Me, but you sent Me to fetch water. I brought you a jug of water.' Some are rebeling: 'What kind of prophet is this?'

Moses turns to those who are waiting: 'Folks, He came and went, I wasn't able to recognize Him. Let's eat.'

So be awake. Be careful in everything.

The inn

Moses set off and arrived at a town. There's a very large inn, people are filing in, nobody's coming out.

Moses went in. Everybody finishes his business and leaves through the back door. The innkeeper, they've placed a bed beside a fountain in the middle of the inn, he's lying there. They're circumambulating that hundred-twenty-year-old man.

Moses asks, the innkeeper answers.

'Does this place belong to you?'

'It belongs to God, your Creator and mine.'

'What is all this?'

'I built this place for charity. I have an incurable illness. God gave me much, so I'm giving, too.'

Moses loves it. He says: 'I'm going up Mount Sinai next week. Is there anything you want?' 'O Moses, we're very close. Still, give Him my regards. I couldn't burden you. Besides, doesn't God hear what we're saying? He hears as soon as I tell you.' Moses says: 'If I hadn't been prophet, he would've been.' That's the kind of faith one ought to have.

Moses and the thief in the cemetery

Moses is going around in a cemetery, he's poking skulls in the open with his staff. Some of them, he's picking up and collecting in a separate place. A thief who had been hiding there watches him, trying to make sense of it all. Finally, when Moses has collected five skulls, his curiosity overcomes him.

'What on earth are you doing?'

Moses says, 'Bring a pick and a shovel.' He strikes a skull with his staff, it goes in one ear and out the other. He strikes another, it doesn't penetrate at all.

'That's how they listened to the Torah. I struck one skull with the staff, it remained inside, they listened to the Torah well. Those are the ones we need, that's why I'm collecting them.'[14]

The thief is impressed, he asks Moses a question. 'If I stole something, what would its punishment be? When is your Divine Law realized?' Moses replies: 'Outwardly, he's in punishment every day. But it is postponed for seven years.'

'Have you any water left?' Moses asks. He takes an Ablution and begins to Pray. The thief steals his headgear and money [which Moses had set aside]. As he's running away, he falls and, *snap!* breaks his leg.

Moses finishes his Prayer and finds him. The thief says: 'Look, you said I would be punished seven years later, but it happened immediately.' Moses smiles. 'My son, this punishment is for what you did seven years ago.' The thief says: 'I shall obey you from now on.'

Solomon

David is the father of Solomon. David has twelve sons from a wife. He marries Solomon's mother, Solomon is her only child.

When Solomon is twelve years old, his father gives some advice to visitors. As they're leaving, Solomon says, 'My father said that, but do it this way.' And he turns out to be right.

---

14. A similar story is related in Sufi lore of Bahlul the Wise. He was giving away the worthless skulls for free, and selling the valuable ones that heeded the instructions of the Quran and the Sayings for a high price.

David has fifteen or twenty sons, some of them older than Solomon. Solomon turns sixteen. David's time is nearing. 'My God, who will be prophet after me, who will continue the path?' God indicates Solomon in a revelation. Three times, Solomon is indicated in all three, even though he has older brothers. His father asks: 'Son, can you manage these people?'

He says, 'Father, you can do better than me, I can't do it as well as you can.' When David insists, he says: 'Father, see how many brothers we are, you're raising us in poverty. I don't want this kind of prophethood. If I can have kingship and prophethood together, that's what I want. I don't want to be destitute like you.' He wants the rule of both the material and the spiritual kingdoms. [This should not be confused with the kingship of Israel.]

'Son, our duty is the afterworld.' 'I know, Father, but this is still what I want.'

This was pleasing to God. David consults inwardly with God, 'Accepted' is the reply. He has power over the air, wind, clouds and rain. He understands the language of all animals and birds.

Among the prophets, Solomon is the only one with kingship [over both realms]. He's said to have lived five hundred years, but there's a sign in the Quran, he ruled for thirty-five years. That is, the duration of his reign [until the next prophet comes] is five hundred years. This world does not last, not even for King Solomon.

King Solomon and the ant

There's a general Unification, you know? Everything in the eighteen thousand worlds, with its own language, its own faith ... That is, Totality is within Unification. Don't look for anything outside Unification. Whatever God has created is within Unification. An ant enlightened King Solomon: with Unification.

King Solomon is going somewhere with his army. A faint voice comes: 'Get off the road!' says an ant. Because King Solomon knows all languages, he also knows the language of ants. He goes in that direction. King Solomon's army fears not even God, the ant is going to get trampled underfoot. So he goes towards the voice, the ant has climbed onto a small, fist-sized stone. He dismounts, he takes the stone: 'What are you saying?'

'Ah, Your Majesty,' it says. 'You feed them and feed them. Nobody sees what's underfoot. We all set out hungry on the road, perhaps we can find a crumb, something from passers-by.' Ants always go on the road, it's still like that today. 'If you command your army not to trample on us, it'd be good. That's why I shouted. We affirm your kingship, but excuse me. I'm *their* king, I'm the king of the ants.'

There and then, King Solomon issues a command: 'Anyone who tramples an ant, who steps on a leaf of grass, who severs a branch, off with his head.' That's where it happens. 'An ant has enlightened me,' he says.

The Queen of Sheba

The hoopoe mediated between Bilqis and Solomon. King Solomon is in Palestine, Bilqis is where ruins are now.[15] Solomon asks, 'Is there a ruler greater than me?' The captain of the birds, the hoopoe, answers: 'Not greater, but there's a ruler like you.' He writes a letter, 'Who will take it?' The hoopoe says, 'I will.' It takes it in its beak and flies for months. According to another account, it was King Solomon's messenger who took it.

She receives the letter of invitation. The hoopoe comes back: 'I gave it, they read it, I came back.'

Bilqis can't resist it. She travels for months and years.

She arrives in Jerusalem. 'Which is King Solomon's palace?' It's a hovel by comparison [with her own]. 'Oh,' she says, 'if only my palace were here, too.'

Solomon learns of this through his genies. 'Who can bring this palace before Bilqis arrives?' A demon among the genies says, 'I can.' Asaf ibn Barakhya (*Hebr*. Berekhya), his vizier, says: 'I can bring it in the twinkling of an eye,' and does so. 'Asaf, how did you do that?' 'I did it with strength from my God and permission from you.'[16]

Bilqis comes, she's astonished. She asks her servants: 'When did you arrive?' They reply: 'We were here all the time.'

Those who are jealous of Bilqis say: 'Her legs are hairy.' Solomon has a pool constructed[17] that gives the appearance of being filled with water. Bilqis arrives, she raises the hem of her dress so it won't get wet,

---

15. Archaeologists believe that the capital of the Kingdom of Sheba/Saba was outside Ma'rib, Yemen.

16. In the Quran, it is mentioned that only Bilqis' throne was teleported, not her entire palace (27:40). An embellishment must have occurred during oral transmission. The Master once confirmed this by referring to the palace account as 'a tale.'

17. Covered with glass.

everyone sees that there is no hair. Solomon fires her detractors. They plead with Bilqis: 'Madam, we were jealous of you.' She forgives them.

The genies informed Solomon: 'Bilqis worships idols.' 'It can't be,' he said, 'she's my wife.' But in fact, a charcoal drawing was found on Bilqis. When he asked, 'What's this?' she replied, 'A picture of my father. I take it out once in a while to look at it.' That's when pictures were prohibited, just like idols.

Comment: *Then we're all idolaters now.*

No. That's not true. People know God now. Pictures aren't idols.

Bilqis wants a kaftan made of the feathers of all birds. Solomon sends for the birds, the owl does not come. Solomon has it summoned. It gives very wise answers. 'Isn't it a pity? What're you going to do with these birds? Winter's coming.'
   Solomon likes this very much and gives a present to the owl: 'May God bring your sustenance to your feet.' From then on, when the owl says '*Hoo*,' it is said that sparrows come to it. It takes one, the others go.

Solomon was making a pillow of down for Bilqis. They asked him: 'Which is greater – the number of the living, or of the dead?' He replied, 'The number of the dead.' 'Why?' they asked. He said: 'I'm a dead man at the hands of my wife.'

The people are jealous of Bilqis. Bilqis has a child. A report comes from the Unseen: 'This child is going to be stolen.' King Solomon pronounces over it every day: 'My God, I entrust him to You.' One day there's an urgent matter, he has to leave without saying it, the child vanishes. It's missing ever since.

Solomon's death

Solomon begins to build the Temple [at the location] of the Farthest Mosque.[18] His time has come. Gabriel brings the news: 'O Solomon, be prepared!'
   He prayed to God: 'My God, my life and soul are Yours. But I have begun this construction. Let me leave a monument.'

---

18. That is, the Mount of the Temple in Jerusalem.

God doesn't change his destiny, he leans on a date tree and expires. He's supported by his cane, he doesn't fall. Asaf, his prime minister, knows. He's there all the time. The temple is supposed to be finished in a year, it's finished in a month. [Genies are said to have helped in its construction.] They're going to perform the opening ceremony, his vizier approaches him. 'Sir,' he says, 'the ceremony?' His glance does not shift. A worm has been gnawing away at his cane, he topples over with a light touch. God's allotment does not change, but the temple is finished.

Ezra

He's of the people of Moses, the people of the Torah, his name is Ezra [Uzayr]. Ezra went to the vineyard to pick grapes, he hitched his donkey, he had been thinking: 'Are human beings resurrected after they die?' [2:259]. He's opposing the Torah, that is, he doesn't believe. He falls asleep, he sleeps for a hundred years. They say, 'He went to the vineyard and was never seen again.' That year his son is born.

When he wakes up, there's no donkey, the vineyard is a ruin. He gets up and goes to town, 'Who are you, stranger?' They say, 'It was said that man went missing.' His son is a hundred years old, he's forty. They've forgotten the Torah too, he teaches them, he becomes a prophet. He stays a week, he says, 'My God, I can't stand this, take my spirit.'

There are many like that. The People of the Cave slept for three hundred years.[19]

Jonah

[Jonah tries to teach his people, but they don't listen to him. Disillusioned, he boards a ship and leaves, but it's dereliction of duty.]

A storm came up. He prayed in the ship. He said, 'My God, calm this storm and take me,' and jumped into the sea. There he's swallowed by a whale. He remains in the belly of the whale for forty days according to one account, and forty hours according to another.

---

19. This event furnishes the title for a chapter in the Quran: 'The Cave.' It is supposed to have occurred in early Christian times. Also known as the Seven Sleepers, the People of the Cave hid in a cave from Roman persecution and slept for three hundred years.

From the belly of the whale, he repeats over and over again: '*There is no god but You. Glory be to You. I have been of the wrong-doers*' [21:87]. They say that with this prayer, Jonah made his Ascension in the belly of the whale.

It doesn't digest him. It takes and regurgitates him on land. His clothes were melted, he was left naked. He covers himself with something. But he doesn't live long after that. Human beings kill him. There are very delicate points here. Don't bother about them, they're not for you to understand.

[According to the Quran, more than a hundred thousand finally believed in him (37:147-8).]

Luqman

(Although the Master did not consider Luqman a prophet, he is included here because he is mentioned in the Quran as a pre-Islamic saint. He was a doctor.)

Luqman is a saint, not a prophet. Between Jesus and Muhammad. They asked Luqman: 'Where did you learn this knowledge, this culture?' He replied: 'In the streets, from the discourteous. [Whatever they were doing, I did the opposite.] I restrained myself until God gave me this knowledge.'

The knowledge of wisdom is superior to Hidden Knowledge (*'ilm al-ladun*). Doctor Luqman was given the science of wisdom. It appears to him in a dream, as a sheet. When he wakes up, he writes it down on three pieces of paper. He was going to cross a bridge and climb a mountain in Tarsus, there he would find a plant. Whoever ate that plant would not die.

Gabriel, in human form, passes by him as he's crossing the bridge: 'Where are you going?' 'To find the plant of no-death.' Gabriel says, 'Where did you get that? Let me look at it,' but strikes his hand before he can give it, knocking it straight into the river. Luqman catches two of the pages, the third one indicating the leaf of immortality goes down the river. Those two pages suffice for Luqman.

Luqman's last lesson

Perfect surrender. To swallow poison as if it were honey.

That reminds me of Luqman. His teacher loved Luqman very much. He came first among a hundred and fifty, two hundred students. He admired his morality, his courtesy, his work.

In February or March, a student brought his teacher a melon, hard to find in that season. But the melon had been punctured, and when a melon is punctured, it becomes bitter like poison. The second day, the teacher says to his servant, 'Go and call Luqman.' He wants him to eat the melon because of his love for him. Luqman comes, kisses his hand, they chat.

The teacher says, 'Wash that melon and bring it over.' They wash and bring it to him, he gives it to Luqman with his own hands. Luqman takes a bite, his mouth is filled with poison, but without the slightest sign of discomfiture on his face, he eats it all. Finally, only one slice is left.

His teacher says, 'You ate with great zest. It's stimulated my appetite. Let me eat this slice.' 'Of course,' he says, 'eat it.' He puts it in his mouth, bites and … throws up. Because he's old, he passes out. Luqman brings a towel right away, he wipes his mouth and chest. He brings water, does a few things and revives him.

The teacher sits up, tears come from his eyes. 'Why, I was killing you because I loved you. How on earth did you eat that?' Yes! 'How did you eat it with smiling face and such appetite?'

He again kisses his hand, 'Teacher,' he says, 'I would give this life for you. *This is coming from your hand,*' he says, 'no matter *what* it might be.'

'I almost killed you with my own hand. Do you want something, something sweet?' 'No,' he says, 'I'm fine, I'm young, don't worry.'

The next day, at school, the teacher fills out Luqman's diploma. 'Two lions can't remain in one place,' he says, 'your studies with me are concluded. Farewell.' And he becomes Luqman.

These are very difficult. Very difficult to believe. To do the bitter part. The other side is light, but to make honey out of bitterness. To be human, to become Luqman.

The voice of command

Doctor Luqman had a student. He said, 'Give me an office so that I can ease your burden.' So he did, and the student began receiving patients.

One day a patient comes, he has an intestinal disease. So he operates on the patient. But he can't put the intestines back in place. He even pleads, they won't go back in. He's helpless, he calls Luqman. He comes. He takes a stick in his hand, 'You good-for-nothings!' he says, 'how dare you! Begone,' he says, 'into your place!' The power of Wrath.

They go in, he sews up the body. They lay the patient downstairs. The student says, 'What was *that*?'

'Some like it that way, son,' he says. 'They don't understand anything else.' That's Luqman's word. 'Sometimes it's necessary this way.'

Jesus

(In speaking of Moses, Jesus and Muhammad, the Master said: 'The important thing is the triad of job–spouse–faith.[20] Moses had all three, Jesus had only the last, and Muhammad had all three also.' This is one of the reasons why Christians still need the Old Testament. The monasticism and asceticism of Christianity probably derives from it.)

'There is no god but God, Jesus is the prophet of God.'

Jesus is one of the five (earlier) Great Prophets: Adam, Noah, Abraham, Moses, Jesus. Muhammad is the last.

Jesus healed the lepers, the sick, everyone, by the power of God. What did they do? They took him and nailed him to a cross. A man of God!

I, too, am trying to do something like Jesus. Am I crazy, or am I sane?

I didn't read it, but I heard about that: the Divine Law of Jesus is to be completed by our Prophet. 'Muhammad will come after me, he will apply the Divine Law' [61:6. Compare John 15:27, etc.].

Jesus was assumed to heaven bodily. With his physical body, so they say. There are many like that, one is Idris and one is Jesus.

Jesus didn't raise the dead. He healed the sick. But in order to 'resurrect' a 'dead' tribe, he did this: 'Are these ants alive?' 'They're alive.' 'Kill a few of them.' They killed them. 'Are they dead?' 'They're dead.' 'Gather them and give them to me.' He took them in his palm.

---

20. See The beginning/The three prerequisites.

Five minutes later, he opened his palm, the ants walked away. Of the thousands of people present, only one became his disciple. The rest said, 'You did magic.' Jesus never resurrected anyone, he healed lepers on the verge of death.

(*Below is presented an eyewitness account to which I myself was not a party.*)

[The Master asked: 'Do you know how Jesus died?' I said 'No.' He said, 'They didn't crucify him, they crucified someone else in his place.' At one point, I understood that this was Judas. 'Jesus is in the realm of spirits now, he will return,' he said. He smiled at me. It was as if Jesus were speaking to me through the Master's mouth.

'Why didn't Jesus get married?' he asked. He said things which I interpreted to mean that being born without a father, it would not have been right for him to marry.

The Master explicitly indicated that the one who was crucified was Judas. He said: 'I don't remember his name – the one who betrayed him.' The soldiers come after the Last Supper, Jesus is 'drawn up' through the window, Judas begins to appear as Jesus to everyone, and is crucified. He said: 'At the Last Supper, God pulled Jesus out of the window. They crucified Judas in his place.']

The Prophet

His life

One step beyond what the Prophet of God said is an abyss. One step behind what the Prophet of God said – that's an abyss, too. Whatever our Prophet called a sin, know that there is harm in it. Whatever he called a merit, know that there is cure, there is life in it.

Muhammad always called Moses and Jesus 'My brothers.' He never denied them.

Our Prophet showed lenience in Mecca for eleven years. He saw that this wasn't going to work, he emigrated to Medina, he took the sword in his hand. If he hadn't done this, he would have been crucified like Jesus – which had, in fact, come within an inch of happening.[1]

One has to defend against sternness with sternness. And lenience calls for a lenient response. Our Prophet showed lenience for eleven years, he succeeded only after he emigrated to Medina and acted with sternness. It's necessary for every ruler. If he had acted sternly earlier, all those hardships wouldn't have occurred. Both lenience and sternness are required in administration.

The war of the Prophet is not egotistical. It's the war to fear God. People were killing each other in Arabia. The war was for establishing peace among human beings.

Our Prophet married several wives, but not for his own self, not for his own satisfaction. He had two wives, both of whom he loved: Khadija, and after she died, Aisha. The others were widowed, they were in the gutter with their children. Their husbands died, they were struck down in battle. He married them in order to look after them, so that no harm would befall them. [And these he wed in honorable matrimony.] Everything else is incorrect. Prophets do not have pleasures, they do not have egos as we do.

Our Prophet, the pride of the universe, leaves Khadija and goes to a cave on the mountain. For years! Why didn't prophethood come to him in his bed? Work! We too have to restrain this cave, our self. He who works wins, whether for good or for ill. God says, 'I love those who work.'

---

1. 'Hence it is that all armed prophets have conquered, and the unarmed ones have been destroyed.' Machiavelli, *The Prince* (1513), Chapter 6.

Right from his birth, there was nothing egotistical or diabolical about our Prophet. His Heart was purified several times. The things the Prophet of God had to endure – forty years in the mountains, in the company of rocks and scorpions. He gave up his children, he sacrificed his life, He gave up his Companions, but he took the flag in his hand. He became a prophet to the whole world.

As you know, our Prophet was of the Quraysh tribe. That tribe was attached to Abraham and Ishmael. It was the most righteous among the tribes that knew God in Arabia. But things came to such a point that they forgot everything. There was the name, but no substance. No practice. They're burying daughters alive, they're doing the worst iniquities. Terrible – in a dark night, morality has been lost, down to zero, that's where God caused the Prophet to emerge.

He saw the greatest malevolence from his uncle, Abu Lahab [the Father of Flame] and his children. And then the Qurayshites, that is, from his tribe. Friendship he found in the Medinans – where's Mecca, where Medina? He escaped from Mecca and came to Medina together with all his relatives and friends. There he started out.

Nobody was ever able to finish their duty. The prophets couldn't do it. Their own people banished them, killed them. Only our Prophet was able to finish his task. During his Farewell Address, he called three times upon God: 'My Lord, be witness.'

Childhood

There was a great priest [named Bahira] who had studied the Torah, the Psalms, the Gospel. He knows the signs of prophethood, the latter-day prophet is due to come. A caravan came by. The Prophet of God is going to Damascus with the caravan. He said: 'Invite them all to lunch.' He recognized the signs in that child. He said, 'Let this one remain with me, some mishap may befall him in Damascus.'

Arbitrator for the Black Stone

The twelve tribes of Mecca had refurbished the Ka'ba. The time came to lift the Black Stone into its place. The Qurayshites said, 'We'll do it,' the others said 'We'll do it,' they couldn't agree among themselves. They decided to fight it out. They're coming to blows. Whichever tribe emerges stronger, that tribe is going to put it in place.

One of them says: 'Let's not do it this way. Let's be patient. Let's wait and gather there tomorrow. Whoever comes first from that [the Stone's] side, let's ask that person and then decide what to do.' 'Okay,' they said.

The leaders of the twelve tribes gathered there in the morning, they're waiting. Our Prophet is fifteen or twenty, he passes by. 'Oh, Muhammad the Trustworthy is coming!' They're all pleased. 'He doesn't lie, he doesn't take sides, everyone is sure of him.' He comes, they exchange greetings, at that time they respect him because of his grandfather.

One of them explains. 'Muhammad, we have a problem. It's a good thing you came by.' 'What is it?' 'The matter is this.' 'Oh, I know,' he says, 'I've known about the construction for two years. What's your problem?' 'Well, we have to put the Black Stone in place. Which of the twelve tribes should do it?'

'You'd better leave this to me,' he said. 'We refer it to you. Whatever you see fit.' He takes the robe of one of those present and lays it on the ground. He puts the Stone in its center himself. 'Twelve tribes, grab a side,' he says. The twelve tribes take hold of the rim of the robe. They raise it up. 'Who's going to set it in place?' 'If you allow me, I'll do it.' And he put the Stone in its place.

Announcing his prophethood

Our Prophet gathered them all together and asked: 'If I told you there's a hostile army behind that mountain, would you believe me?' 'Yes.' Then he invites them to God. 'If I said God has given prophethood to this nephew of yours, would you believe me?' The atmosphere changed immediately. Abu Lahab takes a plate and hurls it at him. He turns his head, it flies by without impact. The Qurayshites said, *'You're going to be a prophet?'* They all leave.

One day our Prophet goes to the Ka'ba, he's going to do his Prayer among the idols. A bearlike man stops him on his way. 'You used to be a shepherd. My father used to pay you two coins for looking after two camels and two sheep. You were an orphan. And now you're trying to become a prophet!'

He grabs hold of his lapel and shakes him. Our Prophet doesn't say anything. When the man leaves, he continues on his way and starts his Prayer among the idols. But his mind is back there. The man called him 'a shepherd.' He's disturbed, depressed. Besides, it's true. He prays to God: 'My God, help me.'

Now watch. Look at this, this game: Gabriel materializes immediately beside him. He's standing to attention. 'Messenger of God,' he says, 'why do you trouble yourself? Your grandfathers, your brothers – Moses, Abraham – were shepherds, too. Then they became shepherds of men. You were a shepherd yourself, and now you're going to be a shepherd of *human beings*.' He delivers revelation from God: 'Beginning with Abraham, your ancestor, I sent the prophets as shepherds. I test them with animals first. If they're successful, I place them over men.'

He heaves a sigh of relief.

The challenge

The Qurayshites selected two representatives from each tribe. They told his uncle Abu Talib, who was protecting him: 'What does this nephew of yours want? Blood is going to come between us. If he wishes, let's make him our ruler. If he wants, let's give him the girl he likes. If he desires, let's make him rich.' Abu Talib says, 'I'll tell him everything.'

In the evening the Prophet comes, he relates it all.

'Nephew, the Qurayshites, the Hashimites, all the tribes gathered and came.' 'I understand. What reply did you give?' 'I left the reply to you.'

'Even if I were ruler, I still wouldn't turn back. I'm going to be a ruler anyway, don't worry. As for women, I love my wife, one woman is enough for me.[2] Money I don't want anyway.

'Uncle, if you were to join forces with the Qurayshites, if they were to put the sun in my right hand and the moon in my left, and make me the leader of the world, I still would not swerve from my cause.'

He stepped outside. He leaned against the mud wall, 'My God, don't remove this last support from me. Where shall I go, whom shall I go to?'

Abu Talib comes out. God gives him strength. He looks. 'I have just one life,' he says, 'I'll gladly give it for you.' They embrace.

If you help God and His Prophet, God will help you.

---

2. As the Master once explained, this is proof that the Prophet regarded one wife as sufficient.

Be truthful

A man came to the Prophet. He said, 'I do everything that's selfish. I want to become a Muslim, but Fasting, Prayer, I can't do any of these. Show me a way.' The Prophet of God replied, 'Don't lie.'

The man went away and thought about it all night. If he should do something wrong, steal something, drink alcohol, he'll have to lie. He came back, 'Messenger of God,' he said, 'what you told me is difficult. Nevertheless, I'll try.' A month later he came back again: 'It's all over, nothing's left [of my old ways].'

The poor

Our Prophet always loved the weak and cherished the poor.

In emigrating from Mecca to Medina, most were hungry and naked. Once there, the Prophet invited the world to peace. Foreign delegations began to arrive. Some residents consulted with Abu Bakr: 'These people are poor and naked, let's send them to another neighborhood so that they won't be seen. Let them stay away from the Mosque.' They agreed on this.

Someone has to tell our Prophet. Abu Bakr said, 'I won't do that.' So Omar told him after the Noon Prayer. Our Prophet said: 'As you wish.' That's all. They specified a neighborhood, about five minutes' walking distance.

After midnight, the Prophet of God got up and went there. He did the Wakeup Prayer [before the Dawn Prayer], he consoled them, both he and they shed tears. 'Don't worry, everything's going to be all right. I'll clothe you, I'll feed you.'

It's almost morning, the Prophet of God is nowhere to be found. Aisha is apprehensive, too. Somebody came and said, 'He's there. He's alive, don't worry.' They went, he's talking. Omar said: 'Forgive us, Messenger of God. Did we make a mistake?' The Prophet: 'Yes, Omar, you made a very great mistake. I came with the poor, I'm with the poor, I shall go with the poor. Wherever the poor are, there I am. My business is with the poor.'

The blind man

They had bad relations with the Persians when this happened, diplomats came from Persia to make peace. There was a blind man called Abdullah, he came along just as they were about to sign the document: 'Muhammad, Messenger of God!' The Prophet said to himself, 'Couldn't you have come some other time? Perfect timing.' As soon as this passed through his mind, *snap*, Gabriel came. 'Messenger of God, God has an instruction for you. You're going to take care of Abdullah's business first.'

How to recognize a prophet

The Governor of Egypt receives an invitation to Islam from the Prophet. He's studied the Torah, the Gospel, he knows his Gospel well. They decide to test the Prophet.

He chooses a foreign delegation. He takes three or four worldly wise people to his side, he sends three presents to our Prophet in Medina. One is the Gospel. They wrap it up. One is a roll of cloth, fit for a king. First rate. They wrap that up, too. And the other is a female slave of ravishing beauty, twenty or twenty-five years old.

'These three gifts,' he says, 'you will bear to the Prophet, but write down carefully what*ever* he says. First you will give the Gospel, then the cloth and finally the maid.'

The Egyptian delegation arrives, reports in, they accept them, they meet in the Prophet's house. All the world of Islam is there. The leader of the delegation says, 'Our master sends his regards. We've brought three presents for you.' 'You're very kind,' he replies.

They bring the Gospel. 'This is the Gospel,' he says, 'as a present from us.' They still had the original Gospel at that time. 'Thank you very much, that is the Book of my brother, Jesus.'

Second, they open the roll of cloth. 'There's no match for it in all of Egypt.' 'Thank you,' he says. 'If I were to wear that, the people around me are poor, they may get jealous, though it wouldn't make any difference to me. Thanks for that, too,' he says. He turns to Omar, 'Wrap this back up, we can send it as a present to someone, to the shahs of Persia.'

'Also,' their leader says, 'we've brought you a female servant.' 'For me, personally?' 'Yes.' She's in a veil, waiting at the door.

'In that regard, there is a religious command to us from God,' he says. Right there, in front of the delegation, they are officially wed.

The delegation stays a week. Then they bid farewell and leave.

'What did you do?' he says. 'This is the situation,' they report.

'I had my doubts until now,' he says. 'I thought he might be a false prophet. That's why I sent this delegation. But I now believe that Muhammad is the latter-day prophet, the Prophet of God.' If he had been egotistical, he would have repudiated the Gospel. He would have worn the cloth, the costume, right away. And he would have accepted the maid without a second thought. But it's official. Everything's official.

The Gospel is our book. The book of our brother, the book of our grandfather.

Declaration of faith is enough

The Prophet said, 'Whoever recites, "*There is no god but God and Muhammad is the Messenger of God*" is your brother, don't draw swords against each other.'

[During one of the Prophet's battles,] at the last moment one of the Qurayshites said: 'I accept Islam, I accept Muhammad,' and recited the declaration of faith. There's no escape, he's going to die. He's also killed many Muslims himself. His opponent said, 'You're lying, you scoundrel,' and finished him off. News of this reached the Prophet.

He asks: 'What did that man say?' 'Sir, he recited the declaration of faith but he was lying, he killed many from our side.'

'Even if it was a lie, once he pronounced it, you shouldn't have killed him.'

How to see an angel

Whoever recites the Chapter of Sincerity [Chapter 112 of the Quran] a hundred times a day will see angels.

One day in Medina, our Prophet said, 'Whoever recites the Chapter of Sincerity a lot will see angels.' Abu Hurayra – [which means] 'the Father of Cats,' he was very fond of cats – is there, he hears this, he begins to recite the Sincerity night and day. Three years go by.

One day, the Prophet of God came to the Mosque early and sat down at the pulpit. Abu Hurayra also arrived, greeted the Prophet and sat down.

At that moment, a revelation arrived. Gabriel comes, greets Abu Hurayra as he passes by, he returns the greeting. Gabriel approaches the Prophet with great courtesy, kneels beside him and delivers the transmission. After the revelation is finished, Gabriel again greets the Companion as he goes away, is greeted by him in return and leaves.

The Prophet says: 'Did you recognize him?' 'The Prophet of God knows best, I did.' 'Who was it?' 'The Archangel Gabriel, the angel who brings revelation.' 'Bravo! Where did you learn this? Where did you get that strength?'

'Prophet of God, when you came to Medina, you once told us in this Mosque: 'Whoever recites the Chapter of Sincerity a lot will see angels.' I kept on reciting it, and God showed him to me for your sake.' 'Congratulations! You're welcome to it.' And our Prophet performs two cycles of Thanksgiving Prayer because someone of his community has seen an angel.

If we recite it, we too will see angels. If we don't see angels, we'll see the Prophet himself, because the one who has given this promise does not go back on it.

Another time, a bedouin approached the Prophet in the presence of some Companions and asked him seventeen questions. One of the questions was:

'I want to be the wisest of human beings.'

The Prophet answered: 'Fear God. That's all.'[3]

What kind of bedouin was that, where did he learn those questions, with what courage did he ask the Prophet? It was the Archangel Gabriel and the Prophet in conversation. We can't know what's in this form.

Don't fall for the same trick twice

Six months to a year after the Emigration, the Prophet comes out of his house as the Companions are talking among themselves. 'What's the subject?' he asks. 'The Helpers (Medinans) deceived us,' they say.

'This is better for you. You'll be able to distinguish between the trustworthy and the hypocrites.'

---

3. 'Fear of the Lord is the beginning of wisdom' (Psalms 111:10, Proverbs 9:10).

He puts his finger in a crack in the mud wall. 'My people are simple. If the mud bricks aren't joined tightly and you put your finger in the crack, a wasp may sting you or a snake may bite you. But it can't do it again. Because you've gained experience, you won't repeat it.'

If a wasp came here, we'd all be disturbed. Let's kill this wasp of an ego and find peace, all of us.

The thanksgiving servant

One day the Prophet says to Aisha, 'Aisha, my spirit wants to worship God, who created me, you, and the whole universe. What do you say? Shall I lie down beside you, or shall I worship God?' Aisha pulls herself together: 'Do as you like,' she says.

That night his feet get swollen. Aisha wakes up, the Prophet is in prostration. She thinks he's dead, she comes close – he's breathing, praying. The next time she wakes up, he's standing, doing the Prayer. They do the Dawn Prayer together. Then Aisha asks him: 'You're the Prophet. God has forgiven your sins. What's this affair tonight?'

'Aisha, God has granted me so many boons, shouldn't I thank Him at least this much?' Aisha feels ashamed.

Health matters

In Medina, they surrounded the Prophet: 'I'm sick,' and so on. He struck his knee with his hand: 'Whatever you do, use this vehicle well,' he said. The body is the vehicle of the soul. If the body moves under the brakes of the ego, it'll collide somewhere. But if it moves under the brakes of the spirit, it'll all go well.

Eat sparingly, drink sparingly, sleep sparingly and talk sparingly. We think that this is for a disciple who has enrolled with a teacher, an Order. Not at all. All the words of the Prophet are general. He enlightened everything. What happens then? One is liberated from the hegemony of the belly, sovereignty passes to the spirit.

In the Prophet's time, a doctor comes to Medina from Venice. He stays two-three years, he heals wounds and diseases. Finally he comes to the Prophet: 'With your permission, I'm going to leave. There's no illness here.'

The Prophet says: 'Whoever acts on my advice does not fall sick. Whoever heeds the Quran and my Sayings will not become ill.'

They get sick in Medina. 'The Prophet brought the air of Mecca, we've fallen ill.' He says, 'Wash once or twice a day, then burn the swamps in teams, dry them and cover them.' They remove the swamps. Then on a Friday he says, 'Now let's pray. My God, change the air of Medina. We've done our duty.' Ever since, Medina's air is cooler than Mecca's. Yes, prayer alone isn't enough.

The importance of work

They say, 'So-and-so is sick,' the Prophet decides to visit him. As they go, a man is leaning against a mud wall, lost in thought. When he sees the Prophet coming, he stands up and greets him. The Prophet doesn't return his greeting, although he greets everyone, even those in error.

On their way back, the man is scratching on the ground with a stick, this time the Prophet greets him: 'May peace be upon you.' They ask, 'Messenger of God, it's the same person, the same place. What happened that you didn't greet him while we were going, but did so on our way back?'

'On our way out, he was heedless, thinking. On our way back, he was working. At least he was doing *something*.' The Prophet didn't even greet those who were lazy.

Egalitarianism

During his period of sickness, the Prophet appointed a slave as commander to the army. Omar, Abu Bakr and Ali asked: 'Can this man command the army?' 'He can with the help of God.' What does the Prophet say: 'Give a task to those who are competent to do it.'

Give good names to children

Children were playing in Medina. Someone named his child 'Dung Beetle.' He grows to be eight years old, it's the lowliest of names. The child is embarrassed. Someone took him to the Prophet, who said: 'Call your father and mother.'

'Why did you give him a name like that?' 'Because we like it, it's our grandfather's name.' 'Let's give him another name. And move to another neighborhood so that his old name is forgotten.'

I've come to improve, not to kill

The Prophet was with his Companions. A man passed by him. He said: 'Fear this man who has no fear. There are hypocrites among you.'

Omar said: 'Let me kill him with one blow.' He replied, 'No. I didn't come to kill, I came to reform. That man is a Muslim externally but he hasn't been able to digest it, he's not a Muslim on the inside. He's a hypocrite, he'll cause you to fight among yourselves. I didn't come to kill, I came to edify.'

The highest knowledge

A stranger came to Medina and wanted to see the Prophet. They showed him. He said, 'With your permission, I'd like to stay with you. I have no one else to go to.' 'Do you know how to read and write?' 'No.' He told one of the Companions: 'Take him home and let him stay with you. Also, teach him the Quran.'

They start at the beginning. They study for two or three months, they go to the mosque together every day. One evening, he has this lesson: 'Whoever does an atom's weight of good will see its recompense, and whoever does an atom's weight of evil will see its recompense' [99:7–8].

The Arab didn't sleep all night. In the morning they had breakfast, he's going to have another lesson, the Arab said: 'I don't want it. This is enough for me. I've learned what I need.' His teacher said: 'We've got a lot more to learn.' 'No, this is enough.' They went to the Prophet after the Noon Prayer for a decision.

'I promise I won't do evil, please excuse me. I'm an old man, I'm not going to study any more.' 'Can you act on that knowledge?' 'Yes, I can. This is enough for me.' The Prophet turned to the Companions in the Mosque: '*His* knowledge is enough for him. This friend of yours has become one of the greatest men of knowledge.' One day that man comes back and kisses his hand, 'May God be pleased with you,' he says. 'You've given me everything.'

Compassion

There are some groups now that say, 'Don't buy or eat the bread of one who doesn't do the Prayer,' and so on. After a battle outside Medina, the Prophet asked: 'Two persons, one is a Muslim, the other is an infidel or a Christian. They both ask for water. Who do you give it to?'

'We give it to our brother,' they say. Omar asks: 'What do *you* say, Prophet of God?' 'First to the enemy, if he's dying. If possible, *divide in two* and give half to your brother first.' First to relatives, then to those more distant. The attribute of Compassion.

Don't embarrass people

The Qurayshites around the Prophet drank alcohol. He said, 'Don't speak ill of them because they drink.' He regarded the drunkard with mercy.

There was a bedouin Arab tribe chieftain. That tribe had faith, they had recited the Word of Witnessing. He said, 'Let me go and see the Messenger of God.'

He came, he asked, they said, 'He's in the Mosque.' He went over and introduced himself: 'I'm from such-and-such a tribe. I've come to see you.' He said, 'Sit down.'

There are lots of townspeople and strangers in the Mosque, he's listening to their troubles, he's making inquiries. The man began to fidget, he had to obey the call of nature. He said 'Excuse me,' the Prophet said 'Okay,' but he didn't say what his problem was. He went to a corner of the room and relieved himself. They're tribespeople, they don't know any better.

The Companions are upset, the Prophet of God looks, the smell spreads all over the place, he signals them: 'Don't say a word,' he says. That man comes and takes his earlier place.

The Prophet cuts it short, 'Come on,' he says, 'let's talk outside.' Without giving that man *the slightest hint*.

They get up, they step outside, he says: 'Give me a dustpan, a broom and some water.' 'Messenger of God, let's …' 'This is my guest. He came for me.' They insist, he says 'No. You go out, too.'

He takes the excrement, throws it outside, digs the ground, covers it, smooths it over, then comes over to them. The Companions are again amazed.

They talk outside, he sees him off, gives him some money, 'Goodbye.'

Three years later he comes again. The same man. They were sitting in the Mosque again, he greets them. He sits down in propriety and courtesy. Religion, good manners have spread everywhere.

He kneels, after inquiring how he is: 'Messenger of God, with your permission I'd like to kiss your hand.' 'Why, what for?' 'I came to you once, and did such an unseemly act. Please forgive my error.' 'No, no, no. Good for you, good for you.'

The first Prayer-call

The Prophet first asks those around him how they should do it. One says, 'Let's use a bell to call Muslims to Prayer.' 'No,' they say, 'the Christians do that already.' Another says, 'Let's light a fire,' 'The Zoroastrians are doing that, too.'

The Prophet says, 'Let's all pray and go to sleep, and await a sign from God. Let's see what dreams we will have.' That night, three people had the same dream: an angel recited the Prayer-call. Whereupon Bilal the Ethiopian sounded the first call to Prayer.

Miracles

There's spiritual power, but physical power is also necessary. That's what the Prophet says: 'A sword for a sword, an arrow for an arrow, a horse for a horse.'[4]

It happened like that at the Battle of Badr. He prostrated in Prayer as though to puncture the sands. 'There are only a handful of Muslims, how shall I prove Your name if You take them, too?' Gabriel came, 'Good news! Take a handful of earth, throw it in the direction of the enemy.' He threw, some of the enemy were ruined, others escaped. A wind, a storm blew up, that was the end of them. 'You didn't throw what you threw, I (God) did' [8:17]. We shouldn't say, 'I won,' we should say, 'God made me win.'

---

4. That is, assets should be evenly matched. Selim the Resolute (Selim I) conquered the Mamluks in Egypt. Their chief said: 'We abided by the Saying: "Use arrows and swords in battle." That's why we couldn't stand against your cannon.'

Selim replied: 'Didn't you ever hear of the Saying: "Counter a weapon with a weapon of the same kind"?' (This is the initial part of the Saying in the main text.)

[The miracle of splitting the moon:] One of his enemies, Abu Jahl [the Father of Ignorance], says: 'Let him show us a miracle. Every prophet has a miracle, show us a miracle yourself.' The others agree. It's nighttime, there's a full moon. 'You're right,' he says. 'Do you see?' he asks, pointing to the moon. He recites: '*In the name of God, the Compassionate, the Merciful,*' and extends his finger. The moon splits in two, the two halves separate a distance that appears like two yards, they join again as he lowers his finger. They still say, 'We won't believe.'

When they were digging a ditch for the Battle of the Ditch, they came upon a boulder. They couldn't break it up. The Prophet of God took a pickaxe, '*In the Name of God, the Compassionate, the Merciful.* My God, all Power and strength is from You.' He takes refuge in God. He shouts loudly, everyone is surprised. Three blows, the boulder splits in four. He gives thanks. Each of the sparks from that rock indicates a different thing: the fall of Persia, the fall of Byzantium.

The Prophet said, 'Bring me some stones.' He put them in his palm. The stones begin to chant: 'Oh God, Oh God.' He opened his palm, it's still the same. Omar said: 'Messenger of God, may I have them?' When he gave them, the stones fell mute. When he took them back, they began Invocation again.

The unforgettable wife

After they come back to Mecca, he sacrifices a ram with Aisha. There's a poor woman, he says, 'Take her a piece.' Aisha takes it, but that woman happens to be a relative of Khadija [the Prophet's dead wife]. She comes back, she chides the Prophet: 'You still love her more than me. You take other wives.'

The Prophet listens patiently to the end, he doesn't say anything. You should do the same thing to those who criticize you. In the end he says, 'Finished? Aisha, I haven't married any of my wives for the sake of my own self. What I love in Khadija is not her property or riches, it's her morality. I love her *morality*.'

Of his line, the Prophet loved Khadija most, then his daughter Fatima and Ali [her husband and his cousin]. Khadija did not frown at the Prophet even once. I'm thinking that she was created especially for him.

Self-reliance

The Prophet is helping Fatima grind barley in a handmill. Barley is difficult, it's hard. It would be easy if it were wheat. 'Father dear, could you tell one of the Helpers [Medinans] to turn this handmill?'

The Prophet: 'Fatima, daughter, I've never asked anyone anything for my own self. Not since the day I was born. Everything is as an exemplar for others, not for myself. Let me teach you a prayer. If you recite it, God will give you the strength to do your own work. I'm in such difficulties, I recite it too and do my own work.' He teaches this prayer: *'O First of firsts, O Last of lasts, O strength of the Firm, O Compassionate Bestower, and O He who is the most Merciful of mercifuls.'*

The Prophet did not accept war booty. They're dividing the booty after a battle, they offered him a share. 'You're human, you have a family, you have children, let's give you some.' 'No, no.' He doesn't take it and further, he brushes off its dust from himself afterwards. That's the kind of prophet he was. He's in need, but he earns patiently.

The morality of the Quran

After the Prophet passed away, the Companions assembled. 'Aisha,' they said, 'you knew how to read and write from the earliest age. You're his wife. You've related many a Verse and Saying. Can you explain to us a little bit about the morality of the Prophet?'

'Yes,' she said. 'Do you know the Quran?' 'Yes, Aisha, we know it, we read it.' 'You want the ethics of the Messenger of God?' 'Yes.' 'His ethics, his character traits, were precisely those of the Quran.'

Love me with all your heart

The Prophet of God was walking with Abu Bakr on one side and Omar on the other. Abu Bakr said, 'Messenger of God, you're so wonderful inwardly and outwardly that I would lay down my life for you.' Omar also collects himself, 'Messenger of God, I too love you more than anything except myself.'

The Prophet doesn't answer. Thinking he hasn't heard, Omar repeats this three times. 'No, Omar, that won't do. Unless you love me *more* than yourself …' Right away, before his next step, 'I agree. I love you more than even myself.' 'That's better, Omar.'

What do we do? What is it we love? It is our own self. You can't get anywhere as long as you don't love the Prophet more than your children, more than yourself. You can't find God as long as you don't love God more than yourself. Where are we going to find the legacy of the saints every day? Let's work and earn.

The meaning of the Ascension

Our Prophet made the greatest Ascension, yet he doesn't say 'I am God.' He doesn't say, 'I saw God during the Ascension.' The Prophet says: 'God is not a form, that I should see Him.' He did not see Him, he spoke to Him, he heard His voice. If God manifests in a form, it is because there is Compassion in them that He does so. The Prophet says: 'Gabriel comes to me in human form.'

During the Ascension, he speaks, he receives orders, there's a veil in between. Some prophets made their Ascension in dreams, others as inspiration. They didn't all perform their Ascensions like the Prophet. For example, the Ascension of Noah is the Ark. With wrath. Adam, as he came to life.

Externalist[5] hodjas say, 'The Prophet made the Ascension thirty-three times.' Some say he did it once. Others say, 'He's constantly in Ascension.' All accounts are acceptable to us.

Prelude

The Prophet is stoned and wounded in Ta'if. Upon that great distress, the Ascension occurs. In those wounds, God opened the doors of Ascension. Why? Because he didn't complain. He prayed both for the people of Ta'if and for all human beings. This was pleasing to God. He flung open the doors of Ascension.

[Escaping Ta'if, the Prophet and Zayd bin Harith, his foster son] came to a vineyard. There the Prophet did his Prayer. You, too, don't miss the Prayer when you're in distress or angry. In that *distress*, you'll succeed.

The gardener, a priest, picks and offers them each a bunch of grapes. [The Prophet says, 'We can't accept these without the permission of

---

5. See The foundation/ Material and spiritual.

the owners or without paying for them.' The gardener is astonished.] 'Who are you?' he asks. He becomes a Muslim, but the owners of the vineyard do not. They remain in doubt. They say: 'Let him eat these grapes, but if he comes to Ta'if some day, let him remember us.'

Let us do the Prayer to see him. If we work in earnest, it won't take a week. To see him is Ascension.

Together with Harith, our Prophet arrives at the house of Umm Hani, his paternal aunt. 'Messenger of God, there's nothing to eat, not even a date.' 'That's okay.' 'You rest.' There's an armor left from her husband, Umm Hani dons that armor, takes his sword and circles the house all night to protect the Prophet.

It happens right after that catastrophe in Ta'if. He goes to Jerusalem and from there, traverses the seven heavens. When he returns, he finds his bed is still warm. That is, we accept that he made this journey both physically and spiritually. Seven [heavens], and then seven more.

The Ascension

Gabriel goes to Paradise. The *buraq*s – a steed smaller than a horse – were dancing and prancing there. All except for one. It's leaning on a rock, it won't touch food or drink, tears flow like threads from its eyes.

Gabriel says: 'What's wrong?' 'Forty thousand years ago, a voice came, I don't know whether from my left or right. It said, 'O Muhammad!' I fell in love with that voice. That voice still nourishes me. I pine for it ever since.'

Gabriel says, 'God has granted your wish.' And he takes it to the Prophet.

This is for us, for us! God tells us, 'I'm closer to you than your jugular vein' [50:16]. What is the Buraq? Spirit, spirit [pointing to his head and his heart]. Buraq is the vehicle of the Prophet, we are the vehicles of God. That poor animal is burning with the love of Muhammad, it refuses food and drink. What about us?

The others are in the midst of fun and games. They eat, drink and make merry. These are all you. Tame the self a little bit, draw near a little bit. A poor animal falls in love with the Prophet. What about you? It fell in love with a voice. You read and hear the Verses, the Sayings every day. Let's rein in the Base Self just a little bit.

The Prophet of God Ascended together with Gabriel. Gabriel said, 'This is as far as I go. If I take another step, I'll burn.' The Prophet of God said, 'If I burn, so be it,' [and plunged into] Totality.

The Prophet goes to communicate with God on the occasion of the Ascension. He apologizes on behalf of all humanity, of his people. God asks: 'My Beloved, do you love Me very much?' He says, 'My God, no doubt it is known to You.' He asks our Prophet: 'Since you love Me so much, what present did you bring Me?' This is very important. *Very*.

He replies: 'My Lord, I've brought You the only thing You don't have. I've brought You my nothingness. I am nothing, that's what I brought You.'

God says, 'What present shall I give *you*? Ask whatever you wish for.' 'I don't want anything. Your servanthood is enough for me. Accept me as Your servant.' Upon that word, Gabriel comments: 'Muhammad, that's what I would expect of you. You did the very best.'

We're all a handful of dust, let's not go too far. Let's live as Muhammadans. He prays: 'I take pride in my servanthood. I am Your servant, You are my Creator.' This was very pleasing to God: 'Muhammad, you asked for the very best. And you received the highest.'

The Meccan idolaters do not believe in Muhammad's journey. They say, 'If you went to Jerusalem, describe it to us.' In that instant, God places Jerusalem in full view before the Prophet's sight. He recounts the domes and columns. That happens spiritually. It's spacefolding.

The Prophet in his cosmic aspect

Present-day scholars leave the Prophet aside and talk only about the Quran. It's a pity.

A greater prophet than the Prophet cannot come, nor a greater Book than the Quran. Because they've left no place for anyone/anything else. They unite their predecessors and successors within themselves. What does the expression say? 'The leader of those before him and those after him.' If a prophet comes from now on, he will say the same things. If a book comes, it will come from within this Book. There's no *space* left for anything else.

God says, 'I first created the Light of Muhammad, and then created the entire universe from that light.' The before and the after of the universe is the Muhammadan Light. [A Saying:] 'When Adam was between water and clay, I was a prophet [already].'[6]

On the face of it, Adam is a visitor to this universe. First the universe was created, then Adam came into it. But on the *other* hand, God first created the Light of Muhammad, and created all the worlds from that. 'The first thing God created was [my Spirit,] my Light.' As Niyazi Misri says:

You're the ore out of which the universe is manifested, Messenger of God.

Muhammad is the First Light. That's the end of it. So the cosmos came as a visitor to Adam (the human). The name of Muhammad is coded into the name of Adam: A, D, M. All the Verses and Sayings are based on the Light of Muhammad.

Another name of the Prophet of God is Ahmad. Say, 'Ahmad, help me.' If you love him very much and take refuge in him, nothing bad will befall you.

In terms of spirit, our Prophet is angelic. Angels don't eat, drink or get married. But physically, he is human – though not human in the same way we are. Nothing can assume his form.

Our Prophet has two attributes: Compassion and Mercy. God addresses the Prophet: 'I did not send you, except as a Mercy to the worlds' [21:107]. He invites from Compassion to Mercy. The attribute of Compassion is difficult, we couldn't bear it. We have to comply with the attribute of Mercy.

One day, while the Prophet was sitting in a vacant lot, he said, 'This is the everlasting Paradise.' Later, that place became a graveyard. Of course, there's a delicate meaning to this, too. [In imitating the Prophet's gesture, the Master circled his hand and brought it back to himself:] It's himself. [The real everlasting Paradise is himself.] God gave him Paradise and everything else. But if he had told them that, they would all have fled. Of course, there were those who understood in that age, too.

We can't get anywhere unless we love him. When you go abroad, they ask you, 'Do you have a passport?' If you do, they say, 'Go ahead.' Otherwise, you're turned back from the border. Without a passport from the Messenger of God, you cannot go to God.

---

6. Compare the saying of Jesus: 'Before Abraham was, I am' (John 8:58).

It was in Muhammad that God proved His Unity. Love him very much. Without his leave, we can't go directly to God ourselves. Our passport is in the hand of the Prophet. Pronounce Blessings on the Prophet continually. Receive the passport from Muhammad, go wherever you want.

Let me tell you something more. You can tell this to everyone. There was an American president, now he's gone. Now they have a new president. The old one is alive, too. But only the new one's signature is valid. Can you give a petition with a former president's name on it to the president in office today?

Now, it's the same thing. Who is the last prophet? Whose word is valid? The Prophet said, 'I'm the last prophet.' Christendom hasn't understood this point for fourteen hundred years.

We're going to find God with Muhammadanhood. If we go without that, the priests are going, others are going, they're all the servants of God. You cannot go to God without Muhammad. You have to conquer with his love. If we don't love the Prophet more than our own life and soul, we can't receive his effusion. There's someone here, he's telling you where you want to go, you tell him: 'Stay here,' you try to find it yourself. Know this to be true: without the Prophet, nobody finds God.

A friend who was interested in Transcendental Meditation went to a conference of the Maharishi in America. He related:

> A Pakistani engineer stood up, he said: 'I'm a Muhammadan. You haven't said anything about Muhammad or the Quran.' He paused. 'You're right. But Muhammad fills the earth and heaven. Muhammad is the universe. How can I describe him to you?'

The universe is the realm of Muhammad. The universe is Muhammad, Muhammad is the universe. They say: 'Outside Muhammad there is nothing.' He has a Saying, 'I am not of the Arabs, the Arabs are of me.' Not just Arabs, the universe is of him.

They ask the Prophet certain things, he says, 'If my Lord informs me, I'll tell you.' He knows, but he doesn't tell. That's because if he told them, they couldn't bear it.

What human beings can't bear, the Prophet concealed. His people who came after him saw it, they concealed too. Anyone who mentioned a corner of it was struck by a blow and departed. Do not reveal any more than what the Prophet permitted. He says, 'I take refuge in my Lord with my Lord, I take refuge in my Lord with my servanthood.' Sainthood, polehood are what is given, but servanthood is what is taken.

They call the Prophet 'unlettered,' I call him an ocean. These colors are not in vain. The sea is blue. You have to dive into the sea – the ocean – of Muhammad. You have to pass beyond color and dive into the sea, the love of Muhammad.

Question: *Did revelation come via Gabriel, or directly?*

Both ways. At many points, our Prophet uttered revelation before Gabriel did. And some Sufis have called Gabriel Intelligence. Say, 'God and His Prophet know best,' and leave it at that.

The poet Yunus Emre says, 'Whoever is human does not die. Whoever dies is an animal.' It's he who's saying that. What about our Prophet? If the universe were to die, he wouldn't, that's how we're going to know it. We're going to know the Prophet not with the Base Self, but with the spirit. Those who say 'He's dead' are those who don't know. Shall I tell you his age? His bodily life is sixty-three years. He was alive before the world was established. He was born into this world fourteen hundred years ago, he is fourteen hundred years old. All prophets had a term, he doesn't have an end. His rules continue. He is the Living.

Follow Muhammad, there is no other way. There are, but those can't enter here. Beliefs remain on lips, they can't descend to Hearts. God polishes, one is cleansed of human attributes, divine attributes are what remains. This is where intense asceticism is necessary, in erasing the human attribute.

God says, 'Follow the Prophet if you want to come to Me.' The Prophet says, 'You cannot go to God unless you obey me.' God praises His Prophet whom He has tested and chosen, His Prophet praises God. The Messenger affirms God, God affirms the Prophet. There's a duality here. There's a delicate point here.

God hasn't left His Godhood to anyone, and the Prophet hasn't left his Prophethood to anyone.

The Prophet's household

The closest are the Family of the Cloak (*Al al-'aba'*): only Fatima [his daughter], Ali [Fatima's husband and his cousin] and Hassan and Hussein [their sons]. The Prophet embraced these people of his household and placed his cloak over them. Just then, Salman the Persian came in. Seeing this, he said, 'Messenger of God, are you going to leave me out?' The Prophet said, 'Come, Salman, you come, too.' Thus Salman was included in the Family of the Cloak.

The People of the House (*Ahl al-bayt*) are Fatima and the Twelve Imams ('Leaders'), that is, Ali, Hassan, Hussein and their nine descendants.

During the Battle of the Ditch, the Prophet said of Ali: 'His flesh is of my flesh, his blood is of my blood, his spirit is of my spirit.'

The People of the House all performed their Prayers, even their grandchildren performed their Prayers. Hussein and all of the Twelve Imams were firmly attached to the Divine Law. They all went to mosque.

One does not give charity to the People of the House. *One gives one's life, one's spirit, but not charity*. We expect from *them*, physically and spiritually. The People of the House embrace the universe, the universe embraces the People of the House.

The caliphs

Abu Bakr

After our Prophet passed to the other world, a caliph had to be appointed. The Qurayshites said, 'We're his tribesmen, the caliph has to be of us.' The Helpers [Medinans] couldn't cope with them. Abu Bakr came forth, Omar pledged his allegiance to him, and so did the rest. Just as we vote today and pledge allegiance.

A beggar comes to Abu Bakr, 'Something for the sake of God.' He's given everything to the poor, there's nothing left to give. He takes off his clothes, there's a straw mat, he secures the mat around himself with some rope and gives his clothes to the beggar. He couldn't go to Prayer, he was late.

They finish Prayer and are coming out. Gabriel comes, he's wearing a straw mat just like Abu Bakr. Our Prophet: 'What's going on?' Gabriel replies: 'Abu Bakr did this. It was very pleasing to God. He ordered all the angels to dress like this.' The Prophet sends clothes of his own: 'Let him put these on and come.' When he comes: 'Abu Bakr! You're the Truthful!' That's where he receives his station: 'Abu Bakr the Truthful.'[1] Muhyiddin Ibn 'Arabi, the Greatest Shaykh, also has a story like that.[2]

Omar

Omar Faruq[3] is just. Of God's Ninety-Nine Beautiful Names, the name of 'Just' has manifested in him.

---

1. *Siddiq*: Sincere lover of Truth, Upright, Honest, Truthful, True. In the above episode, sincerity is emphasized. The term was first applied to Abu Bakr, and later to the first followers of Muhammad.
2. See The saints/Ibn 'Arabi/Generosity.
3. *Faruq*: Discriminator, possessor of sound discrimination (between truth and error).

How Omar became a Muslim

Two meetings are being held: one by our Prophet, the other by Abu Jahl. The Muslims have become thirty-nine people. Omar is at Abu Jahl's gathering. He says, 'I'll kill him.' He goes out. On his way he comes across someone who knows the Prophet. 'Where is he?' 'Why do you ask?' 'I'm going to kill him.' 'You'd better look at your sister Fatima and your brother-in-law first. They're Muslims, too.'

As he nears his sister's house, he hears a sweet recitation of the Quran. He knocks on the door. They hide it in the closet immediately. 'What are you doing?' 'We've become Muslims, we're reading the Quran. We hid it from fear of you.' He delivers two slaps. 'Read, I'm going to listen.'

He leaves and goes to the Prophet's meeting. 'Oh, Omar, welcome,' they give him a good greeting. 'How many people are you?' 'There are thirty-nine of us.' 'With me, now you're forty.'

When Abu Jahl hears of this, he says, 'Oh, no! Now we're done for.'

Omar and the Black Stone

Omar went to perform the Pilgrimage. He's the caliph, the ruler. He's going to start his circumambulations, he stands facing the Black Stone that's in the corner of the Ka'ba, he addresses it: 'You,' he says, 'wherever you come from, whether from Paradise or from Mount Qubays, you are a stone. I am a human being. I am not for you, you are for me. I wouldn't kiss you, but the Messenger of God kissed you and for his sake, so will I.' He stands and kisses it. That is, he reverts to the Divine Law.

Remembrance of things past

Omar is sitting in the caliph's room. There are no servants, no doormen. They're all himself. He remembers how, before he converted, he was burying his daughter and she held his beard. Tears well up in his eyes, tears of compassion. At that moment there's a knock on the door, visitors arrive.

'What's wrong?' 'Well, I remembered, and I shed a tear in spite of myself.' They shed tears, too. 'We used to come together for the New Year, fifty youths, we would collect flour, butter, sugar and make idols out of sweetmeat (*halwa*). After we made our wishes, we would tear them apart – some of us from the hand, others from the arm or leg – and then we would eat them.'

Quarantine

Conquests are being made in the time of Omar. There's typhoid fever in Damascus. The commander said: 'It won't harm us.' News arrives from Medina. 'I told you. The orders of the Prophet, don't enter where there's an epidemic.' Where's Damascus, where Medina? Yet they return. [Earlier, the Prophet had forbade the army from entering Damascus when there was a plague epidemic. That may have been the first historically recorded instance of quarantine.]

The visitors from Persia

During the period of Omar's caliphate, another delegation arrived from Persia for a postwar peace agreement. The Persian minister of foreign affairs asked: 'Is this Omar's palace?' One room, two rooms. 'Yes.'

There was a date plantation near Medina. Omar was resting there. He had a cloak covering him. The minister thought: 'A man all by himself. There aren't any guards or soldiers around him.' The sentry said, 'I'll let him know.' When there were five or six steps left, he removes the cloak and sits up. Whatever the minister saw, his lip cracks from fear and starts bleeding. Omar comes and takes his position: 'Welcome.' It takes half an hour for the minister to regain his composure.

Omar hosts the delegation for a week. A week later, they pull themselves together and write the articles. 'We can't fight these people.' He doesn't have a soldier or anything. 'What did you see?' 'A man.' But of what kind?

The trip to Jerusalem

[The patriarch, Sophronius, insisted that Jerusalem would surrender only to the caliph himself.] 'The people want to see you.' He's a stern man. His servant, his slave is tending the camel. They set out from Medina, every three hours they take turns riding on the camel. He says: 'Get on.' 'Sir, I'm accustomed, I'm young, be comfortable.' 'No,' he says. In turns – no matter how much the slave insists, the answer is No.

As they arrive, the priests are in ranks on two sides, it's the slave's turn again. Omar dismounts: 'Time's up.' 'Oh, sir, you made me do this up to this point, but now? What am I going to do with all these people?' He replies: 'It's God's justice.'

The slave mounts, Omar walks in front of the camel.

This also happened during the conquest of Istanbul. When Mehmed the Conqueror [Mehmed II] takes the city, they're entering with Aq Shamsuddin, his teacher. Mehmed is young, all the Greek girls surround Shamsuddin. The same thing happened there. However much Shamsuddin protests, they all encircle him.

They went.

The military commander came up and embraced Omar. So did the priests who had seen what had happened. They apologized: 'We didn't know, we didn't recognize you, we're sorry.' They saluted the slave! 'No,' he says, 'He is me and I am he.'

Noontime, the Prayer-call is to be recited, he calls for Bilal the Ethiopian: 'Bilal, climb up there and recite a Prayer-call.' 'But Omar,' he says, 'you know I haven't recited a Prayer-call for weeks after the Prophet died.'

No matter how much he declines, Omar says: 'This is a different day. This is Christendom. See? There are thousands of priests. I miss your blessed voice, and they should hear it.' He insists, so Bilal says 'Okay.'

He climbs up [a pillar], he pronounces Blessings on the Prophet. Whatever kind of voice he did that with, the priests all look at him, some prostrate themselves. Then he recites the Prayer-call.

They wait for Bilal to come. Omar is going to lead the Prayer and Bilal is going to be the Caller, his assistant in congregational Prayer. But Bilal isn't coming.

Two people go over to look, Bilal has passed out. They carry him back. He's still unconscious, so someone else acts as Caller.

He stays there a week, he leaves part of the army there, a part goes back with him.

The mosque

In the time of Omar, they're building a mosque on the land of a Jew. [The governor of Egypt wrongfully initiates the construction.] The Jew files a complaint. He says, 'Have you forgotten the justice of the Persian king Nushirawan?'[4] Omar gives orders, they set out to

---

4. Nushirawan (Khosrau I Anoshirvan) reigned in Persia at the time of the Prophet's birth and was renowned for his justice. In his youth, Omar and the future governor-to-be of Egypt went to Persia to sell horses. Their horses were forcibly taken from them – by the Emperor's son, as it turned out. Anoshirvan did not hesitate to execute his own son in order that justice be done. It is this earlier event in Omar's life the Jew was referring to. Omar, in turn, told the governor of Egypt, 'I am more just than Anoshirvan.' The governor immediately halted construction of the mosque.

demolish the mosque. In the face of such justice, the Jew says, 'Stop, Omar, I've become a Muslim.'

The tree

Omar came upon a crowd. 'What's this all about?' 'Well, the Prophet sat under this date tree, he leaned on it, so we're visiting it.' Omar said: ['You're not supposed to do that.'] He chased them away and had the date tree cut down. [There is no place for superstition or instituting superstitious practices.]

The shepherd and the wolves

Omar is a great caliph, he succeeded Abu Bakr. In his time, in one of the villages surrounding Medina, there was a brook with a wooden bridge over it. While a shepherd was crossing the bridge with his flock, a piece of wood broke, the foot of a sheep went through the hole, the others are pressing from behind, its leg snaps. The sheep crossed over, the shepherd comes up behind, one is lying there. He pulls out the leg, it's broken.

He brings it home, he slaughters it. He writes a petition to Omar, the caliph. 'If you're going to be caliph, do it properly. Otherwise, resign. Think of the poor. I'm from such a town, such a village. There's a bridge here. The people are poor, they can't repair the bridge. One of my sheep broke its leg, and you're responsible.'

In Omar's time, the caliphate and justice are very good. They give him that letter, he reads it. In all the cities – Mecca, Medina and so on – all the bridges, all the roads are repaired. Thanks to that shepherd.

Two or three years pass. The shepherd has spread his flock out at the foot of a hill to graze, he's watching them against thieves and harm.

Two wolves come out from behind. Each grabs a sheep. He doesn't move. He just watches, he's an experienced man. They eat their victims, the other sheep flee toward the shepherd. After they're finished, the wolves leave. He gathers the sheep in the evening and goes home. He goes straight to the village chief.

'Any news from Medina?' he asks.

'No. Why, what's up?' asks the chief.

'Omar is dead!' says the shepherd.

'What? Where did you hear that? How do you know?'

'Two wolves came today and ate my sheep,' he said. 'If Omar were alive, they wouldn't do that.' Omar was that just.

'No,' he says, 'there hasn't been any news like that.' The next morning, news arrives: 'Omar has been assassinated.' The chief goes out to the shepherd, who is grazing his sheep again. 'You were right,' he says. 'Omar's been assassinated.'

'I knew it,' he says, 'because if he had been alive, the wolves wouldn't have eaten my sheep.' That kind of justice! Omar was killed during the Dawn Prayer, the wolves ate the sheep at noon.

Who's boss?

Omar dies. The angels of interrogation come to question him. 'Come closer, I can't hear you. You've come from afar, from a distance of a thousand years. Didn't you forget what you have to ask?' 'No, we didn't.' 'I came from here to here. You didn't forget, how can *I* forget? Haven't you ever heard of Omar? Didn't you hear of his justice?' He grabs them by the ears and shakes them. This is just hearsay, of course – angels don't have ears or legs. 'That's what we'd expect of you, Omar. Goodbye.' 'Run along,' he says. Omar's resurrection was over in five minutes!

Ali

Ali became the last of the four 'Rightly Guided' caliphs.

His term was the most difficult. They ask, 'Why wasn't he the first caliph?' If Ali had been intended as the first caliph, the Prophet would have appointed him while he was still alive. He would have told Ali, 'Be Prayer-Leader.' If Ali hadn't become caliph when he did, Islam would have been erased. The Prophet died, unrest began in the time of Abu Bakr. Ali came upon a storm. They had set the Quran aside and were busy fighting.

Ali invited to Islam, the others invited to the Base Self. Mu'awiya desired worldly power and opened a front against Ali. I don't approve of it myself. But all this is long past. We should now try to save our own selves.

The Light of Sainthood ['Saintlight' for short] passed from the Prophet to Ali. The Prophet combined prophethood and sainthood within himself. Prophethood was terminated with Muhammad, but the Saintlight moved on via Ali.

They all loved the Prophet. But Ali was with him from childhood. He took over his state, his ethics. They're cousins. God especially favored him and gave him great power. The Prophet embraced him, he said, 'Ali's blood is of my blood, his life is of my life.'

Ali is entirely in line with the Divine Law. He performed his Prayers. They're all exalted, but among the Four Caliphs, in terms of knowledge, Hidden Knowledge and Reality, people are more inclined to Imam Ali. Ali's knowledge is greater than the rest. [In addition,] he enters some fields that the Divine Law can't accept and remains outside. The other caliphs conform to the Divine Law. In the case of Ali, one says at certain points, 'I wonder?' Those are matters for Hidden Knowledge. For example, one is: 'I wouldn't prostrate to a God I didn't see.' Go figure that! This is for those who know.

Another point emerges from this saying of Ali. He doesn't say 'I am God,' see! Why was Ali, the Lion of God, getting tired? Does God get tired? Why didn't the Prophet, the Master of the *Universe*, allow people to call him God? Why did he make them call him Prophet? You've got to think about these things a little bit.

You want to see God. See the Prophet, see Ali. You can see God after you see them. Say, 'It's enough for me to see the Prophet, to see Ali.'

The letter of Ali [to a newly appointed governor of Egypt concerning administration] is in effect the constitution of humanity. The words of Ali are a constitution, and all constitutions are within it.[5]

Pass the gate and come to the city

The Prophet said: 'I am the city of knowledge, Ali is its gate. Whoever passes Ali can come to me.' That concerns sainthood. It continues through Ali. That is, don't give up the door of sainthood. As for Ali: 'The lock to God's door is opened only with me.' The Prophet gave Ali as example so the Companions could slowly come to the path. The gatekeeper, everything, they're all the Prophet. The Prophet spoke like that in order to avoid assuming everything to himself. And also as a compliment, a delicacy to Ali. No one understands yet! You have to pass from Ali in order to reach the Prophet.[6]

---

5. The Master attached great importance to this epistle. It is reproduced in some of his books. It is also available online in English, e.g. at http://www.amaana.org/ismaali.html.

6. As for Abu Bakr, the Prophet said: 'Whatever was given to me, I poured into Abu Bakr's chest.' The Naqshis are the only Sufi order that trace their lineage back through Abu Bakr to Muhammad.

The watermelon

A Companion bought a watermelon out of season and brought it to the Prophet. It's Ramadan, the month of Fasting. There's an hour left to break the fast. He said: 'Eat!' 'We're fasting, Messenger of God!' 'All right. You eat!' 'I'm fasting, too.' He said the same thing to several people and got the same answer. Then Ali came along.

'Ali, you eat!' 'As you wish, Messenger of God!' 'Go ahead, eat.' He cut and ate it at once.

'How come you ate, Ali? Aren't you fasting?'

'We learned of fasting through the word of the Prophet, we'll break the fast through the word of the Prophet. You instructed me to fast, I fast. You instructed me to cut the watermelon, I cut it.' Ali has daring moves like that, that's where he won. Still, the Prophet does not alter the Divine Law. He says: 'Thank you, Ali. After this month is over, fast for a day to make up for it.'

The 'Father of earth'

The reason why Ali is called 'Father of earth' is that one day, he has an argument with his wife Fatima. Ali leaves. The Prophet comes by, he asks what happened and soothes Fatima. Then he goes and finds Ali. He found him sitting on the ground. He had wrapped a covering over his head. The Prophet compliments him in this way, and it sticks as a nickname.

Abu Bakr has been compared to the sun, Omar to air, Othman to water, and Ali to earth.

God's good pleasure

'May God be pleased with you' is one of the greatest prayers.

Ali and Salman the Pure [the Persian] set out from Medina. They're on the road, it's noontime. An Arab was going to Medina. But he's dying of thirst. Let's appreciate the value of this bounty we have. It's flowing away all around us.

He said, 'Water, water!' and fell to the ground. Ali told Salman, 'Give him water from the water pouch.' He gave him, he came to himself and said 'May God be pleased with you, you've saved my life.'

Ali told Salman, 'Untie that camel back there and give it to this man.'

'What is this?' 'The Master gave this to you.' He doesn't know that it's Ali, they're travelers and so is he. 'May God be pleased with you a *thousandfold*. I was going to Medina with the hope of a small job, perhaps as a porter. To earn my family's sustenance. You don't know me or anything.'

When he said, 'May God be pleased with you a thousandfold,' Ali said, 'Give him the other camel, too.'

'What is this?' 'He's giving this to you.'

'I just don't know, may God be pleased with you whichever way He sees fit,' he says, and hitches the second camel. As Ali is about to present the third camel, Salman flees! He goes some distance away and waits there. Ali says to the Arab, 'Get up. All this stuff is yours, camels and all.' 'But sir, how can that be?' 'Well, you wanted it that way when you said "May God be pleased with you."' He prays, he takes the camels and goes.

Ali waves at Salman: 'Come on.' He comes. 'Why did you run away?' he asks.

'Each time he prayed,' says Salman, 'you gave him something. You gave and gave. The *camels* belong to others, the *goods* belong to others. How are we going to account for this when we return to Medina? Leave that aside, I was afraid you were going to give *me*,' he said. 'That's why I ran away. You were going to give me too to that blabbermouth. Not that it's important, but I'd have been deprived of you.'

Ali and the snake

A snake had twined itself around the branch of a tree. A fire started, it's going to burn, it's screeching. Ali was passing by. He extended his staff, the snake coiled around it: It climbed over, coiled around Ali's neck and began to squeeze.

'What are you doing? I saved you!'

'What can I do? This is our nature.'

'Okay, but who are you? Come to the front so I can see you.'

The snake brought over its head. Ali struck with his sword.

'And this is *our* nature,' he said.

Ali and the devil

I saw it in a book: the devil says to the Prophet, 'You're the one I like least. I have to deal with you all the time. The others are mine anyway.'

The devil assumes the appearance of an old man. Ali gets up to attend the Dawn Prayer. He's going to the mosque, an old man with a shining face falls into the lead when there's a short distance left. Ali can't pass him out of courtesy. By the time they arrive, the Prayer service is over. Ali does his Prayer in a corner.

This goes on for two or three days. The Prophet asks, 'Ali, are you sick? You're late for Prayer these days.' 'Messenger of God, an old man comes in front of me in the mornings, I can't pass him out of courtesy.' 'Didn't you recognize him? He deceives the entire world, he's fooled you, too.'

The fourth morning the old man comes along again, Ali grabs him and ties him to a date tree. They do the Prayer. Everybody waits for the Prophet. Nobody gets up. There's work to be done. The Prophet asks: 'Ali, what did you do with that man?' 'The Messenger of God knows best, I tied him to a tree.'

'Ali, go and untie that man. He has a duty. See, the congregation won't leave even though they have business to attend to. If you don't release him, nobody will leave. It's with him that the work of this world gets done.'

The secret and the reeds

The Prophet says to Ali, 'I'm going to tell you something, but don't tell anyone else.' He kept the secret for a month and couldn't stand it any longer. A deep, dry well, he tells it to the empty well. Then he continues on his way.

The well fills up with water immediately. Reeds sprout, it waters the reeds. A shepherd comes by, the well has filled up. The shepherd drinks some water. He does a Prayer. He likes the reeds. He cuts off one, he makes a flute out of it. [He's playing it when the Prophet and Ali pass by.]

The Prophet understood what had happened, he told Ali: 'I told you not to tell, but you did,' he said. 'It became a reed flute, the shepherd is playing it. But don't worry, nobody will understand it,' he said.

One understands the Quran only to the extent of one's lot. The rest, the eighteen thousand worlds, still remain secret.

The adversary

In the Battle of the Ditch, Salman the Persian says, 'Let's dig a ditch ten yards deep and ten wide.' Our Prophet accepts. The ditch is dug, the battle starts. A wrestler from the other side challenges them: 'Are you all mama's boys, isn't there anyone who'll face me?'

This word offends Ali. 'Messenger of God,' he says, 'with your permission, I'd like to face up to this man.' He insists. The Prophet accepts. Ali's famous two-bladed, cleft sword (*Zulfiqar*) is also given that day. It was a gift to the Prophet from a ruler, he brings it out and gives it to Ali: 'Here, this is yours.'

Ali moves out to meet him. He's a bit young. The enemy wrestler says, 'Couldn't they find anyone but you?' The fight begins.

Ali proves more than a match for the wrestler. Finally the wrestler, in order to anger Ali and force him to strike the fatal blow, spits in his face.

Ali wipes his face and steps back. 'Get up,' he says.

The man asks, 'Ali, why did you release me?'

'Earlier, I was fighting for the sake of God. When you spat, I was angry. If I had killed you then, I would have done it for my own ego. In order to oppose my Base Self, I released you.'

The man says, 'Is *this* Islam?' He replies, 'Yes.' 'Then I'm becoming a Muslim too,' he says, and they fight against the enemy together.

How to transmute mud into gold

Imam Ali said, 'If I could explain the meaning of the Naming, camels couldn't bear its weight.'

Now, about why our prayers aren't accepted:

During the period of his caliphate, the chieftain of a tribe becomes a Muslim. He trusts in his knowledge, he wants to visit Ali. He gets on his camel and comes over. He goes, it's a shack. Omar and Othman were like that, too.

Ali sends him to a rich place for the night. He comes back the next morning. He bothers Ali for four or five days. 'I'm the leader of such-and-such a tribe,' he says. 'I'm very rich, I want to get richer. Give me some advice.'

Ali takes him to where mud bricks are being made. 'What is this?' 'It's mud, it's earth.' He places his hand on one: 'How rich are you?' 'I don't know.' 'Here you are. This mud brick is ten times what you're worth.'

He takes it, the mud brick has become gold! 'This is so many carats of gold. Take it and have it measured, they won't be able to name its price. This is mud from the soil of Ali.'

Before he goes, he asks: 'Ali, how did you turn this earth into gold?' 'The Chapter of Sincerity.' 'Repeat it, repeat it,' he wrote it down. 'Say: God is One,' he doesn't know that yet.

He doesn't say, 'He made gold out of mud,' he says, 'He gave me a gold brick.' His wife is happy, they're so rich. He goes and gathers his tribe. He has thousands of mud bricks made. His greed is insatiable.

The mud bricks dry. He takes five bricks and comes to his room. He places three pieces on this side, two on that, he recites 'Say: God is One' on them all night long. In the morning he looks, it's still the same mud. Twenty days, a month, no change.

He places two bricks on the camel's saddle and goes straight to Ali.

'I've learned it, I've been reciting for a month. Nothing happens. Could the soil be bad?'

Ali smiles. 'I recited 'Say: God is One' in place of the Greatest Name prayer. God accepted it. I gave you the prayer and I gave you the brick, but I didn't give you this mouth or this tongue.'

'The solution?'

'Go, stop eating your daily food, distribute the rest to the tribe in God's way. Give all your wealth to the poor tomorrow, and you'll make gold out of mud.'

'Ali, forgive me, I can't do that. How can I?'

'Then the mud won't become gold.'

'Perhaps another brick? ...'

'Go on, this is enough for you.'

Every prayer is the prayer of the Greatest Name, as long as the tongue is straightened, the tongue, the tongue. This body must become the Greatest Name, it must accept it. Let's work until we find it. *Aha!*

Early history of Islam

Khalid bin Walid

Khalid bin Walid and Uqba [bin Nafi] are the knights of God. They're Muhammad's physical and spiritual soldiers.

Khalid has a fortress surrounded, they won't surrender. The ruler of the fortress says, 'We're dying of hunger, bring your commander.' 'Don't worry,' he tells them, and goes. The ruler is sitting in an armchair. 'What do you want from us?' 'We don't want to disturb you.' 'How come?' He explains. There's a bottle and a cup. 'What's this?' 'Poison. It kills in five minutes.' The ruler is going to drink it and commit suicide. 'Give me a cup!' He drinks it. Nothing happens. 'What on earth? The term of this is five minutes. Sit in my place, you're the ruler of this fort.' 'Open the main gates,' he says, 'these people don't die with what kills us.'

Khalid is in an open expanse. He goes to a village, he enters the church. The priest comes to the fore, he's going to preach, to speak to the congregation, his mind's a blank. The congregation is waiting. 'Whoever is Muhammadan among you, let him come forth!' Khalid steps forward. 'You've cut me off. You all can kill me if you want to, I'm becoming a Muslim.' So did they all. 'Khalid, you made us all Muslims with one word.'

The Umayyads and Abbasids

Mu'awiya delayed the progress of Islam by five hundred years.[7] There was a dispute, religion, knowledge, faith were all left by the wayside. After him, his son Yazid continued in his stead. Schisms arose in Islam. The Abbasids couldn't do very much. The Ottomans did the most, but they did it by the sword.

They fought for five hundred years because of Muawiya and Ali. This craze started in the time of Muawiya. They would behead anyone who named their children Hassan, Hussein or Ali. Whomever they found, they killed, they poisoned. In Muawiya's time, the Umayyad period, no mention is made of religion. It was chaos. There was denial for five hundred years. Muhammadanhood was very advanced, this is why they fell behind.

Abu Muslim of Khorasan was a peasant. He gathers an army. He really worked at it. He conquers Damascus, Mecca, Medina. He did an amazing lot, that peasant son. He takes all of Arabia.

Abbas is the uncle of our Prophet. Abu Muslim asks: 'Who is there from the Prophet's tribe?' The Abbasids. 'I can't be leader where there's one of Abbas's grandchildren,' he says, and returns to his village. Tamerlane was similar [in terms of conquest], but this is different, he saved all of Islam.

In the period of the Abbasids, the Four Imams, the leaders of the Four Schools of religious jurisdiction, united and pulled the religion together.

[The delay of five hundred years points to al-Ghazali, who – building on the groundwork of all his predecessors – was finally able to reconcile the exoteric and the esoteric, namely Islamic Divine Law and Sufism, respectively, which had diverged during those chaotic centuries. Ghazali was instrumental in restoring orthodox respectability to

---

7. By this the Master means that the negative effects lasted for five hundred years, not that the Umayyad dynasty reigned that long.

the mystical/spiritual/psychic dimension of the religion. Ideally, the period of the Prophet should have been directly succeeded by scholars like Ghazali, but this proved impossible due to the political powerlust of the Umayyads.]

Harun al-Rashid

Harun al-Rashid was the [fifth and most illustrious] ruler of the Abbasids.

Harun al-Rashid took Anatolia before the Seljuks. He sent [Charlemagne] a clock as present. [This brass water-clock was a marvel of early ninth-century Islamic technology. Small brazen balls fell down to chime the hours, and twelve horsemen could step out of twelve windows.] There the priests and wise men inspect it, they say, 'This is the devil, it must be destroyed immediately, otherwise it'll be our ruin. You've brought the devil, the devil is shouting.'[8]

---

8. Much later, the alarm clock sent by the Ottoman Sultan Ahmed I (reigned 1603–17) to the Queen of England was again called 'the work of the devil.'

The scholars

The four schools of Islamic law

The Hanafi, the Maliki, the Shafi'i, the Hanbali are all ours. I say, why don't we accept one of these as leader? It's all past now.

Abu Hanifa

General

Among scholars, the rich one is Abu Hanifa, 'the Greatest Leader.' Imam Shafi'i and Imam Malik were very rich, too. And Imam Hanbal. All four imams are wealthy, but the richest is Abu Hanifa. Once you give your collar to God, God gives you ten for one, a hundred for one. Among the sages, the richest – both materially and spiritually – is the Grand Saint Abdul Qadir Gilani, also known as the Greatest Helper.

A child said of his mother, 'She doesn't sleep at night, she does Prayer.' After that, Abu Hanifa didn't sleep at night for forty years.

Is Abu Hanifa more pious, or is his wife more pious? In order to bear his burden, one has to be as pious as him.

It is said that Abu Hanifa talked with Imam Jafar Sadiq (one of the People of the House of the Prophet). He has great praise for him. 'If I hadn't met him,' he said, 'I would doubt my faith. If I hadn't met Leader Jafar Sadiq three years ago, I wouldn't have understood the essence of knowledge, I would have remained ignorant.'

His parents

Abu Hanifa's father came to a riverside. He's going to take an Ablution, he sees a fresh apple. He takes a bite, at that moment he remembers [about the Forbidden and the Allowed.] But the juice has already mingled in his mouth. He leaves his hometown for two or three days, he spots the tree of that same apple, its branch bending over the river.

He finds its owner. 'Will you give up your legitimate claim to that apple? Will you declare it Permitted (lawful) to me? See, I only took a bite, I didn't actually eat it.'

The owner of the orchard has a ten-year-old daughter. 'If you serve me for *seven* years, I'll declare it Allowed to you.' 'Don't, don't say that.'

He works for seven years, the owner says: 'I have another task for you. I have a daughter who is blind, deaf and totally paralyzed. You shall marry her.' He hasn't seen that girl in seven years. Is it due to the girl or the man? The man was working, the *girl* didn't show herself to him.

He looks – why, she's a pearl of a girl! He goes to her father and says, 'There's a girl like an angel in there, I must have gone into the wrong room.'

There are such delicate things in our religion. Her father says, 'Her eye hasn't seen what is Forbidden. Her hand hasn't touched what is Forbidden. Come, let's have a cup of coffee.' The Greatest Leader was born of that, sir! He read the entire Quran when he was five years old. But he had a slight lisp. His mother said: 'If your father hadn't bitten that apple, your tongue wouldn't be like this, either.' Also, because his father Numan bit the apple, he mastered the Quran in a week instead of in a day.

The butter in the milk

To appear as a Muslim and to sow doubts in the minds of Muslims: that is hypocrisy. Those types always exist.

When Abu Hanifa was about seven years old, he went with his uncle on a business trip to a town of Baghdad. They take some goods, they're going to sell them, buy other goods and come back.

They went. The day is Friday, there's the obligatory congregational Prayer. As soon as they sold, they left the bazaar and went for the Friday Prayer. The mosque is close by, a giant bear of a man climbed the pulpit and began to preach. He recited a Saying. He's supposed to preach and lead the Prayer.

He said: 'This is the Verse in the Quran, the Saying of the Prophet: "God is present and conscious everywhere." How can this be?', he asked. 'Now is this true, is there an example of this? Please, there are a hundred, five hundred, a thousand of you, will one of you stand up and show us God?'

Abu Hanifa was so angry, he began to tremble. 'Uncle, I'm going to stand up and answer this man!' 'Son, nobody knows us here.' He challenged them three times. 'Someone stand up and prove this.' The congregation is distressed now. [This] man of knowledge has stood up and is saying, 'Prove it.'

It's the child who gets up. The Greatest Leader. He's about seven years old. His uncle sees him by the pulpit, he waves at him.

'You said something, Prayer-leader.' 'I said this.'

'Please,' he says, 'get down, I'm going to climb up there and answer you.'

The imam is angry, he tells him, 'Don't be angry. Will you give me your turban, too?' He gives that, too, with wrath. He puts it on, but it covers his face! He raises it, 'Give me your robe, too.' He dons it, the robe is too large for him.

He pronounces a Blessing on the Prophet of God. He relies on the strength of God, pronounces the Naming and sits down.

He first recites a chapter of the Quran. He does it beautifully, the congregation is ecstatic.

He opens his mouth and says, 'Congregation of Muslims: whose house is close by, who has milk in his house? Let someone bring me a bowl of milk.'

Somebody's house is near, he has also milked the cow, he says, 'Just a moment,' he goes and fetches the milk. 'Here you are,' he says.

Abu Hanifa calls out: 'Mufti!' This time he says, 'Yes?' 'Is there butter in this milk?' 'There is.' 'Will you give me a piece? If there's butter in it, I just want a piece of it.'

The imam is vexed. He says: 'There is butter in it. Before I can give it to you, it has to become yogurt, it has to be leavened, whipped, the butter has to rise to the top, there will then be a layer of butter. How can I give it to you now?'

'Do you accept this?' 'Yes, I do.'

'You recited Verse and Saying, "God is present everywhere," you said, "show this to me."'

'Now, you have to do the Prayers, you have to Fast, you have to fulfill the requirements of Islam for *years*. After all this, you still won't be able to see God, but at least you will understand a little bit what the Verse means.'

The congregation rises to its feet. 'Why, you! ...' They all chase the mufti [religious official]. Just as they're about to avenge themselves, there's a friend of God there, he says: 'No, that's enough.'

They fall upon the child, they carry him on their hands. They kiss him, hug him, they ask: 'Where were you raised?' The time for the Friday Prayer arrives, he says: 'Somebody lead the Prayer service, because it's not obligatory for me as a child.' They do the Prayer, but the congregation doesn't let go of the imam. 'Who are you? Where did you come from, where are you going?' He says, 'Ask my uncle, he knows best.' His uncle kindly tells everyone: 'He's an orphan. He studies the Quran. He's like this in his Quran lessons, too. It's a grace from God, I hope he'll be well-educated. We live in Baghdad, this neighborhood, this street.' He sells his goods and they come back.

There are such things now, too.

The building

Abu Hanifa had a large building constructed. Gossip starts: 'Where did he get the money?' He continues to live in a shack himself. One day he gave a tea-*fest* to both those who understand and those who don't. Some say, 'Let's leave,' he says, 'Don't go.' He takes them on a tour of the building. The basement, the baths, upstairs is the cafeteria where they eat, sleeping quarters above that and so on. He's still living in that shack.

He showed it to them all. He said, 'Friends, God is witness that this is not for myself. The people of Baghdad are poor,' he said. 'If a visitor comes, one should bring him here. If a businessman comes, there's nobody to host him, nobody to give him bread, friends. But God has given me this wealth, I'm working and God is giving. I built this a bit high so that visitors won't bother you or us. They'll see this tall building, they'll ask, "Who does this belong to?" People will answer, "It belongs to Abu Hanifa, it's a foundation." They'll come here and won't bother you. They can eat, drink, stay and be off. There's nothing in this for myself.' So they surrendered and went away.

Without the rich, what would the poor do? What if the rich were poor, too? If the poor become rich, they'll be engrossed in their own problems. I recommend wealth to all of you. Work with lawful (Allowed) money, lawful salary, honest earnings. Not for our selves, but for God.

The cloth

He had a partner, a draper. He went to visit him. A woman, her husband had died, she's going to sell some cloth for money to buy bread, she brings it in. Abu Hanifa is sitting there.

She says, 'Buy it.' He replies like anyone else, 'The time for this has passed. If it cost ten, I'll buy it for five.'

Abu Hanifa gets up, buys it for twelve and tells his partner: 'Tally your share and leave immediately.' 'Why?' 'You deceive. I can't be friends with you,' he says.

The ship that sank

One day, he's teaching students, they're the graduation class, they're studying the last chapter of the Quran under the Greatest Leader, their diplomas will be presented.

He's in class, someone knocks on the door, comes in and salutes him. He stands up and says, 'What's up, son?' 'Bad news, sir,' he says, 'our ship was loaded with goods, together with nine people, it sank before it reached the Persian Gulf.'

He thought for a moment, 'Too bad,' he said. 'Let's leave the matter to God.' The man left. Then he said, 'Thanks be to God,' and went on with the lesson.

The next day, another man, similar situation: 'Sir, that ship wasn't ours, it belonged to someone else. Our ship was spared. The goods are coming to Baghdad.' Again the Naming, he says, 'It's the wisdom of God,' he says. 'Thanks be to God. You can go, it's over.'

Now because the students are seniors, they ask, 'Thanks be to God for loss, thanks be to God for gain. What is this?' On the third day, one of them stands up and asks: 'Teacher, in great loss, nine people drowned, you gave thanks to God. The second day they brought the good news, the ship was saved, you said the same thing. We couldn't figure this out. Explain it to us.'

He said, 'Thank you. God has given this wealth to me lawfully. The first day, they gave me the news of that loss. All my capital is on that ship. All of it. But I glanced at my heart, it had no effect. No pain, no worry. That's why I thanked God. Now you asked me, and I've explained it to you.

'The second day he brought the good news, again I looked at my heart, and could find no trace of joy in it.[1] The same. I gave thanks for that, too. Thanks both for gain and for loss.' And he went on with the lesson. He was a great man.

If you do this, you'll become very rich. If you can't, you'll be mediocre. If you say, 'Everything comes from God and returns to Him,' you too will be very wealthy.

Wealth is good. For example, if you were to buy and distribute coal for the winter to several poor people or meet some other need, you can do it only if you have riches. What can you do if you don't?

---

1. 'I am not joyed by gain / Nor by loss pained / My consolation is Your love / It's You I need, and You alone.' – Yunus Emre. 'One to me are fame and shame / One to me are loss and gain.' – *Bhagavad Gita.*

The naturalists

There are friends and enemies in every age. Five or ten naturalist professors came together and said, 'Let's go and put the Greatest Leader to the test.'

'Peace upon you,' 'Upon you peace, welcome,' and so on. Abu Hanifa is very famous, in Baghdad and out.

After the greetings, one of them started to talk. He was advanced in the knowledge of his day. 'Leader,' he said, 'I've been thinking about something for a long time. My father was thinking it too, and so was my grandfather. This universe, the earth and the sky, how do these stand without a pillar?'

He replied, 'There is One God. His strength, His power is enough to support a *thousand* heavens like this without a pillar.'

'Are you serious?' 'Yes, I am.'

He stood up. 'Are you still a follower of these things?' 'Of course.' 'But we came to learn something from you.' 'Well then, *learn*,' he said. 'No,' he said, 'nature, a tree stands by itself, too.' Questions, questions, Abu Hanifa understands what is going on. Nature, nature. Parts of nature govern each other.

He said, 'Excuse me for a moment. I have to go to the restroom.' 'Go ahead,' they said.

He went out, he did a couple of cycles of Prayer in the other room, 'My God,' he said, 'protect me from the evil of these people.' He sat down, took a book and began to read. The visitors are waiting there!

Half an hour goes by, the Leader is nowhere to be seen. They smile and wink at each other: 'The imam ran away without answering us!'

He sits like that for fifty minutes and comes back. 'Peace upon you,' 'Upon you peace.'

'Where have you been, where did you go? We're waiting here, we came to ask you questions, to learn knowledge from you?'

He said, 'I'm sorry.' His house is close to the [Tigris] River. Its winding course passes between the houses.

'I went down to the river bank,' he said, 'and relieved myself. I was taking an Ablution from the water of the river, when I saw a big ship, without a captain, without a rudder, passing by at high speed. There's a bend in the river! As I looked at it, I was overcome by amazement. I'm looking at it all the while. A ship without a captain, no steering, no helmsman, *empty!* It's moving on, it went by without colliding with anything, and I was left there in the middle of nature.'

They looked at each other. Was he kidding? They didn't believe him. 'Why,' he said, 'that's quite a claim you've made! A large ship on the river, how can it *move* without a helm, a captain?' 'No, really,' he said, 'I saw it. That's why I was late. I'm sorry.'

'You're either making fun of us or deceiving us. We were talking among ourselves that you had run away, but you're on an entirely different track. How can a ship sail down the river like that?'

'Do you stand by this word? Do you affirm it?' 'Yes,' they said.

'This universe of which you speak: how does *it* turn without a captain, without an engine? How come one star doesn't collide with another, why don't their routes coincide, why don't they hit the moon? How come it all stands in harmony and order? Can this universe move without a captain?'

They couldn't answer him. Most of them thanked him, they said, 'We came to ridicule you. It was wrong of us to do so.' They paid their respects and left.

I've been left alone, and nobody's looking for me! I'm saying this on account of myself.

You too, tell your friends, 'I read a very strange news report in the papers the other day. A plane without a pilot, a stewardess, a crew or passengers, took off from Ankara's airport and went to London without an accident, it landed at London's airport all by itself. They won't believe you, insist on it. Say, 'I read it in the back pages.' Let them look it up, buy it and bring it to you saying, 'It's not here.'

That's when you tell them: 'Of course it isn't there. Can such a ridiculous thing happen?[2] Okay, so you don't believe that a plane can take off from here and land in London unaided. Then how can you believe that this entire universe keeps going like this all by itself, with such harmony and order, without anything colliding with anything else?' Again, give them an example: 'Has anyone ever heard of blood instead of milk coming from a woman's breasts? What is it that ensures this, that milk should come from the breasts of all women?' Speak to them like this and explain to them.

---

2. This is no longer so ridiculous, thanks to advances in UAV (Unmanned Aerial Vehicle) technology. In April 2001, a robot plane, Global Hawk, became the first unmanned aircraft to fly across the Pacific, taking off from California and landing in Australia, all unaided. The Master's example was given in 1980, more than twenty years before that milestone of aviation history. To update the example: the universe, in that case, must have a computerized guidance system of at least comparable sophistication to do what it's doing. But there is no evidence of this in nature. And even if there were, who conceived of, built and implemented that guidance system?

Ibrahim Adham

Comment: *Abu Hanifa showed great respect toward the famous saint Ibrahim Adham. His students ask him about this, he replies: 'We are involved with the shell of the matter. He deals with the core. That's why I was so courteous toward him.'*

True, sir. True. Ibrahim Adham had received sainthood at that time, Abu Hanifa was a scholar, a virtuous man. The knowledge Abu Hanifa had was possessed by Ibrahim Adham also. He became what he was with that knowledge, and he was continuing in the same way, as a dervish. Abu Hanifa said, 'Ibrahim Adham didn't abandon his shell of dervishhood.' A shoot had sprouted from the shell of dervishhood, but he had not abandoned the shell – that is, the Divine Law.

Work and the thief

The famous thief of Baghdad was about to be hanged. The judge and prosecutor are there. Abu Hanifa comes by and says, 'Peace upon you. With your permission, I would like to kiss the hand of this man [a gesture of respect in the Middle East].'

They were all amazed. 'What's the reason for this?' He replied, 'This man persevered. For the sake of his profession, he worked and even gave his head.' They save him from execution. The judge tells the thief: 'Pray for the government.' The thief says, 'No, I owe that old man thanks.'[3]

One has to work. A hodja stepped in through Abu Hanifa's door and said, 'I won't leave until you give me something.' All night until morning. Then they gave him. You too, work and earn. We all want it for free. 'Give!'

His patience

Abu Hanifa was going to a friend. Somebody was running toward him, he stopped when he saw him. 'I have to ask you something, wait.' The man went, but forgot all about it. Abu Hanifa waited for twenty-four hours. The next day the man comes by, 'Why, thank goodness I saw you here again.' He didn't put him to shame. He comes home, takes an Ablution and does a Thanksgiving Prayer. He says, 'My God, thank

---

3. Compare The saints/Bahlul the Wise/The execution.

You, You had pity on me early.' He doesn't even tell his wife. He says, 'I went to a neighbor.'

His death

Islamic Law is very important. It is very great and very delicate.

When he was six or seven years old, Abu Hanifa is going to school, he sees a sparrow in the hollow of a tree. He seals it in with a stone. When he comes back that way in the evening, he's going to take it out and play with it. He's a child. At his age, it's capricious. Anything capricious is Forbidden.

He forgets. When he's passing through the same street again one day, he remembers. He opens it. He finds the sparrow dead.

Time passes, he becomes the Greatest Leader. The Abbasid caliph of the time, he's a despot, he says, 'I need a mufti, I need a minister of religious affairs. Who do we have?' They say, 'There's the Greatest Leader.' 'Bring him to me.'

'Can you do it?' 'We have a Book, we have the Sayings. If I abide by these as God has commanded, I can. But if the caliph's side bears down occasionally, I cannot. I can't take orders from you. Excuse me.'

'*You!* You're telling *me* this?' He slaps his face twice, 'Throw him in jail.' He remains there for a few years. The Greatest Leader has students, lawyers. One day his friends come to visit him. 'We've had a court order issued, you'll be released soon.'

When one comes to a difficult passage, one's record of past deeds appears before one. That is, they don't leave it to the other side. Tears drop from his eyes. 'Why?' He tells them: 'I once confined a sparrow. Children, God is going to exact that sparrow's revenge on me. God is going to take my life in this prison.' 'But sir, you were a child,' and so on. 'That's the way I saw it,' he says. A couple of weeks pass, news arrives, he's dead.

He wanted only four people at his funeral, but it was attended by fifty thousand. Such people have enormous congregations like that. God avenged a sparrow, a bird, on him. The Greatest Leader!

Ghazali

People like Ghazali can remake a man from scratch.

When the Prophet went to the Farthest Mosque (the Temple Mount) as a preliminary to his Ascension, he met all the other prophets there and led them in a two-cycle Prayer. He talked to Moses. He said, 'Some among my Community will excel all the prophets of Israel.' Moses found this hard to believe, so the spirit of Ghazali was summoned from the future. They asked him about an issue. Normally there were three answers to that question, he gave nine.

[Moses asked why he was so long-winded about it. Ghazali, in turn, asked why Moses spoke so much with God. Moses replied, 'Because I wanted to remain in that presence a little longer.' 'My reason is the same,' Ghazali said.] 'Because I wanted to remain in your [the Prophet's and Moses'] presence a little longer,' he said.

There are two kinds of death. One is rooted to the grave [normal death]. The other is linked to the grave, the world and everywhere else. Like the wind. This is the death of saints, they're mobile in the afterworld.

Imam Ghazali didn't see the outside world during his last ten years. Worship, study. One day he rises at daybreak. A couple of much-beloved friends drop by. 'We've missed you,' they say, 'come on outside and take a breath of fresh air. The children have made a garden.'

He's enthusiastic. They go, they sit beside a fountain, they begin to talk. Ghazali is facing the house. 'Why, it's so beautiful! The children didn't tell me. If I had known, I would've come here every day to sit for five minutes.'

They're removing a funeral from the house. 'Come on, let's go too.' They take him by the arms. They do the last rites. They move away as the final prayer is being recited.

He asks, 'I wonder whose funeral that was? I didn't ask, but it came out of my house.'

'That's you, sir, it's your own funeral.' 'Oh, really? Well, I'd better go now.'

'You can't go, sir, and they wouldn't recognize you even if you went. From now on, you're mobile.'

Bukhari

Muhammad bin Ismail Bukhari ['of Bukhara'] is a collector of the Prophet's Sayings (Traditions: *Hadith*). [He collected more than six hundred thousand Traditions, but kept only about two thousand as the most reliable. The following true story highlights the meticulous care taken by this doyen of collectors in his efforts to secure only the most trustworthy Traditions.]

He upped and went to a distant land. Someone knew a lot of Traditions, he's going there to learn something more. Today, our homes are full of Traditions, we don't bother to memorize five of them.

He went and made inquiries, the possessor of Traditions lived in a village. He went to that village. A child took him over, showed him his yard and said: 'The man who knows a lot of Traditions is the owner of that yard.'

The child departed. He leaned on the wall, he's watching the garden. Now the man's horse was unharnessed, he's going to catch the horse, water is to be drawn from the well. There's a waterwheel for raising water, he's going to water the garden. And the horse is unhitched. The animal is tired, as the man approaches the horse, it flees. He can't get close.

The man has trained [the horse by offering it sugar in his hand]. Just as he's going toward the man, he shows his empty palm, when the animal comes near he grasps its gear, he catches it. He brings it and hitches it to the waterwheel. A whiplash, he blindfolds it.

Don't allow yourselves to be blindfolded! Let our eyes, ears and tongue be open. Force it. If they're not opened, continue on the Word of Witnessing [a hundred per day]. Follow that by reciting a hundred Words of Unity. If still not open, pronounce a hundred Blessings on the Prophet. Let this head be opened. We're going to take it and bury it in the ground. Let it be opened!

The horse begins to turn, it's drawing water. He sees a man watching from the wall surrounding the yard. 'Well, hi there!' This is a prominent man, the owner of the garden. Everyone goes and learns knowledge from him. He says, 'Come over, man, the gate's over there, see? Circle around from the gate.'

He waves, [Bukhari] approaches. He says, 'Friend, I'm tired. I've come a long way to this village to see you. You're a possessor of Traditions, a possessor of knowledge. I've come to learn something.'

'Well, come *on*, have a cup of coffee, something to eat, you're tired.'

'Friend,' he said. 'you caught an animal with an empty palm. You'll deceive me, too. Goodbye,' he said.

[Which brings to mind a similar story:]

The mufti who spat towards Mecca

Again, someone[4] traveled a great distance. This is very good, too. Be very careful. Again, a possessor of knowledge. That man was a mufti, the mufti of his district.

As they enter the town, people have finished the Noon Prayer, they're leaving the mosque. He asks: 'Who is he, the mufti, the scholar?' They say: 'That man.' People have surrounded that mufti. He has four or five friends. From outside the mosque, [he calls out]: 'Peace upon you.' 'And upon you peace. Welcome.' 'I came just to see you.' 'Come along,' he says.

As they're going down the road, he coughs: '*Ka-hoo!*' He coughs up a lot of sputum. He turns his mouth around and spits at the roadside. As they take two more steps – pay attention to this point – the one who came from afar, who's going to learn Verses, Traditions from that man, says: 'Friend, excuse me. I'm very tired. Let's talk in the morning, God willing.' 'But we're here, this is my house, that door.' 'Please, excuse me. I'm covered with dust, let me get rid of that. I haven't done the Noon Prayer, let me do that. Afterwards, I'll either come to your house, or we can talk in the morning.' [The mufti] insists, but *uh-uh*.

After they depart, his companion is with him, 'Thanks be to you, Dear Lord!' His friend, he's hungry, they go to a cook, they have some soup. They go to a mosque and perform the Noon Prayer. He says: 'Son' – they're called 'apprentice' – 'let's get out of this town at once.' He says: 'Master, you desired it so much. See, you're going to talk to the man.' 'You don't get it, son. I'm leaving, you can stay if you want.' How's he going to stay? He's in his entourage.

They continue on their way, they do the Dusk Prayer outside that town. But his man is curious. This man came from a month's distance. He spent so much money. He saw the man, he didn't talk, he's leaving. After their supplications, he says:

'Master, God knows I didn't do the Prayer properly [I couldn't concentrate]. I'm assailed by doubts.' 'Why, son?' he says.

'What have you done? You traveled for a month for the love of that man's name. You said hello to him. You've brought us, we're not

---

4. Bayazid of Bistam, according to the *Kitab al-Luma*.

even staying in town, we're on our way again. For God's sake, Master, explain.'

'Son,' he says, 'I've heard much praise of him. He's a scholar, a man of virtue, a possessor of Traditions, of Verses. May God bear witness that this is the sole reason I came to this man: to learn from him. But the man came out of the mosque. We introduced ourselves. His home is close by, too, he said so. Then he coughed with a loud, discourteous voice: *A-how!* And he spat that,' he said, 'towards the direction of prostration [Mecca]. Let's not stay in this town. If the mufti of this town does this, what would its ignorant not be capable of?

'You have your answer?'

'I do, Master, I'm sorry.'

Learn, learn. If you know already, learn again. Let's open up this head, for God's sake.

The saints

The Saintlight

The Prophet emerged like a *light* out of a dark people. They attacked him in order to kill him, to extinguish it. This light will continue till the end of humanity. We can't say it doesn't exist, because it *does*.

Like the Prophets, the saints too are privileged. They are privileged in spirit and they come by command, they fulfill the command. God gives them to a society in order to improve that society. They act on orders, they act not egotistically but with Compassion. Do you see what trials the saints of God undergo, the *sufferings* the Friends of God endure? And alongside those difficulties, they continue in their asceticism. They've put in labor, they're the stars of the universe.

We can't accept *any* hardships, not the slightest *thing*. We *do* love them, but we can't follow in their path. We want it to fall into our lap. Thank God we love them. What would we do if we didn't?

The saint is a person who has gathered the attributes of the four poles, who combines within himself the qualities of the sun, water, earth and night. He is like the sun in loving-kindness, like water in generosity, like the earth in humility and like the night in hiding sins. An ant is his life and soul. A blade of grass is his life and soul.

The saint has taken the universe in hand. If I were to sit in the shade and say: 'Bring me the sun, bring me wind,' you couldn't. One has to be like that. The easiest miraculous feat is to talk with the dead. Go ahead, talk! You have to die before you die, then it's possible. Whatever is difficult for your ego, do that. If one is in possession of those truths, one is not a prophet, but one is fulfilling the morality of the prophets. A person can save a million human beings by taking refuge in God, by depending on God and His Prophet. God says, 'I created human beings for worship' [51:56]. The greatest worship is conscious service.

All the saints have served humanity and endured hardships. They were beneficial to humankind. Rumi served in affluence, Yunus Emre served barefoot, in poverty. His master, Tapduk Emre, served humanity with blind eyes. With his *blind eyes*. Hajji Bayram Wali passed his life under the *ground*.

Beyond Paradise

The devil is the God of some people. One is either a friend of God or a friend of the devil. Now, all the friends of God have said this: 'If we don't desire Paradise, we can't find the Friend.' And if we don't search for the Friend, we can't find Paradise, the two are connected. We couldn't deny one if we wanted to. They started there first: 'Heaven, heaven,' and went on the path that way. That's how they achieved sainthood.

Yunus Emre said: 'My God, those villas of Paradise, those pleasures, those houris and servants, those sherbets, butter, milk, honey and so on – *give them to whoever* wants them,' he says. 'I need You, and You alone' is again found by that path.

If someone does you a favor, meets a need of yours, you shouldn't forget that friend. Because God gave through him. And the basis, the primary school, for this – the basis for finding the Friend, for traveling to Truth – is the Divine Law. One has to carry out the Divine Law to the letter. Then middle school, then high school, it's so difficult to enroll in college now. The same holds in spirituality.

But you did win college, you became the professor of a chair at a university. Can you abandon elementary school? Because you were educated there! This is where everyone falls, acts incorrectly. Once you abandon the Divine Law, know that you've fallen into the sea. You'll be fodder for fish. No one among the friends of God has abandoned it. Let us take refuge in the Divine Law.

Speak little

We said spare talk, right? The Divine Name of 'the Standing' (*al-Qayyum*) is upon the saints, they don't talk. The secret of the People of God is obscure, they speak through hints. Merkez Efendi [Center Master] is preaching. He says: 'This much is for the whole congregation. That much won't be understood by most of the congregation. As for this, it's for the person sitting behind that pillar. He's trying to find a mistake.'

If one cannot carry what is given and overflows, this prevents further development. Yunus Emre, Rumi and Niyazi Misri are all cases of overflow.

Sometimes the friends of God welled over, they revealed the secret. We cannot explain them. We can't do it, we can't go into that. Gilani, Naqshband all went by Quran and Saying, they didn't gush beyond that.

The Twelve Orders

The Twelve Founding Saints have to be descendants of the Prophet (sayyids), to come from that water. Abdul Qadir Gilani, Ahmed Rifa'i, Ahmed Badawi, [Ibrahim] Dasuqi, Mawlana Rumi, Bahauddin Naqshband are all sayyids. They all come from that water. They're the children of our Prophet, they're of the People of the House.

The beginning is Muhammad, the end too is Muhammad. Neither is it lost now, that water continues. Prophethood ends with us [with Islam]. Prophethood is gone, but sainthood continues. Where? It continues in that water. And it will continue till Doomsday. Whenever sainthood ends, know that it's the end of the world. There's time for it yet. A Saying: 'As long as there's someone who says *'There's no god but God,'* the world doesn't end.' The one who says that is the Saint of the Age.

Not all those who come from the lineage of the Prophet are saints. Those who do not come from that line but adopt the morality of the Prophet can become saints, too. I heard it from Hajji Ahmet Efendi: 'Prophets and sayyids are very privileged. But the others, if they strive' – this is exactly what he said – 'if they work by the sweat of their brow, they earn it, too.'

Now, there's good news: by working, a person can surpass the People of the House. Hajji Ahmet Efendi used to say, 'They're favored.' If we work, if we wipe the sweat from our brow, we too can be included. Not by favor, but by striving.

Kinds of saints

The Renovator (mujaddid): Once every hundred years, God sends a saint. He renews the religion.

Madmen of God (majdhub/majzub): They're on duty. They're on duty spiritually.

The Unseen Saints (rijal al-ghayb): Then there are the Unseen Saints. No matter how much they hide it, when a mortal bird (the spirit) flies from this world [its cage], its secret is revealed. Their secret is revealed only after they depart.

The Pole (The Saint of the Age; qutb): This business resembles that of prime minister. As in physicality, so in spirituality. In physicality, forty thousand people gather and elect a member of parliament. From among these, a cabinet is selected. Every minister is specialized in a different field. A fully evolved prime minister is very difficult to come by. He has to manage them all. It's a matter of state [level of being], not a matter of speech. One has to become infused with the state of God and His Prophet. This is nothing like your neighborhood superintendent.

The Assembly of the Pure

The saints come together in a certain place. They convene with their same appearance, their same garb. The Assembly of the Pure gathers once a year. Where it convenes is known to the Prophet of God: at the Ka'ba according to one account, at Medina according to another. Perhaps in a different place every year.

Ibn 'Arabi says, 'I took part in it, a tall person with a pointed beard fell beside me. I looked, he had no shadow.' According to one account, Khidr doesn't have a shadow either, they're stripped of human attributes. [Also,] some feel the thumb to tell whether it's really Khidr – it is said that his thumb has no bones.

Among scholars, Ghazali, among saints, Abdul Qadir Gilani – the spiritual schools and the Divine Law were balanced in these two. In this respect, I say that the worldly and the otherworldly should proceed in balance.

Among scholars, Abu Hanifa was very rich. He also engaged in trade. Among saints, Abdul Qadir Gilani was very wealthy. Wealth is good, that is. It helps.

Among prophets, the one who faced the greatest trials was Abraham. What does it mean to carve up one's son? It's worse than fire. Among the saints, Ibrahim Adham faced many trials. Bahauddin Naqshband faced trials and asceticism. Sayyid Burhanuddin underwent trials.

Khidr

(Although Khidr is pre-Islamic, he is included here because he is the archetype for Sufi saints. In fact, some saints have claimed to be taught by Khidr and not by a living teacher. These are called Uwaysi, after Uways al-Qarani who went to visit the Prophet but never met him in the flesh. Khidr is loved in the Islamic world, and is believed to rush to the rescue of those in distress.)

There are many saints who became friends with Khidr. There are many who say, 'I learned my Invocation (*zikr*) from Khidr.' Many of them enter Khidr's following. And then there are the rare, the very rare, Khidr enters *their* following. Khidr enters the entourage of the Perfect Human. What need do you have to search for Khidr any further? Don't try to catch Khidr yourself. When you're the right person, Khidr will come and catch you.

The soil that turned to gold

The story goes that Alexander, 'He of the Two Horns,' conquered everywhere. In order to enhance the power of his army and state, they set out in search of the Elixir of Life. Khidr and Elias were soldiers in his army.

Now the Elixir of Life is of two kinds: physical and spiritual. The physical kind is water, which we all know. The Elixir of Life is in water. They even say that its source is somewhere in Southeastern Turkey.

Then there is the spiritual Elixir of Life. That is in the most advanced stages of spirituality. Immortality. These are profound subjects.

Anyway, he took his army, and set out after the Elixir of Life. By and by, they came to a zone of darkness. The earth was calling out, 'He who takes me regrets it, he who doesn't take me regrets it too.' The stones and soil are speaking! Some of them picked up handfuls of soil there and put them in their bags.

They left that region, they arrived at a zone of light. A man reached into his bag, he took out some of the earth, it was gold! All the soil had become gold. Then, those who had taken some regretted that they hadn't taken more, while those who hadn't taken any regretted that they hadn't.

This is the knowledge of the Prophet of God. Those who took in this world are going to say, 'Why didn't I take more?' in the other world. Those who didn't take any are going to regret it anyway.

A few months ago, I had a dream. I climb to the top of a mountain. There's supposed to be a gold mine there. I take a handful of earth and squeeze it in my hand, it becomes gold. 'Okay,' I say, 'so it was true.'[1]

---

1. From which it may be inferred that Alexander's 'dark zone' actually exists in the Imaginal World.

The origin of Khidr

During one of their searches on this expedition, Khidr and Elias eat some conserved fish beside a spring. They throw its skeleton in the water, *flit*, away swims a fish. One says, 'I saw a fish.' The other replies, 'There can't be any fish in this water.' They throw in another fishbone, it too becomes a fish and swims away. Finally, one holds a skeleton from the tail and dips it in the water, it begins to squirm in his hand.

They drink of that water, they bathe in it, they don't tell Alexander.

But we have to think: do the times match, are they contemporaries? Moses has to be earlier than Alexander [and Khidr was already immortal by the time he met Moses]. So that's why we have to treat these as stories. They have both physical and spiritual meaning. The spiritual meaning: a poet says in a verse, 'Who drinks from the Elixir of Life does not die.' That is, whoever finds the path of Muhammad, who drinks from his hand.

Alexander's search for the Elixir of Life is to enter the Heart of a Master, to become real with the Real. Then one becomes immortal, like Khidr and Elias. Everybody drinks of that water, but they alone win immortality, because they started out with that intention. Khidr rules the land, Elias the water. With the permission of the Prophet of God, both can rule both.

The stories of the ancients are all true, we have no objection. But decoding these sciences – does that belong just to the ancients, or to all humanity? It belongs to all humanity. Whoever strives, finds it. So we're not striving, we're at fault. May we all drink the Elixir of Life, God willing.

Moses and Khidr

The story of Moses and Khidr is related in the Quran [18:60–5].[2] The ship they board: now if we discuss the matter in terms of the science of Sufism, this body of ours is a ship, too. Plenty of organization is necessary to keep this ship afloat.

The Eye of the Heart must be open. Khidr sees it, but Moses doesn't. Moses, such a great prophet, was able to receive only three words of Hidden Knowledge. When someone comes to the point where – like

---

2. The Master's own account of this encounter is related in the Introduction to the *Meaning of the Four Books*, and has been included at the beginning as the introduction to the Wisdom Base.

Moses – they no longer understand, I take their hand [like Khidr did] and say: 'We've come this far.'

[The meeting of Moses and Khidr is so important that I cannot resist imparting the following further information to be found in Sufic lore. The Quran does not specifically state that it was Khidr who met with Moses, but this is clearly stated in a Saying of the Prophet. Khidr made Moses witness three events: (1) Khidr drilled a hole in the ship they boarded, but this apparent sabotage turned out to rescue the ship from pirates. (2) Khidr killed a young man who would have done much evil had he been allowed to live. (3) They rebuilt a ruined wall so that the treasure buried beneath it would be discovered by its rightful owners years later.

Now Moses had met with Khidr in order to learn Hidden Knowledge, and the reasons for these actions were revealed by Khidr only at the end. But according to Ibn 'Arabi in his *Bezels of Wisdom*, there was a further depth of meaning to these events. In each of these episodes, Khidr was in fact holding a mirror to Moses' own life – which, however, Moses failed to recognize. Each of the three events signaled a parallel event in Moses' biography. The ship that almost sank was a metaphor for the basket of bulrushes, which was snatched from the water by Pharaoh's kin just as it was about to sink. The young man killed by Khidr is a homologue of the Egyptian struck down by Moses (Exodus 2:11). And the wall they built without charging for it corresponded to Moses' drawing water for the sisters in Midian and watering their flock without charging a fee (Exodus 2:16–19).

In fact, this third act has a still deeper layer of meaning. For the wall they built was testimony to nothing less than the edifice erected by Moses himself – the Divine Law (*Torah*) that prevented the hard-won fruits of faith and righteous conduct from falling into undeserving hands. This may well serve as an archetype for religion: *the dividing line*, to use the Master's terms, *between Compassion and Mercy – those who believe and do certain things obtain results which those who do not cannot.*

In a meeting with Shaykh Abul Abbas al-Khidr, of the Haqqani Order, Khidr intimated to him that he had, in fact, had more in store for Moses. 'I had prepared,' he said, 'a thousand cases from Moses' life, from the moment he was born to the time when we met. He wasn't able to stand even three of them.' And the Prophet said: 'If only my brother

Moses had been patient, so that God could have related more of his stories to us' – in the Quran, concerning his meeting with Khidr.[3]]

Waiting for Khidr

A man was looking for Khidr. He was watering the field, the wheat, with a shovel. A man came by, 'Peace upon you.' 'Upon you peace,' he replied. 'What are you doing?' 'I'm planting this wheat to earn a living. I say, I wish Khidr would come and rescue me.'

'How much yield do you get?' 'Two to four bushels.' 'Would you recognize Khidr if you saw him?' 'No.' 'Give me that shovel,' he said. 'What would Khidr do for you if he came?' 'Well, he could turn that shovel into gold, for instance.' 'Really?' 'Sure.' The man said 'All right, wait,' and left.

He took the shovel in his hands, he saw that the color of the shovel had turned yellow. He took it and washed it, it was still the same. He made a scratch on the shovel, again the same. He came back to the village, he asked his wife, she took the shovel to the hodja. The hodja said, 'Khidr did come to you.'

Another man wanted to see Khidr, so Khidr came to him. 'What would Khidr do?' 'He could fetch a stone from afar.' He did it. 'He could lift this cow.' He lifted the cow. 'He can pulverize this stone.' He did that too. But the man still didn't understand. When he told his friends, they all said, 'You've seen Khidr.' 'Oh, no!'

Khidr comes at a difficult moment, so that he'll be dispatched quickly.

Unlisted saints

A hodja is preaching in a mosque, a man's drowsing off. Someone beside him says, 'Listen, brother, jewels and diamonds are flowing from that pulpit.' Two or three times this happens, finally: 'What are you poking me for? If you don't leave me alone, I'll tell this whole congregation that you're Khidr, they'll mob you! You won't be able to escape them. Leave me be.' 'Okay,' he says. He stands up and goes to the rear of the congregation.

---

3. Summarized from Ahmet Avni Konuk, *Fusus-il Hikem Tercume ve Sherhi* (Trk., eds. Mustafa Tahrali and Selçuk Eraydin), Istanbul: Marmara University Press, 1992, vol. 4, pp. 268–9.

After Khidr leaves the mosque, he opens the notebook of saints given by God, he can't find that man. He says, 'My God, I have the book in which the names of all saints are listed, his name is not in it.' God says, 'Some of their names, I haven't given you. I gave you the names of the saints you need to know, not the names of the ones I need.'

How to find Khidr

A man was very poor. People come and go, they talk about Khidr, 'If only you could see Khidr,' they say, 'you'd be freed of this poverty.'

One day he tells his wife, 'Farewell. I may not come back. I'm setting out in search of Khidr.'

Three years he looks for Khidr. From mountain to mountain, from town to town.

He reaches a large city. There's a grocer, he looks, this man is destitute, he's passing by, he calls him over. 'Come here, friend,' he says. 'What's your name, where are you from? What are you doing in this city?'

'Uncle,' he says, 'don't ask. I've been searching for three years.' '*What* are you seeking?' 'I'm looking for Khidr,' he said.

'Oh, my, three years?' 'Yes, I've been after him for three years.'

'*Oh*, if only you had come to me earlier,' he said, 'you wouldn't have exhausted yourself so much.' The grocer is a sage. 'Where do you sleep?' 'I sleep in the streets. I don't have any money left, I'm in a bad way.' The man's hungry, too.

'Come tonight and let's have some supper together,' he says, and goes.

The grocer buys two pounds of fish, pours a lot of salt in it and puts it in the oven. When he comes back in the evening, he slides it before him. 'Eat as much as you can,' he says.

The peasant eats the fish to his fill, the grocer takes him down to the basement of the store. 'The toilet is over there,' he says. 'Sleep here and whatever you dream about tonight, tell me in the morning.'

The grocer puts him to bed, closes his store and leaves.

In the morning he comes, opens the door, he brings him upstairs. His face is ashen, he's in dire straits.

'Did you see Khidr?'

'No, sir, I didn't,' he says. 'What did you see? Tell me.' 'Sir,' he said, 'you fed me the fish last night. It must have been salty, I couldn't sleep all night. I lay my head down, there is water in our mountains, I drink ice-cold water. I go over there and drink water, come and drink – I was preoccupied with water all night.'

There were water jugs there. 'Are you thirsty?' 'I'm dying.' 'Drink all you can.' He drinks.

'You were dealing with water all night without drinking.' 'Yes, sir.' 'If you had dealt with Khidr for *one hour*, son,' he says, 'you would've seen Khidr. You've been wandering for three years. What is this? If you had fallen in love with Khidr the way you did with water for *one hour*, Khidr would've come and found you. You can't find Khidr, son. Take this money and go back to your children.'

If that kind of love binds you, son, Khidr will come and find you.

[In this story, one has to remember that by Khidr, the master is meant.]

When does Khidr disappear?

Aq Shamsuddin becomes friends with the hodja (Prayer-leader) of the village. Now Khidr used to join the congregation of that hodja every Friday. One day, however, Khidr ceases to attend. When two or three months pass like that, the hodja asks Shamsuddin about it. Shamsuddin smiles, 'Okay,' he says, 'Let's look into it.' The next Friday the hodja asks again. Two or three weeks go by. He asks every time. Finally, Aq Shamsuddin says, 'All right, I've talked to him. You admired yourself in the mirror, you said "I'm handsome," that's why Khidr was offended with you.'

The hodja is very sorry. He takes off his turban and tears it to pieces. He takes off his new robe and puts on his old, tattered one.

The following Friday, Khidr joins the congregation again. After the Prayer service, Aq Shamsuddin smiles at the hodja and says, 'Did you see?' The hodja replies, 'Yes, I did. He was among the congregation.'

Aq Shamsuddin

Aq Shamsuddin is the teacher of Sultan Mehmed the Conqueror [Mehmed II], and Hajji Bayram Wali is the teacher of Aq Shamsuddin.

Dervishhood is not in the cloak

One of Hajji Bayram Wali's disciples, Omar Dede [also known as Emir Sikkini], was from Ankara. After the saint's death, the students split in two. Aq Shamsuddin had his cloak, cap and mantle. Omar said, 'This won't do.' They all gathered at Hajjibayram [the location of the saint's shrine] and lit a fire. Omar donned Hajji Bayram's mantle and cap and entered the fire. When the fire went out, the mantle and cap had been burned, but nothing had happened to Omar. 'As you see, brother,' he said, 'the miraculous feat is not in the mantle or the cap.[4] You can still have them, I'm giving them to you.'

This is like Hajji Bayram's story of one-and-a-half disciples. [Hajji Bayram once tested his disciples to see who were the true ones. He set up a tent and all the disciples gathered outside. He said he was going to sacrifice them to God. Inside the tent, he slaughtered a sheep and let the blood run out from under the tent so that it could be seen by all. As soon as the disciples saw that, everyone fled. The only ones who remained were one dervish and a young girl. They entered the tent fearlessly, and understood what had happened.[5]]

Ibn 'Arabi

Muhyiddin Ibn 'Arabi, the Greatest Shaykh, is a man of knowledge, both exoteric and esoteric. That is, he has taken the universe in hand. Ghazali is exoteric only, from the Book. When Ibn 'Arabi saw that they're all running from the exoteric, he spoke esoterically.

Two groups went to Muhyiddin. Afterwards, one group said, 'We visited an unbeliever.' The other group said: 'We visited a saint.' The first didn't understand Muhyiddin's science, the second understood a little bit. He said [of his *Fusus al-Hikam* (Bezels of Wisdom)]: 'Our

---

4. 'Dervishhood is not in the cloak or the crown' – Hajji Bektash Wali. 'If dervishhood had been the cloak and the crown / We too would have bought it for a nominal sum' – Yunus Emre.

5. The Master never told this story in my presence. It is retold from Sufi lore.

words are chickpeas of iron. In order to chew them, one needs teeth of steel.'

Comment: *I'm reading the works of Ibn 'Arabi.*

You shouldn't start building a house from the roof. What happens to a building without a foundation? It collapses.

Muhyiddin inspected whatever is in the Quran and proclaimed it. He always deciphers with Verse. He doesn't step beyond the Quran, he reveals its secrets. Europe took its material side. Eight hundred years ago, he said in the language of that time: 'If two copper wires touch each other, East will communicate with West.' 'If two irons extend together, distances will be shortened.' The railroads. He mentions airplanes.

A German engineer sought out his pamphlet and found it in a bookstore in Egypt. 'How much?' 'Whatever you'll give, fifty cents.' 'Take this and go to the bank.' They fill his handkerchief with gold. He comes back, the German says, 'This treatise of yours is so valuable, even this isn't enough to pay for it.' That man becomes the richest man in Egypt. They take it, we don't know its worth.

He told us of this science eight hundred years ago. And the Prophet did so with the Quran fourteen hundred years ago. Muhyiddin Ibn 'Arabi took this from the Quran, not from anywhere else. Ali says, 'If the forests were pens and the seas were all ink, there would still be no end to explanations of the Naming [the *Basmala*, which the Quran and almost every chapter in it begin with: "*In the Name of God, the Compassionate, the Merciful*"].' 'I am the dot under that Arabic letter B.' The eighteen thousand worlds are within the attribute of Compassion. Let us pass the attribute of Compassion and enter the attribute of Mercy. What other eighteen thousand worlds there are!

The seal of the saints

Ibn 'Arabi drowses away as he's telling his beads [doing Invocation], a dream – he sees himself as 'the last Friend' (the seal of the saints, *khatm al-awliya'*).[6] He gets up and does a two-cycle Thanksgiving Prayer. He drowses again, 'Muhyiddin, there will be many saints after you. But you belong to Me, too.'

---

6. Similar to Muhammad, 'the seal of the prophets' (*khatm al-anbiya'*).

The fast that lasted three months

The Greatest Shaykh started his fast on the first day of the Three Holy Months.[7] He doesn't put anything in his mouth during those three months, not even water. He says, 'My intent is to break my fast on the first day of the Ramadan Festival [at the end of Ramadan].' During those three months, he writes five hundred works. They ask him, 'How did you achieve this?' He replies, 'The pen was in my hand, but an inspiration was doing the writing, it's not my work.'

The scholar and the ass

His father sent Muhyiddin to another town to study. He stayed two weeks or a month and came back to visit his father. He's sixteen or seventeen years old.

On his way back, he comes across an old man, he has old clothes on him. 'Peace upon you,' he says. 'And upon you peace too, son.' He kisses his hand. 'What is it, where are you going?' There's an ass in front of him with a heavy load. The animal is about to collapse.

'Son,' he says, 'I was Prayer-leader in such-and-such a village. Now my lot there is interrupted, they don't want me. I've loaded the animal, I'm going elsewhere. Again to a center of knowledge.'

'Oh, very good. What's that on the animal?' – this point is *very* important.

'On one side, select copies of the Quran, of Traditions. That's one load, on the other side is my correspondence based on them.'

'Bravo,' he said, 'you've really studied higher knowledge. May God help you next time.' Muhyiddin is young, he's still studying.

He said, 'I'm studying, I'm on thin ice in Islamic Law from this teacher.' He says, 'Oh, I know him, I've heard about him.'

'But,' he says, 'this subject I don't understand. Would you help me?' Maybe he can learn something.

The hodja checks himself. 'Son,' he says, 'I'm sorry, it escapes me at the moment. Let's take down the animal's burden, I'll look it up in the books and reply.'

'No need,' he says. He tells him a Tradition, 'Can you explain the meaning of this to me?'

The hodja checks himself once more, 'Son,' he says, 'I can answer both only with these books.' 'No,' he says, 'don't unload them, the animal would rest and so would you, but there's nobody to load them

---

7. Rajab, Sha'ban and Ramadan.

back on. I'm leaving, and you can't load them all by yourself. Let me kiss your hand again. But, don't be angry with me –' he kisses his hand again, he kisses it three times. 'So you're only bearing a load, just like this animal,' he says. This is very important. 'You're only bearing the burden of knowledge, just like this animal. Goodbye, may God be with you.'

Let's work, let's not bear the burden.

The pot that exploded

He goes from Andalusia [in Spain] to Egypt to study knowledge. He goes and goes, there's a body of flowing water like a river, he crosses that. In the evening, sunlight shines on the valley. He looks, he spies someone. He's covered his private parts with a plant, he's naked.

He said, 'Peace upon you. Are you human?' 'Yes, I'm human. Where are you going?' 'Just in this general direction.' 'Be my guest tonight,' said the naked man. 'Okay,' he said, he's tired anyway. Where's he going to go, it's God's desert expanse.

When he says 'I'll be your guest,' the naked man goes straight to the river, he plunges his hand in, he pulls out a fish. He plunges it again, he takes out two. He throws one back in the water, he brings over a couple. He lights a fire, he fries them, it's their supper.

All through the night they don't sleep, they talk.

Because Muhyiddin isn't at that point yet, he's astonished. This man is here, he's doing these wonders. In the morning he says, 'What a good man you are. You're spending time here. How long has it been?' He replies, 'I've been here for thirty-two years. I'm not good, my master is good. You're going to Egypt, I don't know when you'll come back. Will I be dead or alive by then?

'My master is so-and-so, he's in this neighborhood, that street. On your way back, drop by and bring me back news from him, if I remain alive here.'

'All right,' he says, 'if I'm alive too, I'll seek you out and find you here.'

He bids farewell and departs.

He stays there for a year-and-a-half. Muhyiddin studies science and wisdom.

One day, the mosque's great man of knowledge is invited to a feast. Muhyiddin's a student there, he takes Muhyiddin with him. They go, they eat and drink. At the end, dessert – *baklava*, that is – comes in a big earthenware pot. They all eat, while they're still eating, the pot explodes with a *bang!* into smithereens, although nothing has touched the table.

Some of them are ashamed, others are lost in thought.

The master says, 'Let's ask, let's ask the pot what it has to say.' He gathers the burst pieces, the master rebuilds the pot. 'Oh, now it's clear,' he says. 'It's telling. The pot says: "I was broken to pieces and remade ten times on this table, I made ten round trips. Now they've made a delicious dessert in me. You've eaten. Tomorrow they're going to make food with garlic or onions in me, that's not a problem. I'll just burst again. But I'm going to lose the fragrance of this gathering, that's why I was sorry and *burst* away like that." That's what it's saying.'

Muhyiddin is amazed – 'How can he speak with earth like that?' Yes, Muhyiddin was like that, [he found] through his wanderings.

Love of this world

His time there ends, he says, 'Let me see that naked man's – the ascetic's – master in Egypt.' He goes, he asks and finds, they open the door, the stairs are all gold-plated. The stairs! Muhyiddin is astonished. Look at that naked man over there, look at this situation here!

He goes upstairs, he sees the master. He presents his greetings, kisses his hand and sits down. Coffee arrives in gold cups and gold saucers. There are visitors, a gathering. He says, 'Sir, when I was passing through such-and-such a place, there was a servant of yours there. Now I'm going, what news shall I give him? He said: "I've been spending time under these conditions for thirty-two years, for asceticism. Am I going to stay here longer, or does my master forgive me, do I go back to him?" He's been away for thirty-two years.'

His master says, 'And peace upon you, too. Is that so, is he still laboring away over there?' 'Yes, sir, I saw him. I stayed with him for a night. He served me a fish for supper.' He tells his story.

'If he had that long to live,' he said, 'if he were to live in that state for another thirty-two years, it's still no use as long as he has that love of the world in him, he won't be of use to us.'

Muhyiddin wants to ask about those golden saucers, those cups of gold, but he keeps his silence out of courtesy. He's going to say, 'What's this condition of yours, what's his condition? You're buried in the world, that poor man is starving to death,' but out of courtesy he doesn't say it. 'Okay,' he says.

And he comes back. 'Peace upon you.' 'And upon you peace.' His first question: 'Did you see my master?' Yes! Even in that condition. 'Yes, I saw your master,' he says. 'I saw him two days ago.'

'What did he say about me?' he asks.

'You'll be sad if I tell you,' he says. 'Tell me, for God's sake tell me,' he says. That's his first question: 'Is there news for me from my master?'

'First,' he says, 'you've been living here in this condition for thirty-two years.' 'Yes,' he says. [Muhyiddin continues:] 'I saw your master. He's buried in gold, his neck is, like, this thick, tables, feasts ... He's in that condition, you're in this condition, I'm ashamed to speak to you.'

'Yes, my master is like that,' he says. 'God gave him like that, and He gave me like this in order to train me. What else did he say?'

'The master said of you, "If he were to stay there another thirty-two years, it's no use if he still has that love of the world in him."'

'*To me?*' 'Yes,' he says.

He gets up, he prostrates, he says, 'My master spoke the truth. He knows that I haven't been able to abandon the love of this world yet.' He starts to tear his hair out, Muhyiddin stops him. 'But he's in riches himself?' 'Not a drop of it is in his Heart.'

'As long as the love of this world is in you and your master is saying this, it's Farewell to you, and it's Goodbye for me.' Muhyiddin goes back to Egypt, to that master.

The love of this world is necessary – up to a point. After that point, once [the self] submits to the spirit, we're still going to live, eat, drink and sleep in this world.

Fire, don't burn

When the Greatest Shaykh was in Damascus, a Christian priest begins to pester him. He speaks from the Gospel, Muhyiddin speaks both from the Quran and the Gospel. It's winter. Coal is burning in the brazier, he's making coffee. That priest comes, so he makes some for him, too.

The priest asks, 'Was Abraham's fire real fire, or was it the fire of the ego?' 'It was both. But fire can burn only if God desires it. It can't if He doesn't.' 'I don't believe fire didn't burn Abraham.' This is true, it's in the Quran. ['Fire, be cool and safe towards Abraham' – 21:69.]

'Let's do the experiment,' he says. He grabs the hand of the priest and thrusts it into the fire. Nothing happens. He pours some of the fire onto the furry sheepskin, nothing happens. 'Did it burn?' 'No, it didn't.' He takes his hand out. 'Now try it yourself,' he says. The priest burns his finger even as his hand approaches the fire. 'Have you surrendered to God?' 'Yes, I have.' 'Then pour the fire back into the brazier.'

The baby who spoke

Muhyiddin Ibn 'Arabi arrives in Malatya, Turkey. He wants to go to his friend the mufti [religious official], he's tired. He asks a child for directions. The child says, 'Let me take you there.' He's Sadruddin Konevi. To lead a person who doesn't know the way to his destination is part of Islam.

They go. The mufti says, 'Let's get you married. The governor is dead, his widow is a student of the Quran. He was the father of the child who brought you.' 'I'll marry her for the sake of that child.' They get married. They have a daughter called Zaynab.

The lady belongs to the people of the exoteric. One day, in order to open her up, he says, 'I didn't understand this Verse in the Chapter of the Cow.' 'Husband, let's look it up in the Quran.' 'No need to do that, let's ask Zaynab and she can tell us.' The baby takes her mouth from the breast and with that voice, gives a very good explanation. The woman runs to the mufti, 'You've married me to a madman! This is what happened!' 'Oh, really? Come on, let's go.' The mufti tells Ibn 'Arabi: 'Don't do this, otherwise this woman will divorce you.'

Then he goes to Konya for a week, there he meets Bahauddin Walad [Mawlana Rumi's father]. Mawlana is seven or eight years old, he was playing there. His father says, 'Pray for him to become a great man.' 'What are you saying? We're two lakes, following a sea. If I can train Sadruddin, he's going to be like that, too.' He empties that sea of the world [his knowledge] into that child [Sadruddin]. Sadruddin Konevi is from Malatya, not from Konya [contrary to his name].

The Adams before Adam

Ibn 'Arabi relates: 'One year I was circumambulating the Ka'ba. I saw a man with a pointed beard and a long gown of the sort the Persians wear. He had no shadow. There were others, too. "Who are you?" "Muhyiddin, my son" – he addressed me with my name, I was even more surprised – "I belong to your grandfathers who lived fifty thousand years ago."'

Adam is fifteen thousand years ago. Muhyiddin does a brief calculation and says in amazement: 'So you're before Adam!' The man then asks, 'Which Adam are you talking about?' So there were other Adams before Adam.

'I asked, "What is your name?" He replied, "Ahmet." "Well, why don't these people have shadows?" "They've passed into the Realm of the Everlasting. Spirit is light, it doesn't have a shadow."'

Muhyiddin says, 'I saw the same thing later at the Assembly of the Pure. We performed the Dawn Prayer together. Then the sun rose, some of them had shadows, others didn't. They had crossed the threshold to the Realm of the Everlasting, they had become spirit.'

The Adam mentioned in the Quran is the very first Adam. We don't know these others, we have to know only what is in the Quran.

Generosity

In his last days, the Greatest Shaykh goes to Damascus. He stays in the corner of an inn. His friends come together and say, 'This won't do, let's buy him a house, he can stay downstairs and someone can rent the upper floor, that'll pay for his coffee.' They go and suggest it, he says 'All right.' They buy the house and prepare the deed in his name.

A week later, a beggar comes to the door. The Greatest Shaykh hasn't a penny in his pocket. 'Just a moment,' he says, he goes inside right away and comes back with the deed. They go to the real estate office together. He just learned the way recently! He signs the deed over to the beggar.

He comes and sits in his usual corner at the inn. 'What's up?' He tells his friends, 'I've done a great thing. I've applied the radiant way of Abu Bakr. It wasn't as good as what he did, though.'[8]

The secret of Ibn 'Arabi

The Greatest Shaykh called that sort 'the animal who speaks.' One day he goes to the barber. When a rich man comes in, the barber interrupts Ibn 'Arabi's shave midway and begins to shave the newcomer. Once, twice, three times, he got angry. He left the barber shop and went to the Ummi [Umayyad] Mosque in Damascus [Sham] for the Friday Prayer. There he got angry with the hodjas. As he left after the Prayer, he stomped his foot on the ground and said, 'What you worship is beneath my feet.' Then he inscribed on stone with his bare finger:

---

8. See The caliphs/Abu Bakr.

'When S enters Sh, the secret of Muhyiddin will be revealed.'

Those present beat him, some with sticks and some with stones. He couldn't get up, the great Muhyiddin. He died in the house he was taken to. They buried the great saint in a garbage dump.

A few hundred years passed. When Sultan Selim the Resolute read this on his way to Egypt, he thought to himself, '"S" is you [Selim], and "Sh" is Sham [Damascus].' He said, 'Describe to me where he struck his foot.' In the courtyard, between two pillars, he said 'Dig here.' From there emerged three large earthenware pots full of gold.

Behold this miraculous feat of Selim: 'Muhyiddin Ibn 'Arabi would not speak in vain, he wouldn't strike his foot there for nothing.' One pot he left to Muhyiddin in Damascus, one pot he took to Egypt, one pot he sent to the treasury in Istanbul. These are all true. I've gone there, I've done a two-cycle Prayer in that mosque myself.

Why did God stop him? Because there is overflow. One does not say such things. For instance, if you call a Prayer-niche 'stone,' it's as if one is performing the Prayer to stone, they'll say 'He's prostrating to stone.' Where will that leave Prayer? But prostration is not to stone, it is to God. Indeed, because of such statements, some have ventured to say: 'There's no need for Prayer.' My last will and testament to you all is this: do not open the veil of the Divine Law. Don't divulge a secret, cover it.

Bayazid of Bistam

Bayazid (or Abu Yazid) of Bistam was trained by twelve masters. He changed twelve teachers. People think it was the teachers' fault. It wasn't. The fault was Bayazid's. He grew, he matured, he was realized at the twelfth.

What does Bayazid of Bistam say? 'You go to a gathering, they don't recognize you. You give a cry from the heart: "God!" They'll give you a seat, they'll ask: "Who are you?"' And he says: 'It's like when you strike a red-hot iron, the sparks fly.' You too, let your sparks fly.

The loony bin

Many seasoned travelers of the Sufi path say, 'Worship me.'

It was a Sunday, just like today. A bunch of people went to visit Bayazid of Bistam. He took them all to the insane asylum. The insane asylum! Listen!

They went, it's a summer day. The craziest are behind bars. Those with a little more sense are outside. They've gathered in groups. They went to a group, 'I'm Harun al-Rashid.' Someone in that group says, 'You're the minister of foreign affairs, you're the minister of internal affairs.' Bayazid tells his friends, 'Listen to them.' After listening, they give them cigarettes and go to the next group. They change three or four groups. These are the sanest, that is. The others, the worst ones are inside.

They went to the last group. 'Peace upon you,' 'Upon you peace.' They made some small talk. One said, 'You visitors, did you recognize that man?' 'No, we didn't.' 'This is Adam, the first man,' he said. 'Sure.' Whatever they say, 'sure.' 'Do you recognize this one?' 'No.' 'He's very generous, he's Abraham.' He goes through all of them, finally the prophets are finished. They're all prophets. Not one is a follower of a prophet.

There's only one left. 'And who are you?' he says. They're all declaring *themselves*, without Bayazid and his company asking.

'I,' he says, 'am God Almighty.' 'Sure, sure,' they say. 'But I never created any false and lying prophets like you. Where do you invent such lies, aren't you ashamed of yourselves?'

Bayazid of Bistam signals to his friends. 'Sure,' they say, and leave. Bayazid turns to those accompanying him and says: 'At this rate, you'll end up in the asylum too. That's why I brought you here.'

Now, those people have a group, one is Hajji Bayram Wali, another is Rumi, another is a prophet … they're all like that. Tell this story to that group, okay? Don't forget. Tell all of them! If you're sane, separate yourself from the lunatics.

Bahlul the Wise

Bahlul Dana ['the Wise'] was the brother of Harun al-Rashid, the famous caliph. He was a *majdhub* [madman of God], that is, a saint of his times.

The execution

He went downtown, he had some business. He saw a crowd gathered at a market place. He went and looked, they've erected the gallows, they've brought someone in front of it, they're going to hang him.

He asked: 'Who is this, what did he do?'

'This is a famous thief. He's been famous for ten, twenty years, they caught him today, they're going to execute him.' 'Is that so?'

The judge, the prosecutor are all there, he went to their side. 'If you'll allow me, I'd like to kiss this fellow.' 'Okay,' they said. He drew near, he kissed him on the forehead, 'Bravo, son. So you went to the gallows for your craft, eh? I have a task too. Although I've tried to serve God, to follow in the footsteps of the Prophet, I haven't been able to succeed. See? You've succeeded. You came to execution for the sake of your profession. Well done. May God save you.' The people there said, 'Amen.' And he left.

The judge asked: 'Who was that?' 'Bahlul the Wise.' 'Why did he say that?' Those who knew him said: 'You must have misunderstood. Everyone has a duty, a calling, physically and spiritually. This man was so dedicated to his calling that he came to the gallows *without ever relenting.*'

But each one of us has a task, too. We should fulfill those tasks in the best way, and leave the rest to God.

The judge understood then. He said, 'Bravo. Well said.' They have a duty too, everyone has a duty, but God has prohibited them all in the Glorious Quran. But what can he do, he's made this his craft, everyone's calling is different. God's banned it, 'Don't do these things. If you do, it'll be a sin.' May God protect us all.

The judge and prosecutor reconsider his case and decide to release him.[9]

This is for all of us. We walk in the path of God, but we can't give up our lives. What does Yunus Emre say? 'You wish for the Beloved without giving up your life.' We can't even give a finger, let alone our lives. Give your life first, then come to the Beloved. May your sustenance increase, not with wrath but with mercy.

---

9. Compare The scholars/Abu Hanifa/Work and the thief.

A villa in Paradise

To the Five Daily Prayers, the first wife of Harun al-Rashid added five more. A lady who feeds the poor. His father left her his wealth. She doesn't spend from Harun al-Rashid's money, she spends of her father's *honestly earned (Allowed)* money.

'My dear,' he said, 'I'm going to take another wife.' 'As you wish, husband.' 'Are you reconciled with this?' 'I am.' The first wife obeys him. So he brings her over.

One day, one wife says to the other: 'Let's go to the public bath.' On their way, Bahlul the Wise is drawing something on the ground with his finger. They see him. The first wife asks, 'What is this?' 'Villas in Paradise.' 'Would you sell one to me?' – She just wants to give him money. – 'How much?' 'One gold Lira.' She's pleased, the other wife is infuriated. She bickers even at the bath. In the evening, she tells Harun al-Rashid: 'Your crazy wife did this.' 'Leave her alone,' he says.

That night she has a dream. She sees a five, six-storey villa in the center of Baghdad. There's nothing like it in the world. 'Not even my husband has anything like that!' She looks, the first wife is on the top floor. 'This is the villa I bought yesterday,' she tells her.

She wakes up in regret. She goes straight to where Bahlul is still practicing real estate. 'How much?' 'One hundred thousand Liras.' It's worth millions, not a hundred thousand. 'But you sold it for one Lira yesterday?' 'She bought it without seeing it. You saw it and now you're buying.' She doesn't have a clothes-bundle, let alone a hundred thousand.

That evening she tells Harun al-Rashid, he says, 'Didn't I tell you not to meddle in these things?' That first wife, she took the Euphrates in Syria and brought water to Mecca, to Mount Arafat. It's still there.

The Prayer-call

Bahlul the Wise tells the Caller, who sounds a Blessing to the Prophet, 'You're lying.' 'Why did you say that?' 'Because if he told the truth, the minaret would have collapsed.'

It's an insult to the Muhammadan Prayer-call, he has to prove the opposite.

They build a pulpit of iron. As soon as Bahlul calls: 'I bear witness that Muhammad is the Prophet of God,' the pulpit melts down. Someone says: 'Come down! If you finish the Prayer-call, it'll be the end of the world.'

Who's the giver?

Bahlul was hungry and thirsty. He asked a horseman for some water. The man not only didn't give Bahlul water, he also insulted him. But then he regretted doing so. He called Bahlul over and gave [water to] him. Bahlul took it.

The man said: 'If I were in your place, I wouldn't have accepted it. I insulted you.' Bahlul replied: 'Nothing's in your hands. Earlier, they told you not to give, so you didn't. This time, they told you to give, so you did.' This is very good.

Muhammad Birgivi of Bursa

Nine people came to Birgivi, they all had had a fight with their wives. Then the master's wife came in. She sees them there – 'Get out! This man can't solve his own problems. How's he going to solve yours?' She turns on him: 'If you were any good, you'd benefit *me*! What do they find in you?' She *bang*ed the door behind her.

'Do you know who that was? She ruined both you and me.'

'No, Master, we don't know. Ours do this kind of thing too, but not this bad.'

'That was my wife. Now go and get along well.'

I'm always asking you, 'How are you with your job, your spouse and your faith? If they're all okay, you're in Paradise.'

One day, six people went to visit him. One came and complained about his wife, so did the other, so did the other ... The six came together in Bursa within one hour. He listens to their accounts, nothing but complaints.

'Children,' he said, 'You're right, all of you. But I have one, too. I've listened to your accounts, but what can we do, every Muslim needs a spouse. Go and be reconciled to your lot. If they don't listen to you, if they disobey their husbands, if they rebel against you, they'll be infidels. But every Muslim needs one, it can't be helped.'

This word circulated until it reached the ear of the Sultan's wife. 'There's a hodja in Bursa,' they say, 'He's made infidels out of women!' Now this lady is very pious. She does her Five Daily Prayers faithfully. She said to the Sultan, 'I want this hodja. Either he clarifies this, or it's off with his head!'

She summoned him. They took him to Istanbul. He talked to the Sultan, the Sultan liked him. He's learned, virtuous ... 'Did you say anything like that?' asked the Sultan. 'I did,' he replied. He said: 'My wife heard about it. What shall we do? You're in deep trouble.'

'I'll do something,' he said, 'don't worry.' 'You must save yourself.' 'Don't worry.'

It occurs to the Sultan that there is a pasha[10] in the service of his wife. 'Is he married?' 'Yes, he is.' 'Let's talk to him,' he said. He sent word and he came to the Sultan. 'I'm sorry, but I have a troublesome task for you. In the evening – do you have money?' 'Yes, I do.'

'Make a bundle out of stockings, headscarves, lingerie, bedsheets and shoes. Wrap them up in a bundle and take it home. When you arrive in the evening, your wife will greet you, give her the bundle. If she asks what it is, tell her, "My dear, I'm sorry. One of our friends died, the Sultan wants me to take his wife in marriage. She has two children, in order to look after those kids. I brought her this by the command of the Sultan."'

The poor man, what can he do, he did exactly as he was told. When he went home in the evening, his wife greeted him, he gave her the bundle, they went in, she opened the bundle, 'What is this, husband? Did you buy this for me?' He didn't reply. 'I had one of these. Are you lovestruck? What have you done?'

'My dear,' he said, 'here's the situation. The Sultan has commanded me. One of our friends died. I want a marriage in order to take care of those children. What can I do?'

'*You!*' she said. 'The Sultan did this!' 'Yes,' he said.

She took the bundle and threw everything into the stove. She burned them all up. She began to shout: 'Get out! I recognize neither the Sultan, nor any such command of God!'

The man went to his brother's house and spent the night there. He came back in the morning. 'What did you do? It was a big hassle, wasn't it?' 'No, it wasn't.'

They call in Birgivi. The same account: 'What did you do?' 'I did this and I did that.' Birgivi says to the Sultan, 'Please, you did this for me, to save me, you've troubled this man, let him give the same account before your wife, the lady Sultan.'

The same account, they go together with the Sultan. The lady Sultan knows the pasha, he's in her service all the time. 'What did you do?' 'So and so forth.' 'Your wife?' she asks. 'Yes.' His wife, and don't forget this, to her Five Daily Prayers she adds five more, the Quran never falls from her hand. The wife of the Sultan knows that woman.

---

10. Highest official title for the Ottomans.

They send for her, she comes over. The Sultan and the pasha are both there.

'What have you done, daughter?' 'Majesty, how can this be?' she says. 'Sultan Mother, the Sultan commanded it, my husband is going to wed another woman by the order of God. I have three children. What kind of command is this? I said it. I will obey neither the Sultan's order, nor God's order.'

They called Birgivi. He bows, offers his greetings, comes and sits down respectfully. The Sultan Mother is angry anyway, she wants to hang him.

He recites a chapter from the Quran and adds a Saying. 'Your Majesty, a person – whether man or woman – may deny the Sultan's orders. But there's no denying God's commands. This is the meaning of Verse and Saying. If a person denies and repudiates God's commandments, what do they become?' The Sultan replied, 'They become infidels.' 'That's what I said, your Majesty,' he said.

He stands up respectfully and goes to the next room. The Sultan Mother says, 'What a clever one, what a learned man. I forgive him.'

Sirri Saqati

His foot was disabled (*saqat*). He had a shop. They inform him: 'The whole market burned down, only your shop is standing.' He was caught off guard, he said, 'Thank God.' There's nobody there, he comes back without opening it. Before he gets home, *bonk!* it hits him on the head. 'Your little shop of small wares is standing, the entire market has burned down. Shame on you!' He never went back again. Thirty years pass, a friend says, 'You look troubled.' 'Thirty years ago, a shop belonging to me didn't burn down, I gave thanks for that. I've been repenting for thirty years.' He's a Sufi, he knows the Divine Law, he knows the Real. If, from this, we can glean something beneficial to ourselves, to humanity, to God, then it'll be all right. Otherwise, we'll just take on a burden.

[It was also Sirri (or Sari) Saqati who said: 'Like the sun, the wise one shines on all the world. Like the earth, he bears the good and evil of all. Like water, he is the source of life for every heart. And like fire, he gives his warmth to all and sundry.'[11]]

---

11. www.www.sufizikr.org/?p=578, accessed 8/8/2011.

Junayd of Baghdad

Sirri Saqati is the maternal uncle of Junayd. He and Saqati come to Baghdad. They find everywhere full to the brim with exoteric knowledge. They wanted to open a center of wisdom. 'What shall we do for a living?' he said. 'Our Hidden Knowledge is no use here.' A while later he asked again: 'What do you want, nephew?' Junayd said, 'The science of Sufism is missing here. I want permission to open a school of Sufism. Do I have your permission, Uncle?' 'Right,' he said, 'okay.' They rented a house and put up a sign: 'The School of Sufism.' Two rooms, one is the classroom. A few students came from universities, here and there. The place was established in a year. Time passed, there were students who had been there for five or ten years, they're learning.

One day he comes in again, the students are discussing something. The subject is always Sufism. He's giving lessons. 'Good morning,' he says, and sits down.

They were discussing the Divine Law (*shari'a*) and Sufism. A student asks about Sufism: 'Isn't it dangerous?' he says.

'It's dangerous, but we love it. Let me tell you something else,' he says. He gives the analogy of a ship. He says, 'A ship at sea, complete with its crew, gets caught in a storm and capsizes. What are you going to do? You're going to catch hold of a piece of driftwood and not let go until you land ashore. You're going to land without drowning. You're not going to abandon the Divine Law.' Yes! That's Junayd of Baghdad, the teacher of the school of Sufism. 'I learned Sufism and I'm teaching you too, but our basis is the Divine Law. Don't part with it. There's no Sufism without the Divine Law. Sufism is a sea, the Divine Law is the piece of driftwood that is going to bear you safely ashore when the storm breaks.'

This is Junayd's word. You have to be careful. Sufism is very sweet. But it's dangerous!

Shaykh Shibli

[Abu Bakr Shibli is the student and successor of Junayd.] Shaykh Shibli once threw his cloak on the [Tigris River], and a whole army passed over it without getting wet.

Shortcut to the Pilgrimage

Someone had prepared his money, he was going to embark on the Pilgrimage (*Hajj*). Shaykh Shibli is there, a man of knowledge, a Sufi. 'Master, I'm going.' 'The distance is far, son. If I told you something, could you do it? Circumambulate me seven times, just as you would do with the Ka'ba.' He said, 'Master, I couldn't do that.'

How to carry water in a sieve

Shaykh Shibli was sitting one summer day. The flies have invaded, everyone's sweating from the heat, they're all silent. They're thirsty. He said, 'Dervish, my son, we're thirsty. My lips are dry. Take that sieve and fill it with tap water, let's drink water.' These are all true, sir.

They said, 'Did the Master say something wrong?' How can you bring water with a sieve? 'Master, how can water stay in a sieve? Why are you doing this?' 'Oh, really? I hadn't thought of that.'

A bit later he said, 'Mahmud, my son, you bring it.' '*At once*, sir!' He picks up the sieve and goes to the tap. He fills it with water. He brings it over, he fills and distributes without spilling a drop.

'Bravo,' he says. 'You've fulfilled an order of God.' That's the way to do it! He told the others, 'Why don't you listen to orders?'

Praying for rain

It's June, water is cut off, there's no rain in Baghdad. They come to Shibli, 'Pray that we may have some rain.' 'Couldn't you find anyone else to go to in Baghdad? I'll look into it tomorrow.' There's a grocer across the street. 'Give me four pounds of butter. I have no money, I'll pay you later. Put it in a tray.'

'I'm selling *yagh. Yagh!*' (Double meaning: 'Butter'/'Let it rain.') He measures and gives to whoever wants it. He works until nightfall.

The rains begin before he gets home. They last for weeks. The houses are flooded. Finally, the one who asked for rain comes: 'Master, you know best.' He goes to the same grocer, this time he buys walnuts. He goes to a schoolyard, '*Yaghma! Yaghma!*' (Double meaning: 'Free for all'/'Don't rain.')

Repentance

Shaykh Shibli was ill. A neighbor brought him some soup and he got well. He said, 'The neighbor's soup made me well.' But then he repented for thirty years for having said that.

Ashraf Rumi

Rumi, Son of Ashraf (*Eşrefoğlu*) first fasted for forty days in Kayseri with Sayyid Burhanuddin. Just an olive or a drop of water in the evenings. Sayyid Burhanuddin transfers him to Hajji Bayram Wali. He came to Hajji Bayram Wali in Ankara, he fasted another forty days.

When he emerges from seclusion, Hajji Bayram has a beloved daughter, he marries her to him, hosts him for a week, then refers him to Hussein of Hama, one of the descendants of the Grand Saint in Baghdad. He sends them off with an ass and a blanket.

On the day of their arrival, Hussein Hamawi posts five or six men on the road, saying: 'He's a stranger, don't let him get lost.' They see two people. Another forty days of asceticism there. He arrives at such a state that he passes away from himself. No food, no drink. On the thirtieth or thirty-fifth day, the one delivering food to him says, 'He's dead.' The gossip starts: 'Instead of becoming a Man, the one who came from Anatolia died.' [Also implying in a way that Master Hamawi is not quite on top of things.]

When the forty days are done, he asks, 'What happened?' 'He's dead, nobody owns up to him.' He goes and stands by his foot. 'Ashraf, my son, you're still needed here. Get up.' He prods his foot with his own, he gets up. He's a guest for a week.

One day the Master says, 'Let's go somewhere and have tea.' They say, 'There's no water there.' 'Why, God will provide!' They go and talk. Noontime comes, the Noon Prayer, 'Go and find some water.' They smile. They spread out, there's no water in those quarters. 'Didn't you find any?' 'We couldn't.' 'Ashraf, you go and take a look.' He gets up and walks off. After he's gone forty or fifty steps, the Master calls out from behind: 'Ashraf, where are you going? Stomp with your foot or poke with your rod!' Water sprouts. 'Master, I found the water.'

'You see,' he tells them. 'I've prevented you from many things, but I couldn't prevent you from gossip. We give their right to those who earn their rightful due. You can leave, son,' he says. That's how he became Ashraf Rumi.

Hajji Bayram Wali

The district of ill repute

Hajji Bayram is wide, expansive. 'Father Rose' (*Gul Baba*) is narrow. Hajji Bayram Wali used to do his Friday Prayers at a mosque in Ankara, he used to lecture there. They said, 'Let's build a mosque for you.' One day they come out again, fifteen to twenty people are with him. He says, 'Come.' They came to the red light district. 'Master, what on earth are you doing?' 'I know. With the permission of God, let's build a mosque here.' They came to cover a filth.

The videophone of the saints

Listen to this and don't make a mistake later on. Hajji Bayram Wali writes a letter to a friend, another saint, in Damascus. A few of his students are jealous of each other. In the morning he asks for a cup of coffee, one of the most jealous comes. 'Take this letter to Damascus.' 'Yes, sir.' He goes, he takes a look at the envelope along the way. There's no address on it.

'What happened?' 'I turned back from nearby, there's no address on the envelope.' 'Oh, I must have forgotten. Just lay it over there.' Another, another. The best one comes. The same [envelope]. He's brave, he continues on his way. The recipient in Damascus is waiting for him to arrive, he's playing with children. The traveler says to himself, 'Look at that man, he's playing with kids.' The saint goes to him. He hosts him for a week. He gives him three Prayer-mats and some money. He runs out of money on his way back, he sells one of the Prayer-mats and then another. Only one Prayer-mat remains. He brings it and gives it to Hajji Bayram Wali.

'Very good, but there were supposed to be three Prayer-mats.' 'There's one, Master.' 'In that case, let's ask,' he says. He opens the cupboard beside him and speaks into it: 'Hassan, were they three or one?' 'Master, there were three of them, maybe somebody needed them.'

The disciple is embarrassed. He gets up and kisses his hand. 'Master, I'm confused about something. If you're so close, why did you send me?'

'Son, I sent three people before you. You were the best. They're no good and neither are you. We talk every day, all that is for training *you*. So, for this reason, don't be jealous of one another. Be for *God*, live for God. We're talking and working *for you*.'

Niyazi Misri

Niyazi Misri ['of Egypt'] suffered more than them all. Finally, that great man of knowledge, that Sufi, that philosopher [not to mention poet], gave up his soul in a jail on Limni Island. He was thrown in jail twice and died on the third. His tomb is on the island of Limni. He said, 'I am the one who is the original mystery.' He couldn't save himself from the People of the External (exoteric Divine Law). What mysteries these are, sir. That is, the only remedy is to be a servant of God, to work for it.

Niyazi said, 'Do not think, pious man, that Fasting, Prayer, Pilgrimage and Alms-tax will suffice to finish everything.' Whereupon all the scholars say, 'Do you see that unbeliever? He's denied Four Pillars of Islam. All that's left is the Word of Witnessing.' That's when he was banished to the island.

His master, Ummi Sinan, is from Aspozi, which is probably Çirmik [Yeşilyurt, a neighborhood of Malatya]. Ummi Sinan, his eye is unlettered (*ummi*) but he's a sea (*umman*) himself.

Another of Niyazi's couplets is:

> *I used to look right and left in order to see the Friend's face*
> *I used to search for it outside, while He was life within my life.*

Encounter with the saint

Niyazi Misri seeks out Hajji Bayram. When he sees him he thinks, 'This beggar is Hajji Bayram?' He goes off to Egypt. There, he sees in a dream that he has a chain on his neck, and the other end of the chain is in the hand of Hajji Bayram. He comes and surrenders.

Hajji Bayram Wali is in a village of Ankara, he's gathered his disciples, they're eating. Niyazi arrives, he leans against a tree and waits. Hajji Bayram Wali doesn't call him over. When lunch is over he says, 'Throw these crumbs to the dogs.' Niyazi Misri eats them. Hajji Bayram Wali says, 'Now you're ready, come.'

Niyazi's enlightenment

Niyazi came [to Malatya], the people gathered in the mosque, they're going to hear his sermon. He's young, about thirty-five or forty, he came and climbed up to the pulpit. 'By God,' he begins, he's going to pronounce Blessings on the Prophet, there's nothing. Right away he opened [the Holy Book], a Verse, a Tradition, nothing! [His mind's a complete blank.] He's sweating, the congregation is all there. As he came with all that pomp and climbed to the pulpit, Ummi Sinan pulled out a thread from the rug and rubbed it between his fingers, then he placed it in the rug beneath his leg. Niyazi searches his mind, nothing!

He tells the congregation: 'I must be tired, I must be catching a cold, I'm sorry,' and steps down. He goes straight to the Prayer-Caller. 'For God's sake, who do you have here?' 'We're all here.' 'No, no, I mean is there any particular someone here with an open Eye [of the Heart]?' 'There's one sitting there,' he says.

Either at that moment or after the Prayer, he approached him. 'Master? ...' 'No, son, it's nothing.' Ummi Sinan pulls out that thread, he puts it down, 'We gathered you here!' he says. They go home together, that's where Niyazi got his due. But he searched a lot, you know?

Hajji Bektash Wali

Hajji Bektash Wali was the disciple of Hodja Ahmed Yasawi, he didn't abandon the Five Daily Prayers for a single day. He was from the side of Sufism. The Divine Law, Sufism. He built that place [his famous convent at Nevşehir, Turkey] for Prayer.

Two or three people were looking for a master. They went to Rumi, to Tapduk Emre, they brought millet to them. They didn't eat it. Finally they come to Hajji Bektash, he says, 'Cook it and let the dervishes eat.' They don't stay with him, either. They go back to Rumi and Tapduk. They ask, 'You didn't eat, he did. Why?' 'He's a sea, it comes in one side and goes out the other.'

There are many tales about him. When spiritual tasks were being assigned in his later days, he saw that Ahi Evren, Tapduk Emre, Rumi, Rumi's father [Bahauddin Walad], Sayyid Burhanuddin, had all attracted the iron nails [the best students]. What remained was pieces of wood and leather.

One day, during the Dawn Prayer, he says, 'My God, You're All-powerful. You've taken all those whom You love. Grant the drunkard, the thief, the pickpocket to me. Leave these to me, grant them to me.'

There he reveals his secret. He ups and goes to Nevşehir, he tours the city. In the largest coffee-house, he sees people playing backgammon and other games. They're gambling. 'Peace upon you, dervishes,' he says. 'Upon you peace,' they reply. They look, he's a sage. One says, 'Bring grandpa some tea, it's on us.' 'I'm not well, I can't drink it.' 'What is it, this illness of yours?' With that illness, he sets them on fire. 'The medicine of my ailment is God, the one who heals it is the Prophet of God,' and so forth. He's not ill. He doesn't drink their tea. The gambling goes on. 'Thank you. May God help you prosper. May God give you disgust for this.' 'Grandpa, are you going to teach us how to be Muslims?' 'Yes, child, I'm going to teach you ethics.'

'Why, Grandpa, where did you come from? Where are you?' 'I'm poor, I'm from the village of Hoyuk in Kirşehir.'[12]

From there he goes to a tavern. 'Give grandpa a goblet from us!' He pours it under the table, he leaves the empty glass in front of him. They say, 'Grandpa drank, too!' The same thing, 'Kirşehir.'

He goes and sleeps in an inn, the second day he's back. Again he does something.

'Grandpa, maybe we'll need you some day, maybe for a disease or something. Can you give us your address?' 'Sure,' he says, and gives his address.

From there he goes to Kayseri. The same. Wherever there is a tavern, a coffee-house, he goes there. The good ones go to the mosque anyway. He goes here, he goes there, he tours Eskişehir and leaves his address everywhere.

Then he retires to his village. Someone gets sick, 'There was such a grandpa. Here's his address, let's take you there.' Another, his livelihood is a mess, no salary, no money. 'There was this grandpa.' They come together. He attracts them from that distance. Because he came down to their level. Those pieces of leather and wooden pegs. The iron nails are gone, they've all been taken. They all become dervishes. He says, 'My God, thanks be to You. You have bestowed them upon me.'

There, a friend of God becomes a balm for everyone's troubles. That's the way one should work, child.

---

12. This village is now the county of Hajjibektash, under the jurisdiction of Nevşehir.

Mansur al-Hallaj

Why was Hallaj punished?

Mansur al-Hallaj did something that violates the Divine Law. But how did Hallaj acquire that burden? Some saints overflow, then they receive a slap from the Prophet.

Hallaj does the Wakeup Prayer [before the Dawn Prayer], he tells his beads [recites the Names of God]. He thinks of the Ascension.

'During the Ascension, the Prophet of God said, "My Community." He asked for the pardoning of his followers, not a general pardon.' He's doing Invocation, he's wide awake. He says of Muhammad, 'I'm sorry, but it looks as if you're in error here. If I had been at the Ascension, I would have asked for the whole universe.' That's where he went astray.

He continued with his Invocation. A little sleep overcomes him. The spirituality of the Prophet manifests: 'Mansur, my son, what have you done? I was given that much, I did that much. What you say contradicts this verse of this chapter in the Quran.'[13]

Hallaj comes to himself. 'I'm in error, how shall I mend this?' 'You have to do something that contradicts Divine Law. Pay for it with your head.'

Thereupon Hallaj goes to his friends and begins to say, 'I am God, I am the Truth.' 'Oh no, don't say that, you're our teacher.' Everywhere he goes, 'I am the Truth.' The mufti hears of it. He calls Hallaj over and asks him. He doesn't tell the mufti what really happened. That is, he took it upon himself.

Ibn 'Arabi says, 'Ever since he went, we [the saints] have been pleading with the Prophet of God to forgive him.'

The Naming [see Appendix] is three words: God, Compassionate, Merciful. All prophets came with the attribute of Mercy and invited to Mercy. Here, Hallaj remains with the attribute of Compassion. Because of this, don't knowingly exceed the Prophet by even a hairbreadth. But unwittingly – God will forgive.

A shepherd steals a sheep. The judge, the prosecutor will chalk it down to his ignorance and will try to release him with a light sentence. But if a lawyer, a judge were to do the same thing, they would give him the heaviest sentence, because he's supposed to know better. That's how Hallaj was regarded. May we be counted as a shepherd.

---

13. If God had wished, He would have created all human beings as Muslims, belonging to the Prophet's Community (11:118). Both Compassion and Mercy would then have been coextensive.

One has to be very careful. Although they're servants, a lot of saints fancy they're the Creator. That won't do. The Prophet of God is at the greatest station, during the Ascension God says: 'I will give you whatever you want.' He said: 'I'm Your servant, I wish for Your servanthood.' Don't step beyond servanthood, beyond the Community.

Everyone, every nation, every family does to itself (reaps what it sows).

The rose or the stone?

[During Hallaj's punishment for claiming to be the Truth:] They tied him up somewhere, everyone has to throw a stone, to spit on him. Everyone has to throw something. They're punished if they don't. They come and stone him, they go and spit.

He has a friend, he comes too. He came and looked. He had a rose in his hand, it's the season for roses. He threw the rose.

Hallaj says, 'Friend, this is my fate. I'm not complaining. These stones they throw at me don't hurt me, but this rose from your hand did. Because you *know*. They throw without knowing.' The other says, 'What can I do? It's obligatory.'

So it's very difficult to deal with friends. If they turn out to be rotten ...

Ahmed Ibn Hanbal

Ahmed Ibn Hanbal is the founder of an order, he didn't eat anything for ten years. He lived with asceticism and pious worship. But when someone left his side, they would die. Those who looked at his face would die. This isn't the Evil Eye, it's a manifestation of God. He struck like lightning. They told him about this, he said 'Thank you' and covered his face.

Ahmed Ibn Hanbal was going to a village one day. He was wearing a very rich robe [of the kind worn on auspicious occasions]. The Noon Prayer, he had a disciple with him. The water was far away, so they did a Substitute Ablution.[14] 'Pray for me,' he said, 'let me do two more

---

14. When water is not available, one states one's intent to take a Substitute Ablution (*tayammum*), then pats the ground or a clean surface and wipes one's face, pats again and wipes both arms down from the elbows. Also substitutes for Bodily Ablution (*ghusl*) until water is found.

cycles of Prayer.' He departed on the last prostration. His disciple waited for two hours. He touched him, he toppled over sideways. He called someone immediately.

He's buried in a graveyard in Egypt now. That desert has now become a town. They went there, they built houses and gardens.

Hassan of Basra

His mother used to clean the house of the Prophet. A wife of the Prophet suckled him when he was a baby. Once, when a barren [and hence milkless] woman tried to suckle him, her breasts were filled with milk. The child was sated. So Hassan of Basra is a saint.

Later he went to Basra and stayed there for a long time. Then they escaped to Malatya from the reach of Mu'awiya. There he made a great statement: 'There's the possibility I'll return to Basra some day.' He died in Malatya, but the Euphrates river dragged his earth and bones there.

If one were to shed a tear or two for God, heaven would be his, earth would be his, everything would belong to him.

Hassan of Basra got up one day at 2 or 3 a.m. He did his Wakeup Prayer, made up for his missing Prayers. The tears started streaming from his eyes. Someone's going to the Dawn Prayer, a couple of drops fell on his head. He continues on his way. After Prayer, the sun is on the verge of rising, he knocks on the door.

'Who lives here?' 'Hassan of Basra.' 'May I see him?' In that instant the sun rises.

'Didn't you go to Prayer?' 'I'm ill, I couldn't go.' 'While I was going to Prayer, a couple of drops fell on my head. Is this water from an Ablution, or is it urine? I've come to ask what it is.' 'Oh, my son, that's the dirty water from my eyes. I don't go to the toilet.' The questioner later said: 'That was the happiest day of my life. I must have been a lucky servant that those two drops touched me.' Let's be like that, too, God willing.

Rabia Adawiya

Lady Rabia remained in Basra for a long time. She joined Hassan of Basra's circle. One day Hassan Basri is going somewhere. He looks, Lady Rabia is speaking with animals. As Hassan of Basra approaches, they run away. He asks, 'How did this happen?'

Lady Rabia asks, 'Do you eat meat?' 'Yes.' Lady Rabia: 'I haven't put it in my mouth for forty years.'

Then they're going to do the Noon Prayer. Lady Rabia spreads her Prayer-mat on the water and does her Prayer there. Hassan of Basra does it suspended in the air. After Prayer, Lady Rabia says, 'Sir, birds can remain aloft, too. And fish can stay on the surface of the water. So don't be vain about such things.'

Where are they produced?

Appreciate the worth of women.

A group of scholars want to test Lady Rabia. They come to ask her questions. She takes them inside, she serves them coffee. They drink and begin to ask. They ask her ten questions, she says 'Okay' to all of them.

Finally, she says, 'Gentlemen, are you finished?' 'Yes,' they say. 'We're waiting for your answer.' She says, 'With your permission, I'm your child, your sister. You value men so much and look down on women to this extent – tell me, where is the factory of both?'

They're all speechless. 'Right. Rabia, you finished it with one stroke. Goodbye.' One question.

Hatim al-Ta'i

Hatim al-Ta'i was hosted by a young man. He slaughtered a couple of sheep, he removed their kidneys, he offered them to Hatim as the choicest morsels from the sheep. Hatim gives him his address, he says, 'Come and find me if you need anything.'

Two to three years later, the youth has a fight with someone, he goes to the city. Hatim al-Ta'i makes him a gift of a thousand-sheep herd. He told those around him, 'That man is far superior to you and me. He had only two sheep, whereas I have ten herds.'

Eight points in thirty years

(*'The Secret That is Love'*¹⁵ *was one of the Master's favorite reading pieces. It is where the Eight Gates of Paradise are enumerated. On one occasion, the Master drew a parallel between these Eight Gates and the eight points that Hatim al-Ta'i said he had learned from his teacher in thirty years. Both of these are presented below.*)

[The Eight Doors of Heaven are: (1) Compassion, kindness and affection; (2) Righteousness; (3) Loyalty; (4) Generosity; (5) Patience; (6) Discretion; (7) Knowing one's poverty and weakness; (8) Giving thanks to God.]

Hatim tells his teacher, 'I learned eight points from you in thirty years.' 'What a pity,' he replies. 'What are they?' He tells him. His teacher exclaims, 'I swear to God that everything I have taught is within these Eight Doors.' If you fall into the sea, grab hold of one of these eight as a lifesaver, a piece of driftwood. If you do all eight of them, you're in heaven already.

[The eight points of Hatim were: (1) Loving things that will survive one's death (good works, worship). Making virtues one's friends. (2) Combating one's self. Controlling the self until it obeys God. (3) Opening one's heart to the love of God. Dedicating one's most prized possessions to God. (4) Piety and fear of God, which are the most valuable things in God's sight. To rise in intelligence and morality. (5) Freedom from jealousy. (6) To know that the devil, rather than other human beings, is one's true enemy. To become friends with everyone. (7) Not to worry about sustenance. To stay clear of what is Unclean/Illicit. (8) Trust in God, and God alone.¹⁶]

---

15. Currently available at http://hbayman.angelfire.com/en/fourbooks.htm.
16. From *The Revival of the Religious Sciences* and *Listen, Child (Ayyuhal Walad)*, both by Ghazali.

Muhammad Abdullah al-Tunisi

(The story related below by the Master took place between Abu Abdullah (or Abu Abdus Salam) al-Tunisi and the ruler of Tlemcen (Tilimsan), Prince Yahya b. Yughan al-Sanhaji (d. AH 537). Ibn 'Arabi tells the story in his Meccan Revelations (Futuhat).[17])

This happened in Tunisia. I read it in a book. One of the dervishes there, his name was Muhammad or Mehmet, he wants to enter asceticism but his family is holding him back, he climbed the mountain and found himself a cave. He took his pitcher, kissed his wife and children on their eyes. 'Goodbye,' he said, 'I'll come to you from time to time. Give me your permission, I've fulfilled my obligations to you.'

He's busy with worship there for four or five years. On Fridays he takes his pitcher – an empty water pitcher – comes into town, he does his Prayer at the town's mosque, fills his pitcher and goes back.

One day he comes again, there's a big ceremony. After the service and the prayer are over, Father Mehmet fills his pitcher and sets off.

The Sultan and his entourage have also done their Prayer there, they're going back to the palace on the same road, as they advance he sees someone with a green mantle and green turban walking ahead of them.

He asked the grand vizier: 'Who's that?' 'This is his story,' he said. 'I have a question, I'm going to ask him.'

The grand vizier knew him. He said, 'He's like a madman of God.' He's concerned that the Sultan might incur an illness, punishment or something from Father Mehmet. 'He's a madman of God, he doesn't know how to talk.'

He insisted three times, the Sultan said, 'I'm going to ask.' 'Okay, ask,' he said. 'Since you won't listen to me, ask.'

They caught up with him, he moved to the side of the road, 'Peace upon you.' 'Upon you peace,' he said.

'I have a consultation, I need to consult you.' 'I don't have any knowledge,' Father Mehmet replied. 'I have to answer the Sultan of Tunisia of our time, I'm not in that state. It'd be better if you didn't ask.' 'No, I'm going to ask.' Three times, again he insists.

'Go ahead,' he said.

---

17. Claude Addas, *Quest for the Red Sulphur*, Peter Kingsley (Tr.), Cambridge: Islamic Texts Society, 1993, pp. 22–3. Story in Ibn 'Arabi, *Futuhat*, II, p. 18 (p. 23, n. 55).

He said, 'Do you see me?' 'Yes, I see you,' he said. The crown on his head is gold, his clothing is gold-laced. 'I do the Friday Prayer this way, in this costume. Will my Prayer be accepted or not?'

'I wouldn't know,' he said. 'No.' He's *insisting*. 'Tell me what comes to your mind.'

He said, 'Your Majesty, when I was coming down from the mountain this morning, an animal carcass was rotting, either a horse or a donkey. They dragged it to the edge of the city. As I came down, I saw dogs had gathered around and were devouring it. As I approached, a large shepherd dog scared them all away. It ate and ate, it filled its stomach. After separating from it' – That's the way dogs are, they lift one leg and pee that way. – 'it raised one leg and urinated on it. And I said to myself, *'Tsk*, my goodness, everything it ate is unclean, it's unclean itself, now it puts itself there with its urine.' I saw something like that, my mind's busy with that. I'm sorry, I still can't give you a ruling. I'm preoccupied with that.'

As they're standing, Father Mehmet continues on his way. The Sultan turns to the vizier, the court is all there, 'Why, this man made a dog out of me!' 'No, your Majesty, he's a madman of God, he doesn't know,' and so on. 'No, I'm going to kill this man. He put me to shame. I wish I hadn't asked.' 'Well, I told you. I said he was a madman.'

He rears his horse, catches up from behind, draws the sword, he's going to swing one at his neck. His arm freezes in mid-air. The horse, too, where it is, they stand there rooted to the spot.

The vizier catches up. No speech, nothing, he's like a statue. The vizier rears his horse, trots up: 'Father Mehmet, excuse these matters. He's in a bad way, if he goes we can't assign another sultan in his place. Have pity.' He turns around and looks, he's standing like a statue. 'May God forgive you,' he says, and goes on his way. The Sultan revives.

He dismounts the horse. He gives the sword and the crown on his head to the grand vizier, 'Find yourselves a sultan,' he says, 'I'm going to follow that man.' A marvel has come to the rescue!

He goes and catches up, 'Peace upon you,' 'Upon you peace, Highness, welcome,' he says. That's all.

They go and enter the cave. One, two, the third day the Sultan gets hungry. The dervish says, 'I trained my self this way, you can't stand such business, go back to your life.' 'No, I won't let go of you.' 'You can't stand it.' 'I'll stand it until I die,' he said.

'In that case, get up, take this rope of mine, I used to do it but now I'm accustomed to it, take the rope and gather some twigs and firewood. Go and sell them at the bazaar. Buy a loaf of bread, distribute the remaining money to the poor and come back.'

'Right away!' he says. The Sultan's costume is still on his back – everything, he only gave the crown and the sword. He gathers firewood and twigs, it's early in the morning, he's been hungry for three days. Straight to the wood bazaar. People see the Sultan, they stand to attention at once. A close relative of the Sultan comes by, he asks, 'What are you doing?' 'I'm selling this wood, five cents.' The man sizes up the situation, gives him ten cents, and after the Sultan's left, gives the wood to someone there.

He goes and buys a loaf of bread. He distributes the remaining money. Every day it's like that, every day.

As in the case of Ibrahim Adham, his wife, the vizier, his mother, come and plead with him.

On Fridays he comes down with Father Mehmet, they do their Prayers and leave. Some blame Father Mehmet, some say 'He's lost his mind.'

He continues for a year and then dies, the Sultan gives up his soul in the cave. Father Mehmet comes for the Friday Prayer next morning, he says, 'Your Sultan is dead, bring a pickaxe and a shovel so we can bury him there.'

They go and bury him beside the cave. He tells those present, 'God willing, God forgave him. He'll forgive you and me, too. If I don't come down for the Friday Prayer some day, know that I've gone, too. Only, bury me a yard away from his feet. Below the Sultan.' Again the grand vizier asks: 'How come?'

'He was much greater than I. He left those laces and the life of a sultan, I'm just an ordinary man. I knew the Real in five or ten years with difficulty, he found Him in an instant. That's why he has the right.'

Time passes, one Friday Father Mehmet doesn't come, they go and find him resting on his back, he's asleep.

They fulfill his will.

About fifteen years ago [*circa* 1972, someone] came here and said, 'We're going to Tunisia as a group. Do you have anything to say?' 'I've read this,' I said, 'There is such a story. See if you can find such a Father Mehmet. It's a matter of four or five hundred years.'

He went. 'The Dawn Prayer-call was sounded, I got in the hotel,' he says, 'I went down to the mosque and did the Dawn Prayer, I came out and asked the hodja and the elders. Nobody knew.

'Coming back, I came across someone again, I asked him, 'Is there such a man called Father Mehmet?' He said, 'Yes, son. Behind that hill.' I didn't return to the hotel, I went straight on. I found the cave, I saw the two graves. I did two cycles of Forenoon Prayer there, prayed and came back.'

He brought back that much. So it was true. Yes! He came and said, 'Right, I've found it.'

Now why did I tell this? Let them eat the rot! There's no end to it, don't worry. Let them eat the rot.

Ibrahim Adham[18]

[The case of Ibrahim Adham, the Sultan of Balkh, resembles that of the Buddha. Like Sakyamuni, he abandoned his crown and his throne to live the simple life of a dervish. The story goes that a servant girl lay down on his silk bed for a few minutes and was punished for this misdemeanor. All the while she was being disciplined, she went on laughing. Ibrahim Adham was astounded. 'How come you're laughing under these conditions?' he asked. She said, 'I lay on that soft, comfortable bed of yours for only a few minutes, and look at the punishment I'm getting. What kind of punishment are you, who have slept in that bed all your life, going to receive when you die?' These words served as a stimulus that woke Adham up. Another story is that he heard a noise on the roof of his palace at night, and called out: 'What's all this racket?' A voice said: 'I'm looking for my camel.' 'What's a camel supposed to be doing on top of my roof?' The voice retorted: 'And what are you supposed to be doing under it?' He sent the guards up to the roof, there was no one there. He took this as a sign to enter a new way of life.]

He's the one who suffered the greatest hardships: Ibrahim Adham. He suffered much. When he departs from the palace and the government, he lives in the forest for several months. It's close by. They search for him, they can't find him, a shepherd comes by and says, 'I've found the Sultan, Ibrahim Adham.' 'Where?' 'In such-and-such a place.' His mother, his wife, the council, all go to the forest and find him in that place. He's in tatters, he's surviving on plants, hungry and thirsty. His

---

18. Short for Ibrahim ibn Adham.

mother presses him to her bosom. His wife kisses his hand. The council likewise. They shed tears for him when they see the sorry state he's in.

They talk to him. 'Come on, don't do this, God is present everywhere. Don't leave us, come and be a sultan again and still do your worship.' They can't find a way. 'Bear with me,' he says. He kisses his mother's hand. He consoles his wife, the council, the government. They weep, they say: 'He's lost his mind.'

The sea was close by, they take him down to the seashore. They give him food and drink, 'Eat.' 'I won't,' he says. He's got used to it! He's used to eating plants and grass. His own prime minister, the vizier of that time, says to his mother and wife:

'As an act of God, he's lost his mind. Let's leave him be. Let's pray. There's no other way. Let's leave him be and go.'

This word touches Ibrahim Adham. It saddens him.

'My vizier,' he says, 'am I the one who's lost, or are you?'

'Sir,' he says. 'we all have need of you. You won't come, you're reconciled to this state you're in, you're living in hunger off weeds, you've lost your mind.' He insists.

Ibrahim Adham says to his mother: 'Mother dear, do you have a needle on you?' 'Yes, son,' she says, she removes a needle from her lapel and gives it to him.

He throws the needle into the sea. He says, 'If you bring this needle back to me, I'll come with you. I'll be your sultan and look after you.' Some of them weep, others make fun of him. The vast sea. The needle can be found, but in that age, who's going to go, who's going to find it? Perhaps today they could, they'd turn it upside down and find it, today's technology!

His mother sheds tears. 'Don't, son. Don't.' 'Mother,' he says, 'is this possible?' 'It's not possible. Who's going to find it?'

'If' – he says to his mother, to the prime minister, to the council – 'if I bring back this needle and pin it back on your lapel, will you leave me alone?'

His mother is in tears – she's a mother. The prime minister says, 'All right, we accept.'

He comes to the seaside. He addresses the sea. He says: 'With the permission of God, by the power of God, give me back the needle I threw in you.'

A mackerel, a fish, swims *flit flit flit flit* towards him, he takes it in his hand, he opens its mouth, he takes out the needle.

He takes the needle and gives it to his mother. 'Now go,' he says, 'mind your own business, leave me be.' And he goes back to the forest.

Patience and thanksgiving

One day, in Baghdad, he came across a friend. 'Why, aren't you Ibrahim?' Skin and bones are all that's left of him. The friend tells his wife, he brings bread and what food there is. Whenever the stomach is hungry, the love of God increases. Not [by other forms of] asceticism, but hunger.

The householder goes and comes back with some soup, Ibrahim should finish it. At each bite his hand trembles, the soup spills, on the third attempt the spoon falls from his hand as well. 'Don't you see? Enough. I'm not allowed to eat.' The householder thought, 'There must be a reason for this.' His wife said, 'The neighbor brought it. It's food, what can I do?' It turned out that the food was bought with dishonest (Forbidden) money.

The point is to build up this cave [and not to live in a mountain cave]. The cave of the body, the cave of the spirit. When you cut off the Forbidden, it's filled with light.

Produce the spiritual oil. When you strike this oil, other oils will follow. Let's open this oil well.

Hundreds of years later, the Grand Saint Abdul Qadir Gilani said: 'If Ibrahim Adham had lived in our time, we would have trained him in his crown and his throne.' What does this mean? When you cut off the Forbidden, he can be enlightened in that silk bed. Otherwise, the crown and throne are of no consequence.

Adham said, 'If I find, I give thanks. What can I do if I can't? I'm patient.' The householder laughed. 'Ibrahim,' he said, 'when you were Sultan, the soldiers used to throw away food. The dogs would eat it. They would wait if no food was poured. Your situation is like theirs.'

'So what do you do?'

'If we find it, we give food to the hungry. If we don't find it, We give thanks to God.'[19]

---

19. This Sufic story is usually told of Shaykh Shibli and Shaykh Shabistari. Shabistari: 'What do you do?' Shibli: 'If we find we give thanks, if we don't we're patient.' Shabistari scoffs: 'The dogs of Baghdad do that much, too.' 'So what do *you* do?' 'When we find, we distribute. If we don't find it, we give thanks.'

Ismail Hakki of Bursa

A similar story [to the one concerning Nasruddin Hodja and the thief[20]] concerns the famous Ismail Hakki of Bursa. He's a great man. He was studying in his room, he was writing something. His wife opened the street door and called out, 'Husband, I'm going over to the neighbor. I'm going to talk to her for five minutes. I'm leaving the door unlocked, take care so that a thief doesn't enter.' 'Okay, dear,' he says, and she leaves.

Now just at that moment, the neighborhood thief was passing by. The lady left, the thief came and found the door unlocked, he opened it, went in and looked into one or two rooms. The door is open, Ismail Hakki is busy reading. He went into the kitchen, he took a sack and filled it with pots and pans. He hoisted it on his back and left. Ismail Hakki knows, he sees! He doesn't say, 'Don't do it.'

He went away.

Now the man's heard of Ismail Hakki, but he doesn't know him. His wife returns, she's going to cook some soup for the evening, there's nothing in the kitchen. 'Husband, we've been robbed!' 'I don't know about it, dear,' he said. 'Didn't I tell you?' She begins to quarrel. 'My dear, don't worry. If he doesn't come back, I'll buy you everything brand new, don't worry. Let me just finish this subject.' The lady is right. Fight and pandemonium!

As for the thief, he took it to the bazaar. He opens it, he's just about to sell, he sees Ismail Hakki coming from that side.

Right away, he loaded it back in and moved to another location. He opens it up there, he looks, there he is, he's coming again. Wherever he goes, he sees Ismail behind him.

'This isn't going to work,' he says. He loads it on his back without having sold anything, he heads back to the house. The wife is fighting! Quarrel, fight, all that while. He opens the street door, he throws it down with a *clanng!* '*Take* your pots!' says the man.

The wife runs over, she informs Ismail Hakki, he says, 'Son, come on in, come on!' He says, 'Sir, I'm too ashamed. How shall I come in?' 'Never mind, come on in.' He takes him to his room.

'Calm down, son,' he says. 'These things happen. God knows, I wasn't going to bother you, but my wife, as you see, she raised hell. She's right, you know. I was caught between you two. What can we do?

---

20. See The saints/Nasruddin Hodja/Encounter with the thief.

I'm sorry.' He gets up and prepares coffee for the thief with his own hands. 'You're tired,' he says.

He brings it in, they drink coffee together. He takes out one gold piece in that day's currency. One gold piece is enough to buy half of Bursa. The thief says, 'What shall I do with this? It's too much.' He replies, 'You can do some trade, your business will prosper.'

He gets up and kisses his hand, he promises him. 'You've saved me and my family,' he says. That man becomes the wealthiest in Bursa. He goes and does business with that money. He becomes a landed property owner.

The wife returns, he asks, 'Is anything missing, dear?' 'No, no,' she says, 'nothing.' 'I'm sorry, dear, that man was in need. I saw it, but I didn't interfere.'

Kuddusi Baba

Kuddusi Baba is of the Qadiri Order. He said, 'My God, you've given me everything. Countless thanks be to You. But You haven't endowed me with my Master's morals. Inculcate me with my Master's state.' Not with his own master's state, but with that of the Prophet. These are difficult matters. This one takes everything from that one, except his state.

Again, the following sayings belong to Kuddusi: 'Ever since I began to love You, You're always doing what You say, never what I say.'

> *Those who tread the path of Truth – their task is always Unification,*
> *Those who leave all else but God – their task is always Unification.*

Mahmud Hudayi

He's the patron saint of seamen. He was trained by Father Uftade. He was a mufti, a religious judge (*qadi*) of deep exoteric knowledge. Father Uftade said, 'You can't become a dervish.' He said, 'I will.' Father Uftade: 'Then you must sell livers wearing your embroidered caftan.' He sold offal, he broke his self, that was it.

On the other hand, Father Uftade was explaining Verses and Sayings at the time of Murad IV, the Shaykh of Islam said, 'I won't listen to him.' He passes out for a while, he comes to himself. They visit him. The Shaykh of Islam is a strong scholar, he doesn't surrender to Father Uftade. As a joke, Father Uftade says: 'I couldn't cope with you. May Christian priests perform your Funeral Prayer.' And indeed, the Shaykh of Islam's funeral was led by a priest.

The pouch from the sultan

One has to abandon something. The body, food, drink – one has to abandon one of these.

They're poor, there isn't even a cloth to wrap the baby in. The sultan sends him money. He says to his wife, 'My dear, be patient, what you want is on its way to you.' He writes a letter: 'By the power of this Verse, the Ottomans will rule the world. Your back is to the earth [in your dream, yet] you're sad. What is stronger than earth?' There's a knock on the door. 'Give them this letter.' His wife gives it to the man at the door and receives the pouch. 'Wife, do you know gold when you see it? These are all yours. Go and do what you want.' She meets all their needs.

The greatest miraculous feat

Mahmud Hudayi is the master of Sultan Ahmed I. One day, Sultan Ahmed is pouring water from a golden pitcher into a gold basin for Mahmud Hudayi to take an Ablution, and his mother is going to give him a silk towel for him to dry himself. At that moment she thinks to herself, 'I wish he would display a miraculous feat.' Mahmud Hudayi looks up and says, 'The sultan is pouring water for the Ablution, the Sultan Mother is holding the towel. Isn't this the greatest of miraculous feats?'

Another time, they're on the shore of the Bosphorus with Sultan Ahmed, he tells the sultan: 'I'm going to invoke "God" and walk across the sea to the other shore, you repeat "Mahmud" and walk after me.' The sultan replies: 'I can't do that. I can't invoke anyone except God.' 'All right,' he says, 'you stay behind.' Mahmud Hudayi walks across the Bosphorus Straits.

A lesson in alchemy

Mahmud Hudayi is in Istanbul. The child of a poor man failed his chemistry class. He saw a hodja during a Prayer, 'I've failed chemistry for a year, I'm going to fail again this year. Can you pray for me?' The hodja replied: 'I'm a hodja, I don't know chemistry. Let me send you to a teacher, he'll help you pass.'

He went to the address. As he came, Mahmud Hudayi was sitting under the grapevine. 'Come in, son?' 'The hodja of our mosque sent me to you.' He made him eat his fill and gave him some pocket money. Then he picked a leaf from the vine: 'Give this to your father. And this one is for you. Your father should take this to a jeweler, but he mustn't sell it for a low price.' It turned to gold in his hands. 'Son, this is *our* chemistry lesson. Now go.'

His father sold one for ten gold Liras. The other leaf, they preserved until the time of their grandchildren. In time, his father became the richest man in Istanbul. And he passed his chemistry course.

Now, here's *your* chemistry lesson: get up in the morning, do your two-cycle Prayer, *'In the name of God, the Compassionate, the Merciful. There is no power or strength apart from God.'* Repeat this a hundred times. Everything is solved by *In the name of God, the Compassionate, the Merciful.* One should continue the above.

Mawlana Jalaluddin Rumi

Mawlana Rumi – it's not about his age, his height, his weight. One should pay obeisance to his *morality*.

Rumi's father is Bahauddin Walad, of the Naqshbandi Order. Rumi is Naqshi too, the paths separated after [his encounter with] Shams of Tabriz.

Shams corrupted Rumi. Mawlana had studied all sciences from four sources – Sayyid Burhanuddin, Sadruddin Konevi, Damascus and his own father. Shams came and burned him up. What remained was love and Shams.

Comment: *Shams himself said: 'He was ready, I set him on fire.'*

True, he was all that was needed. There was gossip, the people weren't able to understand. Of the people of Konya, Rumi once said, 'My Lord, thanks be to You, You've plunged me in countless bounties. But unfortunately, I'm in this scorpion's nest.'

They killed Shams. They stabbed him. Both saints are at the pinnacle, neither of them could avert destiny.

What good did Rumi see from those close to him? Rumi's own dervishes, of forty or fifty years' standing, avenged themselves on

Rumi, they killed Shams of Tabriz. These creatures are all like that. It's easy to love God but hard to love people. The secret of life is to succeed in this difficult task.

The three successors of Rumi were Salahuddin [the goldsmith who whirled], Bahauddin Sultan Walad [his son] and Husamuddin [to whom he dictated the *Mathnawi*]. [Of them, he remarked: 'Regard all three of my successors as one. If the Sun (Shams) has set, the moon (myself) has risen. If the moon passes behind a cloud, what else remains to show us the path but stars?']

His famous saying, 'Come back,'[21] actually means: 'Come back to repentance.' He also said, 'I am the servant of the Quran and the dust of the Prophet's feet.'

His father

His father Bahauddin Walad [*sultan al-'ulama'*, 'the Sultan of Scholars'] came from Bukhara. The ruler wrote him a letter: 'Two lions can't sit on one sheepskin.' He replied, 'I am your servant.' His disciples said, 'Let's depose him,' he said 'No.' One night he departs with his family for Mecca, and from there to Baghdad. Then he settled in Karaman, Konya [Turkey]. The Seljuks valued him, he was a learned man. When he died, Mawlana took his place. Rumi's father must be buried in Karaman. He doesn't enjoy popularity, it all belongs to his son.

Sayyid Burhanuddin

Bahauddin Walad told his son Mawlana: 'After me, go and receive Quran lessons from Burhanuddin.' Sayyid Burhanuddin is among the children of the Twelve Imams [which is why he is called sayyid]. Sayyid Burhanuddin came from Bukhara. We all come together in Bukhara [the town of Bahauddin Naqshband]. Our essence unites there. And then it unites in Mecca, in Medina. It comes from there like that.

Mawlana went to Sayyid Burhanuddin as a student. One day Sayyid Burhanuddin said, 'let's take a ride among the orchards.' The donkey stumbled, Sayyid Burhanuddin fell off, his leg was broken. He couldn't sleep for a week. Mawlana said, 'You've been moaning for a week, and we're moaning with you. You pray for everyone, you touch your hand and heal them. Why don't you do the same thing to yourself? Stroke your own knee with your hand.'

---

21. See footnote to The door of hope.

He smiled. 'Oh, child, it's a good thing you reminded me. Come on, you pray and stroke your hand.' He lies unconscious for twenty-four hours and is healed. 'Thank you, son, I was cured by your hand.' Mawlana received training from four teachers. He said, 'It was still your hand, Master. I recited with your mouth.' He replies, 'No, it was your hand, not mine. Can the sword cut its sheath?' – that saying comes from Sayyid Burhanuddin: 'A sword can't cut its own sheath.' [A tailor can't stitch his own rent.] 'God bestowed a cure,' he said.

A week later, he signed Rumi's diploma (certificate): 'Mawlana has finished his exoteric and esoteric training with me.' He said, 'You can go.'

Oppose the ego

One day Rumi met a priest. The priest told him about Christianity and miraculous feats. He performed many of these. He could work miraculous feats, he performed them.

Rumi is noncommittal. 'How did you come by this ability?' he asks. The priest replies: 'I did the opposite of what my self desired.' Asceticism, that is. Rumi says: '*"There is no god but God, and Muhammad is His Prophet."* Ask your ego, does it like this?' The priest flushes red, five minutes later he bends down on his knee, *'There is no god but God, and Muhammad is His Prophet,'* he surrenders to God.

That's how the great ones worked. There are three things the self dislikes: hunger, Prayer and death. We're all going to go sooner or later, let's go with faith, God willing.

The house of the Prophet

Rumi comes home one day, There's nobody home. He asked a servant: 'Child, isn't there anything to eat in the cupboard?' 'No, Master.' 'Not even a piece of dry bread?' 'No.' Whereupon Rumi said: 'My God, thanks be to You! My home has become like the house of the Prophet. Thank You.' Yes! The great Rumi, all of Konya is at his service. He does a two-cycle Thanksgiving Prayer. My God, give to those who don't have, too.

Lifeblood

A French doctor came to visit Rumi and inspected him. He said, 'You're anemic.' He stayed for a week and saw how things were, then came back to Rumi. 'Are you staying or leaving?' 'I'm staying,' the doctor said, 'you can live without blood. I want to become a Muslim.'

Greetings from Shams

Shams disappears. One day one of those dervishes comes to Rumi, he says, 'I've brought you greetings from Shams! He's close by at Aksaray, he's coming tomorrow.' Rumi takes off his silk caftan and gives it to him as a gift. He also gives him pocket money and sends him off.

They say, 'He's a fraud, he lied.' He smiles. 'I know,' he says. 'If he had been speaking the truth [instead], I would have given my life.'

No turning back

Rumi used to whirl like that himself. So did his disciples. With state. Invocation, that is. Two dervishes of a master were sent by that master to visit Rumi. 'Go and check, what is Mawlana doing?' It's the night between Thursday and Friday. They begin the Invocation, the Turning (whirling, *sema*). One of the two asks Rumi, 'What are they doing?' 'They say "God" as they turn.' A little later, the same question, the same answer. 'Master, we thought you were in a high station. You all say "God," and then you turn. As for us, we say "God," we don't turn back.' Rumi [is amused]: 'Where did you learn this?' 'From our own master.'

Let's do that, too. Let's say 'God' once, and not turn back.

Shams of Tabriz

The meat cooked by love

Shams is from Iran. During his travels, he used to stop by a village and see a friend there. Let's call him Hassan. That friend, in turn, would greet him, offer him hospitality and respect, lodge him for the night and send him off the next morning.

One day Shams sets off again, he's going to visit him, he wants to give him a present. They were slaughtering a cow there. He buys a large piece of meat and slices it in two with a knife. Shams's name means 'sun.' He places it in his palm, then turns to the sun and says, 'You roast the side facing you, I'll roast the side facing me [my palm].'

He sets out on the road, when he's passed halfway he turns it over and looks. The side facing Shams's palm is beautifully roasted from Shams's love, but there's no change on the side facing the sun. He turns towards the sun, 'What're you doing?' he says. 'You're going to embarrass me.' He takes that side of the meat in his palm and continues on his way. When that side is roasted too, he had a dirty handkerchief, he takes it out and wraps the meat in it.

He arrives at Hassan's house. Hassan greets him. They talk. 'Hassan,' he says, 'I've brought you a gift.' He takes out and gives the dirty handkerchief as they eat. Hassan doesn't turn him down, he says, 'Okay, I'll eat it,' but because of the appearance of the handkerchief he doesn't eat it, he sets it down on the side of the tray.

When they're finished eating, Hassan calls over his servant and says, 'Remove this tray.' The servant takes the tray to the kitchen. He sees the meat. He thinks, 'What's this?' and takes a bite. It's as if all the tastes in the world are in that bite! He eats it all with relish.

Some time later, certain changes come over the servant. Knowledge of the Quran, knowledge of Sayings ... he's a sea of knowledge! But he hasn't studied these before, he didn't know. He begins to teach hodjas and scholars. Hassan is intelligent, he begins to serve his servant.

After a while, Shams drops by Hassan again. He sees the situation. 'What is this?' 'Well, my servant became like this all by himself.' Shams smiles: 'He ate the meat that was intended for you, that's why he's like this.' 'Oh, no! Doesn't anything like this fall to my lot, too?'

'I didn't forget your lot,' said Shams. '*He's* got your lot. It's out of my hands now.'

A game of chess

Shams of Tabriz parts with Rumi and goes off on his own. Because they [Rumi's disciples] don't want him. He stays at an inn at Konya.

We were speaking of waking up, that's how I remembered this. Shams is aged. A young Frank, a doctor. He comes and says something, tells a joke, he likes it, he stays with him for a while.

Now the Frank was a good chessplayer. That Frank comes, his friends haven't arrived yet. He sees Shams there, he thinks, 'Maybe he'll play with me.' He goes and waits, Shams says, 'Upon you peace, son.'

He asks, 'Can you play chess?' 'A little.' 'Let's spend some time together until my friends arrive.'

They begin to play. That first day, Shams yields all games to the Frank. A while later his friends arrive, they say, 'You've found a friend, come and play with us.' He says, 'No, we're playing.' That day he spends the time that way. The next day, he calls on Shams again, *even though* his friends are there. He goes to his table.

'Would you like to play some more today?' 'I would,' he says, 'but I have a condition.' The second day. 'If I beat you – are you French?' 'Yes.' 'You'll become a Muslim. And if you beat me, I'll become a Christian. I'll be a follower of Jesus.'

The Frank is favorably disposed to this offer. 'All right,' he says. He takes out a notebook from his pocket. He writes it down as an article, he's going to sign it. He says, 'I will abide by my pledge.' Shams says, 'I'm a Muhammadan from birth. I have such-and-such states. I'm very pious. But if you best me, I'm going to abandon my religion. As yet, you're ignorant. You haven't learned your religion well. If you lose, you're going to become a Muslim.' 'Okay.'

That day, too, he loses all the games to the Frank. The Frank is pleased. On the third day, he loses again, but before they're halfway through, he begins the attack. The sweat is dripping from the Frank's brow. He reduces him to confusion. At the end of the series, he checkmates the Frank.

Meanwhile, Rumi has heard of Shams' whereabouts. He sends his son Bahauddin [Sultan] Walad over with two of his friends. They find them, they're going on like that in the café.

Now Shams's back was to the door. The three of them come, what do they do, they clasp their hands [in front of them] like this, they stand behind Shams and wait for the end of the game. The Frank sees them, they're handsome young men.

During the game he says, 'You have visitors.' Shams looks, 'Welcome, son,' he says. He continues with the game, they wait there.

He makes the finishing move.

'Are you satisfied with the game?' asks Shams. 'It's okay, isn't it? It's all the fault of these young men, they distracted you.' These are all words of wisdom.

'It's okay,' says the Frank. 'Thank you.'

He turns to Bahauddin Walad and says, 'Sit down, children.' But out of courtesy, they nevertheless sit at another table. He sends them coffee and tea, they drink. After they're finished – Rumi had put some money in a handkerchief, tied it up, and said: 'Wherever you find him, place the handkerchief in front of him like this, with the tip of the handkerchief pointing towards Konya. Don't say anything else.' He brought over the handkerchief and placed it in front of him as instructed.

'Oh, so your father wants me, does he?' That's all.

The inn he's staying at, he doesn't have the money to pay them. He takes that money and pays off all his debts, including the last tea he sent them.

He says, 'I have a teacher in Konya, he's calling me.'

Shams, the Frank and the others all go outside, sir. Bahauddin Walad gives his horse to Shams. 'Son, you're young,' he says. 'I can walk ...' 'No, no,' he says. A friend wraps a blanket over him, two people ride. They arrive, they rest that night. The next morning he takes the Frank to Rumi, he gets up, they embrace. 'I've brought you a son,' he says to Mawlana. He tells the story. The young man recites the Word of Witnessing, the Word of Unity, the doctor becomes one of the foremost students of his master.

Nasruddin Hodja

[Nasruddin Hodja, the comic man of the Middle East, is also known as Mullah Nasruddin.] He's a great saint. [His master is said to be Sayyid Mahmud Hayrani of Akşehir.]

His origin

In the time of Bayazid II and Tamerlane, Nasruddin Hodja, Hassan Sabbah,[22] and Omar Khayyam[23] studied with the same teacher in Iran.[24] These were his best students. The teacher (hodja) had a sheep,

---

22. 'The Old Man of the Mountain' related to the Ismailis. Founder of the Cult of Assassins.

23. Mathematician who worked on cubic equations, as well as a poet famous for his *Rubaiyat*.

24. Sufi sources also relate this story as having taken place between Nasruddin Hodja, Sayyid Nasimi and Mansur al-Hallaj. Note that even if Hassan and Omar are contemporaries, Nasruddin Hodja cannot be if he is a contemporary of Tamerlane. So this is just a story. Khayyam's translator, Edward Fitzgerald, states that it was Hassan Sabbah, Omar Khayyam and Nizam al-Mulk (the Seljuk Grand Vizier) who all studied under Imam Mowaffak of Nishapur. And although Nasimi and Nasruddin's dates appear to match, Hallaj belongs to the first millenium AD.

Another variant of the story is that Nasimi and Kemal Ummi slaughtered the ram of

a ram. He would slaughter it every month. One day, when the time for slaughtering arrived again, some people came and departed with the teacher.

Ten days pass. Hassan and Omar say, 'Let's slaughter the ram.' Nasruddin Hodja said, 'Don't do it. We're not up to it. We're still students.' They didn't listen. Hassan slaughtered it, Omar skinned it, and Nasruddin Hodja laughed at them.

Now the teacher had a custom. He didn't waste the bones of the sheep. He would put them in a bag, he would strike the bag with his staff,[25] and the sheep would be resurrected. They tried to do the same thing, they couldn't do it. Nasruddin Hodja laughed at their predicament.

When the teacher got back, Nasruddin told him what had happened. The teacher said to Hassan: 'May your head be cut off.'
To Omar, 'May your skin be flayed and filled with straw.'
And to Nasruddin, 'May they laugh at you till Doomsday.'
'Begone!' he said.

Encounter with the thief

One day, a thief entered Nasruddin Hodja's home.[26] It's a two-room place, he looked around but couldn't find anything. He looked into the Hodja's room, he's in bed with his wife. Half-awake, the Hodja is watching him. There's nothing that he can take! As he was leaving through the door, the Hodja said, 'Son, just a moment. Don't let your labor go to waste.'

'Wife, wife,' he says. 'What is it, Hodja?' 'Get up, sweetie,' he says. She gets up and goes outside, the Hodja says, 'Son, in order to meet your labor, at least take this bed and go.' The Hodja has nothing else. And if he had, it wouldn't be worth it!

The thief was intelligent. 'Are you serious?' 'I'm serious, son.' 'What about you?' 'Don't worry about us.'

He went over and kissed his hand, he repented. He said, 'I won't do it again,' and he didn't. After that, he would come to visit the Hodja every month. 'You saved me,' he would say.

Sultan Baba. The latter is said to have thrown a razor before Nasimi and a noose before Kemal. While Nasimi was flayed and Kemal was hanged, there is a period of sixty years between their deaths, militating against their being fellow-students under anyone. So this version of the story, too, appears to be chronologically flawed.

25. As a variant of this, he would blow into the bag.
26. See The saints/Ismail Hakki of Bursa for a similar story.

Falling off a donkey

Nasruddin Hodja got on his animal, his donkey. He went to his orchard. On his way back, he fell off the donkey. His neighbors saw him, they brought him back home. One or two ribs were broken.

They call in the chiropractors of that day: 'Come,' in order to mend them. The Hodja has a question: 'Have you ever fallen off a donkey?' 'No.' 'Then you don't know my suffering.' You understand? The other, the other. The Hodja howls.

One of the neighbors heard of the question, he came over. 'Get well quick, Hodja! What happened?' 'Well, I fell off a donkey.' 'So did I, and three times, too. Let me take a look.' '*Aha!* You're the one I need, you'll understand my situation.'

The second spouse

Nasruddin Hodja's wife had died. He married a woman who had lost her first husband. She couldn't forget the first one. The first night they have supper, 'My old husband used to eat like this.' They go to bed, 'My first husband used to lie like this.' For two years the Hodja is patient. Two years!

One day he says, 'My old wife used to sleep on my left side.' '*What?*' She falls, *thud!* out of the bed and breaks her leg. He calls in the chiropractor. The wife: 'So you still haven't forgotten her after two years!' The Hodja: 'You've been telling yours for two years, I mentioned mine only once in two years.' He says to himself: 'Couldn't you have kept silent? Now you'll have to bear this, too.'

Sabotage

Nasruddin Hodja goes to the orchard. He loads brushwood on the animal all day. As they're coming home, the donkey can't bear the load and collapses. The Hodja waits for someone to come by. Three or four friends are coming, they see the Hodja's situation from afar. 'Let's play a trick on the Hodja,' they say, 'let's push down.'

When the Hodja sees them coming, he says, 'Children, give me a hand so that we can raise this animal.' They say 'Okay,' but they do as planned. The Hodja breaks out in a sweat. 'Just a moment, children,' he says. 'Let's leave politics aside. Let's lift for *God's* sake.' 'Okay, Hodja,' they say, and raise it.

That's how we ought to do things, for *God's* sake.

Long wait coming

Nasruddin Hodja is in debt. The man came. Nasruddin Hodja says, 'If he asks, I'm over there, among the bushes.' He goes into the woods and wanders around.

The man comes. 'You came early.' 'What are you doing?' 'When sheep pass by, their wool is caught on the foliage, I'm collecting those. My wife is going to knit them, I'm going to sell and pay back your money. I'm working hard to raise your money.' 'Are you serious?' 'Yes.' 'You can keep it.' 'That's better, son!'

The pangs of desire

Nasruddin Hodja was riding his donkey on his way to the orchard. His donkey was male. Now it was May, and a female donkey had urinated as she passed by. The Hodja's donkey stuck his nose in the soil and wouldn't budge. He hit him, he drew blood, *uh-uh*.

Nasruddin Hodja emptied the fodder sack, he filled it with that urinated soil and tied it to the animal's mouth. That night the animal brayed until morning. He's hungry! The next morning they went again. The neighbor has a female donkey, the hungry donkey didn't even see her. He went to the orchard, he left the donkey hungry for another couple of hours. Then he leaned over and said into his ear, 'If you repent, I'll let you eat.' Then he fed him. [The Hodja's ass, of course, is one of the best symbols for the Base Self.]

Where's my donkey?

Nasruddin Hodja was going to the mill to grind wheat. His wife said: 'Hodja, we haven't separated the wheat from the chaff, expose this to the wind so the chaff is blown away.' The Hodja goes, but he forgets all about it. They grind the wheat at the mill, then the Hodja remembers. 'Let me do what my wife said so she won't be angry with me,' he thinks.

Now the donkey was standing in the direction of the wind, all the flying flour turned it white. The Hodja looks, his donkey was black, this one is white. He asks the miller: 'Where's my donkey?' 'Isn't it that one?' 'My donkey was black, this one's white.'

This is a good story. Now, God doesn't burden one He loves. We assume the burden on our own. We get powdered with dust. Once you shake it off, no dust will be left. Also, don't attach importance to superficial things. Their flour will fly off, they'll go bankrupt.

More where it came from

Nasruddin Hodja has no money, he's talking to his wife, and a spiteful neighbor is listening at the window.

'Be patient, my dear,' he says. 'God won't leave us hungry. I ask for a hundred gold pieces, I won't accept one less or one more. I'll settle for a hundred.'

That eavesdropping neighbor goes, he counts ninety-nine gold coins into a pouch. He drops it down the chimney. Just as it's about to fall into the fire, the Hodja grabs it. '*Ah!* Here it is. Let's see how much we have.' They count it, ninety-nine. He says, 'He who gives ninety-nine will also give a hundred. My dear, one is missing, but God is very generous, tomorrow He'll give that too.'

His neighbor is alarmed. He comes around to the door. 'What's up, neighbor?' 'Well, it's like this ...' 'No,' he says. 'I requested from God, you're nowhere in the picture. I didn't ask you, son. He'll give the other one, too.'

Say, 'My God, You're very generous, give me much so that I can do much.'

Never enough

Nasruddin Hodja's donkey ate clover until it was full. His neighbor across the street called out: 'Hodja, I can fool your donkey.' 'No, you can't.' The man waved a handful of clover. The donkey got up and ran towards it. The Hodja said, 'You fooled this [animal], you'll fool me, too. Begone!'

Donkey of a self

Nasruddin Hodja is going to the orchard. The donkey is unladen. He's thrown its saddle on it, they're going.

A neighbor said, 'Why don't you ride on it?' The Hodja replied, 'You haven't been riding your donkey, your self, for forty years. Doesn't your case bother me more? I don't say anything to you. Nor do you listen to me. I didn't get on it for five minutes, that bothers you.'

The tree climber

One day, Nasruddin Hodja hides some money. He climbs a tree in his garden. He hangs a pouch full of gold on the tree. A neighbor sees him and thinks of a prank. He climbs up and puts dung in it.

A day comes when the money's needed, the Hodja climbs the tree and finds – dung! He understands. 'I'm amazed,' he says [aloud to his donkey:] 'I climbed up there with difficulty on two feet. How did you climb up there on four? And what did you do with the money?' His neighbor explains and returns the money. 'So you were that animal. But since you've returned it, you've become a human being. Again, it turned out to be a human,' he said.

Of course, the Hodja didn't have dealings like this, these are only jokes.

Love

Nasruddin Hodja gave an invitation. Those who loved him a bit came, they're eating. 'Do you love one another?' 'Of course.' 'And me?' 'Yes, we have respect for you.' 'You're lying. You didn't give a spoonful to each other's mouth, nor did you give me.'

To cut the branch one is sitting on

Nasruddin Hodja was up in a tree, sawing off the branch he was sitting on. Someone saw him from down below and called out, 'Don't do that, Hodja, you're going to fall down.' 'That's what *you* think.' 'All right, suit yourself,' he says, and moves on. A little later, from behind him comes a *crack!* and then, *crash!*

The Hodja comes running up, all flustered. 'Quick,' he says, 'tell me when I'm going to die!' 'How am I supposed to know *that?*' 'Well, you knew I was going to fall, so you ought to know that, too.'

Clean–Unclean

Nasruddin Hodja was riding on his donkey. He's eating something in the meantime. As an Unclean bite came, he was throwing it behind him. As a Clean bite came, he threw it in front – into his heart, that is.

The rain prayer

Nasruddin Hodja and his neighbor went out to pray for rain. The Hodja prayed, 'My God, on my land, too.' It rained all right, but the floods left all the flotsam and jetsam on the Hodja's plot.

His neighbor said, 'Your field has ceased to be a field.' The Hodja said, 'My God, if I had a fault You'd correct it, but why did You do this?'

The true owner

A man is going on a road. He sat down under a tree, when he got up he forgot his staff. He remembers it on his way. At that moment, he sees someone coming with a staff, 'Why friend, thank you so much, you've found my staff and are bringing it.'

'Sorry, friend, this is my staff. My father left it to me.' 'Well, my father left mine to me, too.'

While they're arguing like that, Nasruddin Hodja comes by. 'Give me the staff,' he says. 'If I were to divide this in two, it would do neither of you any good. I better keep this to myself,' he says.

Now, the same thing is going to [happen to] these guys.

Tamerlane

Tamerlane [invades Anatolia and comes to Akşehir. He] inflicts much oppression. 'You're not cruel,' says Nasruddin Hodja. 'We oppressed the people a lot in the time of the Seljuks, now we're paying for that.'

The intellectual donkey

Tamerlane asked Nasruddin Hodja, 'You're a very intelligent man, is your donkey intelligent, too?' 'Yes, it is,' he replied. 'It can read. I wouldn't ride on it if it couldn't,' he said.

Tamerlane said, 'Bring it and let's see.' The Hodja said, 'It's sick now, I'll bring it in three days.'

He went home, he left the donkey hungry for two days. The evening of the second day, he put barley between every page of a book. As the donkey ate, he turned the pages.

The next day they went to Tamerlane. The donkey was turning the pages with its nose, looking for barley.

'Now I believe that your donkey can read,' said Tamerlane.

Nur-ul Arabi

Muhammad Nur-ul Arabi settles in Bosnia. There he continues both on Divine Law and a spiritual path. That's where the Melami Order comes from.

His famous saying is: 'Where there is Reality, there is no Divine Law.' This reaches the ear of the Shaykh of Islam. They call him to Istanbul [the capital city]. In the Sultan Ahmed Mosque, they debate after Prayer. Sultan [Abdul] Hamid listens from behind a grating to hear what he has to say.

He says, 'If the Sultan were here, would our individual wills be valid? The Sultan's will would hold. But when we're alone, we can do as we please.' Sultan Hamid says, 'Release that man.'

Shaykh Sha'ban Wali

He lived in the hollow of a tree for years. The mufti came across him, he's filthy, saliva and mucus are dripping from him. The mufti is appalled. But then Sha'ban Wali says: 'God is going to ask us: "My servant, I was with you all your life. Who were you with?"' Then he adds: '[I'm your shepherd,] I'm driving you all.' The mufti takes him home, he washes him and gives him new clothes. He says, 'Drive me first.' He was smart, he became his first disciple.

Hafiz of Shiraz

His conversion

[Shamsuddin Muhammad] of Shiraz memorized the Quran, that's why they call him *Hafiz* [memorizer of the Quran]. His father and mother raised him, he's rich. He later became addicted to drink. He has a wife, she's pious.

One day, as he was leaving the tavern again, he urinated, and at that moment he saw something white on the ground. He looked, it was a piece of paper with '*There is no god but God, Muhammad is His Prophet*' written on it. He doesn't wash it, he rubs it on his face. 'Woe that I should see Your noble name on the ground like this!' he wails. 'Was this what You were going to do? You've brought Your own name beneath feet, you've addicted Hafiz to drink. Can't you protect Your own name? Forgive Hafiz,' he says as he weeps.

He comes home, he's put it in his pocket. He goes straight to bed. In his dream: 'Hafiz, get up. You have honored My name, and I have forgiven you.' He gets up, he takes a Bodily Ablution [ritual bath]. He does a two-cycle Thanksgiving Prayer. He tells his wife: 'Here's good news for you, you will not see Hafiz in taverns again.'

He goes to his old tavern. He reserves a corner for himself. 'Where's Hafiz of Shiraz?' 'He's in the tavern again.' They still run away.

Go and see Hafiz of Shiraz in his own country [where he rests in a garden fit for a fairy tale]. Some come favored into this world.

The ruling of Hafiz

He gave a *fatwa* [ruling of religious law], this is good, too. A mufti, the mufti of the region, is going on Pilgrimage. He had a beautiful daughter, he entrusts her to a hodja as the best choice. After she's stayed a day or two, they chance upon each other at the rest room. The hodja can't restrain himself, he kisses her with lust. He's a Prayer-leader (imam), he leads the Prayer. He exclaims, 'What have I done?!' No one can give him a *fatwa*, he leaves town. He wanders for two or three months, no one can decide.

He finds himself in Iran. They point out Hafiz of Shiraz. He's in the corner of a tavern. The hodja has a robe and a turban, he's in full regalia. He sees him from afar. They say, 'Hodja, you're going to the wrong place.' [When they understand his quest,] they take him over there.

First, small talk. 'Where are you from, what are you looking for?' he asks. The hodja says, 'I did such-and-such a thing.'

'You did well. Hassan, my child, take down that seven-year-old wine.' [To the hodja:] 'Drink while I pass the *fatwa* on this.' As he drinks, he ascends, he sees the Guarded Tablet. 'You shouldn't have done this to me.' Where's he going to see it again? No such luck!

This is Khwaja (Master) Hafiz of Shiraz, he's made a sherbet there, everyone thinks it's wine. Two more glasses, the hodja finishes the bottle.

'Now go home before her father comes back. This time, kiss her as your own daughter, with the kindness of a father. And when her father arrives, explain things to him.'

The imam goes. When he explains it to the girl, she says, 'Thank you. You're forgiven. I'm your daughter, you're my father.'

Yunus Emre

Tapduk Emre had thousands of disciples, only Yunus Emre succeeded. So this business is difficult. The same with the 'Father of Loaves' (Somuncu Baba), there's only Hajji Bayram. How beautifully Yunus said it:

Handless to one who beats him
Tongueless to one who swears
A dervish should not take offense
You cannot be a dervish.

How Yunus became who he was

If you don't get angry, if you don't succumb to your ego, it's good to wait at the door. Yunus served Tapduk Emre for seven years. He always hewed straight logs for him. One day he asked: 'Where do you find these logs?' 'Master, there are crooked ones too, but they're not worthy of this door.' Trials, tests, tribulations, hardships – one day he's fed up. This is the basis. He said: 'Enough!' and left.

On his way, he met two friends. He didn't tell them his name. They came to a brook, they did their Prayers. One said to the other, 'We're hungry. Pray to God so a table spread will be sent to us.' One of them prays, a banquet appears, they dine. In the evening, it's the turn of the other friend to pray for a spread.

Finally, it's time for breakfast, they tell Yunus: 'It's your turn.' Yunus doesn't know things like that yet, so he prays: 'I haven't learned such things. A table spread for the sake of whoever they prayed in the name of.' A breakfast [fit for a king] arrives, with butter and honey.

The two friends are amazed. 'How did you do *that?*' 'Brother, I don't know. I asked in the name of whoever you asked in the name of.' 'There's a much-suffering Yunus Emre. He suffers all night and waits at the door.' 'Is that so? ... I'm going back.'

Now, it's Tapduk Emre who sent these friends. That is, he's not driving Yunus away, he's showing him: 'See where you are, what you are?'

Tapduk Emre's wife opens the door. 'Yunus, my son, where did you go?' 'Mother, I ran away. But I came back. Did the Master ask for me?' 'Yes, he did.' 'What should I do?' The weather is cold. 'Lie down in front of the door,' she says. Tapduk is blind. 'If he steps out at night, he'll step on you. If he asks who you are, say, 'I'm Yunus, your slave.' If he says, 'Our Yunus?' there's nothing to be afraid of. If he says 'Begone!' run, don't wait.'

So indeed it happens. 'Our Yunus, where have you been?' And he escorts him to the rest room as usual.[27]

---

27. The Master indicated that in a variant version of the story, Yunus is driven away by Tapduk, but manages to get his head inside just as Tapduk shuts the door. He then says,

Heaven and Hell

Yunus Emre became very curious. 'Paradise,' he said, 'is for us. But what shall we do about this Hell?' One night he saw himself elevated in the World of Meaning [the Spiritual World], they took him to Heaven. He told the angels, 'This is the abode of the faithful. Now please take me to the abode of woes, to Hell. I want to see that place, too.'

They took him there in his dream for an hour. He looks and looks, he can't see a fire or anything. Nothing's there. He asked the escorting angel: 'Is this Hell?' 'Yes,' the angel said, 'it's Hell.' 'But there's nobody burning, no cauldron, no tar, just nothing. This is a safe place.' 'Wait a bit, take a breath and you'll see.'

By and by, two or three people come along, laden with brushwood. They light bonfires, one should run from fire, they step right into them. Another brought a can full of gas – according to one's reward, whatever the reward is for this side – everyone brought their own chastisement. They lit them and stepped inside. He asked the angel: 'Is this true?' 'Yes, it is. Everyone brings their own fire. There's no fire here on its own.' Yunus said, 'My God, You are All-powerful, Merciful. Forgive the sins of us all.'

He came to himself.

Double duty

A man went to hew wood, he cut a lot of wood. He's far from home, he loaded it all on the donkey. The animal is weak, it couldn't bear the burden, it collapsed. Yunus Emre is there, watching. The man beat it and raised it to its legs by force. A bit later, it collapsed again. This time the man took the wood on his shoulders, got on the back of the animal and said: 'Come on, I'm carrying the wood.' The animal collapsed instantly. 'Why, you good-for-nothing …!'

Yunus came out from there. 'What are you doing?' He took him to the convent. 'You made it carry both the load and yourself.' 'Thank you. I hadn't thought of that. And I'm going to set that donkey free.'

'Thank goodness, I got my head inside. Master, cut it off.' But he stated that the version given in the main text is 'more appropriate. It is the pleasure of God, the knowledge of God.'

Yusuf Bahri

(His case is a classic illustration of the Sufi phrase, 'Forget all you know – transform your knowledge into ignorance.')

Yusuf Bahri is in the time of Mawlana Khalid the Two-Winged.

Yusuf Bahri is from Çorum. His tomb is there. He studies at a religious school in Istanbul. He takes his books, he's going to go to Egypt, he's looking for a wrestler to tackle [a scholar to match wits with].

He's going to Damascus, to Egypt. On his way, he comes to a place where a preacher is lecturing at a mosque. The first thing he hears is, 'Nothing can be told to children.' He continues for a week, he doesn't understand a thing. He attends for another week. The preacher asks: 'Do you have a knowledge you rely on?' 'My books.' The preacher tells him, 'Your mind doesn't comprehend this. Yusuf, throw your knowledge, your books, into the Euphrates River.'

The books are his life and soul! He can't bear to part with them, he has a waterproof bag made. He drives an iron stake in the middle of the Euphrates. He chains the bag – with his books in it – to that stake, and comes out.

It waves there for two days. Then the preacher says, 'Did you do it? You're deceiving yourself, and you're trying to deceive us. Break off the stake, too, and leave it.' Towards dawn he severs the stake.

That's it, it's done. The preacher says: 'Congratulations, you're my guest for a month.'

He hosts him for fifteen to twenty days. One day, as he's listening to the preacher in the mosque, the place is filled by white, blue and green pigeons, pigeons of every hue, coming in through the window. They fill in between the ranks of the congregation. He takes them in his hand, he fondles them, they're real. The pigeons invoke as they weep. Yusuf's eyes are filled with tears. It's all gone, knowledge is gone, his capital is gone. They fly off before the lecture is finished.

That day the hodja catches him again. 'Did you understand anything from the lecture?' 'I saw such a thing.' He says, 'I gave you a month. God had pity on you.' 'Is this an illness, or is it real?' 'It's real. If you'd gone to Egypt and studied there for two-three years, you wouldn't have been able to see this.'

He takes him home, he gives him a lesson [a number of Invocations to be recited daily]. 'Do you want to stay or leave?' 'I should go, Master.' 'Go. Your business is finished. Go and teach in Çorum.' He makes an addition to his name. He calls him 'Bahri' [the Sea], that is, the source [sea] of knowledge. He goes back to his land, he rejuvenates all of Anatolia. He dies in Çorum. He's there, in the big graveyard.

Now, we all have some knowledge. We have a knowledge we like and trust. After that knowledge of the Quran, one has to discard all of it. May God bestow Muhammadan knowledge, wisdom and intelligence on us all.

The Chain

(The 'Golden Chain,' or Chain of Transmission, is the spiritual 'family tree' through which masters pass on their knowledge and spiritual stations to students. In this chapter, the Master's own chain of transmission is introduced.)

General

After Bahauddin Naqshband, there's Imam Rabbani (Ahmed Sirhindi). There are others in between. Imam Rabbani is a descendant of Omar, the second caliph. Again there are others, then comes Abdullah Dahlawi, who trained Mawlana Mehmed Khalid of Baghdad.

The Naqshi Order came to Anatolia as a branch of Mawlana Khalid, in the time of the Ottomans, from Damascus. He trained many successors, he was a great man. There are also Ismail Fakirullah, Ibrahim Hakki. Then came Hodja Bakir, Ali Sebti and Mahmud Samini. There are more than fifty branches of the Naqshi Order, we're from the Samini branch.

Abdul Qadir Gilani (d. 1166)

The attributes of prophethood and sainthood are united in our Prophet. Sainthood continues through the lineage of Ali. They leave Hassan out and continue it from Hussein. God knows best, but sainthood is transferred to the Twelve Patron Saints [the founders of the twelve principal Sufi Orders] and continues from there.

Abdul Qadir Gilani's father comes from Hassan, his mother from Hussein. Love him very much, he's one of the Prophet's descendants. His father is an exoteric scholar. If a prophet had been destined to come after the Prophet, it would have been Gilani. He comes from the Twelve Fountains [Orders]. He encompasses all Orders. If you dress in red, I in yellow, he in black and we all go out into the sun, wouldn't the sun enlighten us all? There's the sun of knowledge, and there's the sun of this world.

He's in command of the Twelve Orders, that is, he's the president. In his day he dispensed justice with the spirituality of the Prophet. He's the Pole of Poles, the Greatest Diver [into the Ocean of Unity] of his age. He doesn't just rule Baghdad, he rules the world. The president of his time. Everything is in his palm! Yet he never strayed, he never strayed an inch from the Prophet.[1]

When the Grand Saint was chosen by the Prophet, fifteen or sixteen people had come to the same level, they were all waiting to be appointed as Diver. But the Prophet of God chose Gilani and the rest bowed to him.

The person who comes to the station of the Grand Saint determines physically and spiritually. He determines the president, he determines the prime minister.

Gilani said, 'I will come to the rescue of a person who loyally seeks help. If a person is in dire straits and calls my name three times, with the permission of God I will arrive to help him.' When you pray for something, say, 'Make my wish come true for the sake of this august name.'

The Grand Saint is from Iran, he studies elementary school in the village of Gilan. His father sends him to Damascus to the Quran course. Then his mother sends him to Baghdad to study. He studies and becomes a superior scholar. He's an esotericist, he's also very rich. Ordinary hodjas keep away from him. They haven't entered this field. They travel on the surface of the sea, but they're not divers.

Having two wings

There are birds with a single wing, they flutter but can't fly. In order to fly, two wings are needed. The hodjas of today have single wings. They're neither where they claim to be, nor can they fly there, nor can they take you there. The hodjas of old were dual-winged, they could fly where they wanted and alight there.

A rich woman brings the Grand Saint her son so that he can learn the Quran. She comes back a year or two later, she sees that her son is eating salt and drinking water in the basement. Upstairs, the Grand Saint is having roast lamb and rice.

The woman says, 'I've lost my patience!' The Grand Saint says 'Sit down,' she doesn't listen.

The Grand Saint says to a roast chicken: 'Get up and walk,' *cluck, cluck*, the chicken comes to life. The woman calms down. 'Your son was going to have a state like this, you didn't allow it.' 'But sir—' '*Uh-uh!* Take him and go.'

---

1. Which is precisely why he was the Pole of Poles.

Now, some hodjas are like they used to be. Some are like those of this day. Some are like the Grand Saint. Don't mind them. Just go to the mosque and do your own duty. If they drive you away from the mosque, too, do your Prayer in the courtyard and leave. Forgive them and don't meddle with anyone.

Old friends

A cowherd, a friend with whom he went to elementary school, goes to visit the Grand Saint. He greets him at the door, gives him his seat, everyone's astonished. He honors him, treats him with respect, he has him take a bath, he gives him two or three thousand gold pieces. When he's leaving, he adds a couple of the largest camels in Iraq.

The cowherd looks. 'This wealth is too little for you, and being a cowherd is too much for me,' he says.

Again, a friend of the Grand Saint from Damascus said, 'Let me go and visit him.' On his way, he passed by five or ten herds. 'Whose are these?' 'They belong to the Grand Saint.' [The friend] gave his own donkey to [the Grand Saint as a present]. The Grand Saint is always smiling. 'You're making fun of me?' 'No, I'm not laughing at anything, I'm smiling at the donkey.' He stayed for a week. The Saint put some silk clothing on a mare for his wife and kids and gave him some money. 'You're going to mount this, it's the gift for the donkey.' 'That bald ass was too much for me. And this wealth is too little for you.' He set out.

Let's think a little bit. Let's wake up.

Keep your wealth in your wallet, not in your heart

(*I include the following story about the Grand Saint from Sufi lore, both because it is a good one and because it ties in with a story about Ibn 'Arabi and one about Mahmud Hudayi. I never heard it from the Master, however.*)

A man decided to visit the Grand Saint. When he was at two hours' distance from his location, he saw people working in the fields. He asked, 'Who do these fields belong to?' The workers answered, 'The Grand Saint.' The same thing happened when he was at an hour's and half-hour's distance. He thought to himself, 'They say the Great Saint is a very spiritual man, but look at all this worldly wealth!'

When he arrives, the Grand Saint honors him as his guest. After a while, he says, 'Let's take a stroll in the garden.' By and by, they come to a river. The Saint says, 'Let's walk across this water. Repeat "Abdul

Qadir, Abdul Qadir" and come after me.' As they start walking, the man hears the Grand Saint repeating 'Oh God, oh God.'[2] He thinks to himself, 'Why should I recite "Abdul Qadir"? I'll recite "Oh God," too.' The instant he does that, *splash!* He finds himself in the water.

The Grand Saint chuckles as he pulls him out. 'Son,' he says, 'All that land and all the wealth that you've seen belong to me, it's true. But I haven't allowed even a particle of them to enter my Heart.'

Do you know what love is?

Someone became the disciple of a master. He heard, 'Love is this,' 'Love is that.' He upped and went to the Grand Saint. He stayed a couple of days, 'I want to learn about love.' The Saint said: 'I don't know about love. I have a brother, Ahmed Rifa'i. Go to him.'

For another week, he pestered Ahmed Rifa'i. 'What is love?' 'Let me show you tomorrow after the Dawn Prayer.'

In the morning, 'My God, with Your strength and power, show this man what love is.' He began to whirl on the toe of his right foot, he rose as he rotated and was lost from sight in the sky. The spirituality of the Grand Saint manifested instantly: 'What have you done to my brother! Quick, beat on this plate!' A plate materialized. He beat on it until, *crash!* the master fell down, unconscious. And the form of the Grand Saint disappeared.

He came to himself in half an hour. 'What did you understand?' he asked. The man also sobered. He threw himself at his feet. 'Forgive me,' he said, 'I disturbed you both. I can't do such states, they're not for me.'

Arrogant scholars

There was a scholar, a virtuous man, in Damascus. Precaution, decision, predestination, he's learned them all. He heard about Abdul Qadir Gilani in Baghdad, he said, 'I wonder if he knows more than I do?' He took five gold pieces, he didn't even leave any for his children and left.

He talked for a week. [Then] he said, 'I've come to like you very much. How am I going to leave you?' He repeated this two or three times. As he was sending him off, the Grand Saint said, 'You have five gold pieces in your pocket. Love me as much as you love them, that'll be enough.' The man can't bear the weight of those words. 'Love me

2. Allah, Allah.

as much as your children.' He goes back to his presence and says: 'Enough.'

Abdul Qadir Gilani became famous. There was a scholar. He said, 'There's a scholar greater than me.' He hears of him again and again, he says, 'I have to go and size him up.' The Grand Saint has hundreds, even thousands of students, he doesn't give the turn to anyone else. He talked without cease for a week.

A week later he says, 'I came to listen to you, but you listened to me.' The Grand Saint says, 'Fine, fine.' Then he asks: 'These things you see, what do you see them with?' 'With the eye of the head.' 'Does that eye see itself, too?' 'No, sir, it sees the outside world.' 'Do you see your mind?' 'No.'

The Grand Saint says, 'A pity. I'm sorry for you. The eye that can't see itself is blind. It's all in vain if you don't see it. You have to open the Eye of the Heart. A lot more work needs to be done on you.'

The scholar is bewildered. 'Sir, would you teach me this?' 'Well, if you won't be embarrassed – son, take him and let him have a Bodily Ablution.' His worship of fifty-two years has gone down the drain. He comes and sits down.

The Grand Saint: 'You've started from scratch. Forget everything you've learned until now. This eye can see both itself and God.'

As long as you see God's face, it doesn't matter how you see it. If there's a Sound Mind, he'll see his mind, he'll see his eye, he'll see everything. You gave twenty years of your life to study law. It's hard to learn these things in a month, in a year!

You can go to every gathering. But don't go to the gathering of the eye that doesn't see itself.

The boy with a sweet tooth

In the time of the Grand Saint, there was a woman near his neighborhood in the same city. Her husband had died, she had a child five or six years old. The woman is poor, she washes people's clothes, she washes dishes, she buys a little food. The child always wants candy. 'Mommy, candy, Mommy, candy.' Whatever little they can give from the places she works at. That time is not like this, candy's hard to find. Today, by God's grace, He's pouring it from all around!

Her neighbors complain, 'Your child is like this.' 'Candy, candy,' day and night, candy's scarce. A woman tells her, 'There's a hodja around here close by. His name is Qadir, in that neighborhood. Go and see him, maybe he'll say a prayer or write you an amulet.' So the woman finds an opportunity and goes. She asks, they show her his house. She takes the hand of the child and comes up.

She pleads on the subject of candy, she tells the child's situation, her own situation. At that moment, the Grand Saint was drinking coffee. Coffee with lots of sugar in it. The blessed man loved sweets a lot. Whether *baklava* or candy, he loved them.

He listened to her account. 'Daughter,' he said, 'I can't say anything to you now. There's no paper or pen, I can't write you an amulet.' Because the lady mentioned that. 'Take the child and go. Come back twenty days later. Count twenty days and come.' 'Hodja, sir, what shall I do these twenty days?' He gave her lots of money. 'Buy candy with this, eat some yourself.' The money he gave the woman is enough to last a year. This is the Grand Saint!

When she went back, she looked for candy, she found some, she bought a few pounds, she brought it: 'Son, eat to your heart's content!' She tells the neighborhood, too: 'The hodja did this!'

That coffee, he drank it halfway. After the lady left, he didn't drink the remainder. He cut off sweets altogether.

A few days passed, on the fifth day the boy stopped putting candy in his mouth. And so it went, until the twenty days were over. When the time was up, the woman went to the Grand Saint and explained the situation. 'I came back twenty days later like you said, to give you the good news.'

His wife was sitting there. 'My dear,' he said, 'so it was I who was causing people all this trouble.' 'How so, husband?' 'It's like this,' he explained. 'The day I dropped sweets,' he said, 'everyone else did, too.' And he did a two-cycle Thanksgiving Prayer.

Gilani and the devil

One night, Abdul Qadir Gilani is wandering hungry and thirsty in the streets of Baghdad. It's midnight. Suddenly, a light, a voice comes, 'My beloved Abdul Qadir, I have made everything Allowed (lawful) for you. You can eat from any garden you want.' Just so he can pick an olive and quench his thirst.

He stops, he thinks. '*In the Name of God, the Compassionate, the Merciful. All strength and power belong to God, the High and the Great.*'

The light fades, it becomes a person.

'*How* did you guess I was the devil?' Because it was him, it was the devil.

'*One*,' he said. 'The meaning of a sacred Verse: "Nobody's property is Allowed to anyone else." The olive is Forbidden, it is Allowed only if you earn it with the sweat of your brow. You tried to make me eat what was not Allowed.

'*Two*, again the meaning of Verse and Saying, "God's voice is fine and strong, it comes from every direction." Your light and sound came from one place.'

God's voice engulfs the whole body. It isn't clear which direction it's coming from.

The devil said: 'Allow me to kiss your hand. You've escaped my influence. Before you, I tricked seventy saints and led them astray on this point. I made them worship me on this count, but now I worship you. If I didn't have my duty, I would've become your disciple. I'm now under your command, I couldn't trick you.'

So one has to be very careful. When you're with the master, the master tells you, 'This is dangerous, that is dangerous.' If one isn't with the master, one should tell him [the things one sees and does].

The cloth on the shelf

A man opened a shop. The Grand Saint went to visit him. A woman brought some cloth, he bought it cheap and put it on the shelf. A little later, he sold it to a man who came by for twice the amount he had paid. Gilani said: 'I wish you would put me on that shelf, too. That way, my value, too, would be doubled.'

They place me on a shelf, they double my value. If they increased my spiritual value, that would be better.

The Friday sermon

The first time the Grand Saint went up to the pulpit, he wasn't sure of himself. In that instant, the Prophet manifested before his eyes: 'The command has been given, continue.' From one mosque to another, finally he bloomed.

One day, a Thursday, they're talking during a discourse. There was a field, a wide area on the outskirts of the city, he said: 'Let's do the Friday Prayer there.' His audience can't fit into mosques. 'How?' they said. 'One can't do Prayer where there is no mosque, no pulpit.' 'Ah!' he said, 'Have all our discourses been in vain? Isn't this entire world a mosque? The responsibility – if any – belongs to me. We're going to do the Prayer there.'

Before the Prayer, they erect a pulpit there. They say *seventy-three* Jews became Muslims that day. And twenty-eight of his followers became Attracted and gave up their souls to God. Each cried 'Oh, God!' and toppled over. In that hour.

The sermon ended, the Prayer-time came, he said, 'Let the dead remain as they are.' They did the Friday Prayer in that vacant lot. 'It was his effusion of that day,' they say. He said, 'This place didn't hold us, either.' He remained in that region for a month in order to disperse the congregation.

He's one of us

Someone was insulting the Grand Saint [behind his back] in the marketplace and elsewhere. A man very close to him was saddened by this. He told him about it. The Grand Saint said: 'Do they mention my name?' 'Yes, Master. They say, "Abdul Qadir is a liar."' 'Well then, they belong to us, too!'

One of the Saint's spiritual children had a father who was a scholar and virtuous. He wanted his father to go to the Saint, too. He told his father about it three or four times, 'Sure, son, we'll go someday.' He's a scholar, a man who knows everything.

He sees that it's hopeless, one day he asks the Grand Saint. 'This is how it is.'

'Where do you live?' 'Two streets down, Master.' It's the same neighborhood. 'Why, he's one of us,' he says. 'Don't worry.' The boy is pleased by this good news.

A few days later, he's alone with his father. 'Father,' he says, 'I couldn't find a way with you. I told the Master, he asked where we lived. I told him we were in the same neighborhood. He gave me great good news. He said, "Why, he's one of us, son, he's a man of knowledge."'

'What, what did he say? Tell me again!' He repeats it three times.

His father says, 'Come on, take me to him.' And thus the young man's wish is fulfilled.

A matter of state

(*This story is not among my records, but the Master did relate it, and I must recount it from memory.*)

[The Grand Saint's son wanted very much to follow in his footsteps. He studied hard to be a scholar, and one day, when he felt he was prepared, he asked his father, 'May I preach the Friday sermon tomorrow?' His father consented, and he was delighted.

The next day he climbed the pulpit and delivered a sermon. It was scholarly, wise and unobjectionable. Yet when he looked, he saw that the congregation was drowsing off to sleep.

His father whispered gently: 'Let me continue from here,' and took the pulpit. He said: 'This morning, we had breakfast with the family. My wife broke an egg into the pan, and it fell into the butter with a *sizzle!*' At that moment, several people shouted 'Oh, God!' and passed out.

His son asked him afterwards: 'How did this happen?' He said: 'Son, this has nothing to do with knowledge or words. It has to do with the state you're in.']

The right time

(The following story is not in my records either, but the Master knew of it and probably told it to others. It is included in a book on Gilani whose preparation he supervised.)

[There was a student of Gilani who had served him for many years. He thought the time had come for the Master to bestow some fruits on him. When he voiced his request, the Grand Saint said, 'Why don't you prepare some sweetmeats (*halwa*), and we'll see what transpires.'

As he was mixing the *halwa*, a delegation arrived from India. 'Our ruler is dead,' they said, 'could you assign a ruler for us?' The Grand Saint called for the servant. 'I will appoint you,' he said, 'under one condition: whatever you gain we're going to share, fifty-fifty.' The disciple happily accepted. He went and became a wealthy raja for eleven years, during which time he had wives and a son whom he loved very much.

One day, news arrived that the Grand Saint was coming. He hosted him and showed him respect, but on the day of his departure the Grand Saint reminded him of his obligation: 'Fifty-fifty.' He reckons his wealth carefully and divides it in two, but the Saint also says: 'You had a son during this period. We have to share that, too.' 'How're we going to do that?' 'We'll cleave him in two, and you can have whichever half you want.'

Just as the Grand Saint is about to bisect the child with his sword, the student draws out his dagger with a shout and says, 'You made me serve you for many years, and now you want to kill my only son!' As he stabs the dagger into the Saint's chest, he realizes he is stabbing the spoon in his hand into the pot of *halwa*.

The Grand Saint chuckles. 'My son,' he says, 'we are not miserly, we give. But not before the time has come.']³

The Grand Saint's visitor

A Jew went to visit the Grand Saint. He ate rice at his table. Someone informed him that this was a Jew. The Grand Saint said, 'Let him eat.'

He stays there a couple of years, then he goes somewhere else and begins to train disciples. But he's still a Jew. Many of his students become saints.

One day, as they were going somewhere, they had to cross a body of water.

All his students walked across the water. They called out to him, 'Come on.' At that moment he was inspired with faith, he said '*In the name of God, the Compassionate, the Merciful*,' and he too walked across.

Miscellaneous

- There was a Jew who used to open and close his shop saying 'Abdul Qadir.' One day he had a dream. Just as the angels were taking him to hell, the Grand Saint stops them. He wakes up in a cold sweat, he takes a Bodily Ablution and goes to the Saint. He converts seventy other Jews like him.

- A genie stole the beautiful daughter of a man. The Grand Saint told her father: 'Give my name to the Sultan of the genies (*jinn*),

---

3. This interesting case raises a question: what would have been the appropriate response for the disciple to make?

(a) When King Solomon was about to bisect a baby to determine its true mother, its real mother said, 'I give up on my share, she can have the whole child.' The disciple could have done the same.

(b) Abraham sacrificed his son to God. It was a tough trial, yet his son was spared. If the disciple had been patient, he could have relied on a similar act of mercy on the part of the Grand Saint.

(c) He could have said, 'Master, I and everything I have belong to you. Take us all!'

recite the Naming and draw a circle on the ground.' The Sultan of the genies threw himself to the ground [in surrender].

- The devil can't draw near the Grand Saint. [Just as in the case of the Prophet.]

- He put the Quranic recitation of a person 'on hold,' the person resumed his recitation when he 'released' him.

- A man came to the Grand Saint: 'I was going to relate a lot of troubles and worries, I forgot them all.' 'That's very good. As long as you don't forget yourself, too.' And what does Ibrahim Hakki say, 'Forget the past that worries you.'

- Again, when he was young, Abdul Qadir Gilani made up his mind: I won't break my fast until someone puts a bite in my mouth.' On the forty-third day someone comes, 'You've placed too much burden on your body. We did all this too, but not in this way.'

- One day he came upon his students. 'What are you discussing?' 'Sir, we were talking about the trials of Ibrahim Adham.' He said, 'If he had come in this day and age, we would have enlightened him in his gold-laced bed.' How? By closing the Two Doors.

- A traveling merchant was attached to a master. He's going to set out on a trip, his master tells him: 'Don't go.' He goes to the Grand Saint and asks him, he says, 'Go.' The night before he arrives in Istanbul, he has a dream that he's robbed by bandits. When he returns, he takes a bolt of cloth to his master. The master says: 'Take this to the Grand Saint, because it was he who made you pass in a dream what would have happened in reality.'

Bahauddin Naqshband (d. 1389)

(The transmission from the Grand Saint to Bahauddin Naqshband, the founder of the Naqshbandi Order, did not happen through a physical link, i.e. a chain of masters in this world. Rather, it occurred by direct spiritual contact.)

The Naqshi split off from the Grand Saint.

One day the Grand Saint is entering a coffee-house, he turns towards Bukhara and remains standing for five minutes. 'What's up?' 'A beautiful fragrance is coming from that direction.' These are signs. Two hundred years later, Muhammad Bahauddin comes to visit the Grand Saint. The Grand Saint says, 'Welcome, Bahauddin, my son,' and extending his blessed hand, he places it on Muhammad Bahauddin's Heart. The imprint of his five fingers is left on his Heart. They begin to talk. Because the imprint of his hand remains on his Heart, he receives the name *Naqshband* ['imprinted']. That is, he took over all the states of the Grand Saint.

These things happened, sir, and they exist even today for those who have come to that state. But Muhammad Bahauddin suffered for *forty* years in order to arrive there. No food, no drink, no life.

His life was spent in discourses. Now, Bukhara has become such that whichever way you turn, there are [the remains of] a saint, a friend of God, a pole.

Those after him are called the Khwajagan ['Hodjas']. He had three or four masters. [He received lessons from the spirit of Abdul Khaliq Ghujdawani (d. 1179), who died a hundred years before he was born.] He studies knowledge with them all.

He's burning with love, he was in the wilderness, hungry and thirsty, for a month. He's going to do his Dawn Prayer at a mosque. He says, 'I saw a wolf before the Dawn Prayer. The Prayer-call was sounded, the wolf lay on its back and raised its legs. The Prayer-call ended, the wolf rolled over on its side and walked away. "My God," I said, "don't I have as much worth as even that wolf? For its sake, accept me. *Enough!*"' For *its* sake, his wish was granted.

The next day, he goes and surrenders to [Sayyid[4] Amir Kulal (d. 1370). It's winter]. They were sitting, warming themselves by the fire. 'Who is it?' 'That mad boy, Muhammad, he's come.' 'Send him away.' He doesn't leave, he rests his head on the doorway. He's starving to death.

Half an hour later, someone coming out sees him. 'Oh my,' he says, 'he made a mistake, but God gave his punishment, should we now punish him too?' He calls inside [to the Master]. His feet are full of thorns. 'My God,' he [the Master] says, You put up with thousands, I couldn't put up with this boy.' He pulls out three thorns from his feet

---

4. *Sayyid*: a descendant of the Prophet through his grandson Hussein. Closely related to *Sharif*: a descendant of the Prophet through his grandson Hassan.

with his teeth. He doesn't let him go back to the mountains. And he becomes Shah Naqshband, Muhammad Bahauddin.

Khalid Baghdadi (d. 1827)

Mawlana Mehmed Khalid is Two-Winged. If someone passes from knowledge to spirituality, they're two-winged, this is very good. If there's no knowledge and one attains spirituality, Sufism, it's one-winged. But once they get to that level, even if they don't know how to read or write, everything is before their eyes. Earlier, if they asked him a Verse from the Quran, he would think.

[Mawlana Khalid goes on the Pilgrimage, he visits the Ka'ba. There he sees his future master, Abdullah Dahlawi, resting with his back against the Station of Abraham. He doesn't say anything, but he finds this discourteous, he disapproves. But he doesn't voice his thoughts.] Abdullah Dahlawi tells Mawlana Khalid: 'Sorry, Mehmed my son, I'm tired. My back may be to the Station of Abraham, but I've given my Heart to God.' [Khalid is flabbergasted: how did he know his name?]

[When Khalid asks around the next day, he learns that the man he met is the famous Abdullah Dahlawi, who lives in the Sultanate of Delhi in India. So his calling is to go there.]

Mehmed Khalid served Dahlawi for seven years. He would draw and carry water from the well. The well was far away. His shoulders became open sores. Two Greek women took pity on him. They made two shoulder pads and gave them to him.

That evening, they do the Night Prayer. He says, 'Mehmed, your task is over. Let someone else bring the water.' 'Master, I'm happy with my work. With your permission, let me continue.' 'No, I'm not more heartless than those two Greek women.' From there he sends him to Baghdad. Baghdad was in upheaval in those days. He suffers a lot there, too. And finally, he becomes Mehmed Khalid of Baghdad.

He suffers that pain, he finds that peace. [The peace that passeth understanding.]

Identify yourself

The shepherd of Mehmed Khalid the Two-Winged sees himself dead in a dream. The angels of interrogation arrive. 'Do you know this?' 'No.' 'Do you know that?' 'No.' 'Who are you?' He remembers, 'I'm the shepherd of Mehmed Khalid.' 'In that case, you're exempt from questioning,' they say. 'You can pass.' These things happen, they're true. The next day he tells Mehmed Khalid. 'Bravo,' he says, 'so you remembered me. Carry on!'

Ibrahim Hakki of Erzurum (d. 1780)

Ibrahim Hakki hasn't met his master, Ismail Fakirullah, yet. In coming to him, Ibrahim begins from afar. He sends greetings by invoking the Divine Names. Now, Ismail Fakirullah accepts them with Verse. Sometimes the beginning, at other times the middle or end of Verses. Yes! He accepts them, 'And upon you peace, upon you peace.'

When he arrives at the door, the greetings end. He's inside, that is. He's got inside. These greetings have been written down and hang near his head now [the head of his tomb].

The wrath of silence

Ibrahim Hakki asks for some water from a child. The child goes to draw water. A horseman comes along, he's going to water his horse. The child comes back: 'He hurled the jug on the ground and broke it.' Ibrahim Hakki says, 'Run back and swear at him!' The horseman was washing the hoof of his horse, the horse gives a kick, his brains are knocked in. Ibrahim Hakki says, 'What a pity. My child, if you'd sworn at him or thrown a stone, this wouldn't have happened.' He was from a neighboring village. They come and take away his body.

So if you say, 'You barbarian!' or something, that state will pass from him. The ego is strongest on three points: to be driven away, love and money.

Ali Sebti (d. 1870)

Ali Sebti, they're sayyids, too. He came from Baghdad, he settled in the village of Palu (Elazığ). Hodja Bakir didn't let him go.

Shaykh Ali Sebti was going from Palu to Bingöl [on horseback]. A wolf took hold of the stirrup. Ali Sebti said something to the wolf. They asked what it was all about. The wolf had said, 'Don't let my offspring perish this year.' 'Go and look, but don't go near.' Indeed, they saw that the wolf was suckling its young.

Mahmud Samini (d. 1895)

They're going to Ali Sebti in Palu from a village. Some of them used to come and go. Samini looks, he's from the same village, he listens to the discussions, he says, 'Take me there too, sometime.' Today, tomorrow, time passes.

He had a mother. He had an animal, he goes to the mountain and cuts wood. He brings and sells it. That's his job, Samini's.

One day he goes for wood again, he sees another convoy going towards Palu. They're people he knows from his village. He asks, 'Where are you going?' 'We're going to the Master.' 'May I come too?' 'Come along.' They went there together. The boy was thirty years old when they met.

They stayed the night. They ate and drank. In the end, Ali Sebti gathered all the leftovers together, whatever's left! He took a spoon himself, 'Come on, eat.' They finished that, too.

At the end, it was the season for pears, they brought in a tray. After supper. They all took one each. They're all full, there's no space left in any of them. There was half a trayful left. He saw Mahmud eat one or two with zest, 'Eat, have another, son.' 'Another one, son, go ahead.' He finished them all. He said, 'Bravo, son, and you score the goal, too.' They went to bed. They got up for the Dawn Prayer, had breakfast and set out on their way back.

As they left, his friends asked: 'Mahmud, did the Master say anything to you, did he give anything?' [Usually a 'lesson' – a *dhikr* to recite with concentration.] 'No.' He was pure and simple. 'He was going to give you something, friend, didn't he say anything?'

He left them there and went back. He came and knocked on the door, the Master opened it. 'Speak up,' he said, looking at him.

'What's your name?' he asked. 'Mahmud, sir,' he said. 'Why did you come?' 'You're giving something to everyone, sir. My friends said so. You didn't give me anything.' 'Oh! Look at me.' He looks and immediately lowers his eyes. 'I looked, sir.' Courtesy! He never saw anyone. He lived like that.

'Look again.' 'Again.' He had him look at him three times. 'Son, would you recognize me if you saw me somewhere?' 'I would, sir.' 'Run along,' he said. 'Don't forget, okay?' Yes, that's all! 'Go.'

He's running to catch up with his friends, when he gets tired he turns back, 'Master, I haven't forgotten.' This is very good!

He catches up with his friends, 'Peace upon you,' they say. 'What did you do?'

Two or three years later they went again with their friends, he favored Mahmud above all the rest: 'Mahmud, why don't you come and go, son? Are you busy?' 'No, sir I'm not busy, either.' 'Well then, why don't you come, son?' 'I'm ashamed to, sir. Why should I come and bother you?'

That night they went to bed again and departed in the morning. The second or third day he went back to the mountain. He's cutting wood with the axe, 'Master ...' *Always* like that: 'Master, I haven't forgotten.' 'Master, I haven't forgotten.'

Two years go by. 'Peace upon you,' says ... the Master! He looks, 'And upon you peace, Master, I haven't forgotten.' He smiles. 'That's why I came,' he says.

'Master, where are you coming from, where are you going?' He says, 'I had a friend in that village over there, I saw him and dropped by to see you.'

They sit there and talk for a while. 'Well, goodbye,' he says. He says, 'Master, I can't forget, but please don't forget me, either.' 'No, no, Mahmud, I won't,' he says. 'From now on, we shall always be together.'

They say that from that day on, he's always with the Master. Always. At the mountain, lying in bed, getting up, they're always together.

In his last days he falls ill, [his disciples ask:] 'Master, may you live long, who shall we go to after you?' He says, 'There's a Mahmud in that village, he'll manage you.' They bring him to Palu and place him in a house, he settles there. They're both buried at Palu in Elazığ [Turkey] now.

So that was Mahmud Samini's lesson: 'Master, I haven't forgotten you.' He became Samini [*Thamini*, 'Eighth' – the eighth renewer of the Naqshi way] later.

That's how he found it, sir. Yes. To act with *courtesy*. To speak little. To be in that *presence*, that repose. *To find the Master. Aha.* This is the goal. It's very easy, but only if you can do it. Very easy! When you leave, take me with you if you can.

There are twenty-four hours in a day. Think about me for one hour, then you'll always see me. If we saw each other just once and didn't forget, that'd be enough. Love and discourses are good. But in the way of God and His Prophet, not to forget. Look at my hair and my beard, do whatever you're going to do. Take a photocopy of me, girl!

Don't look at the floor, look at the center of my forehead. [Because the Light of Muhammad is at the center of the saint's forehead. No angel was able to place that light in Adam, God Himself placed it there when He was adoring His own beauty.]⁵

Othman Badruddin (1858–1922)

Othman Badruddin attained by repeating: 'Oh Samini, Oh Samini.' Samini was very advanced in the esoteric, while Imam Efendi (Othman Badruddin) was very advanced in exoteric knowledge. Consider: a sea becomes attached to a lake. One should be either Imam Efendi or Shaykh Samini. Be either one or the other, then things will straighten out.

Episode 1: how they met

This is how this story comes down to us. Imam Efendi was a Prayer-leader in the army. He requested leave. His orderly was from Palu. He arrived in Palu with the orderly in the evening. It was winter, like this.

He said, 'You're from here.' 'Yes, I am.' He asks, 'Do you know any place here where we can stay?' 'Sir,' he says, 'there's such-and-such a man of knowledge.' 'How is he?' he asks. 'He's good,' he says. 'All right, let's go to him,' he says. So they go.

The ways and states of Imam Efendi are very refined. He used to shun cigarette smoke.

---

5. '[T]he disciple must ... hold the master's image in his imagination even when they are separated, and [drive] all other thoughts and memories from his heart, leaving only the form and memories of his master.

'There is no closer way than this. If the enlightened face of that master – perhaps the middle of his eyebrows – does not leave his mind for even a second, if he is not heedless of it while sitting, standing or eating, if he can always bear it in mind – and this is quite difficult to achieve for the disciple – the wayfarer reaches such a rank in the end that the image of the perfect master takes root in his heart, and he can imagine it at every instant without difficulty.

'But if courtesy (good manners) is violated, this path of illumination can be interrupted in the disciple. It is then very difficult to re-establish ...' – from Henry Bayman, 'The Spiritual Journey of the Sufi,' in *The Meaning of the Four Books*; also in *The Secret of Islam: Love and Law in the Religion of Ethics*, Berkeley, CA: North Atlantic Books, 2003, p. 262 (taken from Ibrahim Hakki of Erzurum, *The Book of Gnosis*). That is to say, the image of the master, which is intimately linked to his spirituality, must become permanently emblazoned on the disciple's consciousness. This is achieved through concentration and abundant respect (courtesy).

The Base Self tries its hardest to make one forget one's master. Here's the yardstick: when you shut your eyes, can you easily visualize your Master?

They became his guests.

They ate supper. They did the Night Prayer. After Prayer, they filled the pipe of Mahmud Samini, they brought it and gave it to him. He smoked. Imam Efendi is his guest, he's sitting across from him. At one point he said, 'Maybe you shouldn't smoke this.' Because outside, he shuns even its smell. Mahmud Samini said, 'What's necessary for one who doesn't prostrate to God?' [See Episode 2 below.] 'Hellfire.' 'Well, I'm burning this here. What's wrong with that?'

Othman Badruddin said to himself, 'I've come to the wrong place. May God forgive my error.'

Towards dawn, Imam Efendi has a dream. In the dream, they go to the mosque. They finish the Prayer behind the Prayer-leader (imam). He turns around, [he's smoking] a cigarette. Imam Efendi is very angry. He looks, the imam is the man who is his host. While he's still in that [dream], Samini gets up, says 'Good Morning' to everyone, looks at the time and says, 'It's close to dawn, let's go for the Prayer.' Imam Efendi pulls himself together, this is what he was just seeing in his dream. He gets up, takes an Ablution and does his Wakeup Prayer. They go to the mosque for the Dawn Prayer. They perform the Prayer.

Samini lights a cigarette. He says, 'It'd be nice if I hadn't got used to this thing, but I did. Now I can't abandon it.' He gives a discourse. They have breakfast. That day, Imam Efendi measures Samini there in terms of knowledge and state. He asks, 'Do you have masterhood?' 'Yes,' he says. 'Can you describe a Divine Name, a prayer for me?' He gives him his lesson there and that day. 'It would be good if you did these. When you have time, do your Extra Prayers, they're good,' he says. He gives his lesson, they depart. So even though there are thousands, Imam Efendi wins the first prize. Othman ceases to be Othman.

Episode 2: years later

In the time of Othman Badruddin, there was a man called Hassan in Istanbul, his master was Hussein. He heard of Imam Efendi's fame, he came over. He found him after a month-long trip. He saw that Imam Efendi is loading his pipe with tobacco and smoking it. His heart sank. He said to himself, 'Is this what I made this month-long journey for?'

They go to bed at night. In his dream, Hassan sees that they're drinking coffee after the Dawn Prayer and he's lighting Imam Efendi's pipe with a cinder. Right after that, Imam Efendi wakes him up, 'Hassan, get up, let's do the Wakeup Prayer, then we'll do the Dawn Prayer.' They do the Wakeup Prayer first, then they go to the mosque and do the Dawn Prayer. When they return from the mosque, it was Imam Efendi's custom, they used to drink a cup of coffee after each Dawn Prayer. The coffee is served, Imam Efendi takes out his pipe and fills it with tobacco. When he's about to light it, Hassan says, 'May I light your pipe, sir?' Imam Efendi says, 'Light it, child.' That's his only remark!

Hassan Efendi was very learned, too. Imam Efendi says, 'Hassan, as you know, all animals and plants prostrate to God, they invoke God in their own language [as is stated in Verse 17:44 of the Quran]. Only one plant wouldn't prostrate to God: tobacco.'

Hassan said, 'Sir, what you just said is written in this book, this page, this line.'

Imam Efendi said, 'Well, son, everyone does things over here and receives his punishment on the other side. So let's burn in this world, so what?'

Who's who?

Mehmed Sa'id was a captain in the army. He first came to Pötürge, where he became attached to Imam Efendi Othman Badruddin. When the British stir up Yemen, they send him to Yemen.

One day Mehmet Sa'id rushes to the Friday Prayer in a sweat. There's a poor man there, he says, 'Charity, sir!' Sa'id says, 'I'm in a hurry.' The poor man clings to his leg, he shakes him off.

He came back. When he returned home, he went to Othman Badruddin and said, 'What kind of master are you? You don't teach these Brits their lesson.' Yes, just like that! And he replies, 'Yes, child, I held on to your leg but you shook me off.'

Shoo fly!

During World War I, the Russians are at the door. Together with the local governor, the townspeople went to Othman Badruddin. 'Master, should we flee?' At that moment, a tray of grapes is brought in and offered, there are flies on it. He shooed away the flies with his hands. 'What are you afraid of? They're of less significance than these flies. They'll go, just like I'm shooing these flies away. *Begone!*'

As they left, the governor said, 'He didn't pray.' Those of his circle who were in the know said, 'He did, he did.' Two days later, the Russian army beat a retreat.

Wild but obedient

Even cats and dogs obeyed Othman Badruddin. One day in winter, they saw this as they were carrying a sick person. A couple of dogs are chasing a wolf, they're going to kill it. He calls out to the wolf. The wolf comes and lays its head on his knee. He says to the dogs: 'Stop,' they stop and wait. He tells the dogs, 'Go away, it didn't harm you.' He turns to the wolf: 'And you, don't bother anyone's cattle or herd again,' the wolf leaves.

Musa Kâzim Efendi (1896–1967)

Before Kâzim Efendi became a teacher, that is, while he was a student, a lot of students became attached to Imam Efendi. Then he separated and went to France to be educated. He came back a month later when the war [World War I] began. His knowledge remains in place. When Imam Efendi dies, Hodja Mustafa Naci substitutes for him.

Kâzim Efendi served Mustafa Naci a lot. When he found the chance, that is. His attachment is to Imam Efendi. His service is not to Imam Efendi, but to Mustafa Naci [who was Imam Efendi's disciple]. He served Mustafa Naci in his last days when he was paralyzed. He did his toilet cleaning and fed him.

He was [trained as a school] teacher, but he didn't teach. He suffered a lot of poverty, of misery. He tried to awaken many. He was the master of Erzurum, of Elazığ, everywhere. He continued for thirty-forty years.

When I come to think of it, we're the ones who killed the masters. Kâzim Efendi, too. They slandered him a lot. I know the gossip they made about him.

I went to Kâzim Efendi in his last days. We went for the Evening Prayer. He showed me the repairs to the mosque. What strength do I have to pray for the master? It came like that. I said:

'May your congregation be crowded, may your life be long, may your sustenance be prosperous, may your deeds be well-accepted.'

He made me repeat it three times. He said, 'Where did you learn that?' This prayer isn't written anywhere. 'Well, there are Verses and Sayings to that effect, I just said it now.' 'Bravo,' he said, 'you've prayed a nice prayer. God willing, may it be so.'

Hajji Ahmet Kaya Efendi (Keko) (1881–1944)

Hajji Efendi was from the Ikizpinar (Ali Bey) village in the Kale (Izol) County in Malatya. He was the son of Othman, he took lessons from Keshef Hodja when he was fifteen. He was a successor of Hajji Othman Badruddin [in the chain of transmission] in Harput, Elazığ. He supervised the Naqshi Order until his death. He was the Pole of the Age, he was the Owner of the Trust. He was a very great man. Hajji Ahmet Efendi died on May 7, 1944, in the afternoon. He was delivered to his place of eternal rest at his own home town.

[Othman Badruddin had three good students: Mustafa Naci, Musa Kâzim Efendi and Ahmet Kaya. They were all fellow-students under Othman Badruddin. When the latter died, several of his prominent students held a meeting. At that meeting, Ahmet Kaya told Mustafa Naci: 'Mustafa, we need a leader. I pledge allegiance to you.' So Mustafa Naci presided over matters until he died.

Unfortunately, Mustafa Naci did not live long. He presided for two or three years after Othman Badruddin, roughly between 1922 and 1925. After that, it was Ahmet Kaya's turn until his death in 1944, and then Kâzim Efendi's turn, who tried to fill in for the master's place until his death in 1967.

Several – probably five – years after Othman Badruddin's death, Hajji Ahmet Kaya visited Othman Badruddin's tomb at Harput, Elazığ. There, he spent three days and three nights without a bite to eat and without a drop of water, in constant Prayer and supplication. At the end of that period, the desired result was obtained. In essence, this is the resolve: 'Until I reach Enlightenment, I will not move from this spot.'

Not all saints possess the same degree of Realization. This is a matter of talent, effort and the grace of God. For example, it is said that Ibrahim Hakki was superior in realization to his own master. Now Mustafa Naci and Musa Kâzim were not of the same caliber as Ahmet Kaya. But even after his own Realization, Ahmet Kaya let Kâzim Efendi preside over the affairs of the people. He preferred to remain in the background.

Even in the case of Ahmet Kayhan, his immediate successor, Ahmet Kaya sent him to Musa Kâzim as well, so that Ahmet Kayhan received instruction from both masters. But his real master was Ahmet Kaya.

Both Ahmet Efendis, the first and the second, were paragons of humility. They didn't advertise themselves. They became known only gradually. Only Keko's close family knew that Ahmet Kayhan had been chosen. And he himself never said, 'He left his place to me.']

I had a master, he wasn't human, he wasn't the son of man [i.e., he was superhuman]. If he's sitting here like this, he would stand up [out of courtesy] if a cat walked by. Reckon our situation by that measure.

God knows, the transmission was from Imam Efendi to Hajji Efendi. That's how I divine it. Hajji Efendi swallowed all those before him. Hajji Efendi, who could bend space and time, who could make it rain and stop the wind. I wanted to see the Pole of the Age, I saw Hajji Ahmet Efendi in my dream.

Truly a great man. What do they call it? 'Perfect Human.' God bless them. I mourn one thing: we weren't able to benefit. He flowed away like the Euphrates River for fifty years. Until he departed, he cast sciences before us such as I've never seen in books, we couldn't appropriate any of them. We went, we listened, we disturbed.

May God not separate us from those we love. Love is of two kinds: one is selfish, the other is Compassionate. May He not separate us from Compassionate love.

They told him, 'Someone wants sainthood,' he answered, 'Give it to him.' They said, 'Another wants to be a dervish,' he said, 'I'm a dervish, I'm a seeker.' That's how one should be. He used to say, 'Don't talk too much with [ordinary] hodjas.' He was a hodja himself, he wouldn't get angry with externalist hodjas, nor did he attach value to them. He would tell me, 'Don't mind them, they're hodjas.'

Encounter with his master

Hajji Ahmet Efendi [or Hajji Efendi for short] finished his military duty. He searches for years for a friend, a master. Othman Badruddin is invited by a *bey* [local chieftain] to Malatya. Then, a man who had an open Eye of the Heart tells Ahmet Kaya, 'I know what you're looking for.' Thus he finds Imam Efendi.

One evening, they had supper with his family, he was sitting. A *majdhub* [madman of God], with hair and beard all disheveled, knocked on the door. He asked for some food, they gave some to him. After eating, he said, 'You're looking for a friend. He's arrived at Malatya. I'll be waiting for you tomorrow evening, we'll go to him.'

This is the first time Ahmet Efendi has ever seen this man. 'Who are you?' he asked. He replied, 'I'm from Malatya. Find me tomorrow evening at the location I describe.'

He got up for the Dawn Prayer, the *majdhub* was gone. He performed the Prayer. That evening he went and found the *majdhub*. He walked for six hours from Izol to Malatya. He found the man at his home, all he has is a straw mat and a pillow, he's in a miserable state. The *majdhub* said, 'You're a good man. You're going to be good.' They did the Evening Prayer. The *majdhub* said, 'We're going somewhere now. The person whose hand I kiss, you kiss his hand, too.'

The *majdhub* enters the door and presents his greetings. He went directly to Imam Efendi and kissed his hand. Hajji Ahmet Efendi goes after him and kisses his hand, too. Imam Efendi says to the person sitting beside him, 'Get up,' and makes Ahmet Efendi sit there.

They do the Night Prayer at the Söğütlü Mosque (New Mosque). Right after Prayer, Hajji Ahmet Efendi began to recite the Quran. He used to recite the Quran with a very beautiful, moving voice. There, too, he began to recite in that congregation. '*I take refuge in God from the accursed Satan. In the name of God, the Compassionate, the Merciful.*' He begins to recite the Chapter of Ta-Ha (Chapter 20).

Before he's finished a third of it, Imam Efendi interrupts him: 'Enough. *God Almighty is the Speaker of Truth. The Opening!*'[6] He called the *majdhub* over and thanked him. 'Where did you find this man?' he asked. 'He burned me up.' And to Hajji Ahmet Efendi: 'If you seek me, I'm at Harput, across the street from the Hamidiye Mosque.' That's how he found a friend.

Trials and tribulations

[It is not to be supposed that the training of a master is an easy task. As Othman Badruddin himself remarks in a book, 'Even under the best of circumstances, the transmission from master to disciple is extremely difficult.' Ahmet Kaya went through a comparable battery of tests, as the following account shows.]

I was present one day at another of his discussions. [He told the following story:]

> A man was doing his military service. Among two- or three-storey houses, he saw one that was five stories high, with walnut boards and

---

6. It is customary to finish any Quranic recitation with these words. Then, everyone present silently pronounces Blessings on the Prophet and recites the Opening Chapter (first chapter) of the Quran, and ends by saying, 'Amen.'

gold plating. He became curious. He knocked on the door. A servant opened it and said, 'Let me inform the Master.' Then he gave him some money and shut the door. Three or four hours later, he came back: 'I want to see the Master.' The servant gave him a bundle of clothes. The third time around, the servant asked: 'Are you crazy?' 'I won't leave until I see the Master.' So the servant informed him.

'What do you want, son?' 'Master, I want neither clothes nor money.' 'What *do* you want with me?' 'Where are you from?' 'Never mind me, where are *you* from?' 'I'm from Izol.'

'Take this man and beat him until he's either dead or he doesn't come back.'

He came again, he's in terrible shape. 'What have you all done? And *you*, why did you come back?'

'What's my fault this time, why did you do this to me? My grandfather enjoined on my father, and my father enjoined on me. Lying and illness comes here from Izol. Master, together with this beating, may I kiss your hand?' 'Kiss it, but don't tell: you've taken the trust from the Prophet of God by force.'

That's the most valuable: to take by force.[7] [Imam Efendi: 'If it's for God, excessive ambition is a cause of Attainment.'] That is, he drove him away fifty times, but he didn't give up. He was so dedicated to his master that he won through being driven away many times.

When he speaks of the soldier, Ahmet Efendi is actually speaking of himself. He used to tell this, everyone would think it's someone else. Years later my mind cleared a little bit, I understood that it was he who did it all, who experienced it all. Saints and shaykhs don't tell events in the form: 'Why and how this happened to me.' They tell it with a story, a simile. For example, he said, 'Someone visited Battal Gazi's tomb once.' *It's himself.* He always spoke like that.

The invitation

[After Hajji Efendi had attained Realization, he told his elder daughter], 'Climb to the top of that hill and call to all sides, "The Holy Sanctuary is open, come."' The girl said, 'I can't do it.' 'Inwardly, not outwardly.'

---

7. Nietzsche's Zarathustra: 'and what you can seize upon, you shall not allow to be given you' (*Thus Spoke Zarathustra*, 3.12:4, Thomas Common translation modernized). C.G. Jung attributes this to the right to become a superman (in his *Nietzsche's 'Zarathustra'*).

The girl climbed up there, she turned toward Mecca and began. In the evening, it's a narrow time, twenty or thirty people came. His first regard was to that village. They did the Evening Prayer and came over. They stayed that night, piled up on top of each other. That's how it started. I remembered this over Abraham. [When the construction of the Ka'ba was finished, God ordered the prophet Abraham to face all sides and invite human beings to the Ka'ba to do the Pilgrimage.]

The course of the Saintlight

Hajji Ahmet Efendi said, 'A sacred trust, a Light' – sainthood, I now understand – 'originated in Mecca. It went to Medina, suffered a lot there.' – See what they did, they didn't give any peace to the children of the Prophet. – 'Then it passed to Bukhara. It stayed there for five hundred years. Then it came to Malatya. Now it's in your village, among us.' He didn't give a name. Later he said to me, 'The brakes slipped and I told everything. Good thing nobody understood.' He would take one's mind first and then put the subject. He would tell, then cover it.

A different lesson

His son Siddik told me the following event:

> I was ten or fifteen years old, I'm serving. [My elder brother] Zeynel had gone to do his military service, it was that time. A ranch owner arrived on his horse, Ali Agha from Bashkir, Elazığ.
>
> The horseman bent his neck low and entered the outer courtyard that way. He got off the horse, he asked, 'There's a Hajji Efendi here, where does he stay?' I said, 'He's in the guest room.' He said, 'Take my horse, take good care of it.' Command, always by command.
>
> I took the horse over and secured it, I gave it some fodder. I made some coffee and went over, there are other visitors.
>
> He slept there that night, I took him some food in the morning. He said, 'Hajji Efendi, I'm from Bashkir, from such-and-such a district. They call me Ali Agha. I own a lot of land, I have many servants, workers and cattle.'
>
> 'That's very good, Ali Agha, very good.'
>
> 'You're giving everyone a *tasbih* [double meaning: prayer beads, or a lesson to be recited on beads]. Would you give me too?' [It's the second he intends.]

My father laughed. He took out and gave him his own rosary from his pocket.

He asked: 'Isn't there anything else?' He said, 'There is, Ali Agha, there is something.' 'Well, give me that too.' 'I will, I will.'

'Do you have servants?'

'Yes, I do, servants, workers, male, female.'

'You're not going to get angry with them. You're going to consider them your own children. You're not going to get mad at your family. Whatever the farmhands give you, you're going to accept as is, you're not going to lose your temper.'

My father counted these off. He replied, 'Hajji, this is a bit difficult, but – it's a bit difficult. Anything else?' 'No. Just these things. I also gave you the rosary. Do your Prayers, don't hurt anyone's feelings. Earn legitimately, eat legitimately, don't follow your ego.'

'Thanks,' he said. 'Well, goodbye.'

I led the horse outside, my father came to the outer door with us. He got on his horse and went back to Elazığ.

It was harvest time when Ali Agha came again.

I tied the horse, I made some coffee, I went, there were other guests. I served the coffee. As I was collecting the empty cups, he said, 'Hajji Efendi, I've made a mistake.

'I said yes to everything, I thought it was easy. Now I don't get angry with the servants. You gave me a lesson.' – See, he considers that a lesson, a duty. – 'I can't get angry with the servant. I can't say anything to the woman [my wife].

'The farmhands steal the harvest, I don't say anything. One or two sheep disappear from the herd … This is tough business. It's not for me. Take your prayer beads back.'

He took the rosary out of his pocket, he set it down, he said: 'Hajji Efendi, I have businesses, I have harvests, this is as far as I go. I came because of the beads,' he said. 'Take your rosary, these things are hard. I can't do them. Goodbye.'

My father laughed, as he bade me farewell I told him: 'My father said, "Ali Agha, the hook's already in place. You're going to come back, what can I do?"'

He went, he came back a year later. 'Hajji, for God's sake, give me back my rosary!'

Against superstition

Villagers used to tie rags to a tree. Ahmet Efendi came, he saw that they were all tying rags and things. [Superstition.] He came with his horse, he said: '*Tsk!* Cut it down!' A villager there threw him a stone: 'How *dare* you cut it!' Whereupon the convoy departed. Six years later, they killed the same man in the same place, with a stone like the one he threw. People have perverted [true religion].

The fruits of one's deeds

Two brethren, one was two years older than me, went to visit Hajji Ahmet Efendi. They made a lot of harmful gossip. [They needed to be taught a lesson.] The next morning, there was a willow – timber – in the yard, he said, 'Chop this up, we're going to burn it.' They strike and strike, all they can manage is a four-inch crack.

It's past noon, Hajji Efendi does the Afternoon Prayer. 'What happened? Didn't you use the axe at all?' 'Master, we hit it thousands of times, it's just no use.'

'Give that to me,' he says, and hits with the axe – but parallel to the grain, not perpendicular to it. He chops it into little pieces, 'There,' he tells them.

Family life

Kâzim Efendi lived well with his wife, Hatija. But Ahmet Efendi did not live well with Mother White ['Beyaz' – her first name]. It was cooking all day long.

[Mother White was a very slim, very well-groomed lady. She was very merciful. She and Ahmet Efendi were cousins. She died twenty-one years after her husband, in 1965.]

Four or five daughters, three sons. How did they stand it, how did they manage, Hajji Efendi, Mother White? You're in Paradise now. In her last days, Hajji Ahmet Efendi's mother asked Mother White, 'What did you see?' 'I didn't see anything. Bake bread, cook wheat. Bake bread, cook wheat. Nothing else.' And they have eight or nine kids. Now all people are in Paradise. You're in heaven. If you could only appreciate it, you're all in heaven. I'm thinking now, we killed the Man.

A house like a hotel

A child's paternal aunt was a relative of Hajji Efendi. One day, at his mother's instigation, he went to visit them. He saw people, some with their feet extended, others sleeping. *He* feels ashamed for *their* condition. Hajji Efendi said, 'Don't mind them, child, these are cosmopolitan people.' When he went back home, his aunt said, 'What you saw is nothing. There's worse.'

I went to my Master one day. I'm going to stay there that night. He spoke to me after everyone left. He said: 'This place is a district. They come from forty or fifty kilometers' distance, they bring me matters that should be solved by a judge, a governor, a doctor, a district official, a watchman. How am I going to do all this? I'm trying to rescue people from the Base Self. If I were to do the duties of a doctor, a judge, they'd be out of a job.' Yes, he said it fifty years ago. 'I work all day long but it's no use. "Sir, give us some advice." Are they crazy, or am I crazy?'

Incomprehension

There was a man, he would swear at Hajji Efendi if he even got mad at his wife. He came one day. The Master said, 'Someone here loves us.' But he's swearing at him every day! Hajji Efendi told him the following story:

'Someone like you went to Malatya. He was going to buy linen. It's fifty pennies a yard. "Can't we make it forty?" "No." "Let's ask your neighbor." They asked, he's selling it for sixty pennies. "What's your name?" he asked. The shop owner said, "Ahmet."'

The man doesn't understand anything, he's smoking his pipe.

'"What's your name? Tomorrow I'm going to complain about you to Muhammad." The shop owner was smart, he immediately begged pardon from the customer: "Don't report me to Muhammad."'

I want to signal him to kiss his hand, he doesn't look, he wouldn't understand. It wouldn't do to say it.

We stepped out together [with my Master]. He told me, 'I must have done something wrong again.' 'Perish the thought,' I said. He said, 'I force open their mouths, give it from between their teeth, they still vomit even that. They won't mature until the time comes. The man wants honey, you give him garlic, he doesn't accept it.' This kind of thing has happened several times to me, too.

A glass of water

During the Second World War, I went to see Hajji Efendi. One day, we went to visit a family. There was a mulberry tree. I ran and fetched a cushion and pillow. His mouth is dry, it's a summer day, the Man is sick. He asked for water. There was a woman at the doorway. Where did you get it, where did you bring it? A jug, a cup, she ran and fetched them before I could move. Ahmet Efendi took a sip and sent it to me. Did you fly? She appeared beside me.

Twenty years later I went there. I returned in order to kiss that mulberry tree from the heart, without showing anyone, because my Master sat there. Now I'm keeping track of that woman. I received news from her a few years ago. Her sons went to Istanbul, she has a villa on the Bosphorus. She became that rich. What mysteries are these, sir?

I want to see that woman. I want to see her because she brought that water barefoot.

Prompt retribution

The captain of the military police asks: 'Who are you, what do you do?' [Hajji Efendi] explains, 'I'm from Elazığ, I'm a Naqshi, my Master is this.' The captain gives him two slaps on the face: 'You don't even deny it! Throw him in jail.'

In the afternoon, news arrives that a town has been invaded by bandits. That captain goes. Before he enters the village, he receives two bullets on his forehead. Hassan, who knew the Master, went to the judge and explained: 'This is the situation. If you don't release him, you'll receive two bullets, too.' He was released.

His Spacefolding

Mehmet relates the following:

> On my way [to a fountain], I got angry with Hajji Efendi. All of a sudden, I found myself beside the fountain.[8] I was so scared, I had to stay in bed for a week. A week later, Hajji Efendi asked: 'Were you frightened?'
>
> I wanted to make some coffee, there wasn't any. Hajji Efendi came, he said: 'There's coffee in our house, fetch some from there,'

---

8. That is, Hajji Efendi instantly teleported him there by Spacefolding.

and gave me the key. I went there running. I looked, Hajji Efendi was there. 'Welcome, Mehmet.' I went back running, he's back there again. 'Are you scared? These are small things. Don't tell anyone, otherwise you'll receive the slap.' I was so scared, I had to stay in bed for another month.

His death

Keko [Kurdish for 'Father'] went just at the right time, at sixty-three [the age at which the Prophet died].

I said to him, 'Stay a bit longer. Let me go in your stead.' He replied, 'You're needed. My time is up, let's not exceed it. I could live longer if I wanted to, but it's not necessary. Give me two days.' He lived two more days and departed.

When he was about to die, I entered his room, he's lying down. Mother White put two spotless-clean pillows on a chair, she said to me, 'Sit down, sir.' I pushed them aside with my hand, I sat to the side and gave the burden to my knees. I thought to myself, 'It's needless that I should live.' He smiled slightly, 'No,' he said, 'everyone has to take their turn. [Everyone has their own life to live.]' His brother Kasim came in, he said, 'Take him and go outside.' We went, we came back, his eyes were open. He went just like that, without batting an eye.

Mother White and his brothers asked me, 'Should we bury him today or tomorrow?' I said, 'What strength do I have? Let's do it today, tomorrow this place will be packed.' His brother Ibrahim said, 'I think so, too.' He 'walked to the Real' [journeyed to God] in the afternoon, we buried him at the Evening Prayer.

[In Islam, the corpse is washed and shrouded before burial.] During washing, there was a hodja who was his close friend. They had agreed between themselves: 'I'll wash you if you die first, otherwise you'll wash me.' We raised the corpse. The hodja is old, I went over to his left side. The hodja struck the Master's arm on the surface with a *thud*. That night, one of his daughters saw him in a dream, his arm was bandaged. He said, 'The hodja struck it, we wrapped it up, it's nothing important. I was going to get up and say, "What are you doing?" But the hodja would have passed out, he would've died, I didn't get up so as not to make things difficult for Ahmet.'

The Master went, everything ended.

The aftermath

After Hajji Efendi, his disciples fell upon each other. They went haywire. After Hajji Efendi, nobody passed through his door. He said, 'A man came from behind that mountain and took away everything.' That's Hajji Ahmet [Kayhan] Efendi in Ankara.

Post-mortem appearances

He said, 'Lessons continue after the master dies.' [That is, disciples continue with their homework just as if the master had not died.] They saw him at his grave.

After Hajji Efendi dies, he appears to someone during Prayer. He sees his foot, the hem of his robe. *Thud!* He falls down unconscious. His brow is soothed on the one hand while he hears Hajji Efendi's voice on the other: 'You saw my foot and this is what happened. What would happen if you saw *me?*' There are *thousands* of examples like this, thousands.

Now, fifty years later, he's still managing [everyone], I'm not doing anything. Which means he's Living, that is. He can add a thousand lives to a life.

I once asked the Master, 'What will we do if you leave?' Here's how he replied: 'His disciples asked Abdul Qadir Gilani the same thing, he answered: "Children, call out to me. I'll emerge from my grave and come."'

It was four to five months after Ahmet Efendi departed. I went to visit Mother White. A visitor came. Mother White began to talk to him: 'Get along well with your children,' and so on. Both her state and her cigarette-smoking were identical to the Master's.

I stepped outside. After the visitor left, Mother White came over to me. 'Why did you run away?' she asked. 'I was annoyed,' I said. She said, 'Forgive these poor people. One has to manage them.' Again, both her voice and her comport were the same as the Master's.[9]

---

9. I can testify that this happens. After my own Master, Ahmet Kayhan, passed away, we observed similar behavior in his wife, Mother Hajar. We knew her intimately well, and the Master exhibited a class of speech and behavior that was totally alien to her nature. Yet after he departed, we would at times see Mother Hajar in exactly that mode of conduct and speech so foreign to her constitution. At such times, it was as if the Master was speaking from her mouth. Yet she was aged and in no position to fake such a show.

Hajji Ahmet Kayhan (1898–1998)

I had a sultan, a Master. A true friend found me. He protected me. He took whatever was in me and left himself in that place. I gave one life, he gave a thousand lives. He loved me very much, I wasn't aware of it. Just when I noticed it, he went away. Just as I was about to understand something, the true friend left. Just as one comes to one's senses, just as we're about to really understand something, the *true friend* departs. What can you do.

I had a Master. He lived in Malatya for forty-five years. He used to solve problems with two words. It's been forty-five years since he passed into the Realm of the Everlasting. I love him more than my own body and soul. That love still continues.

When Keko left, my power and strength departed with him. He went, but he left the burden of the entire world with me. Everything ended when the Master left. He went, love went, too.

[One of his sons] once said: 'I thought to myself, 'Where did my father find Ahmet in the middle of the village, the forest, when there were so many scholars and virtuous people in Malatya?' Why did my father leave it to you, rather than to learned and cultured men?' If he knew, if he loved, he would burn. If he loved, there would be no [he] left.[10] Wisdom – that's what's necessary, wisdom.

A friend should love a friend. A friend should have exchanges with a friend. We sat somewhere with Hajji Ahmet Efendi, we went somewhere together. These are still in my mind. We sat here, for instance.

I understand now that he put me through many tests. He made me know myself. He did so many things, I wasn't aware of any of them. He tested me a lot. He found a bit of refinement – refinement of intelligence – in me, and a little ethics. Otherwise, what else do I have?

I used to listen to Verse and Saying without drawing any distinction. And I would heed my Master's words as if they were Sayings. Whatever Hajji Ahmet Efendi told someone in my presence, I would accept it as if he had told it directly to me.

I received grace through the medium of Hajji Efendi, but I don't know how come. I love worship a lot. I love people very much. I feel

---

10. A Sufi saying goes: 'Love desires that nothing exist at all except the Beloved.' This also explains a conversation between the Master and one of his granddaughters. The granddaughter said: 'How much everybody loves you, Grandpa!' He replied: 'Nobody loves me except you.' When this was disputed, he remarked: 'Maybe they don't know *how* to love.'

sorrow for everyone's worries, I try to solve them. So I think that maybe among all those bandits, I was the one he found best.

When I think about myself, I realize that I found myself in good hands. When I think about my life, I say, 'What would have happened otherwise?' *Aha!* I received my training after I was twenty-four or twenty-five. What would have happened to me if I hadn't found myself in those hands? I would have become a bandit.

It's been forty-six years, when the self begins to move from one side, I still take refuge in him, I say: 'Come quickly!'

A master asked his student: 'Son, you're surrounded by dogs. What do you do?' 'I drive them away.' That's the wrong answer. He said, 'Come back a year later.' When the disciple came back, he asked him the same question, this time the disciple replied, 'I call out to their owner.'

The self is just the same. Whenever something occurs to me, I bring [my Master] to mind at once, and it passes away.

Although it's been so many years since my Master departed, I still ask his help in a pinch. I still take refuge in him. My Master isn't alive now, but I am. You still don't think of me when you're in difficulties.

Give us what we can bear

One day Hajji Ahmet Efendi came to visit me. I had sprained my foot. He looked at it and said, 'Get well quick, it'll heal.' I said, 'May God give what is best for us.' He turned full-face towards me and said, 'Oh, don't say that! We may not be able to bear what is best for us. Suppose I asked you for a glass of water, you'd go to bring it with *love*, you'd break your leg coming back. You'd say, "What have I done?" if you broke it. Do you know what you're going to say? "May God give us the best *to the extent we can bear it.*"'

Can we carry a hundred kilos? We can easily carry five or ten kilos.

Whatever you do, you do to yourself

Fifty people a day used to visit Hajji Ahmet Efendi. He would listen to troubles, he would fix the problem physically and spiritually, then he would tell them all: 'If you do good you do to yourself, if you do bad you do to yourself [17:7]. Whatever you do, you do to yourself. Now go.' There's a lot here. We were created for good. Let us do good, let's not do ill.

He would also give an example. In the Upper Neighborhood of Malatya, there lived a woman. Her son had gone to do his military service. Now a *majdhub* (madman of God) used to live there, he would wander all day saying, 'If you do good, you do to yourself, if you do bad, you do to yourself.' He wandered like this for *years*.

His home was close to that widow lady, she became sick of his calls. He gets up early in the morning, this is all he does. 'Why,' she said, 'this man is disturbing me.' All by herself. A devil came! There's poisonous rat food, they give it to rats, she bakes bread on a hot plate every morning, she said, 'Let me put one or two in a *pita* [a kind of bread], let me give it to him, let him *go to* hell! Let me get rid of his voice.'

Yes. *And she did it!* She got up early, she put lots of rat poison in the bread, baked it on the hot plate and set it there.

She heard the *majdhub*'s voice. She grabbed it hot, she went to the door. 'Peace upon you. Take this and eat,' she said, early in the morning. He just looked: 'If you do good, you do to yourself. If you do bad ...' That's his sole speech, he never says anything else. He said, 'Whatever you do, you do to yourself,' he took the pita from her and left.

He wandered around for a while. He was going along in the noon heat, he would lie down in the cemetery when he got tired. He's wandering about with the pita in his hand, he goes to the cemetery to the place where he's going to sleep. He leaves that pita on a tombstone, he doesn't eat it.

The son of that woman was a soldier. The boy had obtained leave and was coming home. The cemetery is along his way. He came, he saw the bread there, he's hungry. He knows the *majdhub*. He goes, 'Peace upon you,' 'Upon you peace.' 'Let me eat that bread, I'm hungry.' 'If you do good, you do to yourself. If you do bad ...' The man doesn't say anything else!

Well, that's something the boy's known for a long time. He takes the bread. He's hungry. Before he's finished half of it, *thud!* He falls on the road.

Passers-by recognize him. 'He's that lady's son.' They inform her, the woman comes running and spies half the pita in his hand. The boy is dead. Half of it is in his hand! She tears out her hair, she throws herself on the ground. 'I did this myself, I brought it upon myself, I'm not accusing anyone!' They bring the funeral, they bury the corpse, 'What is this, how did it happen?' 'This is how it happened,' she says. 'I did it myself. I was sick of the madman, I was going to shut him up, I killed my own son.'

This really happened, sir. Hajji Efendi would tell this story, then he would say: 'Go and get along with each other.'

How to see Khidr

Some time during the Second World War, I decided to visit my Master. Before I left, I made a wish: 'During this trip, let me see Khidr.' I climbed a hill. From the top I saw a man and a woman down there petting each other. I sat down and began to watch. The Master's voice – the very same! – manifested itself, 'What is their flirting to you?' I continued on my way, I saw two people. 'These can't be Khidr either,' I said. I went and entered his door. I'm telling it exactly like it is. He said: 'There was someone here just before you. He's been pestering me for three days: "Show me Khidr." I couldn't stand it anymore, I told him to get out before you came.' [He was sitting beside Khidr and asking to see Khidr.] At that instant, I couldn't think to kiss his hand.

Courtesy

Every time I went to my Master, he would stand up even if there were a hundred people there. I went to see him once [at age twelve], the place was crowded. He saw me from afar, he motioned me to come over. His brother was sitting beside him, he made him get up. 'Sit on the cushion,' he said, standing up for me. I made him sit on it. Now that I think of it, it was an error, it was disrespect. He told those present, 'Disperse and wash your faces.' He said to me, 'These creatures have killed me.'

I experienced my first Spacefolding with him when I was eighteen or twenty years old. We wanted to go somewhere to take an Ablution. In an instant we were transported there, I saw that we were taking the Ablution.

The testless test

My Master had a saying: 'We cannot bear a test, may God test us without a test.' If they really test us, we can't pass it. We should all say, 'My God, test us without a test, materially and spiritually.' One's failed two courses, but the teacher says, 'You go ahead and pass, anyway.' That's the testless test.

Quality, not quantity

On the subject of Invocation (*zikr*), do you know what Hajji Ahmet Efendi said? He was very wealthy, with God's permission. Spiritually rich.

'If they place a thousand bullets beside you, and if you shoot until nightfall, what would they do to you if you couldn't hit the target even once? That shame alone is enough for you. Further, they'd give you a month's punishment. Shoot just one, score bull's-eye, that's enough for you. Much Invocation is good, there's a Saying about it, but when you hit the bull's-eye, it's okay even if it's few.' He said that and left.

What a great man he was! Of course, we understood this only at the end. I came and went to him for ten years just like that. I understood who he was only ten years afterwards. If I had known at the beginning, I couldn't have visited him.

Now, I've gathered it all in two points.[11] If you don't do those, it's no use if you were to do a hundred thousand Invocations a day.

Mercy, pleasure, grace, favor

I went to Hajji Ahmet Efendi, in that condition he served me. You know what he said? It was after the Night Prayer, nobody's there. He began with Musa Kâzim Efendi. He said, 'The Master loves you very much. Tell me, what do you want?'

'Aid,' I said. Aid (*himmat*) is effusion, training, care.

'Do you know what that means? A beggar opens his hand –' he put his hand in his pocket, brought out a penny, 'see, a penny, the smallest, one puts it in his hand and goes by. That's all there is to the meaning of aid. Do you know what one ought to wish from the Master? Mercy, pleasure, grace –'

At that moment the thought occurred to me: 'One wishes these from God.' He was going to say more, but my lot must have been that much. '– favor,' he said, and stopped. [I hadn't uttered a word.] He went out. I felt ashamed. I saw him coming back through the door. 'What you say is true. We want from God, too. I heard it from my Master, that's why I said it like that,' he said. He didn't shame me, that is. I had thousands of protests like that. If I had known, if I had kissed his hand, if I could only have said, 'One wishes them from you.'

We see their envelope. Their state is not what we think it is at all. There's a saying of Hamid Wali [also known as 'the Father of Loaves']:

---

11. See Closing the Two Doors.

'We are the Living, we don't die. Don't think we ever go into that dark hole.'

Three questions

Without opening my mouth, I asked Hajji Efendi three questions inwardly. My first question was, 'What are these tribulations prophets and saints suffer?' He answered them out loud.

He replied, 'They are born without sin, they bear the sins of the people.

'The second: A bride [wears white, she] goes from one place to another neighborhood, everyone's eyes are on her. She must be spotless clean, there shouldn't be even one stain. Especially if ink drops on her, that won't do at all. The man of religion is like that, too.

'The third: first mention the Verse or Saying, then pass on to the example. There may be a scholar, someone who can swallow you. Do it that way.

'These were your questions, weren't they? Now run along,' he said. I left.

The day of the scorpion

Fifty years ago, I went to visit my Master. I saw two people of his age sitting there, he's sitting on the couch across the room. The distance was from this couch to over there. I kissed his hand. They were his fellow disciples from Othman Badruddin. They're talking. I got to know those two men later, they're learned men. A tall man came in, kissed their hands and sat down. I'm listening like this.

Suddenly, something very light brushed across my face, it was like the wind but it didn't go away. It felt like a fly had alighted on my upper lip. I took it in my hand, it was a black scorpion, this big! I'm telling you exactly as it happened. It's trying to sting me, but I've grabbed it in such a way, by the head part, that it can't strike. I set it down on the ground beside me. Things like this must have endeared me to him.

It got down from there, it headed straight for those two scholars. I'm watching. As soon as it appeared before them, one of them was named Hajji Mehmet, he *jumped* to his feet, *pow!* he stomped on it with all the force of his foot, with the sole of that thick peasant's sock.

'Master,' he said, 'are you going to train us with *this*? We can't stand things like this. Where did you bring this vermin? I almost died! If this had stung me, I would've died right here. Under Divine Law, it's permissible to kill it.' I'm laughing.

The man who killed it went and brought a shovel full of ashes, he sprinkled the ashes on it. *'Did I make a mistake?'* he asked.

'Yes, Hajji Mehmet, you made a mistake,' said Hajji Efendi. 'It's permissible to kill it, but it didn't touch you. Don't touch anything that doesn't touch you. It wanders on the face and lips of others, it doesn't do anything. Is it going to sting you just because it comes in front of you? What's the matter with you?' He had his back turned to me when that happened, yet he's saying this. This is precisely what happened.

'These are on duty, they don't sting anyone *unless God orders it*,' he said. 'They always come on orders, what blame does the animal have?' *'No*, sir, I won't have it,' said Hajji Mehmet.

The hodja who came afterwards got up, 'Goodbye, Ahmet Efendi. Is there anything you want to say?' He said 'No.' As he was leaving, he turned back. 'I have something to tell you in private.' Hajji Efendi got up [to go with him to an adjoining room], but he wavered slightly. I knew he was angry.

Later he tells me: 'This man came to me on his way to Kâzim Efendi. He said, 'I'm going to Elazığ. Do you have a message for the Master?' He didn't relate the greetings I sent correctly, and he didn't relate the greetings he sent back to me correctly. This man' – he recited a Verse [42:11] – 'he recites this Verse every day, he doesn't know God hears and sees everything. These people have become hodjas and scholars, they've become troublemakers.'

Completing the Invocation

My Master used to tell us, 'Recite *"There is no god but God"* a hundred times. At the hundredth, add *"Muhammad is the Prophet of God."*' We were together, the two of us, I said, 'Master, with your permission, could we say *"Muhammad is the Prophet of God"* after every *"There is no god but God"*?' He smiled slightly, he said 'Okay.' We do that to get it over with quickly. I tell those who come and go, 'We learned of God through him [Muhammad], don't abandon him.'

The Master or the Friday Prayer?

One Friday I went to visit Hajji Ahmet Efendi. There were two people with him. I hadn't seen them before. The time for the Friday Prayer arrived. Hajji Efendi said, 'Go ahead, go to the Friday Prayer.' Those two youths hung their necks and said nothing. Nor did they make any motion to leave. He repeated this several times. There's no motion in them. Upon this, I got up and asked permission, partly to serve as an example to them. I went out for the Friday Prayer. They're still sitting there silently with their necks hung like that.

When I came back, those two youths were no longer there. Hajji Efendi said, 'I told them to go so many times, they didn't leave. Finally, I told them to get out.' I had never seen those two before, nor did I ever see them again.

After that, this matter occupied my thoughts for a decade. I come and go, I work, this matter is always on my mind. Was I right, or were they right? I had obeyed both an order and a religious obligation.

Five or ten years passed, I finally reached the conclusion that those youths had been right. [As Imam Efendi remarked: 'Be reconciled to going to hell, do not be reconciled to separation from your master.' Another Sufi saying: 'With you, hell is heaven for me. Without you, heaven is hell.']

The end of my hunting days

In my youth, I was very interested in hunting. I first used a weapon when I was ten years old. I was a sharpshooter. When I was in the military, I scored bull's-eye twice and close to that once [out of three shots].

One day, I bought myself a shotgun for fifty Liras and a gun for another fifty Liras. I'm going to defend myself with these.

As I was coming to my Master's home, I felt ashamed. There are a couple of houses, I thought I'd go over the roofs of those houses and drop into my Master's courtyard without being seen by anyone. And that's what I did. Just as I was on the roof overlooking the courtyard, my Master opened the door to the courtyard. He came out with a pitcher in his hand. He looked at me and said, 'What's this, did you think nobody would see you?' He went to fill water. My knees began to shake. He came back a little later and said, 'Come on, come down.' So I went down. Hajji Efendi was opposed to the weapons I had bought: 'Trust in God, don't trust in these!' he said. 'It is God who protects, not these. Who did you come with?' I said, 'I came by myself.' 'The military police will confiscate these, you'll be left without a gun. Zeynel, take these home.'

That night I had a dream. In that dream, my Master was saying, 'There are many vehicles for us.'

The next day, a military captain I knew came over. He said, 'I won't go away until you give me this shotgun. I'll pay you later for it.' I was forced to give it to him. Some time later, someone else came and did the same thing with the gun. From that day to this, they're still going to pay! Ahmet Efendi [was satisfied. He] said, 'It's good it happened that way.'

Don't test the Master

One day, I dreamt that I and my Master were on our way to visit a sick person. But in the dream I made a mistake, I tried to test my Master. As we were going I thought to myself, 'Let him find the sick woman's house at first try.' I was challenging him to perform a miraculous feat. At that moment he turned around and gave my face a resounding slap. I woke up, my cheek was still smarting.

Now five or six days later, we indeed went to visit that sick woman. I didn't remember my dream on our way there, but I remembered it on the way back, one step from the place where he had slapped me. [I halted, expecting a real-life slap.]

Just at that instant, he turned around and said, 'Is something the matter?' 'No,' I said, 'we're on our way.' He turned to me full-face. 'Be careful,' he said. 'We strike a person once, we strike him real good.'

The guardian

There was a man named Mahmud, he could tear trees apart with his bare hands without using an axe. I was going to go to Gönen with a man, my Master said 'Don't go.' When I wasn't deterred, he sent Mahmud along with us, who also relieved me of my load of onions.

Forty years later, it dawned on me that the man with me was intending to shoot me. Hajji Efendi had sent Mahmud along for my protection. Will you look at the strength and power of the Master?

The frog and the snake

That was a different kind of day. Forty-five or fifty years ago, I went to visit Hajji Efendi. I was at a distance of four or five hours. He asked, 'Why did you come?' I didn't say. I didn't tell him, 'Let me carry you on my back,' I'm still lamenting that.

That day I made a bridge over a brook for ants to cross. I took down a thirsty turtle from a wall. I saw that a snake was trying to swallow a frog by a riverside. It wouldn't do to kill the snake, and it wouldn't do to leave them like that. The snake is swallowing the frog, I bore down on the snake's neck with a shovel. It didn't release it. It wrapped its tail around the handle of the shovel as far up as my hand. Then it saw that it was in danger and let go of the frog, which escaped. I didn't want to kill the snake, so I threw it away together with the shovel.

I went to Hajji Efendi. He asked, 'Where were you?' 'I took a look at the water,' I said. He smiled and said, 'Bravo, you've done a good trade.' He didn't say anything else. 'Go and fetch me a glass of water,' he said.

Two crucial days

[In 1936] I wanted to go to Ankara. I had debts, I intended to earn money and pay them back. Hajji Efendi insisted I shouldn't go. Finally, [in exasperation] he said: 'Let me send you to Kâzim Efendi and let him decide.' This placed a burden on me, a burden the size of Turkey.

Later that day he said, 'In order to go to a master, one has to come to the level of the Tranquil Self first. You all should come to me afterwards. The Base Self ensnares your foot and you don't even glance at it.'

That evening there was one visitor, we sat down to have supper.

Under the influence of that burden, I uprooted and threw away all selfish things from the *root*. From the *root*. I cut down the tree of the self, I ripped it all out, down to the curly roots. A state came over me during supper such that I cut off everything up to the level of the Pleased Self.

Hajji Efendi smiled. 'Bravo, Ahmet,' he said. He's aware of everything. I'm doing it internally. 'Go ahead and eat,' he said. I'm telling you, God watches man through man! Who says He doesn't know what's in you, He knows. During that supper I eradicated evil, then he sent me to Kâzim Efendi.

The next day I set out for Elaziz.[12] There I went to Kâzim Efendi. I stayed there that night, and also did the Wakeup Prayer. I recited the Repentance a hundred times, the Word of Unity a hundred times. That was a *good* night. The night of the *foundation*.

In the morning I asked, 'What about my going to Ankara?' Actually, I was undecided myself, I would've stayed if he'd said 'Don't go.'

'Don't forget God, go wherever you want.'

---

12. Elaziz is the old name of Elazığ.

I was relieved. I went back to Hajji Efendi. 'This is what happened.' Hajji Efendi was angry: 'You didn't listen to me. I was going to resolve your debts and everything. The God of Ankara is very rich. Go on, go,' he said, waving the back of his hand.

I had many troubles in Ankara. At that time I refused to get married. Am I living in a cave or in a forest? But I'm in such a state that in the evenings, my eyes are shut, the Master is giving Quran lessons beside my head. I'm afraid to open my eyes. *Divine Lord, You are my goal and Your pleasure is my request.*

Then I went to a mosque, there was a hodja, he recited a Saying: 'Who doesn't marry, let him choose his place in hell. Whoever marries, let him choose his place in heaven.' It was a Saying narrated by Ali the fourth caliph. I said to myself, 'He's saying this to you.'

So I got married [to Mother Hajar – March 25, 1937]. A month or two later, I'm sitting with my wife, *Smaack!* came a slap. Its place still hurts.

[After that] the Master appeared. There's no one [there physically, but] we're together. The Master said, 'What have you done?' 'It's a Saying,' I said. 'No,' he said, 'that Saying is not for you, it's for those who can't control their selves.' 'Then let me turn back and leave her,' I said. 'No,' he said, 'it's too late. You've done it on your own, now suffer on your own.'

[The problem here is that he got married without asking for the permission of his Master. This trip to Ankara and subsequent marriage apparently postponed his Realization by a number of years.]

The dream of the visit to the Prophet

I saw Hajji Efendi in a dream fifteen years after he had passed into the Realm of the Everlasting. On December 11, 1959. That's my mistake. I said, 'The Master is dead.' We're lazy, that is.

'Get up,' he said, 'I'm taking you somewhere.' There are three or four men in front of me and behind me, they're not saying a word. We're going toward a mountain, someone is standing on top of it looking at us. I know it is the Prophet. He's taller and wider than this door, his head would touch this ceiling. He was unlike others, I saw his majesty. He had a long beard.

We went. Ahmet Efendi pressed his hand to his chest and thus received permission. Next, he went over and kissed his hand. Then they talked a bit, he gave me permission. They stood aside to make way for me. I bent forward and kissed his hand. My first fault – I know it –

was that I didn't want my cigarette odor to disturb him. Hajji Efendi pulled my arm, 'That's enough, don't disturb him too long.'

We left. We came back the same way we had gone there. 'Thank God we've arrived at these days,' he said. 'I was finally able to bring you here. Be intelligent, be careful.'

One day I saw Hajji Efendi in a dream in the form of the Prophet of God. He was awe-inspiring, I couldn't look at him for a long while. Now, there are more than fifty people who have seen me in the form of the Prophet [in their dreams]. I don't know what to make of this, but it happens. These are for you, that is – for you all. Otherwise, where am I, where are they? If I could be dust under their feet, what more could I want?

Yes, it's still he who rules, don't think he's dead and buried. What strength do I have to manage all these people? Each one has a different state. He still bears the burden and does the managing. The departed master rules the disciple remaining in his place. Yes, it's still he who supervises. He and I are not separated, not even for an instant.

I'm the servant of the whole universe. There's a bridge, the donkey, the man of knowledge and the virtuous alike pass over it. I've become a bridge between God and the people. The donkey, the mule pass over it, nobody takes a look at the bridge.

I'm not great, God is the Greatest of all.[13]

Total breakthrough

[The dream of the Prophet turned out to be a harbinger of the Great Realization to come. The Master never spoke to us about his Realization. Fortunately, in a small notebook he used to keep during the years 1960–62, we find the following entry:]

On 16 May [1960], I believed in my God and I saw Him, I knew Him. I experienced Observation of the Compassionate. Thank God. I became real with the Real, thank God. I became one day old. I knew and saw my Lord. The universe ceased to exist, it became ashes, it burned up, only God remained. The name 'Ahmet' remained, he himself ceased to exist. Only God was left. The universe was filled with joy. The meaning of a Saying: 'He who knows his self knows his Lord.' I knew. I knew, I saw, I said: Praised be the Lord, for all eternity. Ahmet.

13. Compare 'Why call ye me good? Only God is good' (Mark 10:18).

Kâzim Efendi died. [Shortly before he went,] in a dream, he made me put on a caftan and a head-cap. He said, 'These belong to Othman Badruddin.'

The night of June 5, 1974, I saw my [secondary] master, Kâzim Efendi, in a dream. He informed me of my duty to train people.

The quest for a successor

In a conversation fifteen years ago, they said: 'Hajji Ahmet Efendi is looking for a racehorse. It has to be purebred.' Someone said, 'I understand, but none of us can do it.' I haven't been able to trap one person! I'm searching, I can't find one. The other professorship is easy. There has to be a spiritual professorship.

I want a man. (It can also be a woman.) He should work such that if he squeezes stone, orange should emerge. An *easygoing* person is required who will say something to someone without hurting their feelings. I'm looking for such a man, I can't find him.

Epilogue

> Such was the end of our friend,
> whom I may truly call the wisest, the justest,
> and best of all the men I have ever known.
>
> Plato[1]

On August 3, 1998, around 9:45 p.m., the Master departed on his journey into the great unknown, on which we must all embark someday, from a hospital room – in full sight of his home – in Ankara. He was a hundred years and seven months old.

No one will ever know the magnitude of the loss we suffered. No one can understand how enormous it was. Two sentences from a book I had been working on stuck in my mind and kept repeating over and over again like crazy music:

> Nietzsche: 'What was holiest and mightiest of all that the world has yet owned has bled to death under our knives …' (For he had said, 'These people are killing me without knowing it.')

> Jouffroy: 'I seemed to feel my earlier life, so smiling and so full, go out like a fire, and before me another life opened, sombre and unpeopled, where in future I must live alone …'

The truth is that the Master's departure left us – all those whose hearts he had touched – shattered. We would have liked to be with him, if only we could. We would have liked to say: 'Either don't go, or take me with you.' We had all grown accustomed to the incomparability that was the Master: we doted on his smiles, his gait, his tiniest movement, his mannerisms. Nothing could have kept us away from his love. We would have followed him to the ends of the earth. But this time, we could not follow him where he had gone – not until our own times came. To almost all our brethren who came to offer their condolences, I said:

'You and I are among the luckiest people in the world. For these eyes have seen, these ears have heard, things which the vast majority of human beings cannot imagine even in their wildest dreams. You may have seen the Master for a long time, or for only a minute. Yet

---

1. Quoting Phaedo, *The Last Days of Socrates*, conclusion.

even if you saw him only in a dream and were unable to meet him in real life, you are among the company of the elect, the most fortunate of human beings. How shall we convey our experience to the outside world? If there are six billion people on earth, nearly all – excluding some thousands or ten thousands – will fail even to understand what we're talking about, let alone believe it.

'But we have an eye debt, an ear debt, to pay Efendi. No matter how difficult it may be, it is our duty to explain the Master to the rest of the world. We should first try to live his wonderful path, that radiant way, ourselves, and then we should explain to others why it is so wonderful.' And everyone agreed.

I added: 'Now is the time, not to fall apart, not to disintegrate, but to support each other more than ever. For in each one of us there is a trace, a sign, an aroma of Efendi. We are his artwork. In you there is a red brushstroke, in me green, in that fellow blue. So if we can continue to love and respect one another, if for no other reason than because of the Master's paint in each one of us, and ultimately because of the Master in each, that will be enough. That would please the Master. The opposite would cause him sorrow.'

Once upon a dream

Two lines of poetry, by the famous Turkish poet Yahya Kemal, summed up our predicament exactly:

> *Few people understand our music of old times*
> *And those who don't understand it, understand nothing of us.*

His life was like a dream, a fairy tale too good to be true – a dream, however, that we had all experienced in real life, in three-dimensional knock-you-on-the-head physical existence. So it wasn't a dream, after all, but a fairy tale come true. Such things could actually happen in real life. If someone had told me and I hadn't seen it myself, skeptic that I am, I would never have believed it.

When three months had passed, I contemplated the lyrics of 'Once Upon a Dream' in *Sleeping Beauty*.[2] There, the princess has her first

---

2. Sung to a tune in Tchaikovsky's *Nutcracker Suite*, in Walt Disney's *Sleeping Beauty* (1959).

meeting with the prince. She has been warned against speaking with strangers, but she has met the prince already – in a dream, she says. So the prince is not a stranger after all, but one immediately recognized, loved and trusted. Moreover, the feelings are mutual, for the prince has had the same dream.

That beautiful fairy tale was symbolic in more ways than one. And it is a fairy tale, not just for children, but also adults. Yes! For in each and every one of us, including yourself, at this very moment, the Master – the Perfect Human – sleeps. Whoever is able to slay the monstrous dragon of their Base Self will gain access to that inner chamber of the Heart, where lies the Wonderful Self in silent repose. Then will come to pass the miracle prophesied by Gustav Meyrink in *The Green Face*: 'the miracle that, even if you are buried, there will be no corpse in your coffin' – meaning that before one undergoes physical death, one will already have attained immortality.[3] But where shall we find that hero, the able person who will vanquish that monster and awaken the Master within? Someday, someone, somewhere, will again be able to unlock that door. But you and I cannot even guess whom it might be.

The Master had stated during his life: 'When I depart, I shall leave behind a thousand Ahmet Kayhans, ten thousand Ahmet Kayhans.' It was up to his followers to turn these words into reality, by adopting the Master's radiant way and explaining to others why it was so wonderful.

In addition, the Master had trained various 'instructors.' These were not themselves *murshid*s (gurus) comparable in any way to the Master, but servants who would continue the task of educating the people in religious and spiritual matters. Poor substitute though they were, in the Master's absence, his flock would turn to them for instruction and nourishment.

Very different, and hidden from public eyes, would be the case of the Singularity, The One whom we might call the Sage of Sages or the Sage of the Age. In that person, all the metaphors of the universe, of science and religion and art and technology and mythology, would converge and come true. This person could only be one. It was a moot point where and when that Singularity would manifest itself. The event could lie years, perhaps decades, in the future. The Singularity would be no ordinary disciple or instructor, but a replacement. This would

---

3. It also means that, when physical death occurs, the spirit of the liberated person will not be confined to the locality of the corpse, but is free to wander.

be a Singularity because the Master himself had been a Singularity, the Pole of the Time, comparable to no one else.

As in a three-dimensional ellipsoid, all the light and sound emanating from one focal point, the Teacher, would converge on the second focus, the student. The self-existence of the student would go up in flames, and from the ashes would arise, Phoenix-like, the self-existence and spirituality of the Master. Taking the metaphor of a laser, the Master would represent the fully reflective mirror and the student, the semi-transparent one. Once the medium between the two mirrors 'lased,' the full force of the Master's *baraka* (spiritual action or power) would explode from the student like a supernova, for the student would have now become entirely Master-transparent. Whatever was broadcast on the radio- or TV-station of the Master would be faithfully reproduced at the receiver of the student. What you saw on the monitor would be a faithful representation of the output from the Central Processing Unit of the computer.

The caterpillar of the student would weave a cocoon of solitude and meditation around itself, and out of that cocoon would emerge, in due time, the butterfly of the Teacher. This metamorphosis was the exact opposite of Kafka's *Metamorphosis*, for while the latter represented a degeneration, the former was a fulfillment and represented an evolution into something higher, an elevation to something more beautiful. Lead would be transmuted into gold. The dark night, the Osiris, of the Master would be reborn in the student's soul as Horus the spirit-child, Sun and daylight. The imploding singularity of a black hole would burst forth as the blinding singularity of a white hole.

Faced with an insurmountable quantum barrier, the electron would dematerialize and, simultaneously, rematerialize on the other side of the wall. For without dissolution, there was no possibility of reconstitution, without death no rebirth.

This transmutation was possible for the same reason that many processes in nature were possible. That is, it did not require infinities or infinite precision. One did not need hundred-percent-pure Uranium 235 to make a nuclear bomb, ninety-three percent ('weapons-grade') was enough. Helium did not need to be cooled down to absolute zero temperature, but turned into a superfluid at two or three degrees Kelvin. In the same way, it was enough that the student approximate a region of 'Lyapunov stability' – simply being in that vicinity, near the 'event horizon,' would be enough for the Master's 'magic' to work itself. Otherwise, infinite perfection is impossible for nature and man, and in such a case none of these phenomena could take place. Crystallization could occur despite – perhaps even thanks to – trace impurities. Even if one could not achieve one hundred percent perfection, God's grace would come to the rescue. Under immense heat and pressure, diamond would be forged out of coal.

Then, the physical body, the outward appearance, would remain as a Clark Kent. But the spirituality would have become that of a Superman – an ethically superior human being. (Recall that the Superman of the comics is also highly ethical.) And like a Superman, whatever powers one was invested with would be harnessed in the service of humanity. Exactly like Superman, one would lay oneself down to span the gap in the rails so that the train full of passengers would not hurtle into the precipice. *Avalokitesvara* (the Lord looking down in Pity), *Arham ar-rahimin* (the Most Merciful of Mercifuls) would, through that lens, spawn a Khidr-manifestation that rushed to the rescue.

So someday, somewhere, the Singularity would return. The only question was, who would it be? No one could know the answer, except God.

There was a Turkish song, some words of which the Master used to repeat frequently, especially in his final years. It went something like this:

> *I searched far and wide, I couldn't find a true friend;*
> *day turned to dusk.*
> *I found the true friend – evening came quickly.*

This reminded me of an English song: 'Keep on looking for a heart of gold ... and I'm getting old.' It also reminded me of Jesus' words in John's Gospel: 'Unless I depart, the Paraclete cannot come. But if I go, I will send him to you.'

The lyrics above, however, conceal a double meaning. If the evening, the end of the day and of life, comes quickly when the friend is found, the departure of the Master could also be interpreted to mean that the friend *had, in fact*, been found. Perhaps the Master, peering far into the future, had discerned that the paths – though seemingly separate now – actually converged on the horizon.

Perhaps, after all, somewhere beyond space and time – perhaps, even, somewhere *within* space and time – the Master found the Friend he had been looking for.

Appendix
Some important formulas

	English translation		Transliteration	
Name	**Formula**	**Name**	**Formula**	
Word of Unity / Unification	There is no god but God, Muhammad is the Messenger of God	kalimat al-tawhid	La ilaha ill' Allah, Muhammadun rasul Allah	
Word of Witnessing	I bear witness that there is no god but God, and I bear witness that Muhammad is his servant and Messenger	kalimat al-shahada	Ashhadu an la ilaha ill' Allah, wa ashhadu anna Muhammadun abduhu wa Rasuluhu	
Refuge (sometimes recited before the Naming)	I take refuge in God from the accursed Satan	a'udhu	A'udhu bi-llahi min-ash-shaytani-r-rajim	
Naming	In the name of God, the Compassionate, the Merciful	Basmala	Bismi-llahi-r-Rahmani-r-Rahim	
Name of Majesty	God (Oh, God)	Ismi Jalal	Allah	
Blessings on the Prophet	My God, may Your blessings and peace be on Muhammad and on the family of Muhammad	Salawat, Salatu Salam	Allahumma salli 'ala Muhammadin wa 'ala ali Muhammad	
Magnification	God, He is Greatest, God, He is Greatest, there is no god but God and God, He is Greatest, God, He is Greatest and praise be to God	Takbir	Allahu akbar, Allahu akbar, la ilaha ill' Allahu wa-llahu akbar, Allahu akbar wa lillahi-l-hamd	
No Strength	There is no strength and power except by God, the Exalted, the Great	La Hawla	La hawla wa-la quwwata illa bi-llahi-l-'aliyyu-l-'azim	
Repentance	I ask for God's forgiveness	Tawba, istighfar	istaghfiru-llah	

Index

Aaron 11n8, 278–9
Abbas 329
Abbasid(s) 329–30, 339
Abdul Hamid 110n1, 113, 164, 404
Abdul Muttalib 267
Abdul Qadir *see* Gilani
Abel 265
Ablution 71, 88, 125–7, 133, 137, 202–3, 228, 231–3, 236, 240–1, 245, 283, 285, 331, 336, 338, 378–9, 390, 404, 415, 420, 428, 445
Abraham 7, 39, 159, 193, 237, 266–7, 270–4, 292, 296, 298, 313n6, 348, 360, 364, 420n3, 423, 435
Abu Bakr (first Caliph) 67, 164–5, 299, 304, 309, 317, 321, 323n6, 324, 362, 370
Abu Hanifa 116–17, 167, 331–6, 338–9, 348, 365n9
Abu Hurayra 301–2
Abu Jahl 308, 318
Abu Lahab 296–7
Abu Muslim (of Khorasan) 329
Abu Talib 298
Ad 270
adab see courtesy
Adam 21, 39, 68, 75, 77, 80, 117, 121, 123, 127, 134, 144, 148, 170–2, 211–12, 233, 265, 267–70, 274, 292, 310, 313, 361–2, 364, 427
Adiyaman 246
administration 175, 295, 323
afterlife 63, 167, 169, 171, 173, 265, 283
afterworld 82, 91, 202, 286, 340
Ahad (the One) 53
Ahadiyya (Absolute Unity) 193, 208, 270
Ahi Evren 375
Ahl al-Bayt see People of the House
Ahmed I 330n8, 390
Aisha 102, 182, 295, 299, 303, 308–9
Aktarla 10, 44
Alawi 11
Alexander the Great 17, 40–1, 349–50
Algeria 114
Ali (fourth Caliph) 63, 82, 115, 159, 164, 167, 194, 208, 268, 304, 308, 316, 322–9, 356, 452
Ali Agha 435–6
Ali Sebti 411, 424–5
Allah 13n9, 206n3, 242–5, 414n2

Allowed *see halal*
Alms(-tax) 53, 61, 127, 154–6, 177, 199, 238, 374
America 13, 16, 25, 58, 67, 79, 114, 116n1, 148, 151, 172–3, 182, 193, 195, 219, 253, 314
Amir Kulal, Sayyid 422
Andalusia 358
angel(s) 19, 27, 50, 60, 64, 81, 92, 94–5, 98, 101, 105, 131–2, 144–5, 150, 161–2, 184, 190–1, 211, 213, 218, 231, 234–5, 250, 258, 265, 268–9, 275, 301–2, 307, 317, 322, 332, 407, 420, 423, 427
Ankara 1, 4, 10–11, 153, 191–2, 194, 215, 244, 248, 251–2, 337, 355, 372–4, 441, 451–2, 455
Anoshirvan *see* Nushirawan
Anqa 256n7
'aql al-ma'isha see Livelihood Mind
'aql al-kull see Universal Intellect
'aql al-salim *see* Sound Mind
'aql al-sultani *see* Kingly Mind
Arabia 295, 296, 329
Arafat *see* Mount Arafat
Arberry Arthur J., 34
art 6, 9, 115, 117, 119, 121, 457
Asaf (bin Barakhya) 287, 289
Ascension (*mi'raj*) 39–40, 183, 194, 211–12, 214, 234, 236, 258–60, 290, 310–12, 340, 377–8
asceticism 83, 97, 133, 192, 196, 228, 250–1, 253, 257, 279, 292, 315, 345, 348, 359, 372, 378, 382, 387
Asiya 275
Aspozi 374
Assembly of the Pure 348, 362
Assisi 7, 22
associationism (*shirk*) 150
astrology 25–7
Ataturk 115
Attainment (*wuslat*) 134, 195, 207, 434
attributes 6, 11, 21, 40, 64–5, 68, 79, 81, 205, 222, 250, 313, 315, 345, 348, 411, 434
Australia 180, 337n2
Avalokitesvara 459
Ayvalik 26, 252
Azazil 144, 268, 269 *see also* devil, Satan
Azra'il (Archangel of death) 64, 196, 268–9

Badawi, Ahmed 347
Badr 165, 307
Baghdad 332, 334–6, 338, 366, 370–2, 387, 392, 411–12, 414, 416, 423–4
Balkh 385
baraka 458
Base Self (*see also* ego, egotistical) 35, 65, 77, 81, 83, 85, 94, 98, 115, 120, 126, 129–32, 135–6, 138, 142, 161, 177, 193, 200–1, 214, 225, 226, 245–6, 250, 253, 257–8, 272, 311, 322, 327, 400, 427n5, 438, 451, 457
  as ass/donkey 400–1
  as fly/sickness/cancer 140
  as serpent/snake 120n2, 130, 132, 257, 277
  as tree (to be uprooted) 214, 451
Bayazid II 397
Bayazid of Bistam 150, 226, 342n4, 363–4
Bektashi 219
Beloved (God) 17, 134, 192, 206, 223, 365, 442n10
benevolence (*ihsan*) 149
Bezels of Wisdom *see Fusus al-Hikam*
Bhagavad Gita 335n1
Bible 19, 169
Bilal (the Ethiopian) 307, 320
Bilqis (Queen of Sheba) 26, 287–8
Bingol 424
Birgivi, Muhammad 367–9
Black Pearl 158n4, 242n6
Black Stone 274, 296–7, 318
Bliss (attribute) 63, 265
Body and Spirit 32
Bosphorus Straits 390, 439
Bradbury, Ray 57n9
Britain 19, 25, 251–3
Bruno, Giordano 26
Buddha 385
Buddhism xv
Bukhara 341, 392, 422, 435
Bukhari, Muhammad 341
Buraq 311
Bursa 223, 367, 388–9, 398n26
Byzantium 308

Cahen, Claude xv
Cain 265
Cairo 23
caliph xv 23, 112, 164, 167, 268, 317–19, 321–3, 339, 364, 411, 452
caliphate xv, 319, 321, 327
Camelot 1
Chain of Transmission 411

charity 155–9, 192, 284, 316
charity stones 158n4
Charlemagne 330
Chesterton, G. K. 23–4
Child of the Heart 253
Child of the Spirit 253
China 86, 115, 172, 257
Christian xv, 18–19, 22, 65, 73, 83n4, 92, 110, 117, 151, 169, 289n19, 306, 360, 390, 396
Christianity xv,18, 23–4, 179–80, 292, 393
Clarke, Arthur 121
Clean *see* halal
Columbus 253
Companions of the Prophet 118, 135, 296, 302, 305–6, 309, 323
Compassion xv, 54, 63–5, 68, 74, 79, 117, 131, 139, 143, 306, 310, 313, 345, 351, 356, 377, 381
constitution (legal) 68–9, 76–7, 112, 148, 323
cosmos 50, 57, 140, 313
courtesy (*adab*) 14, 20, 24, 85, 103, 105, 107, 137, 145, 171, 210, 269–70, 291, 302, 307, 326, 359, 396, 426, 427n5, 432, 445
Critical Self 131, 193
Crucifixion 39, 265, 293, 295
Cuban Missile Crisis 173
culture 9, 73, 113, 178, 290
Çirmikli (Yeşilyurt) 215, 374
Çorum 408, 409

Dahlawi, Abdullah 411, 423
Damascus (Sham) 191, 296, 319, 329, 360, 362–3, 373, 391, 408, 411–14
David 39, 55n6, 78, 285–6
death 64, 106, 119, 127, 132–4, 143, 167–9, 171, 173, 268, 288, 290, 293, 339–40, 355, 359, 381, 393, 422, 431, 440, 455, 457–8
  no-death 290
Delhi 423
democracy 18, 22–3, 25, 69, 73–5, 113, 171
Desiderata 22, 56n8
devil 80–1, 93, 98, 103, 115, 123, 131, 135, 139, 141, 143–5, 190, 210–11, 232–4, 236, 245, 325, 330, 346, 381, 416–17, 421, 444; *see also* Azazil, Satan
Dhammapada 56n7
Divine Attraction 247
Divine Law (*shari'a*) 9, 17, 75, 77, 83, 87, 104, 111, 113, 134, 142, 147–51, 187–8, 192, 194, 205, 210–11, 217–18, 220,

232, 241, 244, 253, 256, 265, 280, 285, 292, 316, 318, 323–4, 329, 338–9, 346, 348, 351, 357, 363, 369–70, 374–5, 377, 403, 427, 448
Divine Name(s) 13, 50, 79, 189, 217, 243–4, 346, 424, 428
Diwan 194
DNA 170n5
Doomsday 170, 172, 183, 347, 398
Dostoevsky 33

Economics 177
Efendi 8, 12, 44, 110, 189, 194, 244, 248, 255, 346–7, 427–43, 445–54, 456
egalitarianism 109, 304
ego 35, 56, 80, 85, 88, 90, 93, 98, 129–31, 139, 141–3, 190, 192, 233, 236, 239, 272, 303, 327, 345, 360, 393, 406, 424, 436; *see also* Base Self, egotistical
egotistical 35, 80–1, 105, 123, 125, 135, 137, 139–40, 150, 161, 209, 220, 223, 232, 234, 236, 241, 295–6, 301; *see also* Base Self, ego
Egypt 57–8, 167, 172, 272, 276–7, 300, 307n4, 320, 323, 356, 358–60, 363, 374, 379, 408
eighteen thousand worlds 51, 60, 63–4, 218, 258, 260, 326, 356
Einstein 251
Elazığ (Elaziz) 424, 426, 430–1, 435–6, 439, 448, 451n12
Elias (Elijah) 40–1, 265, 349–50
Elixir of Life 19, 40–1, 275, 349–50
Emigrants (*ansar*) 182
Empyrean 145
Emre, Tapduk 223, 345, 375, 405–6
Emre, Yunus 51, 83, 134–5, 140, 158, 192, 210, 213, 222–4, 233, 237, 249, 258–9, 315, 335n1, 345, 346, 355n4, 365, 405–7
England 29, 113, 148, 172, 267n4, 330n8
Enoch *see* Idris
entheogens 9
Erzurum 193, 197, 209, 210, 424, 427n5, 430
Eskişehir 376
esoteric 40–1, 58, 60, 115, 117, 181, 187, 189, 218, 255, 329, 355, 393, 427
Essential Realities (*al-a'yan al-thabita*) 26–7
ethics 74–5, 78, 80–1, 85–7, 89–91, 93, 95, 101–2, 112–13, 130, 158, 201, 210, 244, 255, 309, 322, 376, 442
Eucharist 19, 181

Euphrates River 275, 366, 379, 408, 432
Europe 13, 114, 116, 151, 167, 172, 181, 356
European Union 174
Eve 39, 121, 233, 269
exoteric xvi, 58, 60, 110, 115, 117, 187–9, 218, 256, 329, 355, 361, 370, 374, 389, 393, 411, 427
Extra (Supererogatory) Prayers 218, 220, 228, 233, 235, 239–40, 248, 428
Eye of Certainty (*'ayn al-yaqin*) 193
Eye of the Heart 127, 250, 255, 260, 350, 375, 415, 432
Ezra (Uzayr) 289

fana' fi al-shaykh 214n12
fana' fi ar-rasul 214n12
Farabi, al- 116
Farewell Address 296
Farmadi, Abu Ali 7
Farthest Mosque (Temple Mount) 214n12, 253, 288, 340
Fasting 53, 61–2, 92, 127, 148, 194, 199, 210, 238, 258, 299, 324, 374
Fatima 232, 237, 308–9, 316, 318, 324
Field, Reshad xvi
Fisher King 18–21
Five Daily Prayers 4, 124, 144, 148, 201, 203, 218, 232, 235, 237, 239, 243, 366–8, 375
Five Pillars of Islam 53, 77, 85, 142, 147, 155n1, 187, 201, 202, 210, 232, 233, 234
Flood, Noah's 39, 170
Forbidden *see haram*
Formal Prayer (*salat, namaz*) 35, 124, 250
fornication 123, 150, 179, 183, 203, 260, 274
Fountain of Eternal Life 256
Four Books 30, 77, 95, 101, 123, 143, 171, 198
Four Elements 79–80, 83, 104
Four Poles 57, 74, 79
Four Schools (of Jurisprudence) 116, 329
France 148, 172, 430
Francis of Assisi, St 7, 22–5
Friend of God 6, 9, 45, 137, 198, 252, 333, 346, 376, 422
Fusion of the Fusion (*jam' al-jam'*, Unitive Integration) 195, 210
Fusus al-Hikam (*Bezels of Wisdom*) 26, 352n3, 355
Futuhat al-Makkiyya (Meccan Revelations) 382

Gabriel 149, 164–5, 171, 196, 208, 268–9, 272, 274–6, 279, 288, 290, 298, 300, 302, 307, 310, 311, 312, 315, 317
Gauquelin, Michel 26
genie(s) (*jinn*) 208, 267, 287–8, 420–1
gentle(ness) 87, 136
Germany 251
Ghazali, al- 141, 150, 177, 329–30, 340, 348, 355, 381n6
Ghujdawani, Abdul Khaliq 422
ghusl 378n14
Gilan 412
Gilani, Abdul Qadir ('the Grand Saint') 11–12, 118, 150, 189, 194, 206n5, 226, 253–4, 260, 331, 346–8, 387, 411–21, 441
Global Hawk 337n2
Gnosis (*ma'rifa*) 75, 147, 189, 427n5
Golden Chain *see* Chain of Transmission
Gorbachev, Mikhail 13
Gospel (*Injil*, Gk. *Evangel*) 55, 58, 68–9, 77–8, 103, 113, 123, 152, 171, 173, 198, 232, 260, 267, 275, 296, 300–1, 360, 460
Grail 1, 18–22
gryphon 256
Guarded Tablet 258–9, 405

Hafiz (of Shiraz) 404–5
Hajar, Mother (Mrs. Kayhan) 10, 15, 441n9, 452
Hajji Bayram Wali 51, 124, 198, 220, 224, 258, 345, 355, 364, 372–4, 405
Hajji Bektash Wali 214, 219, 355n4, 375–6
hal see State
halal (Allowed, Clean, Licit) 86, 89, 95, 104, 107, 140–1, 154, 177, 179–80, 331, 334, 366, 402, 416–17
Hallaj, Mansur al- 65, 150, 377–8, 397n24
Hamawi, Hussein 372
Hamid Wali (Somuncu Baba) 143, 446
haram (Forbidden, Illicit, Unclean) 35, 94–5, 104, 107, 112, 121, 123, 125–7, 133–4, 136, 140, 170, 177–80, 202–3, 209, 218, 220, 231, 234, 248, 258, 260, 331–2, 339, 381, 387, 402, 417
Haran 272n6
Harun al-Rashid 330, 364, 366
Hashimites 298
Hassan (son of Ali) 167, 316, 329, 411, 422n4
Hassan of Basra 379, 380

Heart 6, 12, 17, 51, 74, 76–7, 79n2, 80, 82, 98–100, 121, 136, 142, 192, 201, 205–6, 208, 222, 239–40, 245–6, 251–5, 296, 350, 360, 375, 414, 422–3, 457, 459
Heartmind 21
heaven 5, 39, 50, 60, 75, 82, 95, 102, 123, 127, 135, 143, 145, 147, 201, 205, 206, 218, 228, 254, 292, 314, 346, 379, 381, 437, 449, 452
hell 82, 95, 102, 127, 143, 147, 388, 420, 444, 449, 452
Heraclitus 2
Hermeticism 23
Hidden Knowledge (*'ilm al-ladun*) 40–1, 115, 187, 189, 255–7, 290, 323, 350–1, 370
Hitler 167
Hobab *see* Shu'ayb
Hodja Bakir 411, 424
hope 71–3, 95, 161
Horus 458
House of Lords 113
Hud 270
Hudayi, Mahmud 389–91, 413
Hundred Sheets/Pages 77, 101, 143
Hussein (son of Ali) 167, 316, 329, 411, 422n24
hypothalamus 256

Ibn 'Arabi, Muhyiddin ('the Greatest Shaykh') 15, 26, 195, 226, 227n6, 270, 317, 348, 351, 355–63, 377, 382, 413
Ibn Hanbal, Ahmed 116, 331, 378–9
Ibn Sina 116
Ibrahim (ibn) Adham 127n1, 338, 348, 384–7, 421
Ibrahim Hakki of Erzurum 61, 90, 106, 197, 209, 253, 411, 421, 424, 427n5, 431
Idris (Enoch) 39, 265, 292
ihsan see benevolence
Illicit *see haram*
'ilm al-ladun see Hidden Knowledge
Imam Efendi *see* Othman Badruddin
Imam Rabbani *see* Sirhindi, Ahmed
Imitation (*taqlid*) 196, 220
India 5, 419, 423
Inspired Self 131, 193
intellect 79, 97, 116, 198
intelligence 8, 59–60, 69, 73, 88, 105, 112, 116n1, 158, 161, 182, 194, 276, 381, 409, 442
interest (money) 178–9
Invisible Royalty (*rijal al-ghayb*) 227n6
Invocation (*dhikr, zikr*) 35, 109, 129, 192,

INDEX

199, 214, 216–19, 223–4, 242, 244–8, 257, 308, 349, 356, 377, 394, 446, 448
Invoke 7–8, 59, 60, 87, 89, 152, 199–200, 235, 244–5, 280, 390, 408, 429
Iran 112, 394, 397, 405, 412
Iraq 272n6, 413
Isaac 237, 271, 273
Ishmael 39, 159, 237, 271, 273–4, 296
Ismail Fakirullah 411, 424
Ismail Hakki of Bursa 388–9, 398n26
Israel 271, 286, 340
Israfil (Seraphiel) 196
Istanbul 13–14, 57, 106, 109, 134, 164, 193, 210, 233, 320, 352n3, 363, 367, 390–1, 403, 408, 421, 428, 439
Izmir 13, 210

Jacob 19
Jafar Sadiq 331
jam' al-jam' see Fusion of the Fusion
Jamshid 20, 254n5
Jerusalem 214n12, 253, 287, 288n18, 311–12, 319
Jesus 5, 11, 18–19, 21–2, 32, 39–40, 55n6, 58, 64, 68, 72, 78, 83n4, 169, 180, 232, 253, 265–7, 271, 283, 290, 292–3, 295, 300, 313n6, 396, 460
Jethro see Shu'ayb
Jew 65, 102, 151, 232n1, 320, 321, 420
Jewish 102, 151, 280
jinn see genie
Jonah 39, 178, 266, 289–90
Joseph of Arimathea 19
Jouffroy 455
Judaism 179
Judas 40n1, 293
Junayd 370
Jung, Carl Gustav 21, 434n7
Jung, Emma 19n13

Ka'ba 12, 69, 121, 172, 274, 296–7, 318, 348, 361, 371, 423, 435
Kafka 458
Kawsar 259
Kaya, Ahmet ('Keko', 'Hadji Efendi') 10, 44, 248, 347, 431–43, 446, 448, 450, 452, 454
Kayhan, Ahmet xiii, 4, 8, 10, 12, 26, 44–5, 189, 194, 199–200, 244, 255, 442–55, 457
Kayseri 175, 252, 372, 376
Kazakhstan 3
Kâzim Efendi 430–1, 437, 446, 448, 451, 454

Kemal Ummi 397n24
Kepler 25, 26
Khadija 225, 250, 295, 308
Khalid bin Walid 328–9
Khalid Baghdadi, Mawlana 408, 411, 423–4
khatam al-awliya' see seal of the saints
Khidr 40–5, 94, 164, 255, 275n7, 348–54, 445, 459
Khidr, Abul Abbas al- 351
Khomeini 112
Khwajagan 422
King Arthur 1, 19
Kingly Mind (*'aql al-sultani*) 97
Kirşehir 376
Knowledge of Certainty (*'ilm al-yaqin*) 193
Koestler, Arthur 25n21
Konevi, Sadruddin 361, 391
Konuk, Ahmet Avni 352n3
Konya 208, 361, 391–3, 395, 397
Kubrick, Stanley 121
Kuddusi Baba 52–3, 79, 221, 236, 389
Kushju, Ali (Alauddin) 116

Laicism 109–10
lata'if see Subtleties
Layla 222, 223
Licit see halal
Limni (Lemnos) 374
Livelihood (Subsistence) Mind (*'aql al-ma'isha*) 73, 94, 97–9, 224
London 337
Lot 274–5
Luqman 212, 290–2

Machiavelli 295n1
madman of God (*majdhub/majzub*) 91, 247–8, 347, 364, 382–3, 432–3, 444
Maharishi 314
Mahdi 21, 169–70
Mahmud Hayrani, Sayyid 397
Mailer, Norman 116n1
majdhub/majzub see madman of God
Majnun 222–3
Malatya 10, 125, 192, 215, 251–2, 361, 374, 379, 431–3, 435, 438, 442, 444
Malik, Imam 116, 331
Mamluks 307n4
maqam see Station
ma'rifa see Gnosis
Mars 26, 170, 261
Mary 11n8, 39
Mathnawi 91, 188n2, 207n7, 392

McLuhan, Marshall 116n1
Meaning of the Four Books 32, 350n2, 427n5
Mecca 4, 44n4, 182, 214n12, 236, 252, 295–6, 299, 304, 308, 321, 329, 342–3, 366, 392, 435
medicine 32, 58, 86, 116–17, 141, 147–8, 181–2, 206, 259–60, 376
Medina xv, 67, 165, 171–2, 182, 295–6, 299–306, 319, 321, 324–5, 329, 348, 392, 435
meditate 50, 53, 61, 90, 190, 205, 269
meditation (*tafakkur*) 9, 50, 52–4, 86, 181, 190, 228, 236, 458
Meeting of Two Bows (*Qaba Qawsayn*) 260
Mehmed the Conqueror 109, 320, 355
Melami 218–19, 403
mercy 65, 71, 106, 151, 170–2, 244, 265, 276, 278, 281, 283, 306, 313, 351, 356, 365, 420n3
merit 59, 154, 295
Merkez Efendi 346
Mevlevi 218–20
Meyrink, Gustav 457
Michael 196, 274
Midian 351
milk thistle 226–7
Mina 273
miracles 165, 307–8
miraculous 14, 98, 148, 165, 234, 249–52, 257, 272, 345, 355, 363, 390, 393, 450
mi'raj see Ascension
morality 14, 50, 68, 73, 78, 80, 85–7, 92, 101–3, 112, 125, 129–30, 140, 191, 198, 201, 255, 291, 296, 308–9, 345, 347, 381, 391
morals 17, 86, 101–2, 177, 205, 389
Moses 11, 32, 39, 41–3, 55n6, 58, 64, 68, 72, 78, 83n4, 164, 175, 225, 232, 255, 259, 265, 266n3, 267, 270–1, 275–85, 289, 292, 295, 298, 340, 350–2
Mount Arafat 39, 273, 366
Mount Qubays 318
Mount Sawr 267
Mount Sinai (Mt. Horeb) 39, 258–9, 278–80, 284
Mu'awiya 322, 329, 379
Muhammadanhood 18, 104, 117, 129, 134, 169, 187, 192, 251, 314, 329
Muller, Herbert J. xv
music 121, 138, 455–6
Mustafa Naci 430–1

nafs al-Muhammadi 214n12

nafs al-murshid 214n12
Naming, the (*basmala*) 63, 65, 101, 136, 184, 217, 259, 327, 333, 335, 356, 377, 421
Naqshband, Bahauddin 346–8, 392, 411, 421–3
Naqshbandi (Naqshi) 7, 10, 217–18, 220, 235, 246, 391, 411, 421, 426, 431, 439
Naqshi *see* Naqshbandi
NASA 57n9
Nasruddin Hodja 388, 397–403
Nevşehir 375, 376n12
Nietzsche 226n5, 434n7, 455
Night of Power 274
nightingale 194, 248
Nile 39, 275, 278
Nimrod 170, 271–2
Nirvana 17
Niyazi Misri 134, 193–4, 199, 205–8, 249, 251, 313, 346, 374–5
Nizam al-Mulk 397n24
Noah 16, 39, 170–1, 212, 265–6, 274, 292, 310
Noah's Ark 16, 170, 212, 266, 310
nucleus (of the two worlds) 256
Nur al-Arabi, Muhammad 164, 403–4
Nushirawan (Anoshirwan) 320

Oman 270
Omar al-Faruq (second Caliph) 67, 164, 167, 299–300, 304–6, 308–10, 317–22, 324, 327, 411
Omar Dede (Emir Sikkini) 355
Omar Khayyam 397–8
Orders (*tariqa*) xvi, 7, 10, 23, 52, 75, 134, 147–8, 193, 202, 217–20, 242–4, 246–7, 303, 347, 351, 389, 391, 403, 411, 421, 431
Osiris 458
Othman (third Caliph) 164, 167, 324, 327
Othman Badruddin (Imam Efendi) 427–33, 447, 449, 454
Ottoman(s) 4, 13, 57n10, 110, 158n4, 164, 167, 173, 268, 329–30, 368n10, 390, 411
overflow 150, 246, 247, 346, 363, 377

Paraclete 460
Paradise 57, 59, 73, 80–1, 121, 123, 135, 154, 182, 197, 222, 233, 244, 259, 311, 313, 318, 346, 366–7, 381, 407, 437
paranormal 8
Partial Will 162–3, 221
Path *see* Order

patience 50, 89, 131, 139, 143, 152, 177, 212, 228, 338, 381, 387, 412
People of the Cave (Seven Sleepers) 289
People of the House (Prophet's Household, *Ahl al-bayt*) 237, 316, 331, 347
Perfect Human Being (*insan al-kamil*) 5–6, 10, 79–80, 171
Perfect Self 131
Persia(n) xv, 20, 254n5, 267n4, 300, 308, 316, 319–20, 324, 326, 335, 361
Pharaoh 80, 112, 144, 170, 265, 267, 271, 275–8, 351
Philosopher's Stone 19
philosophy 8–9, 49n2, 187, 209
Pilgrimage (*Hajj*) 44n4, 53, 61, 69, 127, 154, 199, 238, 318, 371, 374, 405, 423, 435
Piri Reis 253
Plato 22, 25, 31, 455
Pleased Self 81, 131, 272, 451
Pleasing Self 81, 131
politics xv, 110, 175–6, 399
precaution (*tadbir*) 63, 163–5, 182, 414
predestination (*taqdir*) 163–5, 414
Prophet's Household (*Ahl al-Bayt*) 237, 316
prostrate 12, 50, 54, 59, 76, 131, 136, 144–5, 211, 233–4, 238, 268–9, 283, 320, 323, 428–9
prostration 11n7, 53–4, 67, 133, 211, 233, 237–8, 244, 246, 270, 303, 343, 363, 379
Psalms 17, 55n6, 68–9, 77–8, 113, 123, 152, 198, 260, 296, 302n3
Pure Self 131

Qaba Qawsayn see Meeting of Two Bows
Qadiri 52, 217–18, 220–1, 242, 246, 389
Quakers 247n8
Queen of Sheba *see* Bilqis
Quran 6–8, 11, 13, 18, 23, 26, 34–5, 41, 51, 54, 58, 60, 64–5, 68–9, 71, 75, 77–8, 81, 86, 101–3, 109, 113–14, 117–18, 121, 123, 125, 138, 141, 144, 147–9, 152, 161, 167–8, 171–3, 181–4, 187, 189, 194, 198, 200–2, 205, 208–9, 218–20, 232, 242, 244, 256–7, 260, 267, 275, 285, 286–7, 289–90, 301, 303, 305, 309, 312, 314, 318, 322, 326, 332–3, 335, 346, 350–2, 356–7, 360–2, 365, 368–9, 377, 392, 395, 404, 409, 412, 423, 429, 433, 452
in a nutshell 137, 237

Quraysh(ites) 148, 163–4, 296–8, 301, 306, 317

Rabia Adawiya 380
Rabin, Yitzhak 13
Ram Dass 9n5
Ramadan 156, 238, 324, 357
Real, the (God) 54, 187, 193, 195, 202, 205, 207, 269–70, 277, 350, 369, 384, 440, 453
Reality (*haqiqa*) 75, 78, 147, 187–8, 323, 403
Realization (*tahqiq*) 214n12, 220, 431, 434, 452–3
reason (mind) 59, 85, 97, 184n4
reform 83, 92, 113, 156, 211, 305
reformation 113
Renan, Ernest 22
repentance 71–2, 231, 372, 392, 451
resurrection 101, 168, 322
Revelation 28, 75, 118, 265, 298, 302, 315
Rifa'i (Order) 218
Rifa'i, Ahmed 347, 414
Rifa'i, Kenan 98
Rome 275n8
rose 17, 55, 74, 80, 82–3, 85, 193–4, 208, 240, 272, 362, 378
Rumi, Ashraf (*Eşrefoğlu*) 372
Rumi, Mawlana Jalaluddin 72, 91, 124, 188n2, 194, 198, 213, 220, 223–4, 345–7, 364, 375, 391–7
Russia 13, 67, 148, 172

Sabbah, Hassan 397–8
Sacrificial Feast 158, 272
sadaka tashi see charity stones
Safura *see* Zipporah
sainthood 21, 123–4, 126, 161, 169, 172, 192, 203, 234, 248, 322–3, 338, 346–7, 411, 432, 435
Saintlight xiii, 21, 322, 345, 435
Saladin 8, 22–3
Salahuddin (goldsmith) 224, 392
Salman (the Persian) 316, 324–6
Salsal (wind) 270
Samaritan (goldsmith) 275, 279
Samini, Mahmud 411, 425–8
Saqati, Sirri (Sari) 79n2, 369–70
Sarah 272
Sardar, Ziauddin 23
Satan 86, 131, 135, 143–4, 170, 177, 210–11, 233, 238, 252, 268–70, 433; *see also* Azazil, devil
Saud 69

Sayyid Burhanuddin (Tirmidhi) 348, 372, 375, 392
Sayyid Taha 210
sayyids 347, 392, 422n4, 424
Schliemann 2
school of wisdom 61–2, 129, 199
Schools *see* Orders; *see also* Four Schools
Schuré, Edouard 23
science xiii, 2, 8, 25, 49n1, 53, 85, 115–17, 119, 147, 176, 184n4, 187, 208, 213, 241, 251, 253, 255, 267, 290, 350, 355–6, 358, 370, 391, 432, 457
science fiction 57n9, 116n1, 121
Science, Knowledge, and Sufism 20n14
seal of the saints (*khatam al-awliya'*) 356
Secret of Islam 113n2, 427n5
secularism 109, 111, 113
Selim the Resolute 57–8, 110, 167, 307n4, 363
Seljuks 173, 268, 330, 392, 397n24, 403
Seth 265
Sha'ban Wali 404
shabb al-amrad (beardless youth) 255
Shabistari, Mahmud 387n19
Shafi'i, Imam 116, 331
Shakers 247n8
Shams (of Tabriz) 213, 391–2, 394–7
Shamsuddin, Aq 109, 320, 354–5
shari'a see Divine Law
sharif 422n4
Shaw, Bernard 24
Shaykh of Islam 110, 389–90
Shem'i 142, 207
Shibli, Abu Bakr 370–2, 387n19
Shu'ayb (Jethro, Hobab) 276
siddiq 317n1
sin 59, 71, 109, 112, 130, 149, 151, 162, 190, 295, 365, 447
Sirhindi, Ahmed (Imam Rabbani) 411
Sivas 11
Six Pillars of Faith 77, 85, 101–2, 140, 142, 147, 187, 233–4
Smith, Huston 9n5
Socrates 31
Solomon 39, 208n9, 267, 285–8, 420n3
Sophronius 319
Sound Mind (*'aql al-salim*) 52, 62, 73, 89, 95, 97–100, 141, 224, 260, 283, 415
Spacefolding (*tayy al-makan*) 16, 26, 43, 134, 164–5, 251–2, 439, 445
Spain 358
spirituality xvi, 52, 58–9, 88, 90–1, 104, 117, 172, 181, 214n12, 228–9, 233, 253, 268, 346–7, 349, 411, 414, 423, 427, 458–9

Stabilization (*tamqin, taqrir*) 196
Station (*maqam*) 8, 17, 193, 195, 210–11, 253, 258, 260, 317, 378, 394, 412, 423
Station of No Station 113n2
Straight Path 144
struggle (as *jihad*) 224–5
Study in the School of Wisdom 26
Subtleties (*lata'if*), 257
Sufic 17, 21–3, 26, 99n1, 195–6, 282, 351, 387n19
Sufis xvi, 4–5, 23, 32, 71, 183, 195, 210, 251, 315
suicide 26, 95, 328
Sultan Baba 398n24
Supererogatory Prayers *see* Extra Prayers
Superman 434n7, 459
superstition 4, 183–4, 321, 437
Syria 24, 366

tafakkur see meditation
Ta'i, Hatim al- 380–1
Ta'if 310–11
Taliban 113n2
Tamerlane 329, 397, 403
Tao 17
Tao Te Ching 34, 151n1
tariqa see Order
Tarsus 290
tayammum 378n14
tayy al-makan see Spacefolding
technology 22, 57n9, 58, 86, 115–17, 141, 147–8, 169, 181, 259–60, 330, 337n2, 386, 457
teleportation 26, 251, 253
Temple Mount *see* Farthest Mosque
terrorism 113–14
theocracy 109
Third Adam 170–2
Thompson, Francis 5–7
Thompson, William Irwin 116n1
Throne Verse 184
Tien Shan Mountains 3
tifl al-ma'na see Child of the Spirit
Tigris River 336, 370
Tirmidhi, Hakim 227n6
Tompkins, Ptolemy 14, 16
Torah 55, 58, 68–9, 77–8, 103, 113, 123, 152, 171, 173, 198, 232, 260, 267, 275, 279, 280n11, 283, 285, 289, 296, 300, 351
Total Mind *see* Universal Intellect
Total Self 131
Total Will 162, 163
Totality 19, 54, 76, 103, 152, 218, 286, 312
toxic (NBC) weapons 174

Tranquil Self 81, 131, 138, 193, 451
Trial by Fire 272
Truth of Certainty (*haqq al-yaqin*) 193
Turkestan *see* Yasa
Turkey 5, 10, 18, 57, 111, 115, 171, 180, 232, 272n6, 349, 361, 375, 392, 426, 451
Twelve Founding/Patron Saints 347, 411
Twelve Imams 237, 316, 392
Twelve Orders 193, 347, 411
Two Doors 83, 123, 126–7, 140, 192, 446n11, 421

Ubar 270
Uftade, Father 389–90
Uhud 171
Umayyad 329, 362
Umm Hani 311
Ummi Sinan 374–5
Unclean *see haram*
Unification (*tawhid*) 17, 53n5, 94, 198–9, 217, 219, 243, 257, 265, 286, 341, 389
United Nations 173–4
Unitive Integration *see* Fusion of the Fusion
Unity (*tawhid, wahdat*) 15, 53, 195, 217, 218, 234, 245, 258, 314, 411
Unity, Absolute *see Ahadiyya*
Universal Intellect (*'aql al-kull*) 97
university 61, 112, 116, 120, 147, 224, 247, 249, 256, 346
unlettered (*ummi*) 315, 374
Unveiling (*kashf*) 249–50
Upanishads 22
Uqba bin Nafi 328
Ur 272n6
Urfa 272n6
Ushaki 219
usury 179
Uways al-Qarani 348

Uwaysi 348

Vallée, Jacques 26

Walad, Bahauddin (Rumi's father) 361, 376, 391–2
Walad, Bahauddin Sultan (Rumi's son) 392, 396–7
walad al-qalb see Child of the Heart
wali see Friend of God
Watts, Alan 9
Wells, H.G., 121
wisdom xiii–xiv, 14n10, 17, 22, 28–30, 34, 40, 42, 44, 60–1, 68, 72, 82, 103, 144, 189, 199, 205, 222, 290, 302n3, 335, 350n2, 358, 370, 396, 409, 442
WMDs (Weapons of Mass Destruction) *see* toxic (NBC) weapons
Woolley, Sir Leonard 272n6
Word of Unity 53, 141, 206, 209, 217, 244, 397, 451
Word of Witnessing 53, 61, 102, 140–1, 206, 217–19, 306, 374, 397
Wrath (attribute) 63, 265, 292

Yahya Kemal 456
Yalova 18
Yasa 3
Yasawi (Yesevi), Ahmet 4, 202, 219, 375
Yates, Frances 26n22
Yemen 287n15, 429
Yugoslavia 164
Yusuf Bahri 408–9

Zayd (ibn Harith) 310–11
Zenbilli Ali Efendi 110
zikr see Invocation
Zipporah (Safura) 276
Zoroastrians 307
Zulfiqar 327

www.ingramcontent.com/pod-product-compliance
Lightning Source LLC
Chambersburg PA
CBHW020117240426
43673CB00038B/515